FEDERAL HOUSING
POLICY AND PROGRAMS

PAST AND PRESENT

FEDERAL HOUSING POLICY AND PROGRAMS

PAST AND PRESENT

Edited by
J. Paul Mitchell

CENTER
FOR URBAN
POLICY RESEARCH

Published in the United States of America
by the Center for Urban Policy Research
Building 4051—Kilmer Campus
New Brunswick, New Jersey 08903

Library of Congress Cataloging in Publication Data
Main entry under title:

Federal housing policy and programs.

  Bibliography: p. 391
  Includes index.
    1. Housing policy—United States—History—Addresses, essays, lectures.
I. Mitchell, J. Paul. II. Rutgers University. Center for Urban Policy Research.
HD7293.F43   1985   363.5'8'0973   85-5737
ISBN 0-88285-107-1

CONTENTS

v

III. DIRECT FEDERAL HOUSING ASSISTANCE

Acknowledgments

The preparation of this volume owes much to the help and encouragement of many individuals. First, Dean Robert A. Fisher and the College of Architecture and Planning at Ball State University made it possible for me to go back to school for a year at Rutgers University. Dr. James W. Hughes, chair and graduate director, Department of Urban Planning and Policy Development at Rutgers, suggested the topic and provided the needed encouragement to put a reader together. The staffs of the Center for Urban Policy Research's library and Alexander Library at Rutgers University, and Bracken Library at Ball State University, provided cheerful assistance in locating materials. Lu Whitehair, Secretary for the Department of Urban Studies and Planning, Ball State University, typed and retyped portions of the manuscript. Francis Parker, department chair at Ball State University, provided continued encouragement and advice. Mary Picarella has seen the manuscript through to publication. The authors and publishers have granted permission to use the materials included. To all these I am grateful. Finally, I owe a large debt of gratitude to my wife, Lisbeth Reed Mitchell, who has been, as always, my best and most helpful critic.

J. Paul Mitchell

I
Introduction

1

The Historical Context
for Housing Policy

J. Paul Mitchell

Direct involvement by the federal government in housing really began a half century ago, during the 1930s. Since then every Congress has enacted legislation designed to remedy some shortcomings in the nation's housing delivery system, including defects in previous legislation. A simple chronology summarizing major housing legislation and executive actions, prepared for the U.S. Congress in 1975, devoted one-half page to four entries from 1892 to 1931, and 222 pages to those 1931 through 1974. A swift perusal of this compendium confirms that the federal government has generally acted in accordance with the sentiment expressed by the U.S. National Resources Planning Board in 1940:

> The housing problem is not one problem, but a combination of interrelated problems. Land values, building codes, tax rates, materials costs, labor costs, legal problems, adequate financing, zoning and site planning, housing management and the effective administration of the necessary private and public agencies are all problems in themselves, and taken as a whole they constitute the housing problem. . . .
> Immediate or quick solutions are not possible. On the other hand, time alone will not solve these problems. A continued attack in many sectors, often on a trial and error basis, will work toward a better situation.

The trial and error attacks of the past half-century have led to a bewildering variety of housing and housing-related programs. In their broadest outlines these have included:

1. a federally regulated mortgage finance system;
2. mortgage insurance;

3

3. interest rate subsidies to home owners, developers, and landlords;
4. tax deductions for mortgage interest;
5. special depreciation allowances for rental housing;
6. low-rent public housing;
7. rent supplements for low-income households;
8. subsidy packages for central city redevelopment; and
9. anti-discrimination measures.

But a cafeteria list of programs does not a policy make. Over the years, housing experts of all persuasions have decried the lack of a coherent federal housing policy, citing the plethora of programs as evidence. This is to be expected in a society with America's traditions: an antipathy toward government, local and sectional differences, a federal system of governance, and a sense of what historian Daniel Boorstin called "giveness." These factors have not been conducive to articulating coherent goals.[1]

Most critics have attributed the often confusing array of housing programs to either the absence of clear goals or the presence of multiple, conflicting goals. Donald Kummerfeld contended that the lack of clear goals renders measurement of program success or failure impossible. Thus, subsidy programs are vulnerable to criticism which, when it invariably comes, leads to "a scurrying to remedy the oversight, usually through new legislation or a new program emphasis." Kummerfeld concluded that "our inability to specify what we wanted to achieve through housing subsidies accounts for much of the layer-cake, patchwork nature of housing subsidy programs."[2]

On the other hand, Morton Schussheim noted the existence of large national goals into which housing had to fit, and to which housing policies would be expected to contribute. These larger goals included 1) full employment and stable growth of the economy; 2) environmental quality; 3) equality of opportunity; and 4) redistribution of income. Against these, the famed declaration of national policy as stated in the Housing Act of 1949, namely, "The realization as soon as feasible of the goal of a decent home in a suitable living environment for every American family," is, at best, vague and ambiguous. Thus, Schussheim noted, even a sympathetic President Kennedy pegged the subordinate position of housing by emphasizing that meeting his housing goals would "contribute to the Nation's economic recovery and its long-term economic growth."[3]

One of the harshest criticisms of the lack of focus and coherence in federal housing policy can be found in *Housing in the Seventies: A Report of the National Housing Policy Review* (1974), undertaken by the Nixon Administration. It termed the nation's housing laws as of 1974 "a hodge podge of accumulated authorizations" which "contain internal inconsistencies, numerous duplications, cross-purposes, and overlaps as well as outright conflicts and gimmickry." More than any other cause, the proliferation and confusion were attributed to conflicts between multiple goals: government participation v. independent private enterprise; program goals v. budget goals; production goals v. consumer protection; production v. equal opportunity goals; production v. environmental quality goals; production v. stabilizing wages for construction labor; public and political acceptance v. efficiency and cost savings; political reality v. consistency all represented conflicts which buffeted housing from one course to another.[4] President Nixon's response was a moratorium on all federal housing programs pending the Housing Policy Review and formulation of a more unified policy.

If there has been any consistent national housing policy over the past half-century, it has been twofold in objective. First, it has sought to encourage and facilitate widespread homeownership. Second, it has used housing as an instrument to a) stimulate the economy, and b) to achieve social goals such as better neighborhoods, city redevelopment, or the end of poverty. Thus was built, in the first instance, a specialized home finance industry, fiercely protected and regulated. The ready expansion of urban and suburban infrastructure, particularly the improvement of roads and highways, facilitated this objective. In the second instance, for example, monetary policy has not hesitated to manipulate the levels of housing activity through interest rates in its efforts to stimulate or restrain economic activity. Additionally, housing legislation became the vehicle for urban renewal and community development, notably in 1949, 1954, and 1974. All this has occurred within the context of using the federal government to help correct "market imperfections" (e.g., the inability of the private sector to provide adequate housing for the lowest income segments of the population) while bolstering the market system (free enterprise).

As with all historical phenomena, the development of housing policy occurs in two dimensions. On the vertical dimension one can observe the progression of housing programs as time passes. Each new direction or modification reflects experience with particular programs, so that it is possible to discern a thematic history. On the horizontal dimension, each new housing program was enacted and implemented within a larger historical context. Located thus in time, particular programs were both responses to and factors within other events and trends during that time.

MAJOR EPOCHS

Housing programs that began 50 years ago must be viewed against a backdrop of long-standing concern for the poor housing conditions spawned by industrial cities. Unlike many other countries, the United States never experienced multitudes of the urban homeless—nearly everyone was sheltered somewhere. Although Chicago grew from 30,000 to over 1.1 million in the 40 years from 1850 to 1890, the hordes of newcomers were housed. But the quality of their housing was poor. The outcries of housing reformers, a few wavering voices in the 1830s, had become a crescendo by the 1930s. In every city there were active campaigners against the overcrowding, poor ventilation, lack of sanitation, and poor construction so characteristic of tenement and lower-density worker housing. Moreover, by the 1930s a newer phenomenon, dimly understood and most upsetting in a society so new, added to the woes of urban centers: Cities were aging and deteriorating at the core. To the large stock of housing inadequate from the day it was built was added old housing once good, even grand, but now crumbling and overutilized.

Nineteenth and early twentieth century housing reformers tried to eliminate the evils of slums through restrictive legislation. Laws setting minimum standards for light, air, room access, and occupancy were enacted, as were ordinances prescribing plumbing, electrical, heating, and materials standards for newly constructed housing. But such laws could not eliminate existing inadequacies, nor could they induce landlords or developers to undertake projects of marginal potential profitability. Philanthropic endeavors to build solid housing for the industrial working classes were at best sporadic; what few successes there were among limited-dividend apartments seemed only to reemphasize the inability of private enterprise to meet the needs of this large market.

By the 1930s, therefore, reformers were turning their attention toward positive governmental intervention. If slums were to be replaced by decent housing, it would entail large-scale projects. Governmental intervention would be required to clear and assemble large tracts of slum land and then to supply an outright subsidy to make up the difference between the costs of such projects and what poorer families could afford to pay. In the words of Edith Elmer Wood, "a community which has permitted slum conditions to develop has incurred a responsibility to eliminate them, even at the taxpayer's expense, and . . . an industrial civilization, resting on a certain distribution of skilled and unskilled jobs, has a responsibility to see that wholesome housing is available for those in the lower-paid occupations."[5] The fiscal crises which threatened every city and state as the Great Depression deepened shifted the focus of public intervention from municipal to federal government.

The 1930s

The financial and economic disasters of the Great Depression provided the occasion for the first sustained, overt federal interventions in the housing market. The basic framework for housing policy during the next four decades was established: a federally regulated housing finance and mortgage guarantee system, and the public housing program.

The litany of hardships wrought by the Depression is well-known. By 1931, the nation's unemployment exceeded 15 percent; it stayed there for the rest of the decade. It peaked at nearly 25 percent in 1933. In some cities the unemployment rate was much higher. One of the major contributors to the great crash in 1929 was the collapse of the real estate boom in the years preceding the crash. Housing starts, which reached 937,000 in 1925, gradually declined to 750,000 in 1928, then fell to 330,000 in 1930, and to less than 100,000 in 1933. Even worse for the nation's financial structure, real estate values declined precipitously. Rising unemployment and falling real estate prices meant an increasing number of fore-closures—over 270,000 in both 1932 and 1933, nearly triple the number in 1926. Economic necessity and loss of confidence in banks led to increased withdrawal of deposits, just when financial institutions were discovering the illiquidity and deflating value of their holdings. As a result, bank failures increased and the en-tire shaky financial structure, especially that portion that was heavily involved with home finance, began to crumble.

From this economic chaos, three powerful interest groups emerged to press for federal action. The construction industry was extremely hard hit. In 1934 Secre-tary of Labor Frances Perkins reported that 2 million of the 12 million unem-ployed were in the building trades, and Federal Emergency Relief Administration (FERA) Administrator Harry Hopkins estimated that one-third of the families on the relief rolls were identified with the building trades. To the cries for help from home builders were added those of the finance industry, which was in a sham-bles. Their importunities for federal intervention and assistance were met, with the result that a public-private alliance became a permanent feature in the areas of home building and finance.

The Depression also spawned a third interest group, namely, a virtuous class of poor people. Many housing reform efforts had been hampered previously by the tendency of reformers, the general non-poor public, and policy makers to view poor people as improvident, licentious, bibulous, prone to violence, dull-witted, and generally inferior. Should one provide a bathtub for folks who would only use it for coal storage? These "undeserving" poor had always posed a phil-osophical problem. On the other hand, the "deserving" poor had long aroused sympathy and concern. During the 1930s their ranks were swollen—it was easy to perceive unemployed laborers who could not afford to pay their rent, or their mortgage, as temporarily down on their luck. This helped overcome the philo-sophical reservations about lending them a tax-supported hand. And it created a large constituency for public assistance.

The product of these forces was the nation's home financing apparatus and public housing. The Home Owner's Loan Corporation (HOLC), created in 1933 with President Hoover's blessings, provided emergency financing to prevent foreclosures: HOLC actively loaned money, some $3 billion, until 1936, and then passed from the scene in 1953 when the loans in its portfolio had been re-tired. Of greater long-run significance, in 1932 Congress implemented President Hoover's recommendation, eagerly supported by the nation's thrift institutions, to create a Federal Home Loan Bank (FHLB), whose role in housing finance would be roughly analogous to that of the Federal Reserve System. Owned and governed by its member thrift institutions (savings and loan associations and mutual associations), the FHLB has made the flow of mortgage funds more de-pendable, has helped create a national market for mortgages, and has generally strengthened the system that allows individual savings to provide much of the funds for home mortgages. The Housing Act of 1934 addressed, successfully, the twin problems of confidence faced by home finance institutions: savers were reluctant to deposit their money in such financial institutions because of the risky nature of their major investment, and financial institutions were reluctant to lend money for mortgages lest they jeopardize their depositors' money. A twin system of insurance was provided: the Federal Savings and Loan Insurance Corporation insured individual depositors' accounts against the subscribing institution's failure, and the Federal Housing Administration (FHA) guaranteed individual mortgages against their default and fostered the major change from short-term balloon to long-term amortizing mortgages.

The Housing Act of 1937 created the basic structure for the nation's system of public housing. Local housing authorities, chartered under state enabling laws, would build and administer their own housing projects, using the proceeds from sale of their own tax-free bonds, while receiving additional federal moneys to make up the differences between what their tenants could afford and the costs of construction and operation.

Both public housing and the home mortgage insurance were enacted to stimulate the construction industry and thereby the related manufacturing industries dependent on new housing construction. Public housing had the added objective of slum clearance. Mortgage insurance had the added goal of promoting and protecting widespread homeownership.

World War II

World War II had an enormous impact on national housing policy. The War produced massive dislocation and redistribution of population both for military bases and for industrial production. Over 15 million men and women were in uniform between 1941 and 1945; housing markets were very tight around most military installations. At the same time, production workers flocked to old and new industrial centers to work in the aircraft industries in southern California, the shipbuilding yards of Norfolk, Virginia, and the "Arsenal of Democracy," Detroit. Despite the Lanham Act of 1940 which authorized the public construction of temporary workers' housing around defense plants, housing provision was among the most notable wartime failures. Materials allocations did not go to housing, with the result that by 1944 private housing starts were again approaching the depressed level of the early 1930s. Public housing construction had virtually ceased. In all booming wartime cities, housing was in short supply. For the longer range, the economic stimulus provided by the war led to virtual full employment. With relatively few outlets for consumer goods, this prosperity meant a high degree of savings and substantial pent-up demand.

Of even greater long-range significance was the creation of a large, politically powerful, even irresistible, interest group: veterans. They had risked their lives and deferred their dreams in order to protect the nation. Housing subsidies or favored treatment, stiffly opposed for others, were easily awarded to veterans. Only the churlish or unpatriotic could object to the payment of such conscience money. The feeling of gratitude toward veterans was coupled with a fear that once the economic stimulus of war ended, the nation would return to depression conditions. The Servicemen's Readjustment Acts of 1944 and 1945 grew from the desire to show gratitude to veterans, to facilitate their transition from military to civilian life, and to cushion them against the stoutest blows of the anticipated hard times. Among the benefits they could enjoy was the Veterans Administration (VA) home loan program. This provided that the VA would guarantee the mortgages of veterans, which would carry low interest, be for long terms, and require very low down payments. Unlike the existing FHA mortgage guarantee which was financed by an insurance premium, the VA loan insurance represented an actual government subsidy. VA loans helped boost the volume of home construction to over 1 million annually after the war and were a major factor in the expansion of homeownership to a broader range of households.

Post-War Era, 1946 to the 1960s

During the years following World War II, FHA- and VA-insured mortgages became significant factors in housing markets throughout the country. Conventional home financing also offered long-term, self-amortizing mortgages, while 80 and 90 percent loan-to-value ratios became the industry norm. Home construction, as a result, reached unprecedented levels. In 1946 housing starts passed the 1 million mark for the first time, more than tripling the 1945 total. The annual average number of housing starts throughout the 1950s was 1.5 million, ranging from a low of 1.2 million in 1957 to a high of 1.9 million in 1950. Almost 90 percent of these new units were single-family dwellings, which spread around the outer edges of American cities.

This heavy volume of construction put intense pressure on the price of building materials. Average home construction costs more than doubled between 1944 and 1949 and continued to rise thereafter. Moreover, strong demand coupled with inflation drove the price of existing houses even higher. The 1960 U.S. Census showed that the median value for all dwelling units rose from $3,000 in 1940, to $7,400 in 1950, and to $11,900 in 1960. Indeed, steadily rising values lowered the risk of high loan-to-value mortgages and transformed homes into investments as well as shelters. A sustained high level of prosperity was a final factor underwriting the amazing burst in homeownership, from 44 percent of all households in 1940 to 62 percent in 1960.

The high level of family formation, after depression- and war-induced postponements, underwrote this frenzy of borrowing and building. These families also did much begetting, as birth rates temporarily reversed their long-term trend; the higher birth rates in this post-war era produced the now legendary Baby

Boom. Building and begetting were mutually reinforcing; the former was certainly enhanced by federal policy and federally created institutions designed precisely to achieve the homeowning world that was taking shape.

While the federally created home finance apparatus was apparently achieving its goals of wider homeownership and a healthy construction industry, the progress of the public housing branch of federal policy was disappointing to its advocates. The experience during the war was a foretaste of things to come. Efforts to make wartime publicly financed housing part of a comprehensive housing program ran afoul of local interests hostile to large-scale housing projects which might transform their communities, and they had been stymied by a real estate lobby vehemently opposed to government competition in local housing markets. The Cold War spirit of strident anti-communism bolstered the real estate critics, who attacked public housing as socialistic and lambasted its supporters with the extreme rhetoric of that era. (Even "Mr. Republican," Ohio Senator Robert A. Taft, was called a communist by one zealous lobbyist for his strong support of public housing.)

Equally damaging to the hopes that public housing might indeed become the means for creating more wholesome residential environments was its subordination to the demands for urban redevelopment. The environmental determinism upon which the public housing movement built could easily justify programs of massive slum clearance. Public housing and slum clearance had been linked in the Housing Act of 1937. During the 1940s, while public housing encountered stiff opposition in the halls of Congress and in American cities, slum clearance gained momentum. Mayors, community leaders, real estate interests, builders and developers, and professional planners turned to the federal government for financial assistance for the redevelopment of their city cores on a massive scale. Gradually these interests formulated a program whereby a local public renewal agency, using federal funds, would assemble a large tract of centrally located urban real estate, clear it of unwanted structures, make appropriate site improvements, and sell it to a private developer at its market price, undoubtedly far below the costs incurred. Significantly, this program was enacted in the landmark Housing Act of 1949, and was joined with legislative authorization of 810,000 public housing units during the coming six years. Thus was born Urban Renewal.

These twin offspring, urban redevelopment and public housing, were not equally loved by their parents. If this had not been clear during the five years of congressional wrangling preceding the Housing Act of 1949, it became obvious during the succeeding decade. Urban renewal and commercial revitalization cheated public housing of its birthright; the role of low-income housing construction in renewal projects was gradually all but eliminated. Moreover, as a result of President Eisenhower's austere budgets and continued opposition to the very concept of public housing, actual appropriations and administrative authorizations (there were *none* in 1954) never came close to the construction levels provided in 1949. By 1960 only some 250,000 new units had been made available for occupancy. Thirty years after the Housing Act of 1949 only about 1 million units had been built. Urban renewal, made much more explicit as the nation's urban revitalization strategy in the Housing Act of 1954, destroyed many more housing units than it replaced.

During these post-war years federal homeownership programs chiefly beneficial to the prosperous and multitudinous middle and working classes blossomed forth in single-family subdivisions. Housing programs for low-income and inner city households were systematically underfunded and were crowded out by commercial revitalization intended to counteract the effects of suburbanization encouraged by public policy.

The 1960s: Activism

The era of the 1960s and early 1970s was one of activism. Its dominant moods ran from optimism, to discomfort, to fear. The massive demonstrations by southern blacks to destroy the system of legal segregation culminated in the march on Washington in 1963. Northern blacks, not in the mortgaged mainstream of suburbia, rudely intruded on the world of those who were. The racial skirmishes within central city powder kegs exploded into destructive riots, the most spectacular of which shook Los Angeles in 1965 and Detroit and Newark in 1967. But no large city escaped eruptions, and "long hot summer" became a part of the national vocabulary. By 1966 even the children of suburbia were raising their voices and marching in protest against the U.S. military policy in Southeast Asia. This was not a comfortable time.

The era began optimistically with the inauguration of a young president, John F. Kennedy, the first chief executive born in the twentieth century. His can-do rhetoric attracted swarms of social scientists to Washington who were eager to demonstrate that knowledge and know-how would enable a benign government to lead a wealthy society to the solution of its most persistent problems. Even President Kennedy's assassination did not extinguish this optimism. In fact, Lyndon Johnson's presidency provided a rare congruence of political skill, will, and opportunity to implement programs which would usher in the "Great Society." But the Age of Activism burned too fiercely to last for long. The nation's resources were diverted to the rice fields of Southeast Asia and its good will was sapped by fear. Governmentally, the era ended in the resignation of a disgraced president in 1973.

Federal housing policy from the early 1960s to the early 1970s also ran the gamut from optimism, to disappointment, to disgust. Housing policy was imbedded in the various programs and social objectives of the "Great Society." It became clear that if black Americans were to be better housed, the barriers of discrimination would have to be removed. The Civil Rights Act of 1964 addressed a wide range of racial barriers. The Civil Rights Act of 1968 expressly established equal opportunity in housing as an official U.S. policy by prohibiting all actors in the housing market from discriminating on the basis of race, color, creed or national origin. If inadequate housing was the result of inadequate incomes, as most policy makers believed, then poverty was the real enemy. The "War on Poverty," launched by the Economic Opportunities Act of 1965, was intended as a direct attack on urban slums.

The proliferation of housing programs and agencies had posed coordination problems for years. Efforts to unite all federal housing actors under one banner dated from the interagency rivalries of the World War II era. A Department of Housing and Urban Development was finally authorized in 1965 and organized in 1966. On the local level, the profusion of federal programs made a focused approach all but impossible, while also severely compromising the role of municipal government. The Demonstration Cities and Metropolitan Development Act of 1966 created the "Model Cities Program," designed to coordinate these numerous competing and/or conflicting efforts within a designated deteriorated area. It was short-lived.

The activism of the 1960s spawned a host of highly visible study commissions and reports. The National Advisory Commission on Civil Disorders, chaired by Illinois Governor Otto Kerner, produced its famous "Kerner Report" in early 1969. The report warned that "Our Nation is moving toward two societies, one black, one white—separate and unequal." Two other commissions appointed in 1967 issued reports on successive days in December, 1968, which were particularly relevant to housing policies. The National Commission on Urban Problems, chaired by Senator Paul Douglas, produced *Building the American City*, a classic review of urban problems, with summaries and recommendations about housing and urban-related programs. The President's Committee on Urban Housing, chaired by industrialist Edgar F. Kaiser, produced *A Decent Home*, which focused especially on how the private enterprise system could be harnessed to provide more and better housing for the urban masses. It was the Kaiser Commission which first recommended that a production goal of 26 million new and rehabilitated housing units be established as national policy and that 6 million of those units be targeted for low-income families.

The Housing Act of 1968 did, in fact, officially establish that 26-million-unit, 10-year production goal. Among the new programs aimed at achieving that objective was the Section 235 interest-rate subsidy, designed to make homeownership more accessible to low-income families by lowering monthly mortgage payments. From 1971 through 1973 housing starts exceeded 2 million annually, thanks in large part to the provisions of the Housing Act of 1968.

By 1973 federal housing programs abounded. The cost was rising, and future subsidy payments already committed reached levels that were disturbing to the administration. Between 1968 and 1973 some 375,000 public housing units had been made available for occupancy, whereas only 470,000 had been added in the 18 years since 1949. Changes in public housing rentals made by a series of amendments proposed by Senator Edward Brooke in 1969 and 1970 linked payments to tenants' ability to pay rather than to operating costs. But public housing tenants by that time were no longer primarily the working poor temporarily down on their luck and upwardly mobile. They were, increasingly, members of a semi-permanent dependent class whose incomes, often from public sources, were low and whose chances of upward mobility were dim. Public housing authorities throughout the country were faced with overwhelming cash flow problems and dismal financial outlooks. When scandals began to surface, especially involving the new interest-subsidy programs, President Nixon had had enough. As public criticism mounted, he ordered HUD to conduct an extensive national housing policy review. As expected, the review recommended that current programs be suspended until the federal government's role could be assessed and redefined. The 1973 moratorium was accordingly declared and new authorizations were suspended.

While cities seemed to teeter on the brink of disaster and urban housing subsidies flitted from program to program, households continued their march to the suburbs. Houses, still almost all single family, were built at the rate of 1.4 million per year throughout the 1960s. Some 15.5 percent were financed by FHA-insured mortgages and another 3.5 percent by VA-insured mortgages. The white flight which the upheavals of the period accelerated, and which urban policies sought to stem, was thus being underwritten in part by federal mortgage insurance.

Since 1973

The mid-1970s marked the end of intense activism. There was not, however, a return to normalcy. What had become a kind of conventional wisdom (albeit, not one universally accepted), namely, that government was a benign entity that could solve society's stickiest problems, lost its force. Large segments of the population felt that government complicity had compounded racial discrimination, and government policy had hastened the disintegration of central cities. To others, the American government was the major force in the devastation of Viet Nam. The Republic withstood the resignation of a disgraced vice president and president and the succession of an appointed chief executive. But the image of government, especially the federal government, was further damaged. The final withdrawal of the armed forces from Viet Nam represented a military and political defeat; the United States had clearly lost its longest war.

The myth of American invincibility took another beating from economic developments. The Arab oil embargo in 1973 dramatized the nation's dependency on foreign oil supplies. Long lines at gas pumps quickly translated into skyrocketing gas and oil prices. Political instability in the Middle East and the emergence of the OPEC cartel spelled the end of cheap energy; in an energy-intensive economy, prices of nearly everything moved sharply upward. Little cars from Japan threatened the dominance of the American auto industry, which subsequently went into a prolonged slump and dragged down the rest of the economy. By the early 1980s, the United States was no longer the undisputed technological and economic leader of the world.

These developments had major implications for housing. To no longer dominate was not merely unpleasant, it was actually frightening. As Datsuns, Toyotas, Sonys, and Hitachis proliferated, repeated references to Pearl Harbor reflected the national mood of fear. The search for appropriate responses to this new invasion centered on the decline of worker productivity. Some analysts contended that one reason for neglected investments in industrial technology was an excessive investment in housing. Middle-class Americans were scolded for overhousing themselves; despite a shrinking median household size the typical house built in the late 1970s had 1,500 to 2,000 square feet, as compared to the typical 800 to 1,000 square feet of the late 1940s. Warnings that the nation's attention must be turned from housing to investment in reindustrialization abounded. Indeed, reindustrialization became the watchword; hoping to stimulate increases in productivity, federal policy made capital investments its new favorite. It became increasingly clear that housing's days as a protected investment market were numbered.

The special circumstances under which the United States had become a nation of homeowners ceased to exist. But the system went out in a blaze of glory. Annual private housing starts averaged 1.75 million from 1971-80. The pattern, however, was extremely cyclical: 2.4 million in 1972, 1.2 million in 1975, back to 2 million in 1978, then down to 1.3 million in 1980 (and further down to 1.1 million in 1982). This tremendous volume of production afforded substantial housing choices and, on the other side of the coin, substantial household configuration choices to American families. In a time of rapid inflation and soaring interest rates, the old system of housing finance offered exceptional opportunities for investment in single-family dwellings. Low down payments and long-term, fixed-interest mortgages allowed home purchasers easy access to the bonanza of real estate appreciation. Housing prices rose faster than inflation. The median sales price of a new house climbed from $25,200 in 1971 to $64,500 in 1980, an increase of 156 percent; in some markets the rise was breathtaking. By opportune trading, homeowners could parlay a $5,000 down payment into a $250,000 residence; or they could stay put and watch their paper profits, and net worth, reach numbers beyond their wildest hopes. They could even borrow on their new equity and thus extract from their shelters the funds for college tuitions or sailboats. It was a great joyride for those who owned houses.

Savers and would-be, first-time home buyers missed the ride. High inflation meant that passbook savings shrank in real terms; rising interest rates and new investment vehicles offered alternatives for savers. Home financing institutions were forced to compete more aggressively for funds. These market forces coincided with ideological hostility toward governmental regulation, which had gained momentum both inside and outside the federal government in the latter part of the 1970s. The passage of the Depository Institutions Deregulation and Monetary Control Act in 1980 officially marked the end of the protected network of home finance. Henceforth, homeownership would have to compete with other forms of investment for funds. This meant higher interest rates and fewer long-term, fixed-rate mortgages. And it meant that the Federal Reserve Bank, through its manipulation of interest rates in pursuit of its monetary policies, had become the most important player in the new housing game.

Federal housing assistance policy during this era was contained mainly in the Housing and Community Development Act of 1974. The spate of housing studies and reports produced under the auspices of HUD, Congress, Presidential commissions, private foundations, and other public and private urban research centers provided, if not inspiration, at least sanction for the major features of this landmark legislation. The way had also been prepared by the moratorium called in 1973.

Public housing had by the early 1970s come under attack from nearly all directions, not just its traditional realtor enemies. Friends of government housing subsidy now questioned the efficiency of public housing; enormous capital outlays for new projects seemed to be disproportionate to the number of clients served. And on the related grounds of horizontal equity, public housing was woefully inadequate; approximately 3 million people living in about 1 million public housing units in 1971 constituted less than 5 percent of the eligible households.

Public housing was also severely criticized for having failed to provide a decent living environment. Early housing reformers had insisted that improving slum living conditions required large-scale projects; scattered efforts would only leave islands of respectability which would soon be overwhelmed by the surrounding degradation. Most public housing was done on a large scale, which critics in the 1970s found to be one of its major shortcomings. In the years between 1930 and 1980 careful attention to construction and design had too often been sacrificed to immediate cost-saving, with the result that cheap, dreary high-rise projects scarcely improved on the tenements they replaced. Moreover, the clientele in public housing by 1971 had become not so much the respectable poor envisioned in the 1937 Housing Act, temporarily down on their luck but upwardly mobile, but a more-or-less permanent subgroup: either increasingly black, one-parent (usually female) households with several children, or elderly. Public housing offered too many highly visible images of vertical file drawers filled with society's failures and outcasts. Clearly, public housing had become a major contributor to the economic and racial segregation of American cities.

The plethora of other housing-related urban programs was also bombarded by the criticism of urban experts. The urban renewal approach had its share of critics; it was variously judged insensitive to the richness of the urban fabric, discriminatory toward the poor and the black whom it displaced rather than rehoused; a net destroyer of housing, and inappropriately focused on redeveloping the central business district at the expense of the neighborhoods. Other programs drew additional fire: they were too multitudinous and often conflicting; they used federal dollars to determine local priorities, thereby distorting orderly change; and they bypassed duly elected urban governments, creating separate, often conflicting, bureaucracies. By the early 1970s urban mayors felt the loss of control over federal dollars keenly and requested a more unified system that would restore their budgetary control while still providing much-needed federal funds.

The Housing and Community Development Act of 1974 (HCD) had three major features relevant to this problem. It combined a wide range of categorical grant programs into one large block grant, the funds for which went directly to respective municipal governments. These funds could be used for a wide range of capital improvements and human services; they were allocated through the normal budget-making process of the local governing bodies. In many cities substantial portions of these funds were appropriated for housing programs. Indirectly, neighborhood development programs sought to improve residential environments; directly, local programs included revolving funds for home repair, rehabilitation, code enforcement, and a host of supportive services which included tool banks, advisory services and sweat-equity loans.

A second major feature of the HCD Act of 1974 was its rent supplement program. Rent supplements had been suggested by real estate lobbyists and other outspoken critics of public housing ever since the debates of the 1930s. Housing reformers had long opposed them on the grounds that they constituted a dole. But the availability of existing housing in central cities and criticism regarding the efficiency of public housing made the idea of rent supplements for low-income families paid directly to private landlords compelling by 1974. The act, under its Section 8, created three separate programs: one for existing housing units, one for units requiring substantial rehabilitation, and one for new rental housing construction. Under each, qualified low-income tenants would find suitable and affordable housing in the local market and pay one-fourth of their income as rent, the deficit to be made up by Section 8 allotments, usually to the local housing authority. This system of housing subsidy was intended to achieve the final feature of the act noted here: the scattering of low-income housing. If tenants found their own housing with private landlords, there would be no clearly visible subsidized housing projects and, hopefully, no inordinate concentration of low-income tenants in slums.

SUMMARY

The basic outlines of a federal housing policy were drawn during the Great Depression. Widespread unemployment, bank failures, loss of savings, and home foreclosures led to the collapse of the real estate market. These disasters provided immediate objectives for housing programs: to stimulate employment, to preserve and strengthen financial institutions, and to protect and promote home ownership. During the prosperous decades following World War II, homeownership programs were phenomenally successful. High family formation and high birth rates went hand in hand with high wages, high mortgage availability, and high consumerism, so that, despite concomitant high home prices, single-family dwellings sprawled outward from urban centers across the nation. Meanwhile, the aging and depopulation of central cities (the other predictable outcome of this suburbanization) presented problems less amenable to ready policy solutions. A range of housing and housing-related urban programs were tried, from Urban Renewal, to Model Cities, to Community Development. The contemporary context is marked by the end of the Baby Boom, the sobering realities of international economic competition, and the powerful mood favoring deregulation and reduced federal activism. In that setting, homeownership is less valued and no longer taken for granted. Housing subsidy programs remain, as do federally funded and supported housing developments. But, their visibility in the national agenda has been substantially reduced.

NOTES

1. Daniel Boorstin, *The Genius of American Politics* (Chicago: University of Chicago Press, 1953). See esp. Chapter I, "How Belief in the Existence of An American Theory Has Made a Theory Superfluous."
2. Donald Kummerfeld, "The Housing Subsidy System," in U.S. Congress, House, Committee on Banking and Currency, Subcommittee on Housing, *Papers Submitted to Subcommittee on Housing Panels on Housing Production, Housing Demand and Developing a Suitable Living Environment*, Part 2, 92nd Congress, 1st Session, June 1971 (Washington D.C.: Government Printing Office, 1971), 451-52.
3. Morton J. Schussheim, *The Modest Commitment to Cities* (Lexington, Massachusetts: Lexington Books, 1974), 45-64.
4. U.S. Department of Housing and Urban Development, *Housing in the Seventies: A Report of the National Housing Policy Review* (Washington, D.C.: 1976), pp. 22-25.
5. Edith Elmer Wood, "The Economics of the Slums," *Current History*, 39 (November 1933), 187.

2

Rationale for a Housing Policy

Henry J. Aaron

Nearly all countries—rich and poor—have a housing problem. And nearly all—whether centrally planned or free market economies—have a housing policy. The production and distribution of housing are circumscribed, controlled, regulated, subsidized, and taxed in numerous ways in the United States, as in most other countries.

U.S. HOUSING GOAL

Among the Johnson administration's bequests to President Nixon was a national housing goal, a legislated promise to build or to rehabilitate 26 million housing units in the decade 1969–78. The proclaimed objective was to solve the housing problem in the United States. Although 4 million mobile homes have since been redefined as housing units, housing output has failed to keep up with original projections and the likelihood that the goal will be achieved is shrinking steadily. The success or failure of the United States in achieving the housing goal has become for many a symbol of American willingness to reorient priorities.

The Housing and Urban Development Act of 1968 was passed in response to two housing problems. A huge increase in the number of families was imminent, as children born during the post-World War II baby boom matured, left home,

From Henry J. Aaron. *Shelter and Subsidies: Who Benefits from Federal Housing Policies.* (Washington, D.C.: 1972), pp. 3-22. Reprinted by permission of The Brookings Institution.

19

and formed households of their own. Clearly, these new families would create a housing shortage unless residential construction increased rapidly. America had experienced an even worse shortage after World War II when returning veterans and other newly formed households swelled housing demand. The crush of the 1970s promised to be serious, but the earlier experience indicated that with federal assistance, private industry could solve a "too little housing" problem.

The United States had, moreover, conspicuously and embarrassingly failed to fulfill the much quoted pledge of the Housing Act of 1949 to provide a decent home and a suitable living environment to all Americans. Millions continued to live in housing units officially classified as dilapidated, deteriorating, or overcrowded; many others were adequately housed only because they spent a burdensome proportion of family income on shelter. In short, America continued to suffer from a "bad housing" problem.

To deal with the "bad housing" problem, the national housing goal called for construction or rehabilitation of 6 million housing units with federal assistance, a massive increase over the prevailing levels of federal assistance. Nearly all of the direct assistance has since been channeled through five programs—low rent public housing and rent supplements directed toward low income families, and mortgage assistance, rental assistance, and subsidized loans for rural and small town borrowers directed toward lower middle income families.

To deal with the "too little housing" problem, the housing goal called for the construction or rehabilitation of 20 million housing units *without* federal assistance. For this, the numerically dominant part of the overall housing output, the lumber and other materials, manpower, and land necessary to construction reportedly were available. Mortgage credit might be scarce, and here the federal government had a role; it should somehow assure an adequate flow of credit.

The political tactic of tying the two housing problems together succeeded. Congress enacted the goal and passed laws creating new forms of federal assistance, largely as requested by the Johnson administration. Whether the housing strategy expressed in the national housing goal will succeed is one of the issues this study deals with.

EVALUATION OF U.S. POLICY

In evaluating federal housing policies, three questions arise: what services do the programs provide, who benefits from them, and how efficiently are they provided? This study is concerned primarily with identifying the beneficiaries of programs, their income and other characteristics, and the size of the benefits. It first investigates the reasons why public intervention in the housing market may be necessary and then reviews evidence on the amount and quality of housing in the United States. After exploring the theoretical problems of measuring the benefits from public expenditures, the study focuses on federal housing policies. It does not attempt to encompass programs undertaken by state and local governments or activities not principally concerned with housing (such as urban renewal or defense or college student housing). Neither does it cover the dozens of federal programs that might be discussed (Appendix A gives brief descriptions of many of the programs).

The most conspicuous and questionable omission is income maintenance programs. Welfare agencies divide payments into allowances for housing, food, clothing, and other commodities; in 1969 they allocated nearly $1.4 billion for housing allowances for the poor. A substantial part of old-age, survivor's, and disability benefits, veterans' benefits and pensions, and other federal transfer payments is also spent on housing. Income maintenance programs, however, provide general economic aid, not specific support for housing.

Each of the six groups of policies that generate the bulk of all benefits from federal housing policies is evaluated separately. The most important, in its impact on income distribution, is contained in the internal revenue code. Other significant policies are reflected in programs of federal mortgage insurance and loan guarantees, federally sponsored financing instruments, public housing, special assistance through mortgage markets, and aid to residents of rural areas. The net result of the evaluations is to make apparent the need for change; an alternative plan for future federal housing aid is suggested at the end of the study.

HOUSING AND HOUSING SERVICES

Housing can denote the stock of structures in which people reside: living units, occupied or vacant, differentiated by location, by size and type (for example, single-family detached, highrise apartment, garden apartment, mobile home), and in numerous other ways. The housing stock can be increased by new construction or conversions of other property to residential use and diminished by destruction or depreciation or conversion to nonresidential use.

Housing also can denote "housing services"—the commodity produced by the housing stock in combination with maintenance and repair labor, such intermediate goods as electricity, gas, and water; and another capital good, land.[1] The present worth of housing services, after the costs of maintaining the stock are deducted, represents the value of the housing stock.

"Housing policy" is a similarly ambiguous term. Housing policy can influence the number and kind of new structures built and the maintenance, conversion, and removal of old structures. In a larger sense it can influence housing services—the quality of the housing stock and of the individual units and the cost of housing services.

Unfortunately, the boundaries between public policies are not clearly drawn; all public or private actions have some effect, possibly infinitesimal, on most economic units. For practical purposes, housing policy can be defined as encompassing government expenditures, loans, and loan guarantees for investment in structures; zoning regulations and building and housing codes; and legal provisions concerning property rights and tax treatment of residential real property or of income from it.[2] Among the public actions not directly concerned with housing that may affect it greatly is the provision of locationally fixed services such as schools, police and fire protection, and public transportation.

Residential Services

When a homeowner or renter chooses a house or apartment, he purchases not only housing services, but also a wide range of goods and services—public schools, stores, parks, public transportation, neighbors, and other amenities. Though they cost him nothing beyond the price of housing and attendant property taxes, his satisfaction—indeed, his welfare—depends on these commodities as much as on his housing. He does not express in the marketplace his demand for housing but for the entire package. Statistics on housing expenditures therefore really measure the value placed by residents on housing and residential services.

Improvement in the quality of neighborhood schools, for example, usually increases the amount tenants will pay for housing (exclusive of property taxes).[3] The transportation network—mass transit and the road system—affects the value placed on housing because transportation costs both money and time. The importance of transportation is readily apparent in the Watts neighborhood of Los Angeles, which has been described as "clearly . . . superior to most low-income neighborhoods. Many of the major and expanding employment centers of the Los Angeles metropolitan area, however, are practically inaccessible to Watts residents except by private motor cars, which many of them do not own. Bus connections are long, complicated and expensive. . . . Housing in Watts, therefore, is poor housing for many low-income residents and they know it and resent its crippling effects on their efforts to better their economic position."[4]

Housing segregation has been accused of cutting employment opportunities for Negroes in Chicago and Detroit by reducing access to jobs.[5] But the problem of access is a general one—the value of any residence depends partly on its distance from jobs, stores, and recreation and on the quality and price of the transportation network connecting them.

Another commodity the occupant of a residence purchases is neighbors. Their behavior and appearance affect the price prospective occupants are willing to pay for housing. To some extent, personal tastes—aversion to living among people of different races (particularly if they form a majority), dislike for crowds or for empty space—dictate choices.

The intelligence, honesty, or other attributes of his neighbors directly affect a homeowner's welfare and influence the value of his housing. For example, academic achievement depends significantly on the socioeconomic status of fellow students.[6] Scores on standardized tests—used to determine admission to many colleges, to process draftees, to select among job applicants—rise as the socioeconomic status of neighborhoods rises, unless differences in public expenditures somehow offset the influence of peers on academic achievement. Performance by students on reading tests and pupil-teacher ratios are closely linked to home values.[7] The principal means of expressing the educational value of neighborhoods is through the price offered for housing.

The residents of poor neighborhoods are victims of high prices, inferior merchandise, high interest rates, and aggressive and deceptive sales practices.[8] They pay for the costs of doing business where pilferage and default risks are above average.[9] Costs are averaged over all customers, so that reliable households suffer from living where high-cost customers are particularly numerous. Such extra costs of living are among the costs of residential services that affect the price people will pay for housing services. Another social cost that varies by neighborhood is the probability of crime. The major market response the individual can make to differences in crime rates is to alter the price he is willing to pay for housing.[10]

Housing Markets

For households the borders of the housing market are determined by where the household members work and shop. Workers must live within commuting distance of their jobs. They normally choose neighbors with roughly similar incomes. Their spending habits are seldom affected by the price of housing or vacancy rates in other cities, metropolitan areas, states, or even areas only a few blocks away. The penthouse resident on New York City's Central Park West or Chicago's Lake Shore Drive is less likely to change his spending patterns because the prices of Beverly Hills mansions or farmhouses in Idaho change or because four-story walk-ups one mile away deteriorate into slums than because the prices of luxury automobiles or transoceanic air fares change. Households are far more likely to respond to variations in the price or quantity of some complement of or substitute for housing or residential services than to developments in other housing markets.

Each household, therefore, is interested in only a small part of the total housing stock—roughly, that part in which its socioeconomic peers reside and from which members of the household can conveniently commute to work. The housing markets of all households are linked, however, by a process called "filtering."[11] The homes of the rich often become homes for the middle class or for the poor as incomes change and job patterns shift. Housing also shifts among submarkets as a result of new construction or conversion of nonresidential property to residential use. Through this process, changes in the supply of one kind of housing affect other housing markets as well. For these reasons, all housing submarkets are connected, if only tenuously.

For builders and developers, housing markets are determined by licensing or bonding requirements, by preferences for union or nonunion labor, or by building codes and zoning regulations. The skills and materials employed in most

TABLE 1
Major Participants and Influences in the Housing Market

Market Phase	Participants	Influences
Preparation: land acquisition, planning, and zoning amendments	Developer Landowner Lawyers Real estate brokers Title companies Architects and engineers Surveyor Planners and consultants Zoning and planning officials	Real estate law Recording regulations and fees Banking laws Zoning Subdivision regulations Private deed restrictions Public master plans
Production: site preparation, construction, and financing	Developer Lending institutions (interim and permanent) FHA, VA, or private mortgage insurance company Contractors Subcontractors Craftsmen and their unions Material manufacturers and distributors Building code officials Insurance companies Architects and engineers	Banking laws Building and mechanical codes Subdivision regulations Utility regulations Union rules Rules of trade and professional associations Insurance laws Laws controlling transportation of materials
Distribution: sale (and subsequent resale or refinancing)	Developer Real estate brokers Lawyers Lending institutions Title companies FHA, VA, or private mortgage insurance company	Recording regulations and fees Real estate law Transfer taxes Banking laws Rules of professional associations
Service: maintenance and management, repairs, and improvements and additions	Owner Maintenance firms and employees Property management firms Insurance companies Utility companies Tax assessors Repairmen, craftsmen, and their unions Lending institutions Architects and engineers Contractors Subcontractors Material manufacturers and distributors Local zoning officials Local building officials	Property taxes Income taxes Housing and health codes Insurance laws Utility regulations Banking laws Union rules Rules of trade and professional associations Zoning Building and mechanical codes Laws controlling transportation of materials

Source: A Decent Home, Report of the President's Committee on Urban Housing (Government Printing Office, 1969), p. 115.

single-family and much multifamily residential construction are essentially the same, so that differences in price classes and building types are not important.

Financial intermediaries are concerned with the ability of lenders to meet repayment schedules and with the value of collateral in the event of foreclosure. Thus many lenders refuse to provide funds to borrowers whose income is low or irregular or whose collateral is a very old structure or in a poor neighborhood; such borrowers must deal with lenders who specialize in high risk lending, or they must obtain federal mortgage guarantees. Financial intermediaries help set architectural styles by agreeing or refusing to accept certain designs or structures. They also influence the racial composition of neighborhoods; in the past, public agencies such as the Federal Housing Administration were as guilty of discrimination as were private institutions. State and federal banking laws restrict all commercial banks, mutual savings banks, and savings and loan associations to operations within individual states; a number of states prohibit branch banking altogether or restrict branches to the municipality housing the home office. Other laws restrict mortgage lending to areas within a stipulated radius of the lending institution.

Governmental attitudes toward the shape of housing markets may conflict with those held in the private sector. Federal policies differentiate housing by eligibility for explicit subsidies, mortgage insurance or guarantees, or direct loans. Government actions—such as establishment of attendance boundaries for public schools—and development activities—such as construction of highways or preservation of open space—frequently alter housing markets by creating or destroying neighborhood ties.

Clearly, the housing market, like the fabled elephant, is different things to different people. One of the most striking features of the production and distribution of housing services is the number of parties involved in the preparation, production, distribution, or servicing of housing and the variety of laws, regulations, controls, or subsidies to which they are subject (see Table 1). While other industries would utilize a comparable array of professional skills and businesses, few of them are subject to so many different regulations as the housing industry.

INCOME DISTRIBUTION

One of the reasons for governmental adoption of a housing policy is to alter the distribution of income. Graduated income taxes and cash transfers are the most obvious and most common methods of redistributing income. Such policies reflect a collective judgment that general welfare will rise if some groups have more goods and services even at the expense of others. Governments may supply those goods and services directly instead of redistributing money. Such "transfers in kind"—housing, medical care, and food—increase the quantity of goods and services available to recipients.

Economists have long held that public provision of commodities below cost to households is less efficient in improving family welfare than unrestricted transfers of income. If the government were to give a family the cash equivalent of its housing subsidy, the family could purchase unsubsidized housing equivalent to that provided by the government. Normally, a family prefers to spend only part of an unrestricted transfer on any one commodity. From the family's standpoint a cash transfer would leave them at least as well off as would subsidized housing, and usually better off.

While unrestricted transfers may be best from the standpoint of recipients, the taxpayers who finance the assistance may have aims better served by subsidies. The argument for cash transfers presupposes that the provider cares enough about the recipient to offer cash, but not so much as to be interested in how he spends it. An efficient transfer mechanism that includes subsidies to particular commodities may better reflect the collective will in the redistribution of income. Moreover, even in an essentially market-oriented economy, citizens may decide collectively that some tastes are changeable or should be ignored. The majority might decide, for example, that those who have always been poor do not realize how much they would benefit from improved housing, but that after receiving it they will want it. This paternalistic motive for redistributing income with strings attached has been acidly attacked by Edward C. Banfield:

> The doing of good is not so much for the benefit of those to whom the good is done as it is for that of the *doer's*, whose moral faculties are activated and invigorated by the doing of it, and for that of the community, the shared values of which are ritually asserted and vindicated by the doing of it. . . . One recalls Macaulay's remark about the attitude of the English Puritans toward bearbaiting: that they opposed it not for the suffering that it caused the bear but for the pleasure that it gave the spectators. Perhaps it is not far-fetched to say that the present-day outlook is similar: the reformer wants to improve the situation of the poor, the black, the slum dweller, and so one, not so much to make them better off materially as to make himself and the whole society better off morally.[12]

A more practical political argument for redistributing income through commodity subsidies is that, even if they are economically inefficient, they may be more acceptable politically than cash transfers. Provision of direct housing subsidies along with cash, for example, might increase support for income redistribution. If income redistribution were government's sole objective and if beneficiaries' preferences were paramount, no housing policy would be needed. If government should choose, however, to aid households too poor to buy adequate housing, housing subsidies might assume many forms. Government might pay a part or all of rent or home ownership carrying costs for families with incomes below stipulated levels or provide housing to them below cost. It would be wasteful to reduce housing costs for families with incomes above the stipulated levels. Thus it would be wasteful to subsidize construction, borrowing, or other elements of housing costs where benefits did not accrue principally to families with inadequate incomes.

Most federal housing policies are not so limited. They directly assist groups whose incomes and housing are adequate by most standards. Many federal programs subsidize costs of construction, in general, instead of low income or badly housed families. If such programs are to be justified, the desire to redistribute income cannot be the central motivation.

INEFFICIENCIES OF THE FREE MARKET

Even if no one cared about his neighbors' opulence or squalor, each person would probably feel the effect of others' investment in and consumption of housing services. Pride or shame about the general appearance of a neighborhood or town may induce such public actions as zoning regulations to compel each family to take into account the effects on others of its outlays on housing. The justification for zoning regulations might apply equally well to subsidies designed to promote better housing or to taxes designed to promote or discourage expenditures on housing. The conviction, in rich countries and poor, that housing is a problem to be settled publicly must somehow reflect the impact of each family's housing on others. It is hard to escape the conclusion that the reaction against particularly odious housing—"No one should have to live that way"—or the political commitment of the United States to "a decent home and a suitable living environment"[13] for all is founded as much on personal distaste as on sympathetic concern.

The very vagueness of the justification for a public housing policy makes it difficult to decide what public action should be taken. Codes establishing minimum housing standards and subsidies ensuring that all households can meet the standards might be the solution. Conversely, limits on consumption of housing and taxes to enforce those limits might express the public will. In any case, the rhetoric of politicians and others suggests that housing is regarded as a special kind of commodity in that many families care far more about how others are housed than about how they are clothed, entertained, or otherwise provided for. Whether altruism, selfishness, the visibility of squalid housing,[14] or some other reason stirs this concern is far from clear.

Bad housing has long been alleged to cause poor health, low levels of educational achievement, and high crime rates.[15] That these social ills do coincide is beyond dispute, but that the one is cause and the others consequence has never been proved. Conclusive results are hard to come by because adversity is usually hydra-headed. The allegedly adverse effects of housing have nevertheless been used to considerable political effect in support of various housing programs.

For a strong believer in the marketplace as the arbiter of economic decisions the adverse effects would not necessarily justify a public policy on housing. If bad housing harmed only the tenant, then he might be presumed to calculate that harm in deciding how much to spend on housing; and if he were so poor that he had to live in a self-damaging environment, this fact would argue for cash transfers which he could spend as he thought best. But if the consequences of bad housing were visited on his neighbors or his neighborhood, even the strongest advocate of market allocation would concede that a case for public action exists. Recognition of these consequences would not enable him, however, to decide whether housing codes, taxes on bad housing, or subsidies for the improvement of housing would best force owners and tenants to assess the costs imposed on other parties.

Housing Maintenance

One of the most serious consequences of an unregulated housing market is the failure of households to coordinate their actions. The property owner is caught in a predicament like the prisoners' dilemma: Each suspect in a criminal investigation must choose, in response to police offers, whether to confess and receive a light sentence or remain quiet and risk being exposed by his confederates and punished more severely. If each suspect confesses so as to minimize the risk to himself, all will suffer more than if none confessed.

In real estate, if net profitability declines when improvements are made on a single piece of property, no owner is likely to invest in improvements because they yield less to him than they cost. Although the sum of the benefits from investments by all owners in the neighborhood might far exceed costs, no owner acting independently can capture these benefits. Hence, the dilemma—acting in their individual self-interest, all are injured, but no market mechanism exists to induce the coordinated action that would benefit all. Each person pursues the selfish, beneficial short-run strategy to the long-run detriment of all.

Actually the problem is more complex. Investments on one property can alter the value or the rate of return on investments in neighboring properties. For instance, installation of modern plumbing in one building may trigger similar investments in competing structures. The dynamic consequences are probably more important than the static problems arising from the prisoners' dilemma.

Medium or high quality housing may be as much affected by the prisoners' dilemma as is slum and other dilapidated property. Indeed, such visible improvements as elaborate apartment lobbies or expensive landscaping seem likely to affect neighboring property values at least as much as does replacement of a broken toilet or repair of rotted flooring. As an explanation of slums, the argument of the prisoners' dilemma proves too much. It is an overly elaborate analogy from the homely fact that how well each man tends his garden affects his neighbors' too, and that if he disregards his neighbors' interest he may tend it less well than he should. It argues not only that slums may be self-perpetuating, but also that investment in real property in general may be too low. It could be used to justify slum clearance, wholesale or selective renewal, widespread subsidies to real property, strictly enforced housing codes, or investment in public facilities to encourage private investments. Collective action may sometimes improve private investment decisions. Unfortunately, the interdependencies are not well understood; neither are the remedies.

Housing Information

If markets are to operate efficiently, buyers and sellers must be capable of judging the price and quality of commodities. Moreover, markets for all goods and services must exist. Some parts of the housing market are highly competitive; others are virtual monopolies; in many parts information is scarce and dear; for certain goods and services, markets do not exist. In a number of instances, public action may have caused market imperfections or prevented the existence of certain markets.

Each step taken to protect inexpert buyers and sellers in the exchange of housing and of housing services has imposed some costs. Purchasers of housing, like those of many modern products, are protected only by laws covering contracts, negligence, and fraud. Consumers and investors ignorant of the structural and material attributes that affect the durability of a house are free to purchase expert advice; they are presumed to have made well-informed decisions when they fail to secure advice. Since World War II, restrictions on the construction and sale of housing have become common and have significantly decreased low quality construction.

Housing differs from most commodities because it is so costly; the financial consequences of a bad blunder can be catastrophic. Until recently, housing was usually produced not by large corporations, but by smaller firms whose life expectancy was relatively short or uncertain. The long and often sweeping warranties or guarantees that are issued on such complex consumer goods as refrigerators, automobiles, or air conditioners by corporations that will later be interested in replacement sales[16] barely exist in housing. The courts in recent years have, however, broadened the responsibility of corporations for defective products, including housing, by extending the concept of negligence.[17]

In principle, a variety of techniques could be employed to protect investors in housing. Sellers might be required to provide information to buyers, to post bonds, or otherwise to secure buyers against loss or injury due to misrepresentation or faulty construction. Transfers of real property might be made legally binding only after appraisal or inspection by licensed experts beholden neither to buyer nor to seller. In most urban areas of the United States, state and local government have enacted building codes that stipulate acceptable types of construction and materials and housing codes that set standards for all units available for occupancy. Such codes frequently are designed to do more than protect buyers or renters of housing. Many have been adopted to meet the terms of eligibility for federal programs.[18] Often they require building practices that protect certain labor skills or assure demand for locally produced materials.[19] In most cases, codes define acceptable inputs but not the performance of the structure. States also offer a limited protection by licensing real estate brokers and salesmen. That no state requires all sales of real property to take place through a broker suggests that licensing is intended to protect buyers and sellers from unscrupulous brokers rather than from each other. States also license plumbers, electricians, and other building trades and require such protection at time of sale as title insurance.[20]

Far more subtle and more serious than the problem of inexpertness among consumers is the inexpertness among lenders. Because housing is highly durable, its total cost is large in comparison to its current cost and to the annual income of most families. Credit plays a major role at every step in housing markets—builders use construction loans, ultimate owners typically borrow to finance purchases. The interest rate on loans depends in part on the probability of default as perceived by the borrower, a prediction that even lenders are inadequately informed to make. The rules of thumb that govern the award of mortgages testify to the lack of adequate information on which to measure risk. As with all actuarial risks, probabilities of loss can be calculated only from a large body of experience. Analysis of the numerous factors and complex relationships inherent in losses due to defaults demands far more experience than even the largest lenders have. Public action to underwrite losses is probably justified while the needed information accumulates. There is some indication, for example, that federal loss protection has encouraged private lending for longer terms and secured by smaller down payments than would otherwise have been acceptable.[21] Default rates also vary with unemployment, inflation, and other economic circumstances not amenable to actuarial analysis; since public policy alters those conditions, it ought also to protect private households and businesses against their side effects.

Property Rights

Property owners often frustrate efforts to bring about economically desirable consolidation of properties. A single owner bargaining for a disproportionate share of the profits can block a project. And a group of owners agreeing to force a developer's hand may make consolidation impossible. Fear of failure may even keep a developer from trying to consolidate properties.

In putting together the acreage for Columbia, Maryland, James Rouse had to make 169 separate purchases.[22] To avoid driving up prices, the Rouse Company operated with cloak-and-dagger secrecy, using dummy corporations with such names as Cedar Farms, Potomac Estates, and Serenity Acres. Altogether, Rouse accumulated 15,600 acres at a total cost of $23 million;[23] one of the properties—a gasoline station that was to be demolished—cost $75,800. Rouse's experience is repeated countless times on a smaller scale and often with less success by developers seeking to amass land held by separate owners.

Governments encounter the same problems in trying to consolidate the holdings of several owners. Under the law of eminent domain, private owners may be compelled to sell holdings at a "fair" price for "public" purposes. The price is determined by negotiation or by judicial or administrative action. The comprehensiveness of the term "public purpose" is far from clear; it does not, however, include the transactions of private developers, even though their projects may be socially beneficial. Those transactions may sometimes be impossible in free markets. This form of market failure may be both extensive and costly.

Monopoly and Discrimination

Monopolistic control and market power are harmful elements of a free market. By controlling the supply of workers to the construction industry, certain building trades allegedly inflate wages artificially, establish arbitrary work rules, and restrict the introduction of cost-reducing technology and materials, thereby keeping building costs high. It is alleged that contractor associations have united to resist the introduction of industrialized housing, and that building trades discriminate against blacks, Mexican-Americans, Puerto Ricans, and others in their apprenticeship programs.[24] To the extent that they exist, such monopolistic practices justify public action in the names of efficiency and equity.

Public action ought also to be used to prevent discrimination against minorities in the sale and rental of housing. Legal prohibitions against discrimination, even if enforced, may not prevent segregation, however. Thomas Schelling has shown that segregation can occur without discrimination. Nearly complete residential segregation would result even if most people were averse to it so long as most people refuse to live in a neighborhood dominated by members of other groups. Normal movement of people is sufficient to cause this result.[25]

Whatever economic losses or gains discrimination in housing or its abolition might cause, it is clear that concern about the moral reprehensibleness and social divisiveness of discrimination, rather than calculation of economic costs, has motivated efforts to end it.

Collective Protection

Collective action has been criticized for creating worse problems than it solves. For example, inspection of new houses for compliance with housing codes may prevent the relatively few unscrupulous contractors from duping unwary buyers, but all builders must bear the slight delays and attendant costs of inspections, and taxpayers must pay the inspectors' salaries. The unsettled issue is whether the benefits of preventing large losses for some buyers are worth the costs of building inspections, small for each builder and taxpayer, but perhaps quite large in the aggregate.

The same question arises with respect to every form of inspection, licensing, bonding, and other consumer or investor protection device. Government agencies and private businesses must decide whether fraud by employees or clients, shoplifting by employees or customers, and other illicit acts cost more than efforts to prevent them. Often the cheapest policy is to let the illicit act continue at a controlled though high level. Unfortunately, the benefits from collective action often are not measurable, or are subject to special value standards.[26] For this reason, those who doubt the efficacy of collective action to protect the few from large losses at the cost of small burdens for the many face little risk of refutation or hope of vindication, except in the most clear-cut (and therefore uncontroversial) cases.

ADJUSTMENT LAGS AND CYCLICAL PROBLEMS

Each year new residential construction amounts to less than 3 percent of the housing stock. Each year only one-fifth of households change their residence. Thus the character of the housing stock and residential patterns evolve gradually. Several years are required for ordinary market forces to correct housing shortages or deficiencies. These forces include new construction, improvement or deterioration of existing units, conversions of real property to or from residential use, splitting or consolidating existing housing units, and filtering.

If market forces work quickly and efficiently, housing problems due to population movements or income shifts do not persist. Tenants move, owners alter units and change rents, and maladjustments quickly vanish. On the other hand, if the forces work slowly and inefficiently and problems persist, public action might be justified to speed adjustments. Such action might range from efforts to increase the housing stock, in order to raise vacancy rates and thereby facilitate changes of residence, to moving allowances or small loans for property improvement.

Little solid information exists on the speed with which the housing market adjusts to changes in housing demand. One recent study reports evidence that rents respond fairly slowly to changes in income of tenants and capital costs; only three-fifths of the long-run effects are realized after three years.[27] The kind of public action, if any, that is necessary to deal with large changes in demand is thus difficult to choose.

Credit Fluctuations

Because credit is prominent in the construction and purchase of new housing and in the transfer of existing units, changes in interest rates and in the availability of credit affect the price of housing services more than the price of most other capital and consumer goods. For example, an increase in interest rates from 6 percent to 9 percent raises the cost of amortizing a thirty-year loan by 34 percent. Such increases may be partly offset by declines (or smaller increases than would otherwise occur) in the price of housing units or in other costs that enter into the total cost.

Interest rates fluctuate widely around long-run trends, rising when demand for credit is high or the supply of credit is low. These short-run fluctuations may cause large inverse swings in the rate of housing construction; rises in the price of housing services lower the amounts demanded, as a result of which demand for *additions* to the housing stock is greatly reduced. Credit rationing or other imperfections in capital markets may reduce the mobility of households. Normal population movements can cause housing shortages in particular areas during periods of credit stringency. Without new construction, such shortages might persist, unless large and inequitable price increases occur to reduce the amount demanded. Large variations in the amount of housing constructed or in demand that impose excessive or inequitable costs would create strong pressures for public action. Such action might include measures to assure a steady flow of credit to housing.

Family Formation

In the United States, individual households occupy most housing units, and few demand more than one unit. Demand for additions to the housing stock thus depends on the rate of household formation. Because birthrates were low in the 1930s and high in the late 1940s and 1950s, household formation will rise from an annual rate of 890,000 during the early 1960s to 1,340,000 during the early 1970s. This demographic factor alone will require a big jump in housing investment during the 1970s. The promise to eradicate substandard housing, to increase vacancies, and otherwise to expand the housing stock contained in the Housing and Urban Development Act of 1968 will further expand housing demand. The housing act's goal of construction or rehabilitation of 26 million housing units during the decade 1969-78 will require investment of perhaps 4.3 percent of the gross national product in housing in 1975 as opposed to 3.5 percent in 1969.[28] While neither the level nor the increase is extraordinary—nonfarm residential construction absorbed 4.9 percent of GNP in 1950, up from 3.8 percent in 1949—it will depend on a reduction in some other major component of GNP.

Had public decision makers decided to do nothing about the unusually large housing demand during the 1970s, no housing goal would have been set. Fiscal and monetary policies, based on a broad range of considerations, would only by coincidence have made possible fulfillment of the housing goal. In all likelihood, fewer units would have been built in the 1969-78 decade and more units in succeeding years.

The choice between the high goal of the housing act and no official action to meet the bulge in housing demand affects income distribution. Construction costs are likely to rise less if the residential construction rate is low than if it is high. On the other hand, if relatively few units are built, substandard housing units are unlikely to be eradicated and price increases in areas of acute shortage are likely to be severe. Households that spend a relatively large fraction of their income on housing or derive a relatively small proportion of income from investments in housing will be hardest hit by increases in housing prices. A complex system of taxes or transfers could shield personal incomes from the consequences of an uncontrolled housing market. However, income redistribution is a divisive political act. Those who are concerned about income distribution may therefore advocate policies to keep down housing costs, even though such policies might disrupt the workings of a perfectly functioning market.

This concern may explain why many governments adopt rent controls, particularly in wartime when construction must be curtailed. Wartime shortages are apt to increase the price of housing more than that of other goods; real incomes of tenants fall while those of landlords rise. New construction becomes highly profitable and builders will increase their activity if rent control does not apply effectively to new buildings and if wartime priorities do not preclude construction. The application of controls to new units may reduce or stop new construction. Controls on existing units are a kind of tax on owners with proceeds given to tenants. Controls thereby discourage maintenance, repairs, and improvements, even though tenants would willingly pay increased rents to finance improvements. Furthermore, as tenants move, rent control becomes less efficient. It is a plausible instrument, however, if immediate shifts in income distribution are a more important cause for concern than deferred damage to the housing stock and if less costly instruments are not available.

The facts that housing is highly capital intensive and durable and that most families devote a large part of their budgets to housing explain why free market adjustments to shifts in demand may be unacceptable. Housing is sufficiently different from other investments and housing services from other consumer goods to require special public attention.

SUMMARY

A nation committed to market allocation of most resources might intervene in the housing market in order to alter income distribution. It might act to restrict the benefits or costs of housing transactions passed on to persons not directly involved, or to correct imperfections in the functioning of housing markets. It might also wish to offset the consequences of fiscal and monetary policies on the housing sector.

These justifications for interfering in the housing market are extremely vague. Because evidence about the causes for public concern is scarce or nonexistent, it is hard to know which policies most effectively remove causes of concern or whether actual policies achieve their stated goals. Housing codes, for example, may attempt to control the effect of one family's housing on another's welfare or to limit the dangers of consumer ignorance, but their success in doing so is unknown. Therefore it is impossible to know whether they bring about better housing—for the poor, the middle class, or the rich—or even improve methods of production. It has been argued that housing codes—designed to ensure decent housing for the poor—may in fact deny the poor the opportunity to occupy cheap housing below code standards and to use the money saved on housing for such other things as better or more food.

Public policies themselves create hindrances to efficiency. Compliance costs, delays in inspections, added uncertainties, all may result from public action designed to solve particular problems. Once again, the magnitude of these costs is unknown.

Unfortunately, the numerous but vague reasons why public action might improve the functioning of the housing market offer little guidance in selecting among alternative policies. Moreover, the cost of interfering in the operation of the housing market is vague. The problems may well be extremely serious, and collective action may be the only solution. Political leaders may be excused if they act on less than complete information.

They cannot be excused so readily, however, for confusing the inadequacies of housing with the inadequacies of concomitant residential services. Governments tend to treat the problems of decaying neighborhoods—the dilapidated structures, poor schools, inadequate transportation, high crime rates—with programs aimed principally at physical renewal or reconstruction. That tendency may reflect a recognition that it is easier to renew structures than to deal with other problems; it may also reflect the confusion of the physical, social, and economic problems of decaying neighborhoods with the "housing problem."

NOTES

1. See Richard F. Muth, *Cities and Housing: The Spatial Pattern of Urban Residential Land Use* (University of Chicago Press, 1969), p. 18; Edgar O. Olsen, "A Competitive Theory of the Housing Market," *American Economic Review*, Vol. 59 (September 1969), pp. 612-13.
2. For example, in any period the combined investment in housing, business capital, and net foreign trade is limited by the amount of public and private saving. Programs like investment tax credits, designed to spur business investment, succeed in part if they indirectly discourage residential construction.
3. Wallace E. Oates in "The Effects of Property Taxes and Local Public Spending on Property Values: An Empirical Study of Tax Capitalization and the Tiebout Hypothesis," *Journal of Political Economy*, Vol. 77 (November-December 1969), pp. 957-71, shows that an increase in annual public school expenditures by $100 per student raises home values by about $1,200 in New Jersey.
4. *Building the American City*, Report of the National Commission on Urban Problems to the Congress and to the President of the United States, H. Doc. 34, 91 Cong. 1 sess. (1969), p. 56.
5. John F. Kain, "Housing Segregation, Negro Employment, and Metropolitan Decentralization," *Quarterly Journal of Economics*, Vol. 82 (May 1968), pp. 175-97. For a contrary view, see Paul Offner and Daniel H. Saks, "A Note on John Kain's 'Housing Segregation, Negro Employment and Metropolitan Decentralization,'" *Quarterly Journal of Economics*, Vol. 85 (February 1971), pp. 147-60.
6. James S. Coleman and others, *Equality of Educational Opportunity*, U.S. Department of Health, Education, and Welfare, Office of Education (1966).
7. D.M. Grether and Peter Mieszkowski in "Determinants of Real Estate Values" (California Institute of Technology and Queen's University, 1971; processed) report that if a standard New Haven house were moved from a school district that ranks in the 50th percentile to one in the 90th percentile, the value of the home would rise by $1,500 to $2,400; a decrease in the pupil-teacher ratio from 30 to 25 would add $350 to $1,400.
8. See Eric Schnapper, "Consumer Legislation and the Poor," *Yale Law Journal*, Vol. 76 (March 1967), pp. 745-92; *Annual Report of the Council of Economic Advisers*, January 1969, pp. 174-75; and *Report of the National Advisory Commission on Civil Disorders* (1968), pp. 139-41.
9. One study found that profits of furniture and appliance dealers in a black ghetto were below average (U.S. Federal Trade Commission, *Economic Report on the Structure and Competitive Behavior of Food Retailing*, Staff Report [1966]).
10. Efforts to measure the impact of crime rates on property values have not been successful. See John F. Kain and John M. Quigley, "Measuring the Value of Housing Quality," *Journal of the American Statistical Association*, Vol. 65 (June 1970), pp. 532-48; Ronald G. Ridker and John A. Henning, "The Determinants of Residential Property Values with Special Reference to Air Pollution," *Review of Economics and Statistics*, Vol. 49 (May 1967), pp. 246-57.

11. The term "filtering" has been applied to different phenomena, including changes in rents or prices, measured in current or constant dollars, change in the position of a dwelling unit on the value scale, or change in the absolute or relative socioeconomic status of occupants. For a discussion of filtering, see William G. Grigsby, *Housing Markets and Public Policy* (University of Pennsylvania Press, 1963), pp. 84-130.

12. *The Unheavenly City* (Little, Brown, 1968), pp. 250-51.

13. Housing Act of 1949 (63 Stat. 413).

14. This point was expressed forcefully two decades ago by Paul A. Samuelson on returning from England. "It is easy for an observer to see the inadequacies of the London slums. It is much harder to see the vitamins that the pre-war Cockney occupants were not getting. I wonder if the alleged especial inadequacy of housing is not an optical illusion." Quoted by Leland S. Burns in "Housing as Social Overhead Capital," *Essays in Urban Land Economics: In Honor of the Sixty-fifth Birthday of Leo Grebler* (University of California, Los Angeles, Real Estate Research Program, 1966), p. 16.

15. See Alvin L. Schorr, *Slums and Social Insecurity*, U.S. Department of Health, Education, and Welfare, Social Security Administration (1963); and Jerome Rothenberg, *Economic Evaluation of Urban Renewal: Conceptual Foundation of Benefit-Cost Analysis* (The Brookings Institution, 1967), bibliography, pp. 58-60.

16. Federal regulation of warranties and guarantees seems inevitable. In 1970 and 1971 the Senate passed a bill providing minimum standards for guarantees and warranties on consumer products valued at $5 or more; the bill did not pass the House.

17. See Gustav Rinesch, "Warranties for the Protection of the Consumer," *Business Lawyer*, Vol. 24 (April 1969), pp. 857-66; Joseph A. Valore, "Product Liability for a Defective House," *Insurance Law Journal*, No. 558 (July 1969), pp. 395-405; and Clyde R. White, "A 'New' Tort in Texas—Implied Warranty in the Sale of a New House," *Southwestern Law Journal*, Vol. 23 (October 1969), pp. 750-56.

18. Some communities, by remaining without codes or other elements of a "workable program for community improvement" as defined by the Department of Housing and Urban Development, were until 1969 able to remain ineligible for public housing, rent supplements, or other federal programs intended for low and middle income residents. Some members of Congress supported the workable program to enable localities to keep out distasteful programs; others felt that a workable program would contribute to orderly growth.

19. See *Building the American City*, Report of the National Commission on Urban Problems, pp. 254-72.

20. Many economists argue that licensing in any field of activity restricts entry to the field and enables members of the profession to charge high prices. Members typically award licenses, and their interest in earning high incomes may conflict with their devotion to excluding only the unqualified.

21. See George F. Break, "Federal Loan Insurance for Housing," in Break et al., *Federal Credit Agencies*, Prepared for the Commission on Money and Credit (Prentice-Hall, 1963), p. 19.

22. *Redoing America: A Nationwide Report on How to Make Our Cities and Suburbs Livable* (Harper & Row, 1968), p. 171.

23. James W. Rouse, "The City of Columbia, Maryland," in H. Wentworth Eldredge (ed.), *Taming Megalopolis* (Doubleday, 1967), Vol. 2, p. 842.

24. See *Building the American City*, Report of the National Commission on Urban Problems; J.T. Dunlop and D.Q. Mills, "Manpower in Construction: A Profile of the Industry and Projections to 1975," in *The Report of the President's Committee on Urban Housing*, Vol. 2, *Technical Studies* (1968), p. 273; F. Ray Marshall and Vernon M. Biggs, Jr., *The Negro and Apprenticeship* (Johns Hopkins Press, 1967); and "Philadelphia Plan," *Congressional Record*, daily ed., July 30, 1969, pp. S8837-39.

25. "On the Ecology of Micromotives," Discussion Paper No. 2, Public Policy Program, Kennedy School of Government, Harvard University (Harvard University Program on Technology and Society, October 1970; processed).

26. See Thomas C. Schelling, "The Life You Save May Be Your Own," in Samuel B. Chase, Jr. (ed.), *Problems in Public Expenditure Analysis* (The Brookings Institution, 1968), pp. 127-62.

27. Frank de Leeuw, assisted by Nkanta F. Ekanem, "Time Lags in the Rental Housing Market," Working Paper 112-19 (Urban Institute, June 3, 1970; processed), p. 39.

28. Computed from estimates in *Second Annual Report on National Housing Goals, Message from the President of the United States*, H. Doc. 91-292, 91 Cong. 2 sess. (1970), pp. 69, 107.

II
Federal Housing Policy and Homeownership

3

Historical Overview of Federal Policy: Encouraging Homeownership

J. Paul Mitchell

The most basic thrust of federal housing policy during the past half-century has been the encouragement and facilitation of widespread homeownership. In our fascination with the complex, shifting, low-income housing subsidies it is all too easy to overlook this. Yet this effort to stimulate homeownership has been phenomenally successful. The national percentage of homeowners historically wavered between 45 and 48 percent and dropped slightly below that during the depression. But between 1940 and 1960 it shot up to nearly 62 percent and continued upward to nearly 65 percent by 1980. Moreover, this dramatic surge in the proportion of homeowners occurred during an era of high volume family formation, so that the sheer number of new homeowners was phenomenal. To a considerable degree this was due to federal policy.

Homeownership has been accorded a special place in the system of American values. The American colonies derived from their English heritage the concepts of land as a source of liberty and land ownership as the chief guarantor of individual freedom. Land ownership gave one a stake in society, which, in turn, led to responsible participation in public affairs and, consequently, a stable government and a stable society. In a nation where land was abundant and relatively cheap, and where population growth was often dramatic, land ownership also served as a major source of wealth. Thus, while homeownership may be viewed as a heavy financial responsibility, steadily appreciating values could, and often did, make it a profitable investment indeed. The sturdy yeoman of Jeffersonian mythology (the small farmer who owned his land, earned a living on it by the sweat of his brow, and looked any man squarely in the face) was the hard-working repository of national civic virtue, and became, in twentieth century urban settings, the homeowner. A small plot of ground with a house served as both vehicle for and evidence of freedom, responsibility, stability, and virtue. Every President, from Herbert Hoover who started the ball of federal housing policy rolling, to Ronald Reagan who slowed it down, has acknowledged that homeowners are the backbone of the nation and declared his fervent wish that every American household so desiring might join the ranks.

Federal efforts to encourage homeownership have deep historic roots. After every war, from colonial clashes to the Revolutionary War and through the Civil War, there has been some form of land distribution to soldiers. Such distributions, usually as land certificates, were either soldiers' pay or veterans' benefits. Likely most land certificates were sold at a discount to speculators for ready cash, and served chiefly as a cheap way for the nation to repay a heavy obligation for which liquid funds were not available. Nonetheless, the desire to forestall the evils of a collection of landless, disgruntled ex-soldiers by helping them become landowners was also present in these early veterans' benefits. The history of the disposition of federally owned western lands also reveals the intent to render landownership available to the broadest possible range of citizens. Land distribution, from the Northwest Ordinance of 1787 through the Homestead Act of 1862, made land available on ever easier terms; the minimum plots were gradually reduced, unit prices declined, and down payment requirements lowered. (Indeed, after 1862 the head of a family could obtain title to 160 acres merely by living on it for five years and paying a total fee of less than $40.) While speculators and large corporations got much of the land, the intent to make land available to individual owners was apparent and many smaller farmers and homeowners took advantage of these programs.

HOME FINANCE AND FEDERAL HOUSING POLICY

Federal efforts since 1930 to put homeownership within the reach of more citizens have focused on home financing. Within this crucial area federal policies have employed various devices to stimulate the flow of private institutional mortgage funds to residential construction. These devices have diminished the risks inherent in mortgage lending, improved the liquidity of mortgage loans, broken down the barriers of isolated local capital markets, tapped new sources of mortgage funds, and transformed the nature of mortgage lending. Policy makers reasoned that the best way to broaden homeownership was to make borrowing easier: larger mortgages (lower down payments), longer contract terms, lower interest rates, and lower periodic payments.

The creation of an orderly, protected, and easily accessible system of home finance was made possible, even it seemed, imperative, by the financial chaos of the Great Depression. Home mortgages are, like any other form of indebtedness, intertwined with personal savings: those who wish to build or buy a house but do not have the cash must borrow from those who have saved. While savers need income-producing loans, they have been wary of lending to home purchasers because such loans are both risky and illiquid. As late as the 1920s individuals comprised the largest single group of mortgage holders, although more than half the mortgages were held by various types of financial institutions. Most home loans were for short periods, often only two or three years, and due in full. Some had provisions for retiring part of the principal before the loan fell due; others did not. But borrowers could seldom retire the entire debt after only a few years. They were usually forced to refinance with another, similar, mortgage. Still, the short term mortgage reflected lenders' desire and need for liquidity. Low loan-to-value ratios reflected lenders' desire to minimize risk: few mortgages exceeded 50 percent of the property's value, and mortgages of 70 to 75 percent were virtually nonexistent. But such modest financing fell far short of most home-purchasers' needs. Accordingly, home buyers routinely undertook second mortgages and other junior liens, all at higher rates, to compensate lenders for additional risks. The real estate boom of the 1920s piled up a mountain of this kind of layered mortgage debt. The whole mass could be maintained only if real estate values held strong and if existing mortgages could be refinanced (rolled over) as they came due.

Over the years various institutions (mutual savings banks, savings and loan associations, commercial banks, insurance companies) were formed to mediate between savers and borrowers. By the late 1920s approximately 60 percent of the home mortgages were held by such financial institutions. Nevertheless, the problems of risk and illiquidity inherent in mortgages remained intensified for the public because these financial intermediaries served two constituencies whose fundamental interests clashed. First were depositors (savers) whose main concern was the safety of their deposits and whose secondary concern was for income (interest); to these the intermediaries owed fiduciary responsibility. Second were borrowers who needed funds to purchase a home. Liberalized mortgage terms for borrowers (long contract terms, high loan-to-value ratios, low interest rates) jeopardized the interests of savers. Primary attention to the interests of savers, (short contract terms, low loan-to-value ratios, high interest rates) were inimical to the interests of potential borrowers.

The institutional intermediaries were badly burned when the real estate bubble of the 1920s burst. Escalating prices had prompted more liberal lending terms, which in turn added to real estate's investment appeal. When prices leveled off and then started dropping in 1928, existing short-term mortgages could not be refinanced in full. Forced sales dragged prices even lower, with the further result that lenders were forced to carry mortgages in amounts greater than 100 percent of current market price, or to receive less than full repayment of the loan. Either choice threatened the safety of depositors' funds. Small depositors were forced to withdraw savings due to unemployment, which further diminished the flexibility of financial institutions and brought many to a severe liquidity crisis. By late 1932 and early 1933, when depositors began to withdraw their funds out of panic, the entire system of home finance was on the verge of collapse. Institutional intermediaries were not prepared to make new loans. Home construction virtually ceased, real estate markets were moribund, and only the safest, most bankable loans were being made. Home finance was just one segment of a financial system so badly shaken that President Roosevelt declared a national bank holiday immediately after his inauguration in March, 1933.

Less than 100,000 new housing units were started in 1933, a drop from 937,000 in 1925. Because construction generally, and home construction particularly, was a labor-intensive activity, construction workers constituted a substantial portion of every local labor force. By the 1930s, therefore, they constituted a substantial portion of every city's army of unemployed. Putting them back to work was a high local—and national—priority. And how better to put them back to work than by stimulating the flow of mortgage funds to residential construction?

Federal home finance policy, then, established three objectives: (1) broaden homeownership; (2) shore up and protect home financing institutions; and (3) stimulate employment in the building industry. These objectives were implemented in the Housing Act of 1934, which remains in effect, though it has been amended by every subsequent Congress.

Federal policy for home finance was to mediate the risk to savings depositors and lending institutions. For the first, the task was to insure saver-depositors against bank failure. This insurance had been established for commercial bank depositors in the Glass-Steagall Banking Act of 1933 with the creation of the Federal Deposit Insurance Corporation (FDIC). The FDIC took the risk out of depositing money in commercial banks and restored public confidence in banks. Subsequently home financing institutions were protected through a similar Federal Savings and Loan Insurance Corporation (FSLIC) created by the Banking Act of 1934. The second step was to insure lending institutions against the default of borrowers. This was done also in the Bank Act of 1934 by creating the Federal Housing Administration (FHA) which guaranteed long-term loans made by private financial institutions. Neither of these measures minimized the risks undertaken by borrowers; they were left unprotected. But the combined impact of the FSLIC and FHA attracted deposits to mortgage lending institutions, diminished the reluctance of thrift institutions to make mortgages, stimulated the participation of commercial banks in mortgage financing, facilitated more liberal mortgage terms (lower down payments, lower interest rates, longer contract terms, and hence lower periodic payments), and enabled higher risk households to contract for mortgages.

Another facet of the home finance problem was the local nature of home finance and the real estate market. The financial crises of the early depression years once more underscored the need for a mechanism to render mortgages less inflexible so that lending institutions could withstand the immediate pressures of adverse cash flows. The Federal Home Loan Bank, set up in 1932, provided a national structure to mobilize cash reserves. But lenders eagerly sought a quasi-governmental agency which would make a national secondary mortgage market. Such an agency, by purchasing mortgages at a discount from lending institutions, would allow these institutions, in turn, to make more mortgages. President Hoover's scheme to create a secondary mortgage market by private subscription failed to attract investors. The Federal National Mortgage Association was eventually created in 1938 to stimulate a higher volume of mortgage lending by providing a national market for FHA-insured mortgages.

While institutions had to be created and federal programs set up, another, less tangible but equally imperative, transformation was needed. If the United States was to become a nation of homeowners, it would have to become a nation of debtors. A shift in philosophy was necessary to allow a nation which extolled the virtues of thrift to accept, and even encourage, the idea that thrifty, industrious people could simultaneously be almost permanently, and certainly enormously, in debt. This philosophical shift did, in fact, occur as the opportunity for long-term debt, gradually retired, became readily available.

READING SELECTIONS

These fundamental policies were implemented as a result of the special historical circumstances created by the Great Depression. The first selection in this section, Chapter 4, consists of excerpts from hearings before the U.S. House of Representatives on the Housing Act of 1934. It contains the major arguments and rationale for the mortgage insurance system and conveys the mood of the era in which this basic policy took shape.

Chapter 5, by Semer, Zimmerman, et al., chronicles the major developments in housing finance policy, from the last years of President Hoover's administration, including the changes in the FHA, through 1974. This article was part of the massive Housing Policy Review undertaken by the Nixon Administration.

The third selection, Chapter 6, describes the objectives of the Veterans' Home Loan Benefit and is taken from the President's Commission on Veterans' Pensions, *Report on Veterans' Benefits in the United States* (1956). The policy of facilitating homeownership for more and more families by insuring mortgages and liberalizing their terms was firmly imbedded in national practice by a second special historical circumstance. This was the creation, by World War II, of a huge special interest group—veterans. This politically powerful group had strong claims on the nation's gratitude and conscience; objections to special treatment for veterans were easily made to appear churlish and even unpatriotic. The long Cold War which followed, and the hostilities in Korea from 1950 to 1953, meant relatively high levels of continued military activity, and thus a steady stream of new veterans. This more ready access to homeowning was made available under circumstances which made the success of both these programs highly likely. The United States emerged from World War II as the most powerful economic force on earth. Continued long-range prosperity permitted the attainment of a relatively high material standard of living, which of course included, and, in fact, was built upon, homeowning.

In Chapter 7 Hendershott and Villani discuss several important mechanisms for direct federal participation in the home mortgage market. The Federal Home Loan Bank, Federal National Mortgage Association (Fannie Mae), Government National Mortgage Association (Ginnie Mae), and Federal Home Loan Mortgage Corporation (Freddie Mac), were established to stimulate and maintain a steady flow of mortgage funds. Their precise functions vary since each was created to deal with a specific situation and even specific results of other federal housing policies. But each of these agencies has (1) counteracted the local nature of the mortgage market, (2) helped create a national market for the exchange of mortgages, (3) overcome the inherent institutional illiquidity of mortgages, and (4) allowed financial institutions to make a higher volume of home loans.

The mortgage market thus began to operate under conditions fostered and protected by federal guarantees, regulations, and agencies. It became, almost entirely, an institutional market; the increased involvement of insurance companies and commercial banks gradually tied the mortgage market more closely to other capital markets, necessarily national, even international, in scope. Eventually home finance lost its somewhat sheltered status. Outside events, especially high inflation and high interest rates, interrupted the flow of capital to home mortgages. The selections by Sternlieb and Hughes (Chapter 8) and by Colton (Chapter 9) discuss ways in which market changes led to institutional changes in the late 1970s. Both selections share the sense that the American Dream of owning a home may be receding. The federal policy of extending home ownership as broadly as possible has been phenomenally successful, but it may have reached its outer limits.

TAX INCENTIVES TO HOMEOWNERS, AND TAX SUBSIDIES

During the past 15 years housing commentators have paid increasing attention to another, often overlooked, form of encouragement toward homeownership. Now the subject of much criticism and debate, this newly discovered subsidy is the income tax deduction for mortgage interest and property taxes. In the words of Henry Aaron, ''the murky provisions of the Internal Revenue Code contain the most important housing programs currently administered by the federal government. One 'program' costs the Treasury at least $7 billion per year. It subsidizes nearly every homeowner in the United States. Others provide benefits to most renters. Despite their cost and pervasiveness, these programs receive negligible scrutiny within government and, except for occasional academic analysis, almost none from outside the government.'' Aaron contended that the Internal Revenue Code contains massive tax subsidies for housing. The largest accrue to homeowners through exemption from taxation of net imputed rent and deductibility of mortgage interest and property taxes. Smaller benefits accrue to owners of rental housing to the extent that accelerated appreciation exceeds true depreciation by a greater margin on real estate than on other properties.

Aaron concluded that consumption of housing services was much greater as a result of these benefits and that the people who benefitted most were homeowners generally, but especially upper-income homeowners whose tax savings were greatest.[1]

In an article dealing with federal tax reform, Stanley Surrey noted the strong preference of Congress both for encouraging ownership and for not substituting direct expenditures for tax-based subsidies. Surrey further showed why direct assistance was not likely to replace the existing tax subsidy approach:

> If cast in direct expenditure language, the present assistance under the itemized deductions for interest and taxes would look as follows:
>
> —for a married couple with more than $200,000 in income, HUD would, for each $100 of mortgage interest on the couple's home, pay $70 to the bank holding the mortgage, leaving the couple to pay $30. It would also pay a similar portion of the couple's property tax to the State or city levying the tax.
>
> —for a married couple with income of $10,000, HUD would pay the bank on the couple's mortgage $19 per each $100 interest unit, with the couple paying $81. It would also pay a similar portion of the couple's property tax to the State or city levying the tax.
>
> —for a married couple too poor to pay an income tax, HUD would pay nothing to the bank, leaving the couple to pay the entire interest cost. The couple would also have to pay the entire property tax.
>
> While this upside-down result mirrors the tax assistance now provided it would presumably not be followed in a direct approach to federal assistance.

Surrey's criticism of the starkly regressive features of the federal income tax deduction subsidy have been widely repeated.[2]

The intensive Housing Policy Review undertaken by the Nixon Administration in 1974 traced the evolution of income tax deduction subsidies in its report, *Housing in the Seventies*:

> The Internal Revenue Code reflects an evolution of a policy that began with the first income tax experiments during the Civil War, providing that certain tax benefits should accrue to homeownership at the expense of potential Federal revenues and other forms of consumption or investment. In the Revenue Acts of 1864 and 1865, taxpayers were permitted to deduct interest expense and local tax payments. Within these, two categories of expenses related to homeownership: mortgage interest payments and property taxes. The policy was restated in the first statute implementing the 1913 constitutional amendment establishing the Federal income tax system existing today. The policy has remained virtually unchanged.
>
> In 1972, more than 24 million taxpayers who lived in their own homes—almost

one-third of all taxpayers—took advantage of these two tax benefits, now contained in Sections 163 and 164 of the Internal Revenue Code.

In recent years, homeowners were allowed a third category of tax benefits when Congress approved legislation permitting a homeowner to defer the tax on any gain realized in the sale of his principal residence. The Congress approved the new provision (Section 1034 of the Internal Revenue Code) in 1951 at the height of the Korean War with the stated intent of alleviating the hardships associated with relocations brought on by wartime mobilization, and facilitating the purchase of larger homes by growing families.

Pursuant to Section 1034, a homeowner who sells his home and purchases another of equal or higher price within 1 year, will not be taxed at that point on any capital gain realized (calculated generally as the difference between the original cost of the home plus the cost of capital improvements and the purchase price of the new home). The tax is thus deferred until a homeowner finally sells a home without buying another of equal or greater price or when he buys a home at a lower price. In addition, when a homeowner who has been deferring his taxes under Section 1034 dies, the gains realized are totally excluded from taxation pursuant to Section 1014 of the Internal Revenue Code. In sum, the effect of Section 1034 is to promote both social and geographic mobility and to widen the housing market by providing homeowners, when they move, an incentive to buy another home of equal or greater price.

Section 1034 created a potential problem, however, for the elderly person who may have wished to sell his present home and move to smaller, less costly accommodations, investing the gain from the sale to provide for his retirement. Thus, Congress in the 1964 Revenue Act provided (in Section 121 of the Internal Revenue Code) that any gain realized by a taxpayer 65 or older on a house sold for under $20,000 would not be taxed and only a portion of the gain on homes sold for more than $20,000 would be taxed, depending on the amount of the gain and the adjusted sales price. A taxpayer, however, may utilize this provision only once. The result of this provision was to enhance the value of an investment in a house, which represents the most important and, in some cases, the only major investment made by most taxpayers.

Having more or less just grown out of practice over the decades, this income tax subsidy has affected more and more people as home ownership has become more widespread. It may, indeed, constitute a subsidy greater than all others combined, and it does so in an indirect manner that avoids conscious scrutiny in annual budgets. Nevertheless, the large number of homeowner-taxpayers taking advantage of that subsidy constitutes a veritable political army which no policy maker is eager to attack. Moreover, the subsidy does appear to have contributed to the goal of encouraging widespread home ownership.

In Chapter 10, Richard Slitor, writing for the Housing Policy Review in 1974, provides a rationale for the tax subsidy for homeowners.

NOTES

1. Henry Aaron, *Shelters and Subsidies: Who Benefits from Federal Housing Policies?* (Washington, D.C.: The Brookings Institution, 1972), 53-73.
2. Stanley S. Surrey, "Federal Income Tax Reform: The Varied Approaches Necessary to Replace Tax Expenditures with Direct Governmental Assistance," *Harvard Law Review*, 84 (December 1970), 397.

4

Excerpts from Legislative Hearings for the Housing Act of 1934

U.S. House of Representatives, Committee on Banking and Currency

STATEMENT OF HARRY L. HOPKINS, FEDERAL EMERGENCY RELIEF ADMINISTRATOR

Mr. Hopkins. Mr. Chairman, I would like to make a very brief statement in regard to this bill on four points: One, the present unemployment situation as it relates to building trades, and our relief organization and relief work as it relates to building trades; second, on the social value of housing; third, on the importance of moving heavy industries; and, fourth, on the great importance of our getting private credit into this picture rather than Government bonds.

The building trades in America represent by all odds the largest single unit of our unemployment. Probably more than one-third of all the unemployed are identified, directly and indirectly, with the building trades. More than one-third of all of the 4,000,000 families on the relief rolls are identified with the building trades. In other words, 1,350,000 families, representing more than 6,000,000 people, are receiving relief who are identified with the building trades of America. Now, there are a group of people in every city of America, skilled men, the finest workers in America, who are on the relief rolls in much larger numbers and percentages than are represented in any other single group in America. I know of no city in the United States—no city in the United States—where not less than one-third of the buildings trades workers are not now on the relief rolls, and a far larger number are still unemployed.

Now, a purpose of this bill, a fundamental purpose of this bill, is an effort to

From U.S. Congress, House of Representatives, 73rd Congress, 2nd Session, *Hearings before the Committee on Banking and Currency, National Housing Act, May 18, 1934.* Washington, D.C.: U.S. Government Printing Office, 1934.

get these people back to work. Nobody is going to claim, I believe, who testifies before this committee, that this bill is going to put all of these men back to work, but I do not believe this bill ever would have been suggested (in fact, I know it would not have been suggested) did we not have the conviction that this would put substantial numbers of workers in the building trades back on payrolls.

A second interest in this bill is the wholly social value of housing. There has been no repair work done on housing since 1929. Houses have deteriorated from coast to coast; roofs leak; inadequate furnaces; flooring. New houses, as you know, have not been built. I do not believe you will hear many people testify before you that we maintain that this bill will immediately start a lot of new building. We believe that it will start some—start as much as is desirable. We are convinced, however, that it will result, if passed, in an enormous amount of repair and modernization work in America. I would hate to indicate to you the precise figures as to how much of this work can be done; but, in my opinion, it will represent hundreds of millions of dollars in work and employment. Now anything that is done in this field particularly uses goods which are manufactured by the heavy industries, and while consumers' goods industries are employing 70 to 75 percent of this 1929 number of employees, this committee is well aware that that is not the case in the heavy industries. This bill is an effort to move the heavy industries. We believe that there is no opportunity to move heavy industries goods as usefully as in housing, because we believe housing is needed and repairs are needed—socially useful things that will be done.

And, finally, we believe it is essential that we unloose private credit rather than public funds in the repairing of those houses and the building of new houses; that, if we are going to get home with the return of the unemployed to employment, it can only be done, in our judgment, by the releasing of private credit through some appropriate channels and appropriate methods. We believe this will do it to a substantial extent. We believe it is important that it be done; that every possible effort be used to get the money out of the banks; because there are plenty of surpluses in the banks to be used for socially useful purposes that are directed to the heavy industries and to the employment of the building trades.

In general, that represents the fundamental objectives of this bill. The technical details of this bill will be discussed by those who will succeed me on the stand. Thank you very much.

The Chairman. We shall now be glad to hear Mr. Riefler.

STATEMENT OF WINFIELD W. RIEFLER, ECONOMIC ADVISER EXECUTIVE COUNCIL AND CHAIRMAN OF THE CENTRAL STATISTICAL BOARD

Mr. Riefler. My name is Winfield W. Riefler; I am economic adviser to the executive council and chairman of the Central Statistical Board. Prior to that, I was for 11 years with the Federal Reserve Board and am loaned by the Federal Reserve Board to the executive council for this work.

Mr. Hopkins has stated the problem as to the economic situations of these heavy industries that are stagnant. The light industries, the consumption-goods industries, are now coming back to life; employment there is pretty good. The problem of further development and recovery lies in the heavy industries.

Among the heavy industries we can look for a resumption now particularly in two fields. One is the enormous field of replacement demand that exists. Everybody practically has been conserving cash since 1929. I am talking about the replacement demand in terms of homes, in terms of factories, in terms of commercial factories all the way through. There is an enormous volume now needed, economically needed, of replacement demand. If we can get that employment started, that production going, it will generate of itself the other type of activity of heavy industries, new construction. First, I think new construction of homes which will be needed if we can get reemployment and then incomes reestablished; second, new construction of the productive type eventually.

So this program is directed toward unlocking these economic keys. It is not a single program that is all at one moment; it is a developing one, and planned development.

We look for our maximum volume of reemployment from rehabilitation, repair, modernization, during the coming year. At the same time, the program looks toward unlocking the keys which have stopped practically all new residential construction, and permit that residential construction to go forward which is economically needed and desirable. If we are successful in that, the development of reemployment itself will spread the demand for new construction and will have set in motion the forces that will carry this on.

So the program falls into four parts—really into three parts, three different types of influence, in order to use private capital, to use it to the utmost; because it is an extremely difficult problem. The building industry is one that is as decentralized as any industry we have. We need to create forces that will set it in motion everywhere. We plan to use all of the existing private agencies in the field; we plan to do it through three different types of insurance provisions.

The first one, which will be explained to you by Mr. Eccles and Mr. Deane, is insurance of the relatively short-time rehabilitation loans; that is, loans not to exceed 5 years, of small amounts, to be used just as widely as those who can economically afford to use them will participate. On that insurance plan, the Government carries the cost of the insurance. The funds are advanced privately, but the Government carries the cost of the insurance under this program.

The two other insurance plans are designed to be self-supporting. One of them is the insurance of the best type of mortgage on new construction. By that plan, we hope to open the mortgage market, to unlock it to permit new construction of the best type to go forward where it is economically needed.

The third looks to the insurance of building and loan associations and is a set-up quite similar to the insurance of banks. It offers to protect that very important element in the mortgage market in the same way that we have protected banks and tried to rehabilitate them to take their part in the revival of the construction industry. . . .

What we propose in the market for individual mortgages is to offer to insure any lender, who is an accredited lender of good reputation, on first mortgages on owner-occupied homes. That is, if he will advance funds for the financing of owner-occupied construction, the Government will insure the mortgage for him. That insurance is self-paying; it is mutual insurance. The borrower will pay a premium for this insurance, which will be put into a separate fund and, after the mortgage has matured and that fund has borne the risks of the insurance, anything that is over is returned to the borrower to pay off the last part of his loan. So that that fund is self-supporting.

The premium and the cost of the insurance is on a mutual basis. Any lender can use this insurance who is accredited, who can furnish proper service to the loan. But, to do it, he must offer a loan which meets the standard model provisions. Those provisions will be explained to you in greater detail later; but, in general, they are, first, that the loan must be amortized; that it must not be subject to renewal before it matures. In other words, it will be a self-liquidating loan. It will insist that the owner pay for his home out of his income. Second, the borrower must be of financial reputation standing and ability to be able to carry the loan charge. We do not want people buying houses that are more than they can afford to pay for. That would not be a sound resumption of the construction activity.

Third, the cost of the insurance, the rates, will be lower. It will be a competitive rate fixed in the market, but we will not insure any loan carrying more than 6 percent. In general, in those sections of the East where investment funds are in abundance and are looking for safe investment, we feel that the rate will be 5 percent when this type of security is offered to the investor.

As to the way the insurance will work out in general, it will be a very small fund to operate from a mechanical point of view, because it does not disturb the relations between borrower and lender that exist in the market today. If there are difficulties, however, the lender, to realize on his insurance, will have to turn the property over to the insurance corporation and will receive for his insurance not cash, but a debenture guaranteed by the Government, due three years after his original loan would have matured, and carrying a rate of interest not in excess of 3 percent. That means we are not giving him 100 percent insurance, or offering him 100 percent insurance; we are offering to give enough insurance to encourage private capital to go forward and make these loans. It will not be insured completely against loss. If they make an unsound loan, a loan that gets by the standards, that is impossible, they will have to stand part of the loss.

Finally, because of the insurance feature, we feel it will be safe for the one lender to make the entire mortgage financing in one instrument, and we will be able to evade and avoid the dangers and risks of the second mortgage market. Typical in this country, home building has been financed with first mortgage and second mortgage. The first mortgage was one in which conservative investors put their funds; the second mortgage carried very high rates and attracted speculative risk funds. That system meant a plethora of second-mortgage money when conditions were good, and almost no second-mortgage money, or none at all, when conditions were reversed. So that at the present time, even where first mortgage money is available, which is not generally true, but is true in some cases, still home construction cannot be financed because of the absence of second-mortgage money.

We propose, therefore, that mortgages may be insured up to 80 percent of the appraised value, for mortgages on new construction. In that case, the scrutiny of the mortgage risk, from the point of view of the financial standing of the borrower, will be very strict. Of course, they must be amortized mortgages, so that they will soon be down much lower than that percentage of the appraised value. We also propose that these mortgages shall not be more than 20 years amortization. That ends the brief description of these insured mortgages.

We are proposing that same type of insurance of mortgages to be applied to mortgages on a type of housing project that is usually associated with slum clearance projects. That is, many of our states have now passed laws permitting large scale apartment construction for workers, at low rates, to go forward under strict State supervision, with certain exemptions of taxes and other types of exemptions. There is a clause in this that permits low-cost housing projects in general of that type, and also of private owners if they are genuinely low-cost, to offer mortgages for insurance under this plan, so that those projects will be able to raise their funds more cheaply in the general market, because they can offer for them insured mortgages.

Finally, to carry this insurance, to carry this opening up of the mortgage market to all sections of the country, and to have it unloosen the mortgage market, we propose to permit some of the best mortgages on existing properties to be insured under the same plan, same liabilities.

The limits in the bill on that proposition are, first, that the total that might be insured should not be in excess of 1 billion dollars; second, that the percent of appraisal permitted for mortgages on existing properties should not be in excess of 60 percent. By permitting some of the present mortgages to be insured, we will have given liquidity to the mortgage market. Institutions which are frozen and cannot loan new funds unless they can dispose of their present mortgages will be able to take and insure them if they will recast the mortgage to meet certain provisions as to amortization and interest, and thereby put them in a position to sell them so that they can create a more liquid position of their portfolio and be in a position to loan again.

Second, we propose to authorize a Federal charter of a new type of mortgage-lending institution, national mortgage associations, which will be completely under Federal charter and supervision—supervised at every point and examined by the Federal Home Loan Banking Board. These institutions would be permitted to raise their funds by selling their own bonds or debentures in the market, and we expect them to sell in the security markets where funds are most readily available and to form a type of investment by which trust funds and investment funds of that type could go into mortgages. We propose to control them at every point, however, and permit them to sell those debentures or bonds only against insured mortgages. There must be collateral dollar for dollar by insured mortgages of the model type which I have just described.

We expect those associations to carry the advantages of this insured mortgage to the sections of the country which are deficient in funds and where mortgage rates, therefore, are unduly high. In the country in general, you will find, in the more stable sections of the East where the population is not growing very rapidly, that the supply of savings is in excess of the sound demand for new construction, and it would be bad if we channeled all of those savings into local mortgage construction. It would have the effect of unduly inflating prices. There are other sections of the country, on the other hand, which are growing rapidly, where the demand for new construction is in excess of the local supply of savings, and most mortgage loans are made by local institutions. This results frequently in excessively high rates for mortgage loans. These mortgage associations, by being able to sell their debentures and bonds to institutions and others having investment funds in the more settled sections of the country where capital is in abundance, and using them to purchase, under rigid restrictions, approved insured mortgages in those sections of the country where mortgage funds are deficient, will be able to help bring down the mortgage rate and make the advantage of this proposal universally available. . . .

STATEMENT OF JOHN H. FAHEY, CHAIRMAN
FEDERAL HOME LOAN BANK BOARD

Mr. Fahey. . . . It seems to me that the statement which Mr. Hopkins has made to you is convincing as to the need of dealing with this problem from the standpoint of unemployment, as one feature of it. Certainly no one who has studied the unemployment problem in the country can fail to realize the necessity of getting the construction industry again in action and its enormous influence on employment generally and upon what is known as the "capital goods industries," as well as its influence on transportation and the movement of heavy goods on our railroads and over our roads by trucks and by other methods of transportation.

There are two other features of the problem, however, which we have been particularly impressed with in the Board and to which I would like to direct your attention. I have before referred to the fact that the great mortgage debt on the urban homes in this country represents one of our most serious financial problems. The figures show that it grew at a tremendous rate from 1921, or after the depression of 1921, through 1929; that out of our total of perhaps 134 billions of debt of all kinds in the country, the debt against our urban homes of a valuation of less than $20,000 is the greatest single block of indebtedness we face. That debt of 21½ billion is more than all of your deposits in the national banks of this country as they stand right now. It is almost three times the total commercial debt of the country, including the loans made against stock exchange security by our banks.

In its effect on the depression and the economic structure, it has not attracted as much attention as the rapid decline that we witnessed in the value of securities. That sort of a smash is very much more dramatic and more easily understood. But for 4 years, now, we have had the burden of this debt represented by the mortgage situation becoming increasingly serious.

You know that the Home Owners' Loan Corporation was organized to try to relieve that situation. You are aware of the fact that we have already distributed over the country about $681,000,000 and that it has resulted in vast benefit to our people. But, so far, it is only a drop in the bucket. The demands upon the Corporation are still being presented in increasing amounts. During the last 2 months the total of those demands has been greater than at any time. We now have something more than 1,350,000 applications, aggregating close to 4½ billions of dollars.

Now, we feel convinced that with the least possible delay it is imperative that the funds at the disposal of the private lending institutions of this country, which are under their control in abundance in most directions, must be brought into action to meet this situation. Otherwise, it is our conviction that by next year we will be confronted with increased demands for Government help in this field, and making it impossible to say how far we may have to go. To us, it seems out of the question for a Government institution to undertake to shoulder so great a financial problem and burden as is represented by trying to get under 21½ billions of home-mortgage indebtedness in this country.

The other side of this problem that I would like to refer to is that affecting the question of better and cheaper housing in this country, particularly for the great mass of our workers. The well-to-do, indeed, those of that class which we call the "middle class" in this country, have been reasonably well housed, on the average. I do not think we have any right to be satisfied with the type of housing that we have provided for them in the United States and the price we have charged them for unsatisfactory housing. They have in the main acquired cheap houses at high cost, and they have had great difficulty in paying for such houses. As a matter of fact, we are years behind what the most progressive countries of Europe have done for their people, so far as good housing is concerned for the mass of the workers. England, France, Germany, and Italy have all given us an example of what can be done to great advantage with the aid and support and guidance of governmental institutions in providing excellent housing at low cost and, moreover, the experiments of those countries in recent years have likewise demonstrated the great advantage of encouraging construction of that sort in times of depression. The work that has been done in Germany, England, and France, particularly in recent years, has had a large influence in holding up their employment situation and contributing to their economic recovery.

Our trouble is that after these 4 years of difficulty we are still confronted with an average of over 20,000 foreclosures a month. That is nearly three times any normal average, and that in spite of what the Home Owners' Loan Corporation has been able to do and is continuing to do. Now meanwhile, as has been pointed out, the funds in the savings banks of the country, as a whole, are today at their peak and, according to the National Association of Savings Banks at their convention in New York this week, the next couple of months will show a record so far as deposits in savings banks in this country are concerned. The condition so far as the resources of our national banks are concerned has already been explained to you. Our insurance companies have an abundance of funds, but the great difficulty is that these funds have not been widely stampeded into action, and that is our problem today.

It is suggested sometimes, in the discussion of this question, that even if you make the funds available for modernization and repair, and for new construction wherever it is needed, people will not use the money; that there is too much unemployment. As a matter of fact, gentlemen, despite the seriousness of our problem so far as unemployment is concerned, I feel we constantly overlook the fact that a great army of people in this country are still employed regularly, week after week, and receiving good wages, but they are not spending as freely as they should. Our experience in the Home Owners' Loan Corporation in confronting the demand for modernization shows conclusively that there are tens of thousands of people, if they can obtain money readily, without undue hardship, are ready to use it. The amendment of our bill for modernization was approved, as you know, only about 3 weeks ago, and already the demands for loans for modernization are pouring in by the thousands to our offices all over the country.

This matter of using money if you can get it, and spending if you have it, is the same in this field as it is in nearly every other. Most people do not buy securities until they begin to go up. As the real-estate market is stabilized and strengthened, so more and more buyers will come back into action.

The mortgage lenders, particularly the insurance companies and the savings banks, say that one of the principal reasons for their hesitancy thus far has been that they have not seen enough strength in the real-estate market. Now happily the Home Owners' Loan Corporation and the Federal home-loan banks are contributing something in that direction; for, as we take some hundreds of millions of distressed property out of a panic market, it has a great influence in strengthening the situation and we believe that is making a very important contribution toward recovery in many parts of the country. . . .

We are satisfied that there is a real opportunity for the useful employment of money in modernization. These homes have been neglected for the last 4 years. We have had any number of examples of inability of people to borrow money in their own localities, where it seemed to us, on the basis of the information presented to us, that the risks were perfectly good.

There is one thing about this whole question which we consider of great importance, and that is the emphasis upon making money available by those methods at lower costs and the direction of attention more sharply than ever before to the value of the amortized loan. One of the difficulties of the past has been that the poor man has paid such a premium for a second mortgage. In taking up mortgages in certain sections of the country, we have found thousands of cases where the first mortgage on the property represented the entire cost of the land and the building, a handsome profit to the builder and any number of fees and charges as well and, on top of that, the owner had a second trust or second mortgage which was nothing but pure graft. Now, it is upon people who need most the kind of help which ought to be rendered that that burden has fallen. The well-to-do, those who borrow on a 50- or 60-percent basis from insurance companies and savings banks, ordinarily have the cash to make up that difference, and they do not carry in most cases any corresponding burden.

The building and loan associations, cooperative banks and homestead associations are the lending institutions which have rendered greatest service in general. I do not believe that you can deprecate the contributions made by the insurance companies, or by the savings banks, but the eleven-odd thousand building and loan associations of this country have rendered a very great social service. It is important that they should be encouraged, that their operation should be kept within legitimate lines; that they should have such supervision as is necessary to make them safe and sound—for they are essentially institutions of the worker and the small saver. . . .

We are therefore convinced that legislation along the lines we have suggested here is absolutely imperative if we are to head off increasing demands, if we are to contribute to the restoration of employment generally in this field, and if we are also to take definite steps in the direction of providing better housing for the people of the United States.

I think the opportunity presented in that particular direction is one of the greatest that has ever confronted the country. It is not a temporary matter. I think there is a 20-year job ahead of us in developing housing standards of the United States as they ought to be developed, and I do not believe it can ever be done except under Federal leadership. Here we are a country with the greatest wealth and resources of any on the face of the earth, and yet it is an absolute fact that, so far as our housing for the 85 percent of the people is concerned, it is far from being creditable to the people of this country as compared with the older countries on the other side of the water, which we commonly think are far behind us in many ways.

I think that is all I want to say.

The Chairman. Mr. Russell, we shall be glad to hear you.

STATEMENT OF HORACE RUSSELL, GENERAL COUNSEL FEDERAL HOME LOAN BANK BOARD

Mr. Russell. . . . I would say this much, gentlemen, that from my study of the mortgage situation it appears to me the greatest problem confronting us is to find a means of causing money to flow into the mortgage market. Increasingly, money has flowed into Postal Savings and very largely has flowed out of this type of savings, and that began to tighten up back in 1929 and shows, before the depression even started, the effects of Postal Savings draining money out of this type of institution. You see, those building and loan associations have about 10,000,000 members who save in them chiefly by the week or by the month, in small sums. They are the people who walk down the street and the sun shines today, and, because they have a fresh cow and are going to have milk and save $5, they are thinking about where they are going to put it. They are now thinking about putting that money in the Postal Savings or in an insured bank deposit and save it until they desire to use it somewhere.

If they put it in this type of institution, it goes to work tomorrow and puts a man to work for 2 or 3 days, and it is the plan in title III to cause that money to go where it will go to work and not to go in an insured bank, where we are spending our days and nights trying to syphon it out of the banks by some kind of method. But this title III is designed to get that type of saver to put his money into an institution which will use it and I would point out in this connection, that this type of institution today has not more than 2 percent of its money in cash. It has got all the balance, pretty nearly, in mortgages or foreclosed real estate. It has got 85 percent or so in mortgages and a fraction of a percent in foreclosed real estate, and a few of them have a little bit in State or Government bonds of some kind, but very little—not more than 2 percent; not that much, I think—and 1 or 2 percent in cash. In other words, as soon as you start the flow of money into those institutions, they are going to find a means of lending it and putting it to work, and that puts men to work. And this kind of insurance plan—those of us who have studied it, we think it will attract substantial dollars in that direction and very gradually there will be more employment in this field. And, as Mr. Fahey stated a moment ago, those institutions finance in the first instance more than 65 percent in number of all of the small homes in this country, and it will start some employment not only now but a year from now we will have continued employment. I think, personally, it is about as important to have continued employment as it is to start some employment for just a few months. . . .

STATEMENT OF JOHN H. FAHEY—RESUMED

Mr. Fahey. . . . Now, our experience shows, clearly enough, that in many sections of the country there is a demand for money for modernization purposes, which the community is wholly unable to supply. The banks in some instances—at least, until now—have not had surplus funds available, and such as they had they appeared unwilling to use. It seems to us that that attitude has changed very substantially as the result of the insurance of bank deposits and the flow of money back into the banks where it is piling up. Now, as you know, the modernization section of this bill is intended to encourage the use of that money freely, while at the same time leaving the responsibility for a proper checking of such loans, and making such loans, on the financial institutions themselves. . . .

Mr. Cavicchia (New Jersey). Do you mean that these banks have money on hand but they are afraid to lend it on mortgages?

Mr. Fahey. They certainly have been up to the present time. I say the attitude in that respect is changing, in the areas where that money has accumulated.

Mr. Goldsborough (Maryland). Mr. Fahey, as I understood, in the course of your argument the other day, the gist of it was that the Home Owners' Loan Corporation found that its resources would be utterly insufficient to take care of applications that were being received; and if this is true then it seems necessary to subsidize mortgage companies and building and loan associations, in order for them to be induced to make what would ordinarily be considered conservative loans; and with that in view, your recommendation was that they should be subsidized, if necessary, up to 20 percent. Is that about a fair statement?

Mr. Fahey. Yes; with this supplementary statement: You authorized us, in the case of the Home Owners' Loan Corporation, to set aside out of our resources $200,000,000 which we might use for the modernization of homes where we were to refinance the mortgages. We are not allowed to go outside of that. Consequently, we cannot deal with any applications for money for modernization, except in connection with the taking over of mortgages.

Now, of course, that touches only a part of the community where the demand exists. The rest of the field is left wide open. Consequently, because of the demand which we know exists in some localities—information coming to us shows it clearly enough—it seems to us that an effort should be made to induce the private lending institutions to take care of that situation.

Now, so far as guaranteeing those losses are concerned, our conviction is that the losses are not likely to be very large. We do not feel that there will be any such margin of loss as that provided in the bill. That margin was provided only to make assurance doubly sure.

Mr. Goldsborough. As I remember the testimony of yourself and the other witnesses, it was to the effect that the policy of the bill was to confine these loans to very conservative prospects; there was no disposition, insofar as this particular legislation is concerned, to be liberal. . . .

Mr. Fahey. Well, obviously, it would not be sound policy to induce people to incur obligations of this sort; they have no chance of discharging. The purpose should be, however, to make the money available to those who desire it and who have every reasonable chance of taking care of the obligation within the 5 years provided for.

Mr. Goldsborough. Yes; well, I fully agree that, to loan a man money who is not in a position to return it is not doing him any favor. But in view of the fact that this policy is to be conservative and along the ordinary business lines, do you think it is economically sound for society to subsidize loaning organizations under any circumstances?

Mr. Fahey. Under ordinary circumstances, no. We are, however, dealing with extraordinary conditions. In my judgment, it is a far better policy to risk the comparatively small sum of money involved here to induce employment and stimulate and encourage really constructive work, as against facing the possibility of appropriating another $500,000,000 or $900,000,000 or $1,000,000,000 to maintain people in comparative idleness through the P.W.A. In my personal judgment, it is far better to have our carpenters, and our bricklayers, and our plasterers, and all the other workers of the building trades, engaged in truly constructive work, than to have them raking leaves, or helping to widen streets, and do a lot of things that they are not accustomed to do at all, and doing them on a more or less luxury basis, in other words, your "make work" program.

Mr. Goldsborough. Well, of course, there would not be any serious disagreement between you and me on that score. That is not the issue I was raising. The issue that I was raising was whether or not these private loaning organizations have funds, and if the intention is that they shall confine their operations to legitimate loaning operations—why they should be subsidized at all by society? It is a well-known fact that if you ever start a process of that kind it never stops until it has destroyed itself; it continues, and it becomes greater and more menacing, until eventually it is destroyed automatically. That is the history of all other propositions of this kind; I do not think there is any exception whatever.

Mr. Fahey. That is quite true, Mr. Congressman. But when you confront such extraordinary conditions through which we have been passing, the private lenders are unable, or unwilling, to utilize their funds; and then there is no authority to meet the situation except the Government. Now, let us take it in the case of the Home Owners' Loan Corporation—

Mr. Goldsborough (interposing). Well, if these men, or these organizations—if their interests, as they saw it, induced them to retain their funds, rather than loan those funds, and then if your societies should induce them to loan the funds, by saying to them, "If you do it we will subsidize you"—do you think that is a sound proposition?

Mr. Fahey. Well, ordinarily I would not regard it as a sound proposition. But I think it is imperative that we should get men back to work as quickly as we possibly can. Under these conditions, if the $200,000,000 provided for in this act is used, it will mean the expenditure of a billion dollars. A billion dollars expended in the encouragement of modernization and improvement and new construction, where necessary, is certainly better than a billion dollars paid out in P.W.A. and it distributes just as much and better employment. What I was trying to say and to show was this: That when we have to deal with conditions such as these, no matter whether we like it or not, it is only the authority and power of the Government that is effective for common action.

Let us take the problem of the Home Owners' Loan Corporation. Before the Home Owners' Loan Corporation came into existence, mortgages on something more than 800,000 homes had been foreclosed; and when this corporation began business, there was, as the figures show, something more than 4 billions of dollars of mortgages in the country not yet foreclosed, in which there was danger of foreclosure. No private interest could meet that situation. You could not conceive of a situation under which the savings banks, the life-insurance companies, and all the other insurance companies, would come together and join in a common effort to meet it. It required the power of the Government to meet that situation. And the meeting of it has contributed in a very large way to easing the situation. We have already absorbed some $750,000,000 of such loans, and have saved a corresponding number of homes from loss.

Mr. Goldsborough. Yes; that is true.

Mr. Fahey. At the same time, we have stabilized the real-estate market and we have helped to bring about the very situation to which Mr. Luce referred; that is of bringing the private lending institutions to the point where, perhaps, a bit timidly, but to a certain extent, they have been ready to come back into the field. . . .

May I digress to make a remark in connection with the question you raised relative to the insurance companies? Of course, as you know, there is a good deal of debate as to the soundness of the policy pursued by most of the insurance companies of making only short-time loans on mortgages. As you know, their theory has always been that these short-time loans of our mutual savings banks and insurance companies were the soundest kind of loans, because they matured in a comparatively short time, and the expectation was that they would be renewed in full. This depression has furnished a certain amount of evidence that there is great weakness in that theory because when the loan matured the man was utterly unable to meet his obligation of $5,000. Orginally when he made it it was not expected that he would meet it; it was to be renewed. But under the conditions that developed the savings banks and the insurance companies, in a great many instances, either asked for their payment of that loan, or a substantial reduction in the amount, and the mortgagor was unable to meet that situation. And that condition has undoubtedly aggravated the foreclosure conditions in the country as a whole.

Mr. Busby (Mississippi). May I ask you, Mr. Fahey, if it is not true that all of these various theories fail when the buying power, or the paying power of the public fails on which the theory is based?

Mr. Fahey. Of course, that is quite true; but I will supplement what I was saying, Mr. Congressman, that the burden has been much easier to carry where the man has a long-time amortized loan.

Mr. Busby. That is because payment is not called for at a time when the obligor has no funds; that is the reason, is it not?

Mr. Fahey. Exactly, and is able to meet it on a reasonable installment basis. . . .

Mr. Sproul. Mr. Fahey, I did not hear all of your testimony, but on page 6 it is provided (reading):

> No home mortgages shall be insured which involve an original principal obligation in excess of $20,000, or which involve an original principal obligation in excess of 80 per centum of the appraised value of the property offered as security therefor in the case of homes constructed since the passage of this act, or 60 per centum of the appraised value of such property in the case of existing homes.

Are not those percentages rather high? As a matter of fact, no man could get that percentage of loan from a nonresident organization. Some local organization, because of a man's credit and standing in the community and consideration of moral qualities of the man, might extend a loan of 70 percent, but 80 percent of the appraised value, for example, would seem to be rather out of all reason.

Mr. Fahey. Amortized mortgages, loans extending over a long period up to 75 and 80 percent, are not uncommon among the lending institutions, particularly the building and loan associations and cooperative banks.

The other class of institutions have preferred the short-term loans of 50 or 60 percent; that is, the mutual savings banks and the insurance companies. In many States they are restricted to that amount. But the sound mortgage up to 75 or 80 percent, where there is no second mortgage, of course, has proven its usefulness not only here but on the other side of the water and is very common indeed. Of course, where such a loan is made it eliminates, in almost all cases, the necessity for second-mortgage financing, which is very expensive, particularly to the small man; and where such a loan is properly protected by value, the experience does not indicate that the risk is undue. It is economically and socially desirable to eliminate the second mortgage as far as it is possible to do so in our mortgage financing in the future. . . .

STATEMENT OF HON. FRANCES PERKINS, SECRETARY OF LABOR

Miss Perkins. . . . However, I do want to say this: That from the point of view of the Department of Labor and my own experience, this bill seems to me to be of very great importance at this time because of the results which it will have in providing employment for building-trade mechanics who have long been out of work and who are themselves a basic part of our internal market, our purchasing power in this country, and also the importance arising from the stimulation of capital-goods industries, that will flow out of this bill, and the importance that that will be to the program of recovery in this country.

As you undoubtedly know, the amount of unemployment in the building trades has been very great. It has been out of proportion to the unemployment in all the other industries, and there are at this time almost 2,000,000 people regularly out of work, who were formerly attached to the building trades and who believe themselves to be attached to the building trades, the estimate being some 1,800,000 or 1,900,000.

There has been, as you know, only a very modest and very small revival of employment in private building, and such employment as we have had in the building trades, has almost been entirely due to the public-employment program, the Public Works program. . . .

We do know that there is a certain degree of recovery of private business and private industry.

The degree and the stability of that recovery is not quite measurable at this time. It is still necessary, therefore, to give stimulation both to private recovery and to the continuance of public expenditure in order to give people work and in order to get that great market, that great internal market, which is due to purchasing power. There will, of course, I think it is safe to say, hardly be a substantial recovery and a substantial revival of private business in the near future unless there is for the next year a deliberate stimulation of purchasing power in the people who are in a position to be purchasers. If the building mechanics and people working in the manufacturing trades and incidental trades receive wages for the work which they do in this necessary revision and labor program, there will be flowing from them a market for consumption goods and things which they will purchase for themselves, and from that demand for consumption goods, orders for raw materials, orders for machinery, orders for equipment, and out of that it is anticipated, of course, that we will get the cycle of demand and provision for the supply and demand which makes our normal industrial balance and our normal industrial turnover. . . .

Mr. Luce. Until in our own time, our social system left the gratification of desires in this field to the ambition of the individual. The desire to have comforts, the desire to emulate your neighbors, which is known as "keeping up with the Joneses," was left to the individual. The Government had not interfered nor had that sort of thing existed; but in our time there developed the installment system of buying, whereby private enterprise, through high-pressure methods of salesmanship, cooperated with the monthly payment system to induce a volume of buying which developed into a burden upon the wage-earning classes in the community. In this bill it is proposed to add the Government impulse to stimulate still further the contracting of debts in order to gratify individual desires. Do you approve of that as a social desideratum?

Miss Perkins. Sir, you have asked me a question upon which I should like to debate with you privately for an entire morning. It is one of those questions which, if I were a witness, I would have to say, "I cannot answer 'yes' or 'no'." There are, I think, a great many qualifications which should be put around any program of deferred payments. I do say, however, that with a mass-production system, such as one which we have developed today, due to machinery and due to power and due to the extraordinary inventiveness of the American people with regard to the utilization of machinery and the utilization of programs of using human labor, we have developed a system of production which produces so much, and is capable of producing so much, that it can hardly be maintained, can hardly stand stable, unless it has a variable factor. It is almost inconceivable that a means large enough to sustain it should develop in general without some provision for deferred payments for paying the price of an article which is well within the means of a family but not within its actual cash account on a given week or a given month.

There are, of course, great limitations which should be thrown around a program of deferred payments, and I suppose we have not yet come to the point where we know how to measure exactly what are the means of a particular family. But certainly we should never have built up the automobile industry in this country, which now offers employment to so many people, both directly and indirectly, and has so greatly modified the whole American economic life—we should never have built up and sustained or kept up the industry, kept up a market for it, unless some program of deferred payments had been worked out. And, apparently, it has been within the means of the American people to finance the payment for automobiles for themselves rather generally, both among the well-to-do and among the less well-to-do, on the basis of deferred payments. Hardly anybody pays for his car in cash.

The extent to which one should provide for that in certain items is a question that ought to be discussed, I think, with a great deal of social consideration as well as a reference merely to the classical economic theory. There are such things as houses, such things as homes, making extensions to one's home, which have rarely been built on other than the basis of deferred payments. Hardly anybody builds a house or builds an addition to his house by the payment of cash outright, which he has already stored up in the bank. He has some sort of credit arrangement, and therefore handles it through a series of deferred payments.

The difference between deferred payments, or installment buying, as you call it, for durable goods, for durable things, and for durable permanent benefits to a family, and the use of installment buying on deferred payments, maintained for things which are used up within a season, is very different. Certainly there should not be deferred payments, on a coat, a winter coat, we will say, and the payments should not be deferred longer than the first half of the life of the coat. It is a unique situation, if it does; and you and I have probably seen people who were still paying for garments which they have long since worn out and discarded. That is an entirely unique method of deferred payments; but the use of deferred payments for permanent and durable goods, or permanent and durable equipment is, I think on a somewhat different level, and I think should perhaps be treated somewhat differently. It is a form of credit which can be extended to others, to those who have built up credit by way of investment in savings or securities or land or other property ordinarily recognized as property.

Mr. Luce. You have made an admirable statement with which I take no issue at all, but it hardly meets the anxiety which I have in regard to this bill. We may concede that deferred payments are natural in the social structure, but it is the abuse of the system—or was the abuse of the system—in the minds of some of us, which contributed greatly to the smash of 5 years ago, and in respect to that abuse we want to take thought in the present situation.

To get down to a concrete illustration, let me take your reference to the possibility of building a garage. It is proposed by this bill that a man who wants a garage shall undertake to pay $40 a month through 5 years. That is a larger garage than ordinarily would be built, but we will take that case and assume a garage of that value. Now, hitherto we have allowed that man desiring a garage to pass an unprejudiced, undisturbed, and unfettered judgment as to whether he should add to his burden $40 a month for 5 years. In this bill we propose to incite him to do these things by making it possible for him to get a loan of money. We propose to incite him to do a thing that may be beyond a reasonable extension of his obligations. What I am trying to find out is whether it is a proper governmental function to incite a man to take on burdens that he ought not to carry.

Miss Perkins. When you put it in that very definite form, sir, I think no one could fail to answer that it is not the function or duty of the government, nor is it within its province, to incite men to take on obligations which they cannot afford. It is presumed that this would only make it possible for those who can afford to do so, to do it. I am told—and I know nothing about it of my own knowledge—but I am reliably informed that there is at present a great amount of money not finding a useful and profitable investment, which is in the possession of people who can well afford to make additions to the permanent improvement of their homes, and the permanent social improvement of their communities, by just this kind of expenditure; and that they can look forward, if we do stimulate the business life—if we stimulate the industrial life of the community—they can look forward to a continuance of their present general level of moderate prosperity. If we do not stimulate the industrial and business life of the community, perhaps they cannot look forward to that, but it is to the social and economic advantage of the whole community that they should spend as much as they can afford to spend for the improvement of their own premises and for the social improvement and the life of the communities in which they live.

Mr. Luce. But we are being confronted again and again with the proposition that one of the unfortunate features of our social structure today is the tremendous amount of debt. Half of the public is in debt, half of the farms are mortgaged, half of the homes in the cities are mortgaged. We have been terribly afflicted in that way by the developments in various directions, and that debt not yet having satisfied the producers of durable goods, they now come to us and ask a measure to change the methods still further, so as to increase the debt. It happens that I am a New Englander and that in my day I have read something of Ben Franklin's *Poor Richard's Almanac*, and was brought up in the philosophy that happiness ends when one gets in debt, and I am reluctant to see the agencies of the Federal Government used to incite men to add to their troubles—to repeat that language—for debt involves a period of time in which there is grave chance of illness, deaths in the family, other changes, accidents of one sort or another, which make the burden of debt the most serious blow to happiness that one can find.

While I admit that the social agencies that have been developed normally, such as the building and loan associations, are admirable, I hesitate to embark the Federal Government on a policy of inviting debt.

Do you think that I am unsound in that position?

Miss Perkins. Sir, since I have brought myself to that present point of view, I would not want for a moment to say that you are unsound, for I have long cherished the same point of view myself, if I may say so; but I do think that under our present form of production and distribution, which we have moved into quite rapidly over the last 50 years, and so rapidly that some of us have hardly been aware of it—I think that we have got to regard debt as indefinitely more of an asset than we used to regard it. Debt is not serious, provided that you can establish stability of income. If you cannot establish income, and if you cannot establish the velocity of money out of which national income grows, then debt is a serious thing. But if income is moving, that is, moving rapidly from hand to hand, then your national income increases much more rapidly than you have internal indebtedness for those particular things. As long as they add to the social standard of the community and to the improvement of the living of individuals, I do not think that debt is serious.

I think, philosophically speaking, that your view is extremely important, and that it ought to be canvassed thoroughly in the near future; that we ought to think about this whole relationship of spending and income and the velocity of money, and that we ought to arrive, perhaps, at an understanding of the direction in which we are going; but our whole economic system is now apparently built up on a system of credit. Except for that, we should never make any headway in the conquering of the forces of nature and of the social and economic problems which are still ahead of us. . . .

Mr. Cross. . . . I do not think a debt is necessary. I think debt is the greatest demon of punishment in the world, and it makes people unhappy. They begin to tremble and fear that they will die and leave their wife in a helpless condition, and probably be put out of doors, and people who lose their farms by foreclosure come along and get together and you have got the prospects of a revolution.

Debt is a great incentive to trouble and revolution. I do not see how a fellow could be expected to go out and build a house under such circumstances. You know it is common experience. If you build a house and you can hardly sell it for one-half the cost of building it, how could you be expected to build it?

I do not know, and I would like to get your views on it. It would be because of some persuasion or inducement.

Miss Perkins. It is my understanding that a large part of the effort back of this bill will be not for the erection of new homes particularly, but for the renovizing [sic] and rehabilitation of such properties as people already own. There will, of course, be provision for the building of additional buildings by home owners, but the drive will be for the renovizing [sic], and rehabilitation, and repair, and modernizing of such buildings as at present exist, and that is where the greatest need is, probably. . . .

Mr. Goldsborough. [Deferred payments] is an issue which is involved in the consideration of this bill, you know. The only way that a system of deferred payments can increase the buying power of the public is because those deferred payments allow them to spend more than their income would justify, which simply means that sooner or later they are going to reach an impasse of debt, and that is exactly what happened in 1929. When you have a system of deferred payments and encourage and undertake to increase the buying power of the people artificially by that means, you are going to have periodically the same thing recurring, and it is absolutely inevitable.

Miss Perkins. Sir, I do not think I can quite agree with you, that the deferred payment merely means that people buy things which are beyond their means. If one has a stable income, a relatively stable income that runs, we will say, to $200 a month, one can well afford to purchase a cheap automobile, for which one makes a payment of $50 a month, and it is done all the time, so much down and $50 a month. It is done all the time, and it keeps people well within their income, because their income is a monthly income and not an uncertain matter. If it all came at one time, on the 1st of January, in one lump sum, you could afford not to pay cash for the automobile, but if it comes due in monthly installments or weekly installments, you can afford to pay a proportion of your income for the automobile, just as you pay a proportion of it for rent, just as you pay a proportion of it for your monthly payment of rent. You have got an annual contract to pay so much a year for the house in which you live, but you agree to pay that in monthly installments. You make a budget or plan, which is kept on that basis.

Mr. Goldsborough. Let us take the case of an automobile, which is the illustration that you have just used. The individual who receives $200 a month could ultimately purchase this automobile and pay for it outright if he would save $50 a month and defer the purchase of a car for a few months. Do you not think he would be better off?

Miss Perkins. Ordinarily he would not be as well off. I am familiar with hundreds of people who by the purchase of a car have been able to do business which they would not otherwise have done. . . .

Mr. Goldsborough. When I was a young man a fellow had just paid off his last mortgage and he said to me that that burden had been so severe on him for a great many years that he had reached the conclusion that a man just as well be in hell as to be in debt. At that time I was too young to appreciate what he said, but I fully agree with him, from my own experiences now.

The Chairman (Mr. Steagall). Miss Perkins, what you have in mind under this legislation is that the thing desired is where the heads of families are in position, if they could obtain necessary extensions of credit, to improve their homes, and elevate the standard of living without adding a burden which they would not be able to meet, and at the same time afford employment for labor now idle, which is dependent in part upon public charity for the time being.

Miss Perkins. Yes, sir. . . .

STATEMENT OF CHARLES A. MILLER, PRESIDENT
SAVINGS BANKS' TRUST CO., NEW YORK CITY

. . . Mr. Miller. . . . Owing to the tremendous condition of fright which has been felt throughout the mortgage market, the ordinary lender will be unwilling to incur what he regards as a risk, or will be unwilling to buy mortgages in the market, and feel that his money is tied up in them, unless he has some sort of guarantee behind him—a guarantee either by the Government or someone else. This gives the Government an opportunity to help in that way. At the same time it involves a minimum chance of loss on a minimum expenditure of Government money. . . .

STATEMENT OF HUGH POTTER, HOUSTON, TEX., PRESIDENT
NATIONAL ASSOCIATION OF REAL ESTATE BOARDS

Mr. Potter: . . . Our association wants to urge the passage of this legislation, feeling, after a study of it, that it will accomplish these things:

First, a lowering of the interest rates available to those who build homes or make repairs on homes.

Second, that it will eliminate the second mortgage, which has been an abuse in the home building field for many years, particularly in our section of the country, that is, in the South and Southwest.

Third, we believe it will relieve unemployment in the construction industry, where according to our survey, there are still 80 percent of the three and a half million men normally engaged in that business unemployed.

Fourth, we believe that there is a real necessity for more homes, particularly, in the single-family field and in the lower-price brackets. . . .

I want it understood I am not advocating the usage of governmental money for building purposes in any way; that I only seek to set up instrumentalities which will tend to restore confidence to those who have money to lend, to make it easy, if you please, for one who really wishes to invest money, and there is plenty of it for investment in long-term real-estate and development securities, and to sell them when the time comes when the need is for money.

All of the institutions that are declining at this time to make loans except upon very rigid appraisals, and upon low percentages of those appraisals, are doing it, I think, because of their fear that their liquid position may be endangered, if and when another depression comes. . . .

Mr. Goldsborough. Let me tell you, because it will help that explanation, I think, that I have been on this committee for 14 years watching the course of measures that are handed to us—not our creations, but are handed to us—and, without exception, in the 14 years I have been on this committee, back behind somewhere was a selfish interest that wanted to be served. Now, as one member of the committee, I am utterly unable to see anything in this bill except relieving the selfish interests of people who are in trouble about mortgages they hold. Now that is all I can see in the bill—that and an inducement to people who are not able to do it to incur debt. As far as the housing feature is concerned, that to me is a joke; honestly, I am sincere in that. It is a pure joke. And whoever named this bill, of course, misnamed it.

Another thing that I have seen—and I am only speaking as one member of the committee—in all my experience, is the more flamboyant the name given to the bill, the more snakes there are in it. . . .

Now, then, I just want to tell you what I see in this bill. I cannot tell it all briefly as I am going to speak, but substantially I see in this bill these things: First, I see the fading out of a lot of mortgagees who have worthless mortgages; second, I see the sale of what amounts to Government bonds on a 5-percent basis if you win and on a 3-percent basis if you lose. By that I mean the person who buys the bond is going to get his principal and 5 percent if he wins; and if he loses, he is going to get his principal and 3 percent. That is another thing I see. The third thing I see in this bill is inducing people who are not able to do it do something around their premises. It is perfectly evident to me that you can loan to people by and large, to build garages and other things, and if they are not able to do it and if the Government is going to give them $3,000 for that purpose, it cannot be anything but an evil thing in the last analysis.

Now that is all I can see in the bill.

5

Evolution of Federal Legislative Policy in Housing: Housing Credits

Milton P. Semer, Julian H. Zimmerman, Ashley Foard, and John M. Frantz

GENERATING HOUSING CREDIT THROUGH INFLUENCING THE FLOW OF SAVINGS—THE FEDERAL HOME LOAN BANK SYSTEM

The President's Conference on Home Building and Home Ownership in December 1931 is often cited as providing the impetus for the original basic home financing legislation of the United States, especially that establishing the Federal home loan bank system. Essentially, the President's Conference was a fact-finding body that identified the weakness and inadequacies of housing and home financing in the United States, as distinguished from an organization developing specific recommendations for home financing legislation.

The Federal Government's leadership in establishing a forum for consideration of these problems at a national level was of great historical significance. Although the documents produced by the conference did not directly call for increased or new Federal involvement in the national housing credit market, the fact appears to be that the President's initiative in calling such a conference and the reverberations of its discussions had much to do with the pioneering legislation which was shortly to follow. The conference highlighted for the Nation the existing inadequacies of home construction and rehabilitation, the need for further research and distribution of information on the subject, the crucial problems of building and loan associations and other lenders arising from the Great De-

From U.S. Department of Housing and Urban Development. *Housing in the Seventies: Working Papers. I. National Housing Policy Review.* Washington, D.C.: U.S. Government Printing Office, 1976, pp. 3-27.

pression then existing, and the flaws in foreclosure, zoning and other State and local laws.

The Federal Home Loan Bank Act of 1932

Even before the convening of the Conference, President Hoover announced his intention to recommend to the Congress what he called " ... a system of Home Loan Discount Banks," with four purposes:

1. To take pressure off sound home mortgage lending institutions and permit them to recover;
2. To stimulate home construction and increase employment;
3. To prevent repetition of the mortgage industry's collapse in the face of economic difficulty; and
4. To create a structure for the promotion of homeownership.[1]

In contemporary terms, it is instructive to note that the President considered as a sufficient basis to invoke Federal participation the fact that new home construction had then fallen drastically below a level of 200,000 units per year of "normal times"—as contrasted with a general agreement in the private and public sectors that the national need in the period of the 1960s and 1970s is a rate of new building on the order of 10 times that figure or more.

The Federal Home Loan Bank Act of 1932[2] authorized the establishment of a system of Federal home loan banks, roughly parallel to, and with functions in the field of, housing credit roughly analogous to those of the Federal Reserve system. Initially, the banks were to be capitalized by investment of Federal funds (originally intended to be appropriated funds, but later converted into capital subscription of the Reconstruction Finance Corporation), with the intent that the Federal capital would ultimately be retired by the investments of the member institutions—building and loan associations (later and now generally called savings and loan institutions) and, on a lesser scale, mutual savings banks, insurance companies, and similar major mortgage lenders.

The regional banks were to provide guidance, standards, and supervision. In addition, they were to provide an expanded source of credit to members by making advances on the security of mortgage loans held by them. To raise funds for this purpose—in addition to the provisions for members' subscription to capital stock in amounts fixed in relation to the volume of their business—the regional banks were given power to issue consolidated debentures in the private capital market. The security of these debentures was enhanced by making them all the joint and several obligations of all the banks—thus throwing behind each issue the underlying assets of the entire system.

Thus, taken as a whole, the system served:

- To provide national identity to a structure of home mortgage financing institutions;
- To introduce standards and criteria of sound performance;
- To provide the mechanism for a more dependable flow of mortgage funds;
- To facilitate the flow of funds from areas of adequate to those of short supply.

Theory of Long Term Savings Institutions and Their Role in Home Financing

The Federal Home Loan Bank Act and the various pieces of perfecting and strengthening legislation that followed it did not seek to create an entirely new form of institution to provide funds for homebuilding and purchasing. Rather, they were intended to improve, rationalize, and strengthen institutional forms which had existed for at least a century, generally under the name of building and loan associations, and to reform their policies and practices so as to make them more responsive to the housing and economic needs of the country.

Underlying this approach were two closely related propositions: First, that encouragement of long term savings and habits of thrift was in the best interest of people generally—especially those who were heads of families—by virtue of encouraging individual responsibility, family stability, homeownership, and upward social and economic mobility of the industrious and provident. The corollary proposition was that long term individual savings are a peculiarly appropriate source of funds for home mortgage investment, as distinguished from the more volatile flow of funds in and out of the general investment markets.

In a simplistic way, it might be said that the objective of the system as it took shape and evolved was to provide for the ordinary citizen a way of investing his savings with reasonable security and at a reasonable rate of return, to the end of accumulating resources that would permit him in due course to achieve homeownership.

In this light, the institutions intended to be served and strengthened were not considered to be banks in the ordinary sense, but were conceptually distinguished from commercial banks in a number of ways, of which the following were perhaps fundamental:

1. Funds of individuals in the hands of these savings institutions were not regarded as deposits in a custodial sense, but as investments in the institutions themselves—thus the special terminology that arose, referring to account holders as "members" or "shareholders," rather than "depositors," and to the funds themselves as "shares," rather than "deposits." Similarly, the earnings credited to shareholder accounts were referred to as "dividends" rather than "interest."

2. Consistent with this theory of individual savings as investments, the holders of accounts in savings and loan associations had no right to demand withdrawal. Instead, the associations had the power (consistent with regulations of the Federal Home Loan Bank Board) to impose a waiting period after an account holder made application for what was referred to as the "repurchase" of his shares in the association.
3. Checking privileges and other general banking services were considered to be outside the range of normal operations of these kinds of institutions.
4. The appropriate scope of investment activity for such institutions was deemed to be rather narrowly limited to the making of first mortgage loans on residential property.
5. Although participation of stock institutions owned and operated for profit of the stockholders was not ruled out, the thinking of the time placed heavy emphasis on encouragement of mutual institutions owned by their shareholders and operated for their common benefit.

Thus, the system of institutions which engaged new and significant forms of Federal support beginning in 1932 was conceived, broadly and simply stated, to have a dual function: First, to provide a means of accumulating the long term savings of individuals and families, and encouraging such savings; and second, plowing the capital thus accumulated back into housing in the form of first mortgage loans for the building or purchase of homes. While many variations and even idiosyncrasies have developed within the system over the years, these conceptual threads have persisted throughout its history and have influenced its development along lines parallel to, but always distinguished from, the commercial banking system.

The Rescue Operation—HOLC

The Federal Home Loan Bank Act was designed to restructure the home savings and mortgage lending facilities of the Nation, and to rationalize their operations over the long haul. Before this could be done, however, there was an emergency situation to be dealt with of such immediacy and magnitude as to require other more drastic short term measures.

In brief, the home mortgage lending industry was in a state of virtual collapse. New mortgage lending and new home building were almost nonexistent. The characteristic format of mortgage lending—a balloon-type loan for 5 years or less, at a high interest rate which had to be refinanced or paid off in full at the end of its term—had appeared to function reasonably well during boom times. Subjected to severe deflation and unemployment, it broke down. Lenders could not or would not refinance mortgages coming due; homeowners could not or would not pay them off. Values of both mortgages and the underlying security declined precipitously. Lending institutions with a large proportion of their assets in mortgages found themselves insolvent when the value of the mortgages evaporated. Vast holdings in junior liens—second, third, and even fourth mortgages—were wiped out as values fell below even the primary claim. Some 50 percent of all home mortgages in the country were in default. Foreclosures reached the astronomical rate of more than a thousand per day.

Less than a year after the establishment of the Federal Home Loan Bank Board, the Congress passed the Home Owners' Loan Act of 1933.[3] The act established a Home Owners' Loan Corporation, headed by a Board of Directors composed of the members of the Federal Home Loan Bank Board. HOLC's mission was to refinance home mortgages in default or process of foreclosure, and even to make loans to permit owners to recover homes lost through foreclosure or forced sale. To accomplish these purposes, it used Federal capital and funds borrowed in the private market on the security of federally guaranteed bonds. The original Federal Home Loan Bank Act had authorized the banks to make mortgage loans to individuals directly, as well as indirectly through the provision of credit to member institutions. This little-used authority was repealed by the act which established HOLC.

When HOLC's active lending program ended in 1936, it had made loans of more than $3 billion to refinance mortgages, pay delinquent taxes, and make essential home repairs, modernization, and improvements. In the course of liquidation of the Corporation's program in the years that followed, this investment was fully recovered, both for the Treasury and for the private bondholders.

HOLC, however, did more than stop a one-time panic and contribute to the restoration of confidence in mortgage lending as an economic activity and in mortgages themselves as valuable investments. In the course of carrying out its emergency mission, it pioneered the long term amortized mortgage, and demonstrated the feasibility of homeownership for people of only moderate means when financed through reasonable monthly charges related to income and credit rating. Thus it laid much of the basis for the complete restructuring of home mortgage finance that was to take place in the years that followed.

Rounding Out the System

In the same act that created HOLC, the Congress took another major step toward creating a modern, effective mortgage lending industry for the country. It authorized the Federal Home Loan Bank Board to provide for the "organization, incorporation, examination, operation, and regulation" of Federal Savings and Loan Associations, in order to "... provide local mutual thrift institutions in which people may invest their funds and in order to provide for the financing of homes. ..." (It is interesting to note that as recently as 1968 the authorizing statute was amended (among other purposes) to write into law the prohibition which had long existed in regulations against checking privileges on members' accounts (Public Law 90-448).) Charters were to be issued "... giving primary consideration to the best practices of local mutual thrift and home-financing institutions in the United States.''

As investment outlets, the new associations were virtually confined to making first mortgage loans on homes or "combinations of homes and business property" within a 50-mile radius from their home offices. Provision was made for initial capital subscriptions by the Treasury. Indeed, the Congress felt so strongly about encouraging growth of these new institutions that not only the associations themselves but the earnings of shareholders on their savings accounts were made exempt from income taxes. (This exemption was eliminated in 1942. (Public Law 834, 87th Congress).)

Each association was declared to be automatically a member on incorporation of the appropriate Regional Home Loan Bank. Provision was made for voluntary conversion of State-chartered member institutions to Federal status.

Thus the Board, which had been called into existence to create a reserve banking industry for mortgage lending and which had been used as the parent agency for HOLC, became the chosen instrument for a new and even more far-reaching reform—the effort to bring into existence and institutionalize sound and progressive home mortgage lending practices through a national system of local savings institutions built around federally chartered associations which were to serve both as leaders and examples.

Within a few years, the Federal associations, though only about a third in numbers of member institutions, held well over half the assets of member savings institutions nationwide.

Insurance of Savings and Loan Accounts

Nothing deepened the effects of the Great Depression on the financial community more severely than the catastrophic loss of public confidence—confidence in the integrity and stability of banks and savings institutions themselves, and confidence in the safety of private funds entrusted to their care. The bank holiday, banking reforms, and the establishment of the Federal Deposit Insurance Corporation did much to restore confidence in the commercial banking system. Perhaps no one thing did as much to renew confidence on the part of the small depositor as FDIC, which gave him the assurance of the Federal Government that, no matter what happened to the bank itself, his funds would be protected.

The analogy to individual savings in savings and loan associations was obvious, and indeed it seemed evident that such associations would be at a hopeless disadvantage in competing for individual savings unless they could offer comparable protection. In the National Housing Act (1934), the Congress took this logical next step, creating the Federal Savings and Loan Insurance Corporation in a now familiar format: The members of the Federal Home Loan Bank Board were to serve as the Board of Directors of the new Corporation, and initial capital was to be provided from Federal funds, to be provided, in this case by the HOLC.

Federal savings and loan associations were required to be insured by FSLIC; State-chartered member institutions were permitted to be so insured, upon providing satisfactory assurance to the Corporation that their operating and lending policies and reserve provisions met standards which the Corporation was empowered to establish. A premium was imposed of .25 percent of accounts of insured members, plus creditor obligations. In case of liquidation of an insured institution, the Corporation was required to be appointed conservator or receiver for Federal savings and loan associations, and authorized so to serve in the case of State-chartered insured institutions.

Recapitulation and Summary

The successive initiatives of the 3 years 1932-4 served to lay in the structural foundations of a complete overhaul of what is now called the conventional mortgage lending industry in the United States. Central to this overhaul were four major concepts and instrumentalities:

1. A specialized form of reserve banking system, tailored to the needs of family savings and home mortgage lending, and structured so as to maintain a flow of funds in times of short credit, as well as to permit a geographic flow of funds from regions with surplus funds for home mortgage investment to those where funds were in short supply;
2. A loosely integrated national system of local savings institutions primarily engaged in home mortgage lending, and built around a broad base of federally chartered institutions designed to illustrate the benefits of mutual ownership and serve as models of good practice and community service;
3. Federally underwritten insurance which guaranteed the safety of individual savings in Federal and insured member institutions; and
4. Overall, a Federal Home Loan Bank Board with broad regulatory, supervisory, and, within limits, disciplinary powers.

The institutional unity of the system was both strengthened and rendered more visible when the Board established a single Division now called the Office of Examination and Supervision to perform the functions of audit and examination both for the regulatory and supervisory functions of the Board and the Regional Banks, and for the protection of the insurance system. While serving the obvious purpose of efficiency and avoidance of duplication, this joint operation served as a continuous reminder to member and insured institutions both of a national purpose to strengthen and improve the savings and home mortgage lending system, and of a continuing Federal presence directed to the achievement of that purpose.

Nearly 40 years later, this basic structure is essentially intact. Over the years, as might be expected, a multitude of detailed changes has been made. FSLIC insurance coverage has increased in successive increments from an original figure of $5,000 for a single insured account to $20,000; concurrently, the insurance premium has been reduced, first to 1/8 and later to 1/12 of 1 percent. Restrictions on the investment powers of savings and loan associations have been progressively relaxed—in maximum mortgage amount; loan-to-value ratios; geographical coverage; and types of investments permitted. Within statutory guidelines, a wide variety of investments other than first mortgage home loans may now be made, and, in fact, savings and loan associations may now act as trustees for certain types of investment trusts—a function clearly falling in the category of "banking services" originally considered out of bounds for these institutions. But these are incidentals, however important. The central fact remains that the system is what it was designed to be: An organized structure for individual savings and home financing, characterized by a high degree of stability and providing by far the largest single (in the sense of organized or coherent) source of capital in the Nation for residential building and the movement of existing properties in the housing market.

The Federal Stamp

The record is clear that the earliest originators of the initiatives which led in logical steps to the existing Federal Home Loan Bank System—using that term in the broad sense—intended a far more limited and temporary Federal involvement than that which actually occurred.

The proceedings of the President's Conference of 1931 are replete with warnings against excessive Federal encroachment, and appeals for reliance on private endeavor with some degree of State and local regulation. It appears that President Hoover to some extent shared this view, while recognizing that Federal initiative and support were essential at least at the beginning. Indeed, he was to write, looking back on these events:

> . . .Nineteen years later, on Dec. 31, 1951, the eleven banks . . . had a total of over 4,000 member institutions with aggregate assets of more than $15,000,000. During that period the banks had made loans of more than $3,000,000,000, all repaid except for a current outstanding balance.
>
> Under the provisions for the absorption of capital by members, the government had been entirely paid off. As I had planned, *it had become in effect a private institution*. (Emphasis added.)[4]

It is difficult to avoid the conclusion that the former President's hopes and preferences here obscured his perceptions. For it seems abundantly clear that—whatever symbolic significance may be thought to attach to stock ownership—the Federal Home Loan Bank Board from its creation in 1932 was a Federal agency, and still is. So, too, was the HOLC during its temporary but indispensable existence. So, too, was and still is the Federal Savings and Loan Insurance Corporation.

In 1950, Congress further underlined the Federal character of the system by placing a billion-dollar line of credit (since raised to $4 billion (Public Law 151, 91st Congress)) to the Treasury (discretionary with the Secretary) behind the operations of the Federal Home Loan Banks, and a (mandatory) $750 million line of credit behind those of FSLIC.[5] This was done not because such emergency sources of funds were then needed or expected to be needed, but simply because the Congress thought it good public policy that they should be there if the need ever should arise.

The above discussion is not intended to consider one way or the other the merits of Federal involvement in housing credit, but rather to reflect the historical fact that under the impact of the Great Depression the Federal Government did in fact assume such an involvement on a theretofore unprecedented scale, and that the involvement continues to the present day. While the means and mechanisms adopted were financial, the motivations were social, as is reflected in President Hoover's own characterization of his purposes:

> . . . above all . . . [to promote] . . . home ownership, and employment on home construction.[6]

GENERATING HOUSE CREDIT THROUGH THE REDUCTION OF RISK: THE MORTGAGE INSURANCE SYSTEM

Purposes of the System

The National Housing Act, enacted June 27, 1934, established the Federal Housing Administration to administer a new function of the Federal Government—the insurance of long term mortgage construction and sale, and the insurance of lenders against loss on shorter term loans for repairs and improvements of housing and commercial properties. Its basic immediate purpose was to combat unemployment in the Great Depression, and its original long term purpose was to provide more and better housing through a general improvement in mortgage-lending practices and a general expansion of the residential lending and home-building industries.

As with the Federal Home Loan Bank system, the mortgage insurance program was brought into being by the urgencies of the Depression. It had resulted in the freezing of mortgage credit and an almost complete cessation of residential construction. Production of homes in 1933 dropped to 93,000 units, less than a tenth of the number built in 1925, and onsite construction throughout the country employed only 150,000 persons.[7] In addition to losses of jobs on the site, about an equal number were lost in the production of materials and equipment going into home construction.

At the same time, improvements to existing homes and other small buildings proved almost impossible to finance. Even apart from the depression condition, mortgage financing had been too cumbersome to be used extensively for the relatively small sums involved. Personal installment credit, on the other hand, failed to meet the credit needs in this field because the items involved in a modification job, such as a new roof or bathroom, could not be replevied. Manufacturers of the products used were generally not in a position to sponsor the needed credit because the materials involved came from a number of sources, and because labor (often self-employed) made up a large part of the local cost of the job.

As with much domestic legislation enacted during the Depression and recovery days, unemployment furnished the underlying impetus for the enactment of authority for the mortgage insurance and loan program. In the throes of the Great Depression, the executive branch and the Congress gave prime consideration to measures designed to reduce the massive unemployment existing throughout the United States. Where feasible, such efforts were directed to programs which could also help meet some additional critical depression needs. Legislation to restore the housing industry and promote home construction and repair work, with the resulting benefits to home buyers, builders, and lenders, was a natural mechanism for helping to solve not only employment but other vital social problems.

In testimony before the House Banking and Currency Committee on May 18, 1934, the Federal Emergency Relief Administrator, Harry L. Hopkins, spoke first of employment:

> The building trades in America represent by all odds the largest single unit of our unemployment. Probably more than one-third of all the unemployed are identified, directly and indirectly, with the building trades. . . .
>
> Now, a purpose of this bill, a fundamental purpose of this bill, is an effort to get these people back to work. . . .
>
> . . .There has been no repair work done on housing since 1929. . . .
>
> And, finally, we believe it is essential that we unloose private credit rather than public funds in the repairing of those houses and the building of new houses. . . .

Basic Statutory Functions Under the Original Housing Act

Home Mortgage Insurance

Section 203 of that act provides for the establishment of a "mutual mortgage insurance system" under which FHA could insure first mortgage loans made for the construction, purchase, or refinancing of one-to-four family homes which would not exceed 20 years in term, or either $16,000 or 80 percent of the appraised value of the property.

The FHA was authorized to insure a mortgage loan only if made by a responsible lender able to service it. It had to contain provisions for periodic payments "not in excess of the borrower's reasonable ability to pay," and such provisions with respect to insurance, repairs, reserves, foreclosure, and other matters as

FHA prescribed. The project with respect to which the mortgage was executed had to be "economically sound."

The interest rate on the loan could not exceed 5 percent per annum on the outstanding balance (or up to 6 percent under special circumstances).

The insurance provided gave the lender the right to receive in the event of foreclosure (and conveyance of the property to FHA and assignment to it of all related claims): (1) United States-guaranteed debentures (equal to the unpaid principal of the loan plus certain other allowances) maturing 3 years after the maturity of the mortgage; and (2) a "certificate of claim" (equal to the unpaid earned interest on the loan and foreclosure costs) payable only to the extent that FHA realized net proceeds from handling the property.

In return for this insurance protection, the Act required FHA to fix a premium charge of not less than .5 percent nor more than 1 percent per annum of the outstanding balance of the mortgage loan, which charge could be passed on to the borrower in addition to the interest on the loan. The FHA was required to classify the insured mortgages into separate groups "in accordance with sound actuarial practices and risk characteristics" and to set up a separate account for each such group. Whenever all the mortgages in a particular group account had been paid in full (or the money available in the account met certain requirements for payment), FHA was required to distribute the balance in the accounts for the benefit of the mortgagors, or homeowners. Hence the system was called "mutual" mortgage insurance.

Rental Project Mortgage Insurance

Section 207 of the original National Housing Act authorized FHA to insure mortgages on housing projects of Federal or State instrumentalities or private limited dividend corporations for persons of low income, if those projects were regulated as to rents, rate of return, and methods of operation. That project carried substantially the same insurance benefits as described above for home mortgages.

Repair Loan Insurance

Section 2 of the original National Housing Act authorized FHA to insure approved financial institutions against losses they might sustain as a result of loans for financing repair and improvements to real property. No such loan could exceed $2,000, or other limitations prescribed by FHA. The insurance to any one such institution could not exceed 20 percent of the amount of all its loans made for such purpose. This was changed to 10 percent by Public Law 486, 74th Congress, approved April 3, 1936. Thus, while the insurance payment was triggered by a default in the individual loan the outer limit of FHA liability was limited to a percentage of the aggregate of eligible loans made by the particular institution.

This was an important safeguard since FHA did not initially process or approve the insurance of the individual loans.

Theory of FHA Mortgage Insurance System

Basically, the new mortgage insurance system was designed to protect lenders against loss on long term, amortized, high ratio mortgage loans. The protection was afforded through an FHA obligation to furnish, on default and foreclosure, insurance benefits up to the unpaid balance of the loan, with virtually no coinsurance by the lender. The system was to be self-supporting through the payment of premiums and fees to FHA that would establish an insurance reserve fund on an actuarily sound basis.

The Mortgage Instrument

The housing benefits of the new mortgage insurance system sprang largely from the government assumption of risk on this form of mortgage loan. Each of its features was important to the future of home finance.

Long Term Mortgage. Prior to the HOLC operation, it was customary in almost all cases for a home buyer to obtain two or three separate home mortgage loans, with the first mortgage being limited to what is today considered to be a very short term. Testimony[8] by Marriner S. Eccles, Assistant to the Secretary of the Treasury, given at the time the National Housing Act was being considered in the Congress, indicated that a 10-year mortgage was considered a long term mortgage by lenders at that time, and many home mortgages ran only 1, 2, or 3 years.[9] At the end of that short term, the home purchaser faced the expenses of refinancing and ran the risk resulting from changed market conditions. He faced the uncertainties of higher interest rates or even the unavailability of refinancing on terms he could afford, in which case he could lose his home and his equity investment through default and foreclosure. This characteristic of mortgage financing, along with the characteristics referred to in the next two paragraphs, contributed to the wave of foreclosure that came with the Great Depression and increased its impact.

Amortized Mortgage Loan. Generally, most of these earlier home mortgages were not amortized, and the payment of the entire principal or large balance ("balloon payment") fell due at the end of the short term of the mortgage. As it provided no system of regular level payments geared to the purchaser's ability to pay, the purchaser was either unable or lacked the inducement to make payments that would increase his equity and reduce his personal risk. That feature increased his dangers of default and loss.

Single First Mortgage With High Ratio Loan. The earlier first mortgage loans had such a low ratio of loan amount to value (State laws generally limited the ratio to 50 or 60 percent), that junior mortgage financing prevailed. Second and third mortgages bearing progressively steeper mortgage rates reflected their greater risks. Investment in these junior liens was considered speculative and interest rates up to 18 to 20 percent were common.[10] The speculative nature of this secondary financing reflected a risk to the home buyer as well as to the lender. His added interest cost and multiple financing charges increased the chances of default and loss of his property.

Relative Uniformity of Mortgage Requirements. The relative uniformity of the FHA mortgage requirements, quite apart from the Federal insurance itself, helped to encourage the flow of credit across State lines to areas of greatest shortage. For the first time, a home mortgage instrument was recognized and made marketable throughout the country on a substantial scale.

Cumulative Value of Long Term Low Ratio Mortgage. Almost all of the above benefits to homeowners were designed to have a corresponding benefit for homebuilders and lenders. The reduction of risk features for a purchaser reduced the risk and expense of foreclosure proceedings for lenders and provided more assurance of timely payment. The favorable financing terms for the home purchaser or owner broadened the housing market, bringing financing within the reach of persons of lower income and also benefiting builders and lenders.

Generation of Housing Credit Through Insurance Features of the System

Of course, the Federal insurance feature of the National Housing Act afforded the Federal financial backing necessary to the success of all the benefits of the Mortgage Insurance System. It was the key to generating additional credit for housing construction. Prior to mortgage insurance, the principal protection to the lender was the property covered by the mortgage. As this property, and the lender's rights to it in event of default, were wholly local, the mortgage loan did not lend itself to interstate transfers, or ownership by distant investors. With the Federal financial backup, the lender could look to the insurance as security, and the greatest risk of the mortgage investment was switched from the lender to the Federal Government.

Thus, along with the relatively uniform mortgage instrument, this novel insurance encouraged the flow of mortgage funds on a substantial scale from one part of the country to another where the need might be greater. Nonlocal lenders, such as insurance companies, could invest with confidence in mortgages originating in other areas of the country, relying primarily on the Federal insurance against losses in the event of default.

Actuarial Soundness—Lender Protection Without Loss to United States

Although the full faith and credit of the United States stood behind the FHA insurance obligation, there was an intent that the income to the FHA insurance fund would equal or exceed payments of insurance claims and other expenses. To accomplish this, the plan embodied in the Act had these prime characteristics:

Debenture System. Protection was afforded to the United States as well as to the lender through the unique authority to settle an insurance claim by furnishing long term obligations (debentures) to lenders, backed by the full faith and credit of the United States. Settling claims in debentures rather than cash permitted the FHA fund to avoid heavy cash withdrawals from the Treasury. In addition, a policy of orderly liquidation of acquired properties over a substantial period avoided the adverse effects of wholesale dumping of properties in an already distressed market. Taken as a whole, this plan was to permit the FHA to operate within its own resources even during a severe depression.

Premiums. The statutory authority for insurance premiums and fees was designed to enable the system to function on a sound businesslike basis, paying all administrative and other costs out of receipts and accumulating an adequate reserve against losses which might occur in the worst periods. Of course, in estimating the amount of reserve needed, consideration could be given to the advantages of the debenture system and other characteristics of the insurance. The administrative discretion given in the Act for determining the amount of the premium was considered adequate for adjustments to meet that objective. That is, the initial discretion to set premiums as low as .5 percent or as high as 1 percent was deemed appropriate because the system was too new to permit judgment to be made as to the precise rate.

Mutuality. The statutory plan of "mutuality" (returning to the homeowner, in effect, the unneeded portions of the premiums he had paid) was intended to assist in establishing an adequate insurance fund. As the future ratio of expenditures to receipts under the system was originally uncertain, the mutual feature enabled the premiums to be sufficiently high for soundness of the system, while at the same time assuring the borrower that his premium payments were not excessive.

Mortgage Form. All of the features of the long term low ratio amortized mortgage loan which benefited the borrower, as described above, had a corresponding effect in strengthening the actuarial soundness of the whole insurance system. As they reduced the dangers of default and loss by the borrower, they reduced the degree of insurance risk to FHA and the amount of insurance claims that could be expected.

Individual Mortgage Transaction. Because the soundness of the insurance system was dependent on the soundness of the individual mortgage loans insured, the original act required each loan to meet the specific standards listed above. The FHA approval of each lender was a unique characteristic of the insurance system which entailed regulations and procedures as to his financial and other qualifications.

Intended Beneficiaries and Scope of Market

The several features of the mortgage insurance system that were intended to revitalize the housing industry and make home financing attainable for a vastly greater number of American families certainly benefited those of modest income more than others. However, the original system was not particularly concerned with the special housing needs of poor persons.

The mortgage insurance system was designed to help home purchasers and homeowners throughout the broad scope of the housing market, excluding only the abnormally expensive luxury homes where Federal assistance would be unwarranted. The originally authorized $16,000, 80-percent mortgage gave full insurance benefit to a $20,000 home. With today's costs, that home would be comparable to one costing 3 or 4 times as much. The repair loan insurance (as noted above) was not even limited to residential structures.

The only part of the original Act relating particularly to low income families was the embryonic authorization for mortgage insurance with respect to rental housing. Of course, its application was very restricted in any event, since it applied only to regulated projects of public bodies and limited dividend corporations.

Mortgage Insurance Benefits Having Indirect Credit Impact

The FHA mortgage insurance system embodies additional major features designed primarily to benefit the housing consumer but which have an indirect impact on general housing credit. These flowed from provisions in the original National Housing Act or from amendments:

Minimum Property Standards and Inspections

The importance of these standards is indicated by the title of the original act, which read as follows: "An Act to encourage improvement in housing standards and conditions, to provide a system of mutual mortgage insurance, and for other purposes." Pursuant to that language on standards, all housing to be financed with an FHA-insured mortgage must meet specific requirements formulated and promulgated by FHA. These are detailed and, in total, quite voluminous. They apply to the design of the structure, the quality of materials and construction, mechanical equipment, water supply, and sewage disposal. The location and condition of the site and where appropriate, the subdivision planning must also meet specific FHA requirements.

Compliance with the minimum standards in the case of new home construction is obtained through inspections at three stages of construction. A more continuous supervision of construction is maintained, of course, in the case of new multiple units.

These various standards are designed to make the property more attractive and valuable to the home buying public in general or to help assure preservation of the property over the life of the mortgage. In either case, the standards increase the value of the property as security for the mortgage by reducing chances of default and increasing recovery in event of default, foreclosure, and sale. Of course, this helps to make FHA-insured mortgages on such property attractive as investments, and to that extent helps to generate credit for housing. It also tends to encourage investment in conventional mortgages on the property in case of its subsequent sale or refinancing: investment in housing in general is further encouraged to the extent that FHA standards affect the quality of construction of non-FHA housing in the locality or the quality of materials and equipment at the point of production.

Appraisals

In general, under the regular FHA mortgage insurance programs, the appraisal procedures have been a necessary and successful means of helping to establish the FHA-insured mortgage as a sound investment encouraging credit for housing. The original statute made appraisals necessary because maximum mortgage amounts were related to "appraised values." The appraisals were made by the FHA itself, generally through its own employees but sometimes through fee appraisers where essential because of workload.

Builder's Warranty

As supplemental to other construction compliance and with similar credit impact, a "builder's warranty" was required by the Housing Act of 1954. The act (Section 801) directed that the seller or builder of any new home assisted with an FHA-insured mortgage, or a loan guaranteed by the Veterans Administration, must be required to warrant for 1 year to the purchaser or owner that the dwelling is constructed in "substantial conformity" with the plans and specifications approved by the FHA or VA. This requirement grew out of investigations by the Housing (Rains) Subcommittee of the House Committee on Banking and Currency and the Teague Select Committee on Loan Guaranty Programs. It was determined by them that in many cases homes had not been built in conformity with the approved plans and specifications, sometimes leaving the purchaser or owner without legal recourse under his contract.

Although there had originally been strong opposition to the warranty as a mandatory requirement in the law, this opposition seemed to subside after enactment.

FHA Payment for Construction Defects

As further assurance that FHA-assisted property would meet construction standards, the Housing Act of 1964 (Section 121) authorized FHA to pay the owner of an FHA home any costs he incurred in correcting "substantial defects" in the home (or FHA could itself make the repairs) if such payment were requested within 4 years of the mortgage insurance.

Previously, the FHA had always correctly taken the position that it had no legal obligation, or even authority, to compensate homeowners for defects in FHA-assisted housing. The FHA standards and inspections were solely for purposes of assuring adequate security for the mortgage and no legal obligation in this regard ran to the homeowner. Actually, in cases where substantial defects occurred, the FHA often pressured the builder, frequently with success, to make adequate improvements. However, there remained a few "horror" cases, as where the builder was no longer in the business or had no assets.

The above authority was extended (by the Housing and Urban Development Act of 1970, Section 104) in a broader form to existing housing, as distinguished from new construction, under the FHA Section 235 subsidized homeownership program discussed later. The construction defects covered include "structural or other defects which seriously affect the use and livability" of the dwelling. The Senate Banking and Currency Committee indicated in its report on the legislation that some FHA appraisers allowed blatantly defective homes to be sold to lower income families under the program when the purchasers understandably believed the Government was protecting their interests.

Cost Certification

The cost certification procedure was another protection against excessive mortgage amounts; this protection helped to preserve the investment quality of FHA-insured mortgages. The term "cost certification" refers to the builder's certification as to the dollar amount of his costs for specific items of construction, and related expenditures recognized by FHA. As first brought into the FHA mortgage insurance system for limited purposes by the Defense Housing and Community Facilities and Services Act of 1951 (Section 201), the cost certification requirement meant that the mortgage amount must be reduced, where necessary, to bring it within the builder's cost certification made after the completion of construction. Thus, the mortgage could not exceed 100 percent of the cost of physical improvements, so that the builder had to invest his land, time, overhead, and know-how. That act applied the requirement only to the new special mortgage insurance program (Section 908) provided in the act for rental housing in critical defense housing areas established during the Korean War. The same provision was soon applied to Capehart housing (Armed Services housing mortgage insurance, title VIII of the National Housing Act) by the Housing Amendments of 1953 (Section 10).

The above cost certification requirement was given little attention and is not well remembered. When "cost certification" is referred to now, it means a tighter and more stringent requirement enacted as part of the Housing Act of 1954 (Section 126).

That provision (Section 227 of the National Housing Act) is more specific, and sharper in defining the housing project costs to be allowed in the computation of cost. More importantly, it requires the mortgage to be reduced (after the construction and certification) to a fixed percentage of those costs—the same percentage prescribed by law as the maximum ratio of mortgage loan amount to value (or to replacement cost). Thus, where the law prescribes a maximum 80 percent ratio and the credit cost is $900,000 on a project where its estimated value had been $1 million, the mortgage has to be reduced to 80 percent of $900,000. This more onerous restriction was applied to all FHA multifamily projects.

This cost certification requirement was one of the principal responses of the Congress to the "FHA scandals" of national proportion that rocked the housing industry and Government agencies in 1953 and 1954. The World War II and postwar veterans housing of multifamily rental units (Section 608 housing) came into disrepute largely because of "mortgaging out" in a substantial portion of all projects under the program. That term means that excessively high values and mortgage amounts were authorized by FHA, resulting in the sponsor's walking away with possibly large amounts of leftover cash from the mortgage, after paying all his costs and with no money of his own in the project. At that time, there had been heavy pressure on FHA to get sponsors to undertake projects rapidly, and rising prices of land, materials, and labor had made it difficult to estimate future costs. Indeed, some of the cases of mortgaging out resulted from FHA's recognition of high costs during 1948, when the estimates were made, when actual construction took place during 1949, when costs had dropped.

Forebearance

In addition to the obvious benefit to the home purchaser, liberal forebearance procedures of the mortgage insurance system provided a direct accommodation to lenders with default problems. Also, the increased consumer demand for mortgage assistance, resulting from these favorable terms for the borrower, further increased the attractiveness of home mortgages for investment.

Originally, any concession by FHA to forebearance, which the lender requested for the borrower, was done administratively. When, on request of the lender, FHA found a default on an insured home mortgage to be due to circumstances beyond the control of the mortgagor, it could approve an extension of time for curing default and a recasting of the amortization.

Notwithstanding FHA's foreclosure procedures, considerable concern developed in the Congress over the plight of home purchasers faced with foreclosure through no fault of their own. Special attention was given to unemployed wage earners in depressed areas, or others who had been employed in industries curtailing production. Various bills had been introduced on the subject. In response, the most effective forebearance procedure was authorized by the Housing Act of 1959 (Section 114(a)). To avoid foreclosure, the FHA was permitted to accept a home mortgage in default, along with the property securing it, and pay the insurance benefits to the lender. Thereafter, the lender had no connection with the mortgage, and FHA was free to carry out such foreclosure arrangements with the homeowner as it determined best.

The Housing and Urban Development Act of 1965 provided for "moratorium" relief to "distressed mortgagors" who were homeowners with FHA insurance or VA guaranty in an area with a closed military installation, if the mortgages were in default because of the homeowners' inability to make mortgage payments. In such cases the FHA or VA was authorized to assume the obligations of those homeowners for a limited period.

Interest Rates and Discounts

Although the FHA maximum interest rates on mortgages are intended as consumer protections, the administrative increases or decreases of ceilings within the statutory maximums also can affect housing credit generally. The interest rate ceilings have also been one of the factors in providing uniformity in mortgage terms that has helped to generate credit for housing. Until the statutory interest rate maximums were suspended and left to administrative discretion under temporary authority beginning in 1968 (Public Law 90-301), the original statutory ceiling for regular Section 203 mortgages had been virtually unchanged.

Throughout FHA's history, its maximum interest rate ceilings have undoubtedly prevented excessive rates and abuses that would have occurred otherwise at certain times and in certain places. Also, it is fair to say that these FHA maximum rates have been kept at or below market interest rates on noninsured mortgages.

In times of severe credit shortages, however, when market interest rates are unusually high, lenders on FHA mortgages have resorted to charging substantial discounts in addition to interest rates. Actually, the amount of the discount, which is charged as a lump sum, plus the amount of the interest, often constituted the price which had to be paid to get the mortgage funds at the particular time and place. Generally, the amount of the discount was the amount the originating lender would otherwise lose in selling the mortgage in the secondary market. The FHA did not permit the lender to require the borrower to pay the discount, so the lender charged the seller or builder of the dwelling. Naturally, this tended to increase the sales price of the house, because the increase was not effectively prevented through the appraisal process.

At times, discounts were so large in connection with FHA-insured and VA mortgages that the Banking and Currency Committees became very alarmed, and fully investigated the subject. Of course, the Congressional concern grew out of consumer complaints and publicity concerning the problems. As a result, the Housing Act of 1950 directed the FHA and VA to issue regulations, applicable uniformly to all classes of lenders, which would limit the charges and fees imposed upon the builder or purchaser in connection with construction or sale of housing.

These regulatory controls were adopted and were almost completely unsuccessful. In the case of VA, a maximum 1-percent discount was imposed which curtailed use of the program so extensively that Congress modified the statute in the Housing Amendments of 1953.

Basically, however, the controls were unsuccessful because they were inconsistent with the economic facts of life, and were impossible to enforce. There was no practical means of preventing a discount to be paid to the lender by a builder in the form of some collateral benefit not overtly tied to the mortgage transaction. The controls were repealed by the Housing Act of 1954 (Section 813).

Amazingly, the Congress (in Section 605 of the Housing Act of 1957) required the FHA and VA again to impose discount controls in a form that would vary them by areas and mortgage terms. Those controls were equally ineffective and soon repealed (Section 6 of the Emergency Housing Act of 1958). In reporting that bill, the Senate Committee on Banking and Currency said that the complication of the controls reduced investment in FHA mortgages, particularly for low income families.

Equal Opportunity

As with many requirements adopted for purposes other than credit expansion, the application of equal opportunity requirements to housing has had a direct effect on the availability of mortgage credit.

Through the earlier portion of FHA history there was no involvement or concern with equal opportunity for the purchase or occupancy of housing. In fact, race was not regarded as a factor in any mortgage insurance operations except as to the effect of changing racial patterns in the locality on the value of the proposed housing. The first real response to heavy pressure for some action in this area was the administrative decision in 1950 not to insure any more mortgages on real estate subject to covenants against ownership or occupancy by members of certain races.

The first step of sufficient magnitude to affect FHA housing production or credit was President Kennedy's 1962 Executive Order (E.O. 11063) on Equal Opportunity in Housing, which applied to all new FHA or VA housing and related properties which could be covered (in the view of the Department of Justice) without Constitutional objection, in the absence of legislation dealing specifically with the subject. There was strong objection from the industry on the ground that the Government-assisted housing would be shunned by lenders and purchasers alike, who would shift to conventionally financed housing which was not then subject to equal opportunity requirements. Some objective observers also felt that the FHA production would be greatly reduced to the detriment of home purchasers who would otherwise receive the FHA consumer benefits not available under conventional financing. Others felt the Executive Order was not sufficiently enforceable to prevent the unscrupulous from profiting at the expense of those who would comply.

There may have been some adverse effect on FHA operations from the Executive Order, at least initially. However, it did not reach any significant proportions as some predicted, or convince anyone in hindsight that the policy of the Order was wrong. Even at present, experts cannot measure the effect of the Order on the FHA market at that time, but generally content themselves with the conclusion that increasing availability of credit offsets any possible adverse effect the Order may have made on FHA operations.

As to enforcement, the old reliable threat of withholding future mortgage insurance from the violators of an FHA regulation proved to be a reasonably adequate enforcement mechanism.

Presumably, if a sponsor was set initially on large-scale avoidance of equal opportunity requirements, he would not follow the mortgage insurance route in the first place.

The special concern of FHA's being singled out for regulation came to an end with the enactment of Title VIII of the Civil Rights Act of 1968 (the "Fair Housing" law), which, through a staggered application, covered all housing (and related transactions) as to both sale or rental, excluding only a single-family house sold or rented by the owner without any use of a broker or similar agent, and units in certain rooming houses. That act contains specific enforcement mechanisms.

Although the credit impact of the Issuance of the Executive Order on Equal Opportunity cannot be quantified, it constituted at that time a typical example of two program policies that have divergent, if not inconsistent, objectives—production versus another social purpose. Although the application of equal opportunity regulations to housing has been resolved by statute, similar policy conflicts exist with respect to production versus other consumer benefits such as low interest rates and high property standards. More frequently, the conflicting social objectives have not been adverse to production but to other features of the mortgage insurance system generally considered basic. Thus, looseness of property standards and mortgage terms to enable FHA construction to proceed in outlying areas is inconsistent with the objectives normally sought by FHA. That is, quality is sacrificed to obtain quantity.

Whenever volume production, or another desirable objective, is in conflict with another social purpose, there are generally some persons with extreme views who would support one to the exclusion of the other. In general, however, there continues to be acceptance of a modification of the traditional mortgage insurance system to accomplish a special social purpose if production and other basic features of the insurance are not substantially thwarted.

It must be emphasized, of course, that the Fair Housing Law of 1968 presented a quite different relationship of civil rights objectives to housing production, because the law applies to virtually all housing. Instead of restricting any portion of production, the overall effect of the law tends to increase the volume of production by broadening demand. By making new homes and rental accommodations available to minority families, which have the most urgent need and an increasing ability to purchase or rent new units, a substantial segment of the population is brought into the market for new FHA (as well as other) homes and apartments, especially in metropolitan areas. . . .

Selected Use of New Underwriting Concepts

The original National Housing Act contained two basic underwriting concepts: (1) The property or project with respect to which the mortgage is executed must be "economically sound," and (2) the maximum mortgage amount cannot exceed a percentage of "appraised value." These two requirements are still effective with respect to the regular basic FHA mortgage insurance, that is, the program for one-to-four-family dwellings under Section 203, and the program for multifamily projects under 207 (excluding certain special purpose housing).

No one can question the merits of these two concepts for underwriting purposes. However, the application of them in FHA became very controversial and continued so for several years in the late 1940's and the 1950's. It was contended by groups favoring FHA mortgage insurance for special social purposes that FHA consistently used its underwriting procedures in an unreasonably conservative manner in order to defeat those purposes and avoid the burdens of new or unfamiliar activities. This view was shared by many in the Congress and by some non-FHA offices in the National Housing Agency and later in the Housing and Home Finance Agency. It was true that although the term "economic soundness" in mortgage insurance originally had no different meaning from the usual sense that those words are used, they came to be words of art encompassing the elaborate minimum property standards and established underwriting procedures of FHA.

Accordingly, when proposed special FHA programs were developed in the Executive Branch, or sometimes in the Congress, care was taken to avoid the term "economic soundness" in order to assure that the class of housing intended to be assisted with mortgage insurance would go forward as intended. Generally, the term "acceptable risk" was substituted. The special FHA programs are discussed later under a separate heading.

For similar reasons, "replacement cost" was generally substituted for "appraised value" in these new programs, as indicated above in the cooperative housing program. This substitution of terms had a more substantive meaning, however, than the one substitution above. Because "replacement cost" is only one of the three limitations normally used in determining "value," a maximum mortgage amount computed on the basis of replacement cost alone usually results in a higher maximum amount. "Value" is the lowest of (1) replacement cost, (2) prevailing sales price of similar real property, and (3) capitalized value based on "estimated net return" and "estimated fair return."

As a later supplement to substituting "replacement cost" for "value" in special insurance programs, the Congress began injecting into such programs a provision that required "replacement cost" to include "an allowance for builder's and sponsor's profit and risk of 10 per centum of all" the other items of cost except land, unless the agency certified that the 10 per centum was unreasonable. It was first applied by the Housing Act of 1956 (Section 107(a)) to the FHA Section 220 special insurance program for housing in urban renewal areas.

The provision was adopted because the Congress felt that assurance of that large a sponsor's return was extremely important to the entire urban renewal program, which had been floundering because of difficulties in getting housing underway on urban renewal sites as planned. Section 220 was the only feasible instrument for doing that, and sponsors had not been very interested in it. In reporting the Housing Act of 1956, the House Committee on Banking and Currency said the profit margin being allowed sponsors under Section 220 was not sufficiently high to attract them, and was unreasonably low. (The FHA had allowed a percentage, based on local custom and project size, that had varied between about 5 percent and 10 percent).

Clearly, the above new underwriting standards were designed to force FHA into a more liberal insurance system for the special purpose programs. At the same time, however, the changes certainly were not intended to be used as justification for unsound or "bad" loans. The term "acceptable risk" preserves the connotation needed for keeping the mortgage insurance system on an actuarially sound basis. In general, the FHA programs using the new terminology have been so operated, particularly the Section 213 program discussed above, which has had one of the best records in accumulating a reserve of insurance funds sufficient to cover possible insurance claims in the future.

In any event, to determine that a loan is reasonably sound, the underwriter must ultimately find reasonable expection of mortgage payments. In the case of rental property, this means reasonable prospect of project income adequate for those payments, taking into consideration all relevant factors over the life of the mortgage. This was often the controlling factor.

Growth of the Mortgage Insurance System

Insofar as Federal legislation was concerned, the FHA mortgage insurance system was a viable program from the beginning. The system would have grown and prospered, although in a truncated fashion, if the National Housing Act had never been revised (except as to extensions and changes made necessary by inflation and the passage of time). The program got underway with surprising swiftness, considering the novelty of the system and the enormous number of institutions and agencies throughout the United States which were involved.

Perhaps the most important delay factor was the need for State legislation to make FHA-insured mortgages legal investments for banks, State savings and loan associations, insurance companies, and other State-regulated financial institutions or other public or private investors. State laws generally restricted these investments to 50 percent or 60 percent of the value of the property securing the mortgage, and frequently limited the eligible term of the mortgage. At that time all States except New York and New Jersey met in regular session only once every 2 years, and those sessions were in even years in almost all States. However, a number of States had begun holding special sessions to help meet depression problems, including the enactment of enabling legislation to permit participation in Federal programs. Accordingly, within 2 years, most of these State law problems were removed by specific State legislation. Similar Federal legislation authorizes investment by national banks in FHA mortgages.

During 1934, the FHA insurance was all on Title 1 (Section 2) repair and rehabilitation loans amounting to $27 million. In 1935, total FHA insurance amounted to $297 million, including home mortgage insurance of $93 million and mortgage insurance on rental projects amounting to $2 million.[11]

Major changes in the legislative authority for the basic mortgage insurance program which affected its growth were:

1. Amendments making eligible for mortgage insurance a multifamily project with a profitmaking sponsor.
2. Liberalization of the maximum loan-to-value ratio of an eligible mortgage, which permitted increasingly lower downpayments by the purchaser or sponsor.
3. Lengthening the maximum loan period of the eligible mortgage, which permitted smaller monthly amortization payments.
4. Increasing the maximum dollar ceilings of the individual mortgages, especially in the case of home mortgages.

Other legislative changes in program scope and mortgage terms had appreciable effects on volume and growth. Also, of course, other Federal legislation and administrative actions had major impacts on the size of FHA operations, such as actions affecting the secondary market of residential mortgages and monetary controls of the Federal Reserve Board.

The legislative changes affecting mortgage insurance followed no pattern through the years other than that of broadening its scope and liberalizing its terms. The changes were often spasmodic, but there were recurring justifications or reasons behind similar enactments. The liberalized mortgage terms enacted through the years increased the volume of FHA-assisted housing, and generally each amendment changing those terms increased volume appreciably.

Economists are inclined to express these changes in terms of countercyclical steps. At times, a major motive behind the legislation, particularly on the part of some officials of the executive branch, was the desire to expand those Federal activities that could spur the economy in times of recession. Just as housing construction usually is affected more quickly and severely than any other industry by adverse economic conditions or shortages of mortgage funds, steps which will increase housing production can have a more immediate and substantial effect in providing or maintaining employment and bolstering a lagging economy. Because of the Government's ability to affect production through its administration of residential mortgage insurance, it has been a prime target for manipulation in times of recession.

As a matter of political reality, however, the reason FHA programs have been repeatedly made more liberal, encompassing additional techniques and objectives, has been the desire, both in the executive branch and the Congress, to bring adequate housing to more American families. This generally has meant liberalized provisions to reach more families with lower income.

Of course, large segments of the increased FHA volume built up through the years has been under new special mortgage insurance operations, discussed later, which were established for the benefit of special groups or for special purposes.

The development of the above changes in the FHA legislation may be viewed more specifically:

Multifamily Rental Housing

The National Housing Act Amendments of 1938 completely rewrote the insurance provisions relating to multifamily housing projects (Section 207), particularly to cover mortgages on rental housing built by profit motivated sponsors. As a result, mortgage insurance for rental housing became for the first time a substantial part of the mortgage insurance system. Individual mortgage ceilings were prescribed, including an 80 percent loan-to-value ratio and a $5 million maximum. The part of the property attributable to dwelling use could not exceed $1,350 per room. The maximum mortgage term was 25 years. The insurance was similar to that for home mortgages except that advances on the mortgage were insured and, in case of default, the lender need not foreclose but could, if he wished, transfer the mortgage to FHA and receive the insurance benefits (which would be reduced slightly in view of the shift of the foreclosure burden to the FHA). As previously indicated, the sponsor was regulated as to rents and other operations.

The 1938 act also provided for a program known as Section 210, which authorized insurance of a relatively small mortgage (not over $200,000) covering multifamily dwellings or not less than 10 single family dwellings. The unique character of this provision was the authority to insure advances on a mortgage covering a single family home. The Section 210 authority was little used and was repealed the following year.

Undoubtedly, there were countercyclical motives behind those multifamily provisions, as well as other provisions of the 1938 Act, but they served chiefly to extend FHA mortgage insurance to the whole scope of residential construction. The mortgage insurance operations for rental housing got underway almost immediately. However, they did not reach a volume of $100 million annually until 1947, when there was a sudden increase to $360 million for that year. In 1950 they were up to more than $1 billion for that year. The annual volume varied drastically until, in 1962, it was again up to more than $1 billion.

Liberalization of Mortgage Terms and Volume Operations

The 1938 Act also substantially liberated terms of eligible home mortgages, both for the purpose of fighting a substantial recession and to make adequate housing available to more families. (From 1938 until the Housing Act of 1956 (Sec. 102), a higher maximum mortgage amount was authorized for new construction than for existing construction): The ratio of loan-to-value was increased from 80 percent to 90 percent for a mortgage of $5,400 or less on a new house, which was not an unrealistic figure at that time or for almost a decade later. A mortgage could be up to $8,600 if it did not exceed the sum of 90 percent of $6,000 of the appraised value and 80 percent of the value between $6,000 and $10,000.

In all such cases the dwelling had to be for occupancy by the owner, who must have paid 10 percent of the value in cash or its equivalent. The maximum term for those mortgages was increased from 20 to 25 years.

With the help of the above provisions, the total FHA insurance volume tripled by 1940 from the 1935 level, reaching an annual volume of almost $1 billion,[12] notwithstanding continued recession conditions.

During World War II years, the overall production of housing was curtailed due to the war effort requiring scarce materials and labor to be used only for priority purposes. Normally, no housing could be built except with specific Government approval. However, war housing could be built with the allocation of scarce materials if so approved by the Government. The special FHA war housing programs (Sections 603 and 608), discussed later, provided mortgage insurance for private war housing on liberalized terms. As FHA administered the priorities system for private war housing in nonfarm areas, the portion of private housing built during those war years with mortgage insurance was abnormally high, reaching about 75 percent at one time, in contrast to a typical percentage of about 20-25 percent in other periods.

After World War II, FHA suspended commitments under its war housing programs and resumed operations under the regular Section 203 and Section 207 programs. The enormous postwar backlog of demand by veterans and other pro-spective buyers started an expansion of housing production, even without FHA assistance.

Shortly, in 1946, the Congress enacted the Veterans Emergency Housing Act of 1946, which contained an array of drastic measures to provide quick housing construction, especially for returning veterans. The Sections 603 and 608 pro-grams were revived, with increases in mortgage limits and with use of more lib-eral underwriting standards.

The Housing and Rent Act of 1947 repealed most of the above 1946 Act, but enacted additional provisions including authority for FHA to finance the man-ufacture of prefabricated houses.

Total FHA operations expanded greatly during the above period of veterans housing construction, reaching a volume of $3,341,000,000 in mortgages and loans insured during 1948.

The Housing Act of 1948 further liberalized FHA programs for lower and moderate income families. The maximum dollar amounts on home mortgages were moderately raised, and FHA was authorized to raise the maximum loan-to-value ratio to 95 percent for certain lower cost homes. In the case of multifamily units, a mortgage could be eligible up to 90 percent of value and $8,100 per unit. In the case of nonprofit cooperative ownership housing primarily for veterans, the mortgage could be up to 95 percent of replacement cost.

During the 1950's, the annual volume of FHA insurance reached $4.3 billion. The credit represented by the mortgages covered, together with a rapid expansion of other home mortgage and consumer credit, greatly disturbed the Federal Re-serve Board and other Federal offices concerned with inflation and Federal debt management. About half of the rapid expansion was due to FHA and VA mortgage insurance and guaranty.[13] In large part, that was due to the liberal mortgage insurance operations under the veteran insurance programs, the 1948 Act, and also liberal terms provided under the 1949 Wherry Act insurance pro-gram for military rental housing. Those liberal FHA operations accounted for the growth in multifamily units insured from 1,526 in 1946, to 126,729 insured in 1950.[14] Other factors that encouraged production, however, were the end of price controls, ample funds, and the purchase of mortgages by the Federal National Mortgage Association in 1949 and early 1950 on an unprecedented scale. On the demand side, housing production was encouraged by new family formations re-sulting from the large number of returning World War II veterans.

The general inflationary pressures which were meanwhile making themselves felt, largely because of the Korean War, led Congress to authorize the President (in the Defense Production Act of 1950) to control real estate credit, including specific authority to regulate and reduce loan amounts, loan maturities, and in-creases in the amount of downpayments on loans. The President gave this au-thority to the Housing and Home Finance Administrator with respect to Govern-ment-aided housing, and to the Federal Reserve Board with respect to new construction otherwise financed. That authority was used and the resulting increases in downpayments and reduction in long terms were effective in sharply reducing the volume of FHA operations as well as other housing starts. The controls were gradually removed by the Congress until, in 1953, they ended.

The volume of FHA operations did not increase dramatically during the 1950's, but there was a gradual increase, to an annual $6.3 billion volume by 1960.[15] The statutory changes liberalizing and expanding the mortgage insurance system during the 1950's were made principally in the new cooperative housing program described earlier, and in new special programs (discussed later) carrying liberal mortgage maximums and underwriting standards. The additional programs were enacted to assist Korean war housing in 1951, housing in urban renewal areas in 1954, housing in outlying areas in 1954, housing for displaced families and servicemen in 1954, trailer courts in 1955, military (Capehart) housing in 1955, nursing homes in 1959, and rental housing for the elderly in 1959.

Although the 1950 changes in FHA mortgage terms were made mostly in new programs, there were some significant changes made by the Housing Act of 1954 that further liberalized the regular Section 203 and 207 FHA insurance programs. They followed a recessionary condition in the general economy, and quickly stimulated FHA construction, particularly of moderate and higher priced homes. That act increased the maximum home mortgage amount to $20,000, and permitted a loan-to-value ratio as high as 95 percent on the value up to $9,000 in case of new construction. The maximum multifamily mortgage was increased to $2,000 per room, or $7,200 per unit if less than 4 rooms per unit. A per-room limit was adopted in the Housing Act of 1950 to discourage a tendency that had developed under the "per unit" limit for builders to build "efficiency" or one-bedroom units. Modest adjustments upward were permitted for elevator structures and high cost areas.

The Housing Act of 1957 further increased that maximum mortgage amount for the regular Section 203 home mortgage program so that the mortgage could cover 97 percent of the value of a new house up to $10,000, with adjustments downward on the remainder of a $20,000 valuation. A further small relaxation was made by the 1958 act "to stimulate residential construction" (Public Law 85-364). Such changes in those 1957 and 1958 acts helped increase production in the moderate price range.

During the 1960's, the most important new legislative responsibilities given to FHA were those relating to subsidy operations. However, important relaxation in FHA mortgage terms was made by the Housing Act of 1961 as one of the efforts of the Kennedy Administration to fight the recession beginning in 1960.

Under the 1961 Act, the maximum amount of an eligible home mortgage was increased to $25,000, and the portion which could be covered by a 97 percent ratio of loan to value was increased to $15,000. The maturity of the mortgage could be 35 years in the case of new construction. In addition, the special FHA program for displaced families (Section 221, discussed later) was broadened to apply to low and moderate income families generally. Thus, in a sense it was made part of the general mortgage insurance operation, rather than a program for a special group. The changes in that program permitted insurance of a mortgage up to $15,000 in a high cost area with only 3 percent downpayment, including closing costs, and with up to a 40-year term. Upward adjustments were also made for rental housing mortgages under the program.

These changes, with provisions in the 1961 Act liberalizing other special FHA programs, helped boost FHA operations to over $7 billion during 1963. They remained at more than $7 billion during the 1970's and exceeded $8.5 billion in 1965.

The Housing and Urban Development Act of 1969 increased the maximum home mortgage amount to $33,000 and made a modest increase in the mortgage ratio for higher cost homes. The mortgage maximums for the regular rental housing program were increased substantially (as were all FHA mortgage ceilings for rental housing). Consequently, such ceilings are now left almost entirely to administrative discretion because they are as high as $28,050 per large unit in a high cost area where elevator construction is necessary, and all ceilings may be increased by 45 percent when FHA finds cost levels so require.

The above amendments through the years show that the continuing trend of almost all FHA legislation has consisted of more and more liberalization of mortgage and other insurance terms (whether to benefit more consumers or increase credit or production). Little further liberalization is possible, so that this particular source of benefit has been almost exhausted. Incentives, if any are desired, to spur additional credit and production must come from other directions.

Extension of FHA Insurance into Blighted Area

Of importance to the whole mortgage insurance system (but in terms other than volume) was the enactment of Section 223(e) of the National Housing Act (as part of the Housing and Urban Development Act of 1968), which gave legislative sanction to waiving or relaxing FHA property standards to permit mortgage insurance for housing in blighted areas of central cities.[16] Of at least equal importance was earlier administrative action taken in the same direction by the Federal Housing Commissioner. He forcefully directed his field officers to insure properties in blighted areas wherever possible to do so under the law. The new Section authorized mortgage insurance in an "older, declining area" where conditions prevent compliance with one or more regular eligibility requirements. The area had to be "reasonably viable" and the property "an acceptable risk," giving consideration to the needs of "families of low and moderate income in such areas." The insurance of a mortgage under this new authority was made the obligation of a "Special Risk Insurance Fund" established for a broader purpose contemplating heavier than normal losses.

The background of the above actions was a long history of only small FHA involvement in slum or blighted areas, except, of course, where areas were being rebuilt or improved through urban renewal or similar actions. The practice of excluding these areas, often referred to as "declining," had been criticized for years by certain private organizations and by many members of the Congress.

The field instructions of the Federal Housing Commissioner, together with the above provisions, made a substantial change in FHA operations in blighted areas. For the first time, many such areas in large cities were benefited by mortgage insurance, including several which had been affected by riots, such as Los Angeles and Detroit. Of course, that meant looser FHA property standards insofar as those areas were concerned. It should be mentioned, however, that the FHA instructions did not relax the credit standards applicable to a home purchaser.

This new authority and practice was not limited to FHA subsidy operations but applied to all insurance in the affected areas. This was significant from the standpoint of identifying reasons for abuses and defaults constituting some of the recent FHA "scandals" in Detroit and elsewhere, because properties subject to excessive defaults and foreclosures included much housing under nonsubsidy programs where the looser standards of the above new section were applied.

Open-End Mortgages

As one step in keeping up with innovations emerging in the private mortgage market, the Housing and Home Finance Agency recommended and the Congress enacted authority to insure "open-end mortgages." This was done as part of the Housing Act of 1954 (Section 126). An open-end mortgage is one which provides that the outstanding balance can be increased in order to advance additional loan funds to the borrower for improvements or repairs of the home covered by the mortgage without the necessity of executing a new mortgage. That avoids the expense of a new title search, recording, and other mortgage costs, while permitting the borrower to get funds for repair or improvements at the relatively low rate of interest established in the original mortgage.

Under the provision in the 1954 Act, an added insurance fee has to be prescribed in the open-end mortgage. The original principal amount of the mortgage, and the maximum amount otherwise controlled by statute, could be exceeded if improvements added an additional room or other enclosed space.

One basis for proposing this legislation was the absence of adequate incentive for extending mortgage credit to rehabilitation work. Many States had enacted laws permitting open-end mortgages, and in other States those mortgages could be valid without specific authorization. There had been little use of this type of instrument throughout the country, however, and application of mortgage insurance did not increase its use extensively. The low mortgage interest rate proved unattractive to lenders for use in connection with the small dollar amounts involved in individual repairs and improvements.

Cash Payment of Insurance Claims

The Housing and Urban Development Act of 1965 authorized FHA, at its option, to pay insurance claims (under any of its programs) in cash rather than debentures. Similar authority had been granted in 1961 with respect to certain special purpose programs. Payments in cash constitute an added advantage to lenders that helps encourage housing credit.

The authority to pay claims in cash was not intended to undermine the basic concept of debenture payments previously discussed. The Committee on Banking and Currency stressed in its reports on the 1965 bill that the authority to issue debenture instead of cash was not repealed, and that FHA could use that authority if it determined that discontinuance of cash payments would be desirable.

Also, an important question presented to FHA is whether it elects to agree in its insurance contract to pay claims in cash, or retain in the contract the option to pay in cash or debentures as the circumstances warrant at the time of payment. At present, the FHA retains the option in its programs to choose the method of payment at the time of payment.

Present Posture of the Basic Mortgage Insurance System

Because such a large portion (some 23 percent) of all FHA mortgage insurance is being written under programs involving subsidies, it is difficult properly to appraise the current posture of the basic mortgage insurance system in the terms of volume operations. Because of the effect of outstanding commitments under the FHA subsidy programs, the production incentive impact is enormous, and clearly the overall FHA operations remain higher ($14.8 billion and 830,500 units insured in fiscal year 1972) than they would without subsidies. The 1971 volume was $15 billion, higher than any previous year, and equal to nearly 10 percent of all cumulative FHA business since 1934. On the other hand, a substantial but unknown volume of additional units would have been built under the nonsubsidy program if the subsidy operations had not existed.

The overall mortgage insurance programs are being used for a large portion (over 1.6 million units in 1972) of all housing construction and home sales throughout the country. Of the 2.1 million housing starts in the country last year (excluding almost 600,000 mobile home shipments), about one-fourth of these were assisted with FHA mortgage insurance. FHA-insured repair and rehabilitation loans also remain high—about $900 million last year.

It must be noted that the very recent trend of FHA operations is down, but because of factors which, viewed historically, can be regarded as quite temporary. It is reported that FHA mortgage insurance applications in the first quarter of 1973 amounted to 139,790, which is down from 293,909 in the same period of 1972.[17] Of course, the current suspension of the FHA subsidy programs abnormally affects the overall volume of applications. Also, due to the shortage of mortgage funds during the last few months, housing starts in the whole market have fallen substantially.[18]

Although the recent FHA "scandals" are generally associated with the FHA subsidy operators, they have brought the whole mortgage insurance system under critical review for various reasons and purposes. First, the regular insurance programs are properly subject to review and criticism insofar as they were directly involved in the scandals. As previously indicated, the lowering of property standards was a major factor in mortgage defaults and foreclosures of housing in blighted areas financed with mortgage insurance under the regular programs with the looser authority permitted in 1968. Similarly, the bad management or personnel practices applied to housing under the regular programs, as well as to subsidy operations. Although that obviously points to the need for corrections throughout the system, it does not logically discredit the merits of the FHA insurance system itself. If the system were responsible in any way for the current type of evils, the fact would have emerged years ago.

Questioning of the more fundamental aspects of the system has come largely from private groups, particularly certain segments of the lending industry, which challenge the need for any FHA in view of the broadened scope of home lending by savings and loan associations and the rising volume of business being done by private mortgage insurance companies—matters with no direct relation to the recent scandals. Possibly some of the force of that attack has waned, but the issue remains. There has always been a small group which has opposed the use of FHA mortgage insurance for any "social purpose," such as those initiated after 1950, and which believes that mortgage insurance will continue to be corrupted if linked with other Government operations.

Those who suggest private mortgage insurance companies or other existing institutional types as a substitute for the basic FHA system overlook primarily two of its features: (1) its many consumer benefits of importance to the Congress and the general home buying public, discussed elsewhere; and (2) the value of the Government financial backing represented by the insurance, together with its debenture feature, which makes it possible to have an insurance obligation that will withstand any depression, and with the least potential loss to the Government.

Accomplishments of the FHA

Reform of Residential Financing

With the leverage of the mortgage insurance obligation, the FHA greatly benefited the entire field of housing and home finance. That was a major factor in generating mortgage credit on an adequate, permanent basis. The scope of this encompassed mortgage financing techniques, and practices by lenders, builders, architects, and producers of building materials, and affected State mortgage laws and building codes.

The most important contribution of FHA to home financing was the assistance it gave to the general acceptance and use of its uniform long term, low down-payment, amortized mortgage, which had been pioneered some time earlier by the HOLC for its special purposes. With a standardized mortgage instrument that all States recognize, and on which banks and other institutions can lend, mortgage funds can now move freely across the country to where they are needed. This one feature of the system materially affects the volume of credit for housing, as large-scale nationwide investors, such as insurance companies, have become regular purchasers or direct investors in FHA mortgages.

The soundness of the FHA mortgage loan with its low downpayment and amortization, and without a second mortgage, made the investment more attractive.

The FHA system helped change the whole investment approach of lenders toward residential mortgages. Under the greater financial risks previously existing, lenders had to contemplate and allow for substantial costs resulting from foreclosures. Under the FHA system, they could look to sounder loans and the Government insurance backup.

Volume of Production and Credit

Throughout its history, FHA has helped generate credit for mortgages and loans under its insurance programs totaling 164 billion dollars, which can be compared with a 1934 total national investment in home mortgages of $18 billion.[19] This FHA total includes over 11 million home mortgages totaling over $119 billion. About 40 percent of FHA home mortgages, or about 4.4 million, are on new construction. The total amount of FHA-insured mortgages includes of $23 billion, for 1.8 million units, under project mortgage programs [sic]. About 20 percent of all nonfarm starts in home construction have been under FHA home mortgage insurance programs.

The volume of FHA operations has meant that over 11 million families have been assisted in purchasing or building homes with the favorable financing terms and consumer protections of FHA insurance. The successive occupants of an additional 1.7 million units receive the benefits of adequate accommodations and at reasonable rentals made possible by favorable FHA financial assistance.

It is difficult to determine, at any given time, the volume of production that results solely from mortgage insurance. One study of the increasing residential construction during the post-World War II years estimated a stimulus of 375,000 to 500,000 additional units a year or about $4 to $5.5 billion.[20]

As previously indicated, FHA programs have been successfully changed at times to increase credit which was needed to spur construction during recession as an aid to the housing industry and the general economy.

Channeling Housing Funds to Lower Income Families and Other Special Needs

From almost the beginning of FHA mortgage insurance, inducements in the form of special mortgage terms were designed to help channel funds to housing within the reach of lower income families who would not otherwise be able to purchase homes. For them, FHA insured a mortgage with a lower downpayment and a correspondingly higher risk than for higher income families borrowing with larger mortgages. Also, the fact that under the FHA insurance system the downpayments are generally lower than under other financing tends to channel credit to lower income families. These features of FHA mortgages have influenced other financing and have been followed to a large extent in non-FHA financing by institutions such as savings and loan associations.

The mortgage insurance programs for special groups (such as elderly, veterans, defense workers and servicemen, displaced families, and cooperatives) have carried special inducements to channel credit to them. In all cases, a controlling factor has been the low or moderate income character of these consumer groups as a whole.

Pioneering Consumer Benefits

The FHA has taken the lead in providing the additional consumer benefits discussed earlier. Some of these have had a substantial effect throughout the housing and home financing industries. Thus, maximum property requirements have set a norm for all housing. They have tended to standardize home equipment and materials and have enabled building codes and other requirements to be more nearly uniform.

Homeownership

Homeownership has been a guiding principle of FHA since its inception. The increased availability of home financing credit under its programs has helped increase not only the volume of individual homes, but the ratio of ownership to rental. In 1930, only 46 percent of families owned their own homes. The 1970 census indicated that this had increased to about 63 percent.

Establishment of Mortgage Banking Industry and Large-Scale Builders

Prior to 1934, mortgage bankers handled only an insignificant amount of business. The mortgage bankers now service FHA mortgages amounting to over $50 billion, as estimated by the Mortgage Bankers Association. Their function of channeling the flow of funds from national investors to builders and home purchasers was made practical by the FHA insurance protection of large-scale mortgage investments throughout the country, regardless of State variations in foreclosure procedures and expenses and other applicable State requirements. Concurrently with the development of the mortgage banking industry and its national credit services, many large-scale builders of homes came into existence throughout the country. Only a very few existed before 1934. Because of mortgage insurance, funds from large national investors became available on liberal credit terms. These large-scale builders were encouraged by the resulting prospect of sustained stable production essential to their operations.

Consumer Credit for Repair and Rehabilitation

The insurance of institutions against losses on borrowing for repair and rehabilitation was the first FHA program to start operating, and is still continuing on a large scale. Over 30 million such loans have been made, amounting to more than $20 billion. This form of short term financing operates on a discounted loan proceeds basis, which results in a higher finance charge to the borrower than the interest charge on an insured mortgage. Yet it is a practical procedure for lenders and repair contractors everywhere, and affords the borrower a discount rate substantially lower than he would pay on relatively small unsecured loans without FHA insurance.

The only serious failure in this program occurred in the year 1953, and shortly before, when scandalous abuses occurred that constituted a part of the "FHA scandal" that year. Hundreds of homeowners throughout the country had been defrauded by promoters (called "suede shoe boys") of repair and rehabilitation jobs who took advantage of loose lending practices that FHA had not adequately controlled. It was also the year of greatest operations under the program. Therefore, the Housing Act of 1954 imposed new drastic safeguards, including a 10-percent coinsurance requirement on each loan (in addition to the previous 10 percent maximum on the portion of the institution's loans that could be insured). There were predictions that this would kill the program, but it continued at almost the same rate as the average of years immediately preceding that change.

It may be noted that experience during the priorities and credit control days following World War II made clear that any serious curtailment of this program will produce an enormous reaction from the thousands of suppliers and contractors who use it.

What FHA Mortgage Insurance Has Not Accomplished

Although the mortgage insurance system was adapted, through legislation and sometimes through administrative action, to meet emerging social problems, new forms of ownership, and new industry techniques, it failed in other respects to meet major problems in the housing field. Often, that was because the problems were beyond the scope of mortgage insurance rather than because of any weakness or failure in the mortgage insurance system itself.

Major failures were:

Neglect of Small Cities, Towns, and Rural Areas

Of course, nothing in the legislation—explicit congressional intent or regulations—restricts mortgage insurance to large cities. (There was even an early amendment, Section 110 of the Housing Act of 1954, which is still in effect, that attempted unsuccessfully to extend FHA insurance to a farm dwelling.) In practice, the FHA programs have operated largely in big cities and their suburbs, to the neglect of small towns, and rural areas. Several reasons can be given: (1) the failure of small town banks to learn and participate in the rather complex FHA procedures and requirements, (2) an FHA conservative view of the housing market in a small town or a one-industry small city, (3) a lack of investment by the FHA field office because of the remoteness of a small city or town in relation to the volume of housing involved, considering difficulties of inspections, etc., and (4) concentration during the 1960's on the emerging urban problems of the very large metropolitan areas. Some special purpose housing, such as housing for the elderly, has moved substantially into small communities.

Notwithstanding the real obstacles to providing FHA assistance in small places, those obstacles are not insurmountable, as the Veterans Administration and the Farmers Home Administration have proven, using different legislative and other techniques. . . .

Incoherent Suburban Development

Perhaps FHA is most frequently criticized by professionals for producing "urban sprawl." That is valid to the extent that most FHA insurance on new construction has been on housing in the suburbs that was developed in an incoherent manner from the standpoint of overall community planning and the needs of all income groups. Often, recreational facilities have been inadequate or nonexistent. The usual criticism runs to the dreary scenic appearance and sameness of the housing.

In fairness, it is difficult to say that FHA caused this type of construction, because it frequently occurred in areas where building was done without FHA insurance. It does represent a lack of initiative by Federal and local officials to take whatever steps are required to compensate for the failure of local planning and other controls.

Failure to Produce Housing in Volume
Through Mortgage Insurance for Rehabilitation

No greater effort has been put forth unsuccessfully by HUD and its predecessors than in their consistent and vigorous (but unrewarding) attempts to produce a large volume of adequate housing through mortgage insurance for rehabilitation. Successes have occurred on a small scale with very limited special legislative (such as Section 221(h) and the similar section 235(j) beginning in 1968) and administrative actions, but general legislative authority has not been effective.

Outstanding in this regard were the rehabilitation measures in the Housing Act of 1961 which had been proposed and heralded as one of the main features of that landmark legislation (Section 303(k) and Section 220(h) of the National Housing Act). They produced almost nothing. Apparently, very favorable financing terms are inadequate incentives for overcoming the basic obstacles inherent in rehabilitation jobs.

Lack of Minority Housing In Suburbs

It is obvious that, notwithstanding the application and substantial enforcement of equal opportunity requirements to housing occupancy and financing, the needs of minority families for housing in the suburbs are not being met in a meaningful way. Apparently, nothing FHA does causes this result, but the present mortgage insurance system, together with other Federal and local controls, are failing to meet these needs.

Decline of Central Cities

This is closely related to the above-mentioned failures with respect to suburban development and the needs of minority families. Generally, the FHA has produced housing in the suburbs that is unavailable to blacks and the poor and has facilitated the movement of whites with moderate or higher incomes to the suburbs. This has helped accelerate the decline of central cities. At the same time, the present FHA mortgage insurance system is inadequate for substantially meeting the problems of blight and deterioration in central cities. In fact FHA is being criticized for going too far administratively in liberalizing its programs in attempts to bring mortgage insurance to some areas which continue to deteriorate. Indeed, it has been one of the prime financial losers in older blighted areas. . . .

NOTES

1. Press Statement of the President, November 13, 1931.
2. Public Law 304, 72nd Congress.
3. Public Law 43, 73rd Congress.
4. Herbert Hoover, *Memoirs—The Great Depression*, p. 115.
5. Public Law 576, 81st Congress.
6. Op. cit., p. 111.
7. H.R. Report No. 897, 81st Congress, 2nd Session, Committee on Banking and Currency on S. 2246, pp. 56-67.
8. National Housing Act (H.R. 9620) hearings before Committee on Banking and Currency, House of Representatives, 73rd Congress, May 18, 1934, pp. 1, 2.
9. Ibid., p. 8.
10. President's Conference on Home Building and Home Ownership, December 1931.
11. Allan F. Thornton: "The Economic Impact of Federal Housing Administration Insurance Programs" (HUD Library 332-72-T36) pp. 17 et seq.
12. See President's Conference on Home Building and Home Ownership, supra.
13. Ibid.
14. Ibid.
15. Allan F. Thornton, supra.

16. The provision was substituted for an earlier one (Section 203(1) added by Section 302 of the Demonstration Cities and Metropolitan Development Act of 1963) which waived economic soundness in riot threatened areas.
17. *Wall Street Journal* (May 14, 1973) citing FHA as source.
18. *Time Magazine* for June 11, 1973, p. 79, reports housing starts have fallen from an annual rate of 2.5 million in January of this year to 2.1 million in April.
19. Allan F. Thornton, supra.
20. *The Economic Impact of Federal Loan Insurance* (Washington: National Housing Association, 1961), p. 62.

6

Objectives and Historical Development of Veterans' Loan Benefits

U.S. President's Commission on Veterans' Pensions

The loan guaranty program was originally conceived in 1944 as a part of a three-pronged attack on the harsh aftermath associated with wars. The overall objectives of this attack were to diminish to the greatest possible extent the economic and sociological problems of postwar readjustment of millions of men and women then serving in the Armed Forces. While the loan guaranty, the education and training, and the unemployment compensation programs all originally shared common objectives as transitional devices, each had its own specific objectives and each one had had somewhat different courses of development in the 11 years since the original enactment of the GI bill of rights on June 22, 1944.

INITIAL OBJECTIVES AND PHILOSOPHY OF THE LOAN GUARANTY BENEFITS

The loan benefits were first incorporated in a bill drawn up by a committee of the American Legion and introduced in the Senate in late 1943 as a part of S. 1617[1] and in the House of Representatives as H.R. 4157[2]. During the hearing many amendments were suggested. In common with other aspects of this bill, the objectives of the loan program were, as stated by one witness[3] at hearings:

From U.S. President's Commission on Veterans' Pensions. *A Report on Veterans' Benefits in the United States*. Staff Report No. 1x-c. Washington, D.C.: U.S. Government Printing Office, 1956. pp. 5-19.

" . . .to deal with the bread and butter things as to which the veteran should have assistance the first week or the first month or the first 90 days after his discharge."

While this statement referred primarily to unemployment benefits, the objectives of the loan program were similar. On the theory that many veterans would either be married before or immediately after leaving the service and that they would have neither homes nor money with which to buy them, loans should be immediately available to them. The legion representative pointed out that the purchase of a home gives the veterans "a fixed interest in their community immediately" and thus "helps the veterans and the community."[4] . . .

Congressional Intent with Reference to Title III

With so many cross currents in terms of procedures for carrying out the loan benefits it is difficult to get a clear picture of all the objectives. However, the basic objectives are fairly clear and may be summarized as follows:

1. The veteran should be able to take up his life where he left off when entering the service by aiding him to obtain a home, a business, or a farm. In other words, the benefits were to help him readjust to civilian life.
2. The Federal Government was to supply him with a basic credit standing since he had had little opportunity to build up an equity payment.
3. The loan should be low in cost to make the benefits available to as many veterans as possible.
4. The cost and terms should be uniform in all areas.
5. The veterans should have to deal with only one agency.
6. The benefits were designed to help the economy adjust as well as the veteran.

Implications of Title III

The implications of title III of the Servicemen's Readjustment Act fall into two major groups: (1) Those related to the needs of the veteran himself and (2) those related to the general housing situation.

The Needs of the Returning Veteran

The veteran who had spent 90 days or more in service was assumed to have had his normal opportunities for obtaining a home interrupted. The implication was that in comparison with the civilian who had been earning high wartime wages, the veteran had less opportunity to have accumulated funds for buying a home.[5]

A further implication was that many of the veterans would be immediately in the market for a house after leaving service. It was assumed that many had already married or soon would after leaving service and in view of the then current housing shortage would have no place to live. It was felt that the veteran would benefit by settling down in a home of his own in which he had a direct interest.[6]

The sponsors of the legislation believed that the Veterans' Administration should have responsibility for determining the veteran's eligibility, but that the technical work of seeing that the loan was of a proper amount should be delegated to another appropriate agency.[7] Furthermore the sponsors intended that not only Federal agencies would be used but also local agencies to assure loans in small towns and nonmetropolitan areas, generally not serviced by the Federal housing agencies.

Another implication of the legislation was that the veteran should be protected from ill-advised farm and business loans by requiring that he show some aptitude and ability in the fields of business and farm loans.[8] He was to be further protected by determining that the property purchase was capable of being used as he proposed and that the purchase price bore the proper relationship to his present and anticipated income and expenses. There was every intent in the legislation that the veteran be successful in whatever phase of the loan benefits he undertook.

Considerable stress in the legislative planning was laid on the fact that the loan guaranty was to be one of the several benefits that the veteran could choose. If he was not ready to marry and settle down, he could go to school, or if he wanted to work and no job was available, he could get unemployment insurance. It is doubtful that proponents of the legislation intended that each veteran should be limited to only one benefit, but in general, little multiple use was expected.

The Needs of the Economy and the General Housing Situation

While not specifically in most of the hearings on the loan guaranty there was always at least the implication that title III would stimulate construction activity and thus provide employment opportunity; not only in direct construction but in the building material supply industries. Construction has long been considered in the past the spark plug of the economy because of its use of a wide range of materials. Evidence of this was seen in the effort to stimulate construction in the 1930's and thus overcome the effects of the depression.[9] Furthermore construction offers fairly immediate employment provided materials are at hand. This, however, turned out to be the critical part of the program since materials, other than for war use, were scarce in 1945.

Due to restrictions on housing production during the war, housing had nowhere near kept up to the demand. In addition there had been a net shortage of housing even before the war as an aftermath of the depression. Family formation had far outstripped the construction of new housing. During the war most essential needs had been met by temporary construction, conversion of existing structures, and doubling up of more than one family in a dwelling unit.[10]

In view of the critical nature of the general housing situation at that time, the provision of any mechanism which would produce more houses would not only aid the veteran but would also be extremely important to the general public.

Problems Encountered in Early Operations

It soon became apparent after the program got into operation late in 1944, that there were many problems to be overcome to make the loan-guaranty program operate successfully. These problems tended to fall into three groups: (1) Administration of the program, (2) those created by rising real-estate prices, and (3) the period of eligibility.

Correction of these problems in many instances involved a change in basic philosophy of the law. Consequently extensive congressional hearings were held during 1945.

Problems of Administrative Organization

The principal administrative problem encountered was the time it took to process the loan-guaranty applications. These delays of course were in part due to the newness of the program, but the physical task of clearing each application caused significant delays and tended to discourage both the lender and the veteran applicant. The seller of the property also was affected by delays of this sort and may frequently have refrained from offering property to veterans because of the expected delay.[11] To make the program a success some change was required.

The Impact of Real Estate Price Increases

The basic $2,000 guaranty in the original legislation even at the time of passage was barely enough to represent half of the purchase price. Few houses were available for sale at $4,000 even at that time. Based on Bureau of Labor Statistics of permit valuation it can be estimated that very few new dwelling units were below $5,000 and prices were continuing to rise. This meant that the veteran frequently had to supply significant amounts of cash in order to make the purchase. New housing for sale was at least as high priced and usually higher than existing housing. Thus, even though the objective of setting a low amount was to keep down the prices veterans had to pay, it was evident that an increase would have to be granted.

Another delimiting factor due to real-estate inflation was the appraisal technique implied in Public Law 346. The appraisal was to determine reasonable normal value and set that as the selling price. Reasonable normal value was interpreted as a normal price level which might have existed without wartime inflation rather than current market value. Thus appraisals were too low to enable the veterans to effectively bid against nonveteran purchasers of housing.

A third aspect of the price inflation that affected success of the program involved the required maturity. Where the above problems were overcome in one way or another, the veteran's prospective income and expenses frequently were such that they did not bear the proper relationship to the size of the monthly payments he would have to make on a 20-year amortized loan.

The Period of Eligibility

After a year's operation of the program when relatively few veterans had applied for the loan guaranty it became obvious that either many veterans could never use it with the 2-year eligibility limitation and that a rush of applications as terminal dates approached would cause inflation. Inflation already existed because of the scarcity of used houses for sale or new houses being built. Furthermore, many veterans had not yet settled down or were going to school. The American Legion in consultation with leading bankers and institutional lenders, recommended extending the 2 years to 10 years.[12] The Veterans' Administration concurred in this as did the American Bankers Association (p. 351, Senate hearing). Other suggestions were for a 5 or 6 year extension.

CHANGES IN THE PROGRAM AND ITS PHILOSOPHY

The congressional hearings in 1945 produced a great deal of testimony relative to the loan-guaranty program. The suggestions given ranged all the way from abolishing title III completely[13] to liberalizing it to a 100 percent guaranty with no fixed requirement that the veteran pay it back. From the testimony of various witnesses it appeared that some veterans misunderstood the original act to the extent that they thought all they had to do was to take their discharge certificates to a bank and ask for a $2,000 loan with no obligations attached.[14]

Of the proposed changes, the one dealing with the question of whether "reasonable normal value" or simply "reasonable value" should be used in appraisals, probably received the most attention. The proponents of the original concept argued that the word "normal" was in the act to protect the veteran.[15] The opponents argued that in a time of rising prices, the concept used in appraisal would have to be equivalent to current market value or the veteran would have no opportunity to purchase any house.[16] The opponents quoted one veteran as stating that he would "rather pay five or six hundred dollars above the normal value now, have possession of the house, the use of the house, rather than to pay that out to some landlord."[17]

The dividing line between the groups favoring "reasonable normal value" and those favoring a more liberal concept was not by type of organization as might be expected. Veteran's groups were divided on it as were governmental agencies. The witnesses representing lenders seemed to be the only group quite consistently in favor of dropping the word "normal."

Legislative Changes in 1945

When these hearings were completed Congress passed Public Law 268. The changes were (1) $4,000 maximum guaranty up to 50 percent for real-estate loans and $2,000 for nonrealty, (2) maturity of 25 years for nonfarm realty, up to 45 for farm realty and 10 for nonrealty, (3) appraisal concept was changed to "reasonable value," (4) extension of eligibility period to 10 years (5) lifting the requirement of prior approval by VA for loans made by lenders under State or National supervision and (6) loan insurance as an alternative to loan guaranty.

These changes constituted an almost complete revision of the loan-guaranty program. It changed many of the basic objectives, such as holding the price of properties to a preinflation level. An even more basic philosophical change was that the original act was considered only as a readjustment aid for the veteran who wanted to start a home, a business, or buy a farm when he got out of service. The extension of readymade credit by the Government was to make up for his lost time. The new act provided something different. It could no longer be considered solely as an adjustment benefit for the few who had immediate and specific plans after leaving service. It was now open to all veterans who might decide to avail themselves of the benefit at any time within 10 years after the official end of the war. In terms of aiding the economy over the reconversion period the objective had also changed. It was now a long-range housing program for veterans. This last of the new objectives has been held to consistently throughout the subsequent changes in the program. Nearly all changes have been presumed to help the veteran become a homeowner by extending the terms, making money available, protecting him from excessive charges, faulty construction and so forth.

With these new objectives the veteran loan-guaranty program moved ahead rapidly especially with reference to the home-loan portion (sec. 501) of title III. . . .

THE PROGRAM IN OPERATION, 1946-50

During late 1945 and early 1946 demobilization of the Armed Forces took place rapidly. Marriage rates were at an all time high and the demand for housing was far in excess of any goal that could be met with many materials still under control. The net shortage of housing which had accumulated during the war years now made the pressure for housing even greater. The postwar migration of war workers back to their original homes did not take place as expected. The consequence of these many factors was an intensifed doubling up of families.

Congress, recognizing the emergency, passed legislation designed to encourage production of building materials and to channel materials and labor into residential construction. As a result, residential construction reached a total of 670,500 new dwelling units in 1946.

Character and Volume of VA Home Loans

Because of the shortage of materials and labor the bulk of the home loans in the early days of the program were on existing homes. Less than 20 percent of the total loans closed by the end of 1946 are estimated to have been new dwelling units.

Volume of Loans

The monthly rate of applications increased by about 50 times from the first quarter of 1945 to the last quarter of 1946. During 1946 the monthly rate rose from about 8,000 per month at the end of 1945 to 55,000 in the third quarter of 1946. From then on through 1947, a monthly rate of about 50,000 was maintained.

During 1947 the flow of applications was stimulated by purchases of loans by the Reconstruction Finance Corporation Mortgage Company. Although purchases were discontinued on July 1 of that year, the backlog of commitments outstanding at the end of the last month helped to sustain the rate of applications and closed loans throughout the year. By early 1948 the rate for both fell off precipitously and continued to decline until the middle of 1949. At that time other sources of mortgage money had become available and the volume of business in VA home loans climbed to new record heights by late 1950.

Automatic and Prior-Approval Loans

The legislation in 1945 (Public Law 268), providing for automatic approval of loans made by supervised lenders, was an almost immediate success. The first month for which data are available (November 1946) showed that automatic guaranty loan applications were nearly two-thirds of the total. While that relationship did not continue, automatic guaranty loans quite consistently represented at least half of the volume of applications up to the middle of 1949. Several factors probably accounted for a lessening of the importance of the automatic guaranty:

1. As mortgage company and broker operations became more important factors in VA loans the relative proportion of prior approval loans would increase since such companies usually did not qualify as supervised lenders.
2. Small banks and savings and loan associations each doing a small amount of GI business could not afford the staff work necessary to keep up with VA regulations and therefore used prior approval loans.
3. Large lenders who had submitted automatic approval loans that were unacceptable because of some technicality were likely to use the prior approval loan at least for a while.

Appraisal Procedures

The most important factor influencing the character of the home loans before 1950 was the improvements and refinements of appraisals. In the early period panels of local appraisers were used exclusively. In December 1946 appraisal sections were established in the field offices to make assignments from the panel and review the work of fee appraisers. This was instituted in order to select competent appraisers and to protect the veteran from possible collusion between fee appraisers and the builder, seller, or lender. Later the appraisal sections were given still more authority to assist in the determination of reasonable value. Another change in appraisal procedures consisted of use of appraisal committee for project housing, thus obtaining a uniform opinion on all houses in the project. The committee (usually 3 to 5 appraisers) approach also was presumed to give the veteran greater protection in that the CRV (certificate of reasonable value) did not represent one appraiser's opinion but that of a board of experts.[18]

CRV Advance Commitments

As the volume of construction increased during 1946 and 1947, builders wanted to know in advance whether their projects would qualify for VA loans. In November 1947 the Veterans' Administration instituted a procedure for advance issuance of CRV's through the use of appraisal committees and property compliance inspection during construction. Upon examination and approval of the project plans and specifications, the Veterans' Administration would issue to a builder a certificate of reasonable value for a proposed project which could result in approved loans on the dwelling units in the project provided the builder complied with the original specifications and sold the houses to eligible veterans. The check on this compliance was made by fee inspectors who had to qualify as construction experts. Three inspections were made at varying stages of construction. The CRV was usually valid for a period of 8 months.

The advantage to the builder of these CRV's was that it provided him with a form of assurance of guaranty of long-term loans which helped him obtain the latter and that in turn helped him to borrow construction money. This enabled more builders to get into the program with the result that newly constructed units became a much more significant part of the loan guaranty program than in the early years. Prior to 1947, loans for new homes were only 16 percent of the total, but in the last half of 1950, they represented nearly 60 percent and have been an even larger proportion in some periods since then.

Other Factors in Changing the Character and Volume of Home-Loan Activity

Several other factors have had a significant impact on activity in the program not only prior to 1950 but up to the present time.

(1) *Incontestability.*—By legislative action (Public Law 864, 80th Cong., July 1, 1948), the apprehensions of some lenders about the soundness of the loan guaranty were overcome by a provision making any evidence of guaranty or insurance issued by the Administrator of Veterans' Affairs conclusive evidence that the lender would be protected from loss within the limitations of the guaranty except in the case of fraud or substantial failure to comply with VA regulations.

(2) *Government support in the secondary market for mortgages.*—This support, . . . or lack of it, has been closely tied in with the volume of activity throughout much of the program.

(3) *Operating improvements within the Veterans' Administration.*—Changes in processing applications, use of forms, introduction of uniform procedures throughout regional offices were introduced during this period with a view to speeding up service to veterans, builders, and lenders.

(4) *Changes in collection policies.*—In 1947, the Veterans' Administration issued a statement of policy on collection of losses from veterans in the event the settlement of defaulted loans left the Government with a loss. Briefly this policy was that the veteran was responsible for such losses. Collections could be made from compensation payments or national service life insurance dividends or other benefits. The effect of this policy was presumably psychological in that it made the veteran realize that the loan guaranty was a contractual arrangement which he had to meet even though he gave up the property. To the extent this made the veteran a better risk, the loan program was made sounder.

(5) *Acquisition of defaulted properties.*—In 1948, the Veterans' Administration revised regulations relative to the transfer of properties (when the loan was in default) to VA for liquidation of the security immediately after foreclosure. This procedure involved paying the lender the full appraised price for the property if he elected to transfer it. A final settlement would be made at the time of liquidation by the Veterans' Administration. The effect was to protect the lender from risk of loss in liquidation by forced sale. Under this new procedure the lender also could elect to keep the property (if the appraised value exceeded the unguaranteed portion of the loan) and gamble on a firm market or he could transfer immediately with a full cash settlement at appraised value. This tended to make the loan program more acceptable to all lenders. At the same time, the regulations provided that the Veterans' Administration always could step in to protect the veteran from a lender liquidation of the security that was less than the appraised value.

Character and Volume of Business and Farm Loans

Business and farm loans have never been a significant part of the loan program. The period in which these loans reached their greatest relative importance was soon after demobilization in 1946-47. About one-half of the farm loans and a third of the business loans of the whole program were made by the end of 1947.

Farm loans were divided about half and half between those made for purchase of farms and those made to buy equipment, livestock, seed, and the like for farms they had previously owned or obtained by means other than through the loan guaranty program.

Business loans throughout the whole period have been made primarily to buy shares in existing enterprises or to buy equipment, fixtures, and tools for individual or partnership ventures. Only 15 percent have been made to buy business real estate. The business loan, particularly the nonrealty loans, have been substantially the only part of the loan program for which the insured loan was used. The reason the insured loan was attractive was due to its 3 percent discount feature, which provided nearly a 6 percent return. In addition, the lender could build up credits from which he could deduct his losses, if any.

THE HOUSING ACT OF 1950

In the years 1948 and 1949, residential construction reached successive new alltime highs each year. Yet the demand for new dwelling units was still far from satisfied. Consequently, in the spring of 1950, Congress enacted legislation changing both the National Housing Act and the Servicemen's Readjustment Act.

Changes in GI Loan Benefits and Objectives

There were eight basic changes in the loan program included in the Housing Act of 1950 (Public Law 475, 81st Cong.). Five of these changes involved, or at least implied, a change in objective from the original legislation. However, these changes in objectives were in a sense, extensions of the changed objectives which were started by the 1945 amendments, that is they liberalized the benefits, so that more veterans could participate.

Seven of the changes were concerned with loan guaranty. The eighth was a provision for direct loans.

Change in Guaranty Amount

This change, raising the maximum guaranty for home loans to 60 percent of the loan but not to exceed $7,500, was actually an implied admission that the price line represented by the lower maximum, i.e., 50 percent, not over $4,000 could not be held if the objective now was to provide the benefit for all veterans who wished to buy a home. Since the original objectives, which appeared to have included that of a low-cost home as a means of adjustment to civilian life, had been changed in the 1945 amendments, the increase in guaranty was simply a necessary step in accomplishing the new objective.

The second step in the same direction was the lengthening of maximum maturity of loans from 25 to 30 years. This enabled more veterans to get into the program through the consequent lowering of monthly payments.

Other Extensions of Benefits

The number of persons who could make use of benefits was also enlarged somewhat by the less important changes:

(1) Unremarried widows of veterans who had died in service or as a result of service-connected injury or disease were given the same loan privileges as the veteran;

(2) Veterans whose homes (or farms or businesses) were obtained with a GI loan but lost through fire or other natural hazards, or were taken by public condemnation, or were disposed of for other compelling reasons not the fault of the veteran were given back their full entitlement on a loan provided the VA no longer had any liability on the original loan.

Changes Which Tightened the Provisions of the Loan Guaranty

Three of the eight changes were designed to keep the cost to the veteran down or to provide him with a better property on which he had a loan. They did not restrict participation in any sense.

The first of these provided authority for the Veterans' Administration to establish minimum construction standards, similar to those that had been used by Federal Housing Administration. In order for any new residential properties to be eligible for loan guaranty, they had to conform to these standards. These standards were intended to lend additional support to the appraisal procedures and thus protect the veteran from getting an inferior product for his money.

The second change was intended to keep the veteran from having to pay a higher interest rate than 4 percent. Section 505 of title III, which had provided for the combination FHA-VA loan, was repealed. The combination loan carried an effective interest cost of about 4.8 percent, 4½ percent interest plus one-half percent insurance on the 80-percent portion insured by the Federal Housing Administration and 4 percent on the remaining 20 percent or less guaranteed by the Veterans' Administration. The combination loan was popular with builders because the FHA firm commitment procedure facilitated the borrowing of construction funds. The 505 loan with its higher yield also was popular with the lender and was easier to dispose of in the secondary market. Furthermore the veteran was more likely to be able to get a no-downpayment loan under section 505 than under section 501. The increased maximum guaranty was presumed to enable the veteran to continue to get 100 percent loans but at a 4 percent interest rate. It was reasoned that with 60 percent of the loan carrying no risk to the lender, it was as good or better than a conventional loan where 60 percent of the loan or more was unprotected.

The third change intended to benefit the veteran was to assure the veteran that no hidden charges would have the effect of raising his interest rate. The provision required the Federal Housing Administration and the Veterans' Administration to issue regulations setting the amounts of fees and charges which the lender might impose on the builder and the veteran or other purchaser.

Direct Loans

In addition to changes affecting the guaranty loans, the Housing Act of 1950 further extended the possibility of veteran participation in the loan program by providing for direct loans in areas where guaranteed or insured loans at 4 percent—later changed to 4½ percent—could not be obtained readily or where private mortgage money was not available. These loans could be used for the purchase or construction of homes or for construction or improvement of farmhouses. The authority for the Veterans' Administration to make such loans was granted for about a year but was extended from time to time.

The purpose of the direct loan provision was to give all veterans an equal opportunity to get a home even though they lived in areas where private lenders either were not interested in 4-percent mortgage money or had insufficient funds to make such mortgages. The large secondary market investors were not interested in buying mortgages originated in smaller communities or in semirural areas except at discounts, therefore, there was no readily available source of funds for banks in such areas.

CHANGES IN THE PROGRAM SINCE 1950

Since 1950 the changes in the loan guaranty have in general been designed to improve its operations or to adjust to credit problems rather than changes in objectives. The only exception to this was the passage of the Korean GI bill, Public Law 550, 82d Congress, on July 16, 1952.

Objectives of the Changes Under Public Law 550

The Korean conflict posed the same problem for its veterans as World War II in terms of its impact upon schooling, jobs or building up an equity for the purchase or construction of a home, starting a business, or buying a farm or farm equipment. Congress readily recognized that these veterans were also entitled to aid in readjusting to civilian status upon leaving the service.[19]

The act made all veterans of service after June 27, 1950, eligible for the same loan-guaranty benefits available to World War II veterans for a period of 10 years after the date of official termination of hostilities. This date was set later as January 31, 1955. Thus the same objectives still held, that is, providing time enough to allow practically all veterans to make use of the program if they wished. The act also made adjustments in the entitlement of veterans who served in both periods, World War II and Korean.

Other Changes Resulting from Public Law 550

An increasing number of complaints as to the quality of new houses constructed under the provisions of the loan-guaranty program led to extensive congressional investigations in various cities by the Subcommittee on Housing of the House Committee on Banking and Currency. In addition a special committee (the Teague committee) was established to investigate the education and training and loan provisions of the GI bill. These committees reviewed many individual complaints on construction quality, methods of land development, and sales practices. Their recommendations[20] were considered in the preparations of Public Law 550 and measures to correct some of the worst abuses were included in the final version of the act. The corrective measures included:

1. Veterans' Administration was required to establish minimum planning and general acceptability standards relative to land development, sanitary and drainage systems, water supply, and other development improvements. The 1950 legislation had permitted only approval of actual construction standards.
2. In order to give added enforcement powers to both construction and planning standards the Administrator of Veterans' Affairs was given authority to refuse to appraise any dwelling unit or project owned by a person or firm who had previously sold housing to veterans under title III and which had been found to have substantial deficiencies or to those whose transactions had been in other ways unduly prejudicial to veteran purchasers.
3. The Administrator was also empowered to refuse to guarantee loans made by lenders who had failed to keep accurate records or otherwise willfully engaged in practices detrimental to the veteran's interest.

Other recommendations not included in Public Law 550 were indicative of the types of problems the investigating committees uncovered.

1. Uniform sales contracts: In many instances it was found that the veteran unwittingly signed a contract absolving the builder from all responsibility for defective construction.[21] Because of the administrative difficulties of enforcing a standardized contract under differing local laws nothing was done about this recommendation.
2. A related recommendation was that contracts include a builder's warranty of at least a year's duration.
3. The Teague committee recommended that civil service provide sufficiently high ratings for appraisers and inspectors to attract competent employees and that close supervision be exercised by the Veterans' Administration. This recommendation was to eliminate possibilities of collusion between Veterans' Administration employees and builders.
4. Closely related to the above was a recommendation that title III contain a clause specifically forbidding the acceptance of gratuities, favors, or gifts by Veterans' Administration employees from persons or firms doing business with the Veterans' Administration.
5. Recommendations for strengthening the Inspection and Investigation Service of the Veterans' Administration to help eliminate irregularities in the operation of the loan-guaranty program.

Other Legislative Changes Since 1950

Nearly all of the other legislative changes since 1950 had to do with credit problems. . . . The only ones not discussed . . . are the voluntary home mortgage credit program and the builder's warranty provision each established by the Housing Act of 1954.

The first of these changes is only applicable to direct loans. Under this provision a veteran's application for a direct loan is first referred to a voluntary regional committee. They try to place the loan with a private lender and if successful within 45 days—now 20 working days—the loan becomes an ordinary guaranteed loan. If not placed, the veteran may be considered for a direct loan.

The VHMC program has been criticized by the House Veterans Affairs Committee because a direct loan would be granted only if the veteran faced an "unreasonable" discount which is defined by Veterans' Administration as 2 percent or more. The veteran is not allowed to pay it directly under present regulations; therefore, according to the committee's criticism, if the builder refuses to absorb it the veteran cannot purchase the house.[22] The objective of this program was of course to give private lenders a chance to make the loan and thus cut down on direct cost to the Government. Since veterans' loans in non-direct-loan areas often involved a discount, the 2-percent discount rule was considered fair for the direct-loan areas.

The other change, the builder's warranty, provides that all veteran-purchasers of houses in projects where a CRV has been given prior to the start of construction shall be given a warranty by the builder that the construction substantially conforms with the plans and specifications as approved by Veterans' Administration and the seller.

SUMMARY OF OBJECTIVES AND PRINCIPAL ELEMENTS OF THE LOAN GUARANTY PLAN

As it now stands the objective of the loan program and the elements[23] of the program aimed to accomplish these objectives can be divided into three main groups.

A. The objective of enabling the veteran to get a home, a business or a farm loan on a favorable basis is presumed to be met by these elements:

1. A low-interest rate;
2. Small monthly payments by use of a long amortization period;
3. Fixed charges or fees to be paid but no premiums or commission for obtaining the loan;
4. No required downpayment;
5. Loan can be fully repaid at any time or payments can be accelerated without penalty;
6. Refinancing can be arranged for veterans in temporary financial straits.

B. The objectives of protecting the veterans' interest is assumed to be met by these elements:

1. The loan may not exceed "reasonable value" based on a proper appraisal;
2. Newly constructed dwelling units must meet minimum standards of construction and of planning as to site development;
3. The veteran must meet certain risk standards;
4. Builders, lenders or sellers found guilty of willful conduct prejudicial to the veteran purchaser may no longer use the loan program.

C. The objective of making the program attractive to lenders, upon whom the success of the first objective really depends, is met by these elements:

1. Most important of all is that the Government will assume the loss, in the event of default, up to the percent of the initial guaranty on the outstanding balance;
2. The guaranty or insurance certificate is incontestable except in cases of proven fraud;
3. Prompt cash settlement of claims after default including interest owned and costs of foreclosure, loss by waste of property, etc.;
4. Opportunity to adjust the contract terms with the consent of the purchaser and the Veterans' Administration in order to cure defaults;
5. The option to convey property for which loan is in default to Veterans' Administration or to retain it under a net settlement plan if the value of the property exceeds the unguaranteed portion of the loan;
6. If hazard insurance has been maintained the full guaranty ratio applies even though the property is damaged or destroyed;
7. The provision whereby Veterans' Administration will accept whatever title the holder of the mortgage acquired at foreclosure.

NOTES

1. *See* 78th Cong., 2d sess., Senate Committee on Finance, hearings on S. 1617, January 14-March 10, 1944.
2. *See* 78th Cong., 2d sess., hearings before the Committee on World War Veterans' Legislation on H.R. and S. 1617, House of Representatives, January-March 1944, p. 146.
3. Warren H. Atherton, national commander of the American Legion. See p. 8 of the citation in footnote 1 above.
4. U.S. Congress, House of Representatives, 78th Cong., 2d sess., op. cit., p. 19.
5. Op. cit., House hearings on S. 1767, pp. 397-398.
6. Op. cit., Senate hearings on S. 1617, p. 19.
7. Ibid., p. 120.
8. See secs. 502 (3) and 503 (3) of title III, Public Law 346.
9. For example, *see* Twentieth Century Fund, *American Housing*, 1944 or National Resources Planning Board publications, *The Structure of the American Economy*, 1939; and *The Role of the Homebuilding Industry*, by Miles Colean; also see Clarence D. Long, *Building Cycles and the Theory of Investment*.

10. For a general review of this problem at the end of the war *see The Housing Situation*, Housing and Home Finance Agency, June 1948, and *Housing Needs*, National Housing Agency, Bulletin No. 1, 1944; *see also* statement of Senator Johnson of South Carolina, quoted in H.Rpt.No. 171, cited above, p. 283.
11. U.S. Congress, Senate, 78th Cong., hearings before a subcommittee of the Committee on Finance on H.R. 3749, October 8-12, 1945, p. 350.
12. Ibid., p. 113.
13. Ibid., pp. 132-134 and 220.
14. U.S. Congress, House of Representatives, 79th Cong., hearings on H.R. 3749, June 19-21, 28, and July 5, 1945, p. 193. Also Senate hearings cited above, p. 220.
15. E.g., *see* Senate hearings, pp. 262 and 330.
16. Op. cit., House of Representatives, Hearings on H.R. 3749, pp. 44-48.
17. Ibid., p. 44.
18. This discussion on appraisal procedures is taken from *The First 10 Years*, VA pamphlet 4A-11, pp. 13-14. . . .
19. U.S. Congress, House of Representatives, 82d Cong., 2d sess., rept. No. 1943, May 16, 1952, pp. 24 and 27.
20. *See* H. Rept. No. 2501, 82d Cong., 2d sess., September 11, 1952.
21. *See* pp. 27-35 of H. Rept. No. 2501 for example of defective contracts.
22. Reported in *Wall Street Journal* for February 6, 1956, p. 2.
23. The elements listed are based on those given in *The First 10 Years*, VA Pamphlet 4A-11, June 22, 1954, pp. 29-30.

7

Direct Intervention in the Mortgage Market

Patric H. Hendershott and Kevin E. Villani

The federal government initiated its role in the home mortgage market when home mortgage lending came to a standstill in the Great Depression. The first federal action was the establishment of the Federal Home Loan Bank (FHLB) system as a central credit facility for the principal mortgage lenders, savings and loan associations. Other early efforts focused on reducing the risk and increasing the marketability of the mortgage instrument to renew the confidence of private mortgage lenders. Federal Housing Administration (FHA) default insurance for a standard fixed-payment mortgage and the creation of the Federal National Mortgage Association (FNMA) to aid in the establishment of a secondary market represent federal efforts to improve the efficiency of the mortgage market. The federal initiative has been expanded during the past decade to encompass substantial direct market intervention; FNMA has rapidly built up its mortgage holdings and the newly created Federal Home Loan Mortgage Corporation (FHLMC) has also acquired a significant mortgage portfolio. Moreover, efforts to reduce the risk and improve the marketability of investment in mortgages have been carried to their logical extreme in the creation of the Government National Mortgage Association (GNMA) guaranteed mortgage pools. The pools and FHLB loans to savings and loans are indirect sources of mortgage credit.

From Patric H. Hendershott and Kevin E. Villani. *Regulation and Reform of the Housing Finance System* (Washington, D.C. 1978), 25-45, by permission of the American Enterprise Institute for Public Policy Research.

TABLE 1

Holdings of Home Mortgages by Federal Agencies

(billions of dollars)

	1965	1966	1967	1968	1969	1970	1971	1972	1973	1974	1975	1976
FNMA (off-budget)	2.5	4.4	5.5	7.2	11.0	15.2	16.7	17.7	20.4	23.8	25.8	26.9
FHLMC (off-budget)	—	—	—	—	—	0.4	0.9	1.8	2.4	4.2	4.6	3.9
Federal (on-budget)	3.9	4.5	5.3	6.2	6.4	6.2	5.6	5.0	4.2	5.0	6.9	4.1
Total (including FLB)	6.4	8.9	10.8	13.4	17.4	21.8	23.2	24.5	27.1	33.4	37.8	35.5
Mortgage rate (percent)	5.81	6.25	6.46	6.97	7.81	8.45	7.74	7.60	7.95	8.92	9.01	9.00

Source: Mortgage quantities are from issues of the *Federal Reserve Bulletin*. The mortgage rate is the FHLBB series for conventional new homes and is published in the FHLBB *Journal*. The on-budget agencies include the Government National Mortgage Association, the Farmers Home Administration, and the Federal Housing and Veterans Administrations.

Although the goal of federal intervention remains unchanged—an increased supply of home mortgage credit—the increased emphasis on direct intervention and creation of the mortgage pools implies a change in the philosophy and goals of U.S. housing policy. Whereas early federal initiatives were aimed at increasing the allocation of funds to the mortgage market by making a poorly functioning mortgage market "efficient," the effect of recent direct intervention has been to exploit institutional and regulatory rigidities in order to stimulate a greater quantity of mortgage credit than efficient markets would provide, and the guarantees have made mortgage investment as riskless and liquid as investment in any other private endeavor. Thus economic efficiency is now being sacrificed, rather than achieved, in the pursuit of housing goals presumed to be socially desirable. And this is in addition to the housing subsidy implicit in the federal tax code.

AN OVERVIEW OF THE AGENCIES:
THEIR ACTIONS AND OBJECTIVES

Two federally sponsored credit agencies, the Federal National Mortgage Association (FNMA) and the Federal Home Loan Mortgage Corporation (FHLMC) supply credit to the home mortgage market directly. A number of on-budget agencies of the federal government also hold mortgages, but to a lesser degree. These include the Government National Mortgage Association, the Farmers Home Administration, and the Federal Housing and Veterans Administrations. The level of support by these agencies is indicated in Table 1. The on-budget agencies are aggregated into a federal category, and the total includes small holdings of the Federal Land Banks (FLB) accumulated in recent years ($0.6 billion during the 1973-1976 period).

FNMA responded to the 1966 liquidity crunch by increasing its mortgage holdings by 75 percent during the year. As can be seen, this growth has continued. The holdings of FNMA increased tenfold between 1965 and 1975, rising from $2.5 billion to $25.8 billion. While the rise has been monotonic, the rate of increase seems to have varied directly with movements in the home mortgage rate. The rise in the mortgage rate from 1965 to 1970 was accompanied by a rapid buildup of holdings, a rate of increase that slackened markedly between 1970 and 1972 when the mortgage rate fell. Again, FNMA net purchases accelerated in 1973 and 1974 in response to the increasing mortgage rate and slackened in 1975 when the rate stabilized. Net purchases by the FHLMC in recent years also appear to be related to the interest rate cycle, rising sharply in 1973 and particularly 1974, slowing down in 1975, and even turning negative in 1976. The holdings of on-budget agencies rose modestly between 1965 and 1969 and then declined gradually into early 1974. As a result of the Emergency Home Purchase Act of 1974, GNMA aggressively purchased mortgages for its own account during the rest of 1974 and 1975 and liquidated them in 1976. The total support for the home mortgage market increased by about $15 billion between 1965 and 1970, and by a similar amount between 1970 and 1976.

The growth in the two forms of indirect federal supply of mortgage credit, FHLB loans (advances) to savings and loan associations (SLAS) and mortgage pools, is indicated in Table 2. The net credit extended to SLAS consists of advances less equity that SLAS must hold in the FHLBS. The latter is approximately equal to 1 percent of each SLA's mortgage portfolio.

While advances to SLAS can support purchases of assets other than home mortgages, home mortgages have consistently accounted for three-quarters of total mortgage holdings and SLAS hold few assets other than mortgages and required liquid assets. Thus it is reasonable to assume that increases in advances largely support acquisitions of home mortgages. Two facts seem pertinent regarding advances. First, this form of federal support is even more strongly related to movements in interest rates than are other forms of support. This is indicated by the sharp increases in advances in 1969-1970 and 1973-1974 and particularly the declines in 1971 and 1975-1976.[1] Second, the repayment of advances, while significant, is never enough to lower the level to the previous trough. That is, there is a continual upward trend in this form of support as well as in the holdings of the other agencies. Neither of these facts should be particularly surprising. The demand by SLAS for advances is largely related to recent deposit flows; when inflows are heavy, SLAS repay loans, and when inflows slacken, SLAS borrow more. And significant periods of disintermediation (reduced deposit inflows) and reintermediation (extraordinarily large inflows) are related to movements in open-market interest rates relative to yields on deposits that are nearly constant, given deposit rate ceilings. The general growth in advances is also understandable in light of the growth in SLA total assets and the relatively low cost of advances.[2]

In recent years another indirect form of support for the home mortgage market has expanded rapidly. Since 1970, GNMA and FHLMC have been effectively issuing federally guaranteed securities to finance pools of home mortgages (the agencies guarantee the interest and principal payments of the mortgages).[3] To the extent that the pools are held by institutions that would not have otherwise purchased home mortgages, such as insurance companies and pension funds, increases in the pools are equivalent to direct mortgage purchases. At the other extreme, if the securities are purchased by institutions that would otherwise have bought home mortgages, then the impact on the mortgage market is negligible. The outstanding pools have grown from $3 billion in 1970 (these were largely guaranteed by the Farmers Home Administration) to $44 billion in 1976. A reasonable working assumption is that the funds that SLAS invest in pools would have been invested in home mortgages anyway, because SLAS are so limited in their investment possibilities, but that funds invested by others would have been invested in low-risk agency or corporate bonds, because these institutions (mutual savings banks, pension funds, and insurance companies) hold large

TABLE 2
Indirect Federal Holdings of Home Mortgages
(billions of dollars)

	1965	1966	1967	1968	1969	1970	1971	1972	1973	1974	1975	1976
Mortgage pools	0.1	0.5	1.0	1.4	1.8	3.0	7.3	10.7	14.8	20.1	30.0	43.9
SLA holdings	—	—	—	—	—	−1.0	−2.6	−4.0	−4.8	−5.7	−9.3	−10.6
Pools other than SLAS	0.1	0.5	1.0	1.4	1.8	2.0	4.7	7.6	10.0	14.4	20.7	33.3
Advances (net)	4.7	5.5	3.0	3.9	7.8	9.0	6.3	7.2	13.0	19.2	15.1	12.9
Pools other than SLAS plus advances (net)	4.8	6.0	4.0	5.3	9.6	11.0	11.7	14.8	23.0	33.6	35.8	46.2

Sources: Data on total mortgage pools and net advances (indebtedness of SLAS to FHLBS less equity of SLAS in FHLBS) are from the *Federal Reserve Flow of Funds Accounts.* Data on SLA holdings of mortgage pools for the 1973-1976 period are from various issues of the *Savings and Loan Fact Book;* earlier estimates have been constructed by the authors.

TABLE 3
Direct and Indirect Federal Holdings of Home Mortgages
as a Fraction of the Mortgage Market
(billions of dollars)

	1965	1966	1967	1968	1969	1970	1971	1972	1973	1974	1975	1976
(1) Direct plus indirect federal support	11.2	14.9	14.8	18.7	27.0	32.8	34.2	39.3	50.1	67.0	73.6	81.6
(2) Stock of home mortgages	218.3	231.6	245.0	262.1	280.2	294.6	323.2	365.8	412.2	446.7	487.4	551.9
(1) ÷ (2)	.05	.06	.06	.07	.10	.11	.11	.11	.12	.15	.15	.15

Source: Row (1) is the sum of the total row of Table 1 and the last row of Table 2. The data on the stock of home mortgages are from the *Federal Reserve Flow of Funds Accounts*.

amounts of such assets. An estimate of the home mortgage pools not held by SLAS is given in Table 2.

The sum of advances (net) and pools other than those held by SLAS is a measure of the credit extended indirectly by the agencies. As can be seen in the last row of Table 2, the growth in this form of support of the home mortgage market has been phenomenal, rising from $12 billion to $46 billion between 1971 and 1976.

The data in Table 3 attempt to put the federal support of the home mortgage market into perspective. The first row combines the direct and indirect mortgage holdings of the agencies (the total row of Table 1 and the last row of Table 2). The second row is the stock of outstanding home mortgages, and the last row is the fraction of the outstanding stock supported by the agencies. In 1965, federal support amounted to only 5 percent; by the middle 1970s the support was up to 15 percent.[4] The jump was largely limited to two periods, 1968-1970 and 1972-1974, when interest rates rose sharply.[5]

Recent testimony on the Financial Reform Act of 1976 in the House renewed interest in the role these agencies should play. Both the objectives and the ultimate impacts of these agencies are difficult to pinpoint, a fact that intensifies the controversy surrounding their operations. The objectives of the enabling legislation for the agency activities are explored in the following sections. The institutional arrangements by which the agencies function are then measured against these objectives. The last part of this section deals with the impact of these activities on mortgage rates, credit, and housing outlays.

The FNMA

The Federal National Mortgage Association was created in the 1930s to aid the establishment of a national secondary market for FHA mortgages. Congress always intended the secondary mortgage market facility to be privately owned. But because of the financial risks involved, there were no private initiatives in response to the initial FHA legislation in 1935. The federally sponsored FNMA secondary market facility was chartered in 1938 with the view of eventual private ownership. The agency gradually took on additional responsibilities and operations as a result of the Servicemen's Readjustment Act of 1948 and the Housing and Urban Development (HUD) Act of 1954, but these other operations were spun off in 1968, leaving a new private FNMA with only the secondary market facility.

The secondary market facility was made private because it served and benefited private financial institutions, particularly mortgage bankers. There was no long-term need for federal involvement, because the users of the secondary market service have always been willing to pay for the service. At the same time, the private FNMA operations serve the public interest by providing liquidity to the mortgage instrument.

Congress indicated very strongly in the original legislation the intent that FNMA be a "dealer" in mortgages, but not an investor in competition with private mortgage investors. Section 304(a)(1) of the Charter Act specifically provides: "the volume of the Corporation's purchases and sales . . . should be determined by the Corporation from time to time . . . *as will reasonably prevent excessive use of the Corporation's facility*" [italics added].[6] In spite of this safeguard, the FNMA, for one reason or another, has for the most part been a net purchaser of mortgages. The following statement taken from HUD's 1972 budget illustrates why the facility accumulated mortgages in its early years:

> During World War II, it [FNMA] was primarily interested in providing necessary credit for war housing, without great concern for whether the mortgages were potentially saleable on the private market. Similarly, in the postwar period, a primary purpose was to provide quickly a large volume of credit for housing veterans. It purchased FHA-insured and VA-guaranteed mortgages with minimum regard to whether there was a reasonable early prospect of their resale at the prices for which they were purchased. Meanwhile, as the FHA undertook to assist special classes of housing such as cooperatives, housing in Alaska, and housing near military installations, so did the FNMA.[7]

Congress resisted the trend to a large net volume of purchases by reaffirming its intention of maintaining the "dealer" status of the secondary market facility with enactment of the FNMA Charter Act of 1954. The FNMA was rechartered into a three-part corporation in an attempt to separate those activities that required mortgage investment from secondary market facility. The facility was, as a result of this legislation, to relinquish its role as an investor. During the second half of the 1950s, FNMA accumulated some mortgages, but it liquidated them during the first half of the 1960s. Total holdings were only around $2 billion in 1965. The sharp reduction in the availability of private mortgage credit in 1966 marked a turning point in secondary market activity, however. In the next five years holdings grew at an average annual rate of about 35 percent, rising to $15 billion. This growth rate has declined to about 15 percent during the past five years, but net purchases in absolute terms have increased. By the end of 1975, FNMA's portfolio of home mortgages exceeded $25 billion.

Although amendments in 1968 and 1974 required FNMA to *purchase* mortgages for low and moderate income families through various arrangements with GNMA, the initial cautions against excessive use of the secondary market facility are still part of FNMA's charter. Further evidence that the facility was to remain a dealer is obtained in section 301, Title III, of the National Housing Act. This section indicates that the goal of the secondary market facility is to "provide supplementary assistance to the secondary market for home mortgages by providing *a degree of liquidity* for mortgage investments, thereby improving the distribution of investment capital available for home mortgage financing" [italics added].[8] This suggests that strict adherence to the Charter Act would prohibit substantial mortgage investment and raises the issue of why the FNMA portfolio has grown so rapidly since 1965.

Two separate explanations are required, one for the period before FNMA became public in 1968, and another for the period since 1968. The growth during the earlier period largely reflected the combined forces of rising mortgage rates and the FNMA auction procedure. Prior to 1968, FNMA established an administered price at which it would buy mortgages and another price at which it would sell. These prices were typically set with a lag, partly because of administrative procedures and partly because FNMA felt that this lag helped stabilize interest rates. Because rates rose (prices fell) fairly continuously during this period, the FNMA "buy" price was generally above the market price, and the sell price below market. Beginning in 1968 FNMA introduced the Free Market Auction System. The current practice is for FNMA to receive offers for commitments at its biweekly auctions and then determine the volume of commitments to accept. Consequently, FNMA can control its long-run rate fairly accurately.

A guide to the desired future growth of FNMA is the proposal the FNMA Corporation Planning Department made in late 1976 to the FNMA board of directors that the FNMA continue to accumulate mortgages as long as their yields exceed the FNMA's cost of funds.[9] (This is what might be expected from a profit-maximizing institution.) The question of FNMA growth then becomes a question of what determines the spread between mortgage yields and the FNMA cost of funds and how this spread is likely to change as FNMA grows. The low cost of FNMA debt issues is discussed below. . . .

FNMA's most important advantage in the debt market is the perception of investors that the default risk of FNMA debt is close to zero. This perception is probably accurate, but not because FNMA has a high rating in measures of risk, such as the debt-equity ratio, usually applied to private corporations. FNMA is highly leveraged and therefore extremely risky by these standards. Rather, the perception reflects FNMA's origins as a public agency and the awareness that the federal government is not likely to let FNMA fail. FNMA operates the secondary mortgage market facility, providing a dealer function for HUD as well as private mortgage originators. Moreover, the secretary of HUD has broad regulatory authority over FNMA, and federal regulators have always been extremely reluctant to allow regulated firms to fail, especially when they are large, visible, and important to the entire mortgage banking and housing industries. A second advantage enjoyed by FNMA in the capital market is the special status of FNMA debt as legal investments for federally supervised institutions.[10] In this capacity, FNMA securities can be counted as meeting SLA liquidity requirements and used as collateral for FHLB and Federal Reserve advances; they can be used to meet pledging requirements against government deposits at banks; they can be employed by the Federal Reserve in its open market operations; and so forth. It is noteworthy that although FNMA is private, its ability to intermediate in the capital markets derives from its federal sponsorship and federally granted privileges.

It was for this reason that Congress maintained federal regulation of FNMA when it made the corporation private.

The GNMA

The Government National Mortgage Association (GNMA) was created in 1968 to assume the management and liquidation and special assistance functions previously carried out by FNMA. The special assistance function involves purchase of below-market rate mortgages under various sections of the National Housing Act. These mortgages are then typically sold to FNMA on the private market at a market price. Because the private market requires a market rate of return, the mortgages are sold at a price below par. The loss to GNMA is financed by congressional appropriations. The procedure of GNMA buying and then selling to FNMA is known as the Tandem Plan, because the institutions are acting in tandem.

The GNMA tandem program was initially perceived as a means of maintaining high levels of subsidized housing starts during periods of rising mortgage rates. When mortgage market conditions tightened in the summer of 1971, for instance, the discount on FHA 7 percent home mortgages widened to a range of eight to ten points (the price fell to ninety to ninety-two).[11] Reducing the discount required an increase in the FHA ceiling rate, a move that is always politically unattractive. It was felt that a rise in the FHA coupon ceiling rate and/or an increase in the points charged the borrower would slow the ongoing boom in subsidized construction. In order to avoid a housing crunch, GNMA implicitly "paid" the points by buying the mortgages at par and selling them at a discount.

By 1974, the tandem program was perceived as a major countercyclical housing tool. In January, GNMA was authorized to purchase 200,000 FHA/VA 7.75 percent mortgages. In May, the purchase of another 100,000 FHA/VA mortgages was authorized, this time at a rate of 8 percent. GNMA sold these mortgages at a price averaging about five points less than they paid. The tandem program was expanded to the conventional mortgage market with the passage of the Emergency Home Purchase Act of 1974. As a result, the current tandem program has the capability to subsidize the demand for mortgage credit and simultaneously act as a vehicle to provide additional mortgage funds during a housing downturn. GNMA increased its holdings of home mortgages by almost $3.5 billion in 1974, 1975, and early 1976 and has since liquidated them. There is, however, one undesirable aspect of the tandem programs, that being the giving of the commitments to builders rather than directly to households. The supply of commitments in any given market area is likely to be limited to only one, or at most several builders. Builders without commitments may be forced to cut prices to reduce excess inventories, whereas the builder with the commitment lowers the effective cost without cutting price. Thus, some of the value of the below-market interest rate accrues to builders, rather than to homebuyers.

In addition to operating the tandem program, GNMA has been instrumental in creating an extremely successful new mortgage instrument, the pass-through mortgage-backed security. GNMA guarantees timely principal and interest payment on these securities, but does not hold the mortgages directly. Almost all of the pass-through securities have been issued by mortgage bankers who originate and service the mortgages. The mortgage banker is responsible to GNMA for the interest and principal payments, regardless of the experience of the pool. GNMA limits its risk exposure by establishing capital requirements for participating mortgage bankers and requiring them to hold reserves with GNMA.

Beginning in the summer of 1975, the Chicago Board of Trade implemented a futures market for GNMA pass-through securities. A GNMA future is the right to buy a GNMA security for a specified price at a specified date in the future. This market, which has been extremely active, provides thrift institutions, mortgage bankers, and other originators of mortgages with a vehicle to hedge against the interest rate risk associated with origination. For example, a mortgage banker may obtain a forward commitment from a dealer to underwrite a GNMA pass-through in three months. If mortgage rates fall in the interim, the mortgages he originates for the pool will be valued below par, and the mortgage banker will be forced to absorb the capital loss by selling mortgage interest rate futures contracts. The price of these contracts will fall with the price of his mortgages in the pool; thus the mortgage banker can buy back the futures contract at a profit, offsetting the loss on the mortgage pool.[12] It is worth noting that the short-term horizon of the market prevents thrifts from using it to shift the interest rate risk associated with their investment of short-term deposits in long-term mortgages.

The FHLB and FHLMC

The Federal Home Loan Bank system is yet another product of the Great Depression, created to provide liquidity to a fundamentally illiquid savings and loan industry. Many SLAS failed during these depression years, including many sound institutions with insufficient liquidity. Commercial banks had provided liquidity prior to this, but when faced with a serious liquidity shortage of their own, they were in no position to assist the SLA industry. The advances mechanism of the Home Loan Banks—which have backup authority to borrow from the Federal Reserve System—filled the liquidity void. The level of advances is largely determined by deposit flows. When inflows are large (1971-1972, 1975-1976) advances are repaid; when inflows are small (1969, 1973-1974) advances are built up.

The FHLBS receive no federal appropriations and therefore rely exclusively on income from advances to cover borrowing and administrative costs and to earn a return on equity. Prior to 1970 the system charged its average borrowing cost on its outstanding stock of advances (plus a small markup). Since then the rate on advances has often (1970-1972 and 1975) been set about a half percentage point below the average cost of funds. This has been achieved by a conscious decision to forgo return on equity. Because FHLBS are owned by member SLAS, the decision to lend at below-market rates amounts to a subsidy from institutions (their borrowers and depositors) that borrow relatively less to those that borrow relatively more.

The two periods of below-cost lending are instructive. In April 1970 the FHLBS began to offer one-year fixed-term advances at a cost 25 to 75 basis points below the cost of funds. The stated purpose of this subsidy was to discourage the expected repayment of advances in response to anticipated deposit inflows. Further steps were taken in November 1970 to limit repayments. This program has been estimated to have induced SLAS to purchase $2.5 billion more in home mortgages between the second quarter of 1970 and the first quarter of 1971 (and $2.5 billion less in the following year) than they otherwise would have. The second episode was initiated in May 1974 when $3.5 billion of five-year advances were made at 50 to 80 basis points below the cost of five-year issues. This subsidy program was billed as a response to the 1974 housing slump. The estimate here is that SLAS purchased $1.5 billion more of mortgages during the first half of 1974 (and $1.5 billion less in the first half of 1976) than they otherwise would have. The decision to encourage (subsidize) borrowing during a downturn in housing cycles, such as occurred in early 1970 and 1974, seems quite consistent with the stated objectives of the FHLB Board to stabilize "residential construction and financing in periods when monetary or financial conditions create a dearth of mortgage money."[13]

In June 1978, a third below-cost lending program was announced. Under this program up to $2 billion a year for ten years will be advanced to thrifts that "demonstrate leadership in revitalizing urban housing" at 50 basis points below the FHLB's borrowing cost. This Community Investment Fund is part of the Carter administration's urban program. Rather than using direct tax dollars to subsidize mortgage lending in older urban neighborhoods, other borrowers and depositors are subsidizing this lending through higher charges on their loans and lower returns on their savings.

The Federal Home Loan Mortgage Corporation (FHLMC) was established in 1970 to purchase conventional mortgages from SLAS with the intent of improving the liquidity of the SLA mortgage portfolio. Since that time, FNMA has also been authorized to purchase conventional mortgages, resulting in overlapping authority in this area. The FHLMC steadily accumulated home mortgages through 1975, with their portfolio reaching a peak of $4.5 billion. In 1976 they liquidated over a half billion dollars. While the willingness of FHLMC to reduce its holdings during a single family housing boom contrasts with FNMA behavior, the reduction is quite modest. The rationale for the apparent desire of FHLMC to maintain a mortgage portfolio may be analogous to that underlying the behavior of FNMA. Because mortgage rates exceed the average borrowing costs of FNMA and FHLMC maintaining a portfolio is profitable. Moreover, these profits, as well as most of the servicing and origination fees, accrue to savings and loans which effectively own the FHLMC and sell the mortgages to FHLMC initially.

THE IMPACT OF THE AGENCIES ON INTEREST RATES, CREDIT FLOWS, AND HOUSING

The severe cycles of housing construction during the past decade have been attributed primarily to periodic shortages of mortgage credit. Prior to 1966, efforts to increase the supply of mortgage credit focused on smoothing the flow of funds to the mortgage market by providing liquidity both to mortgage lending institutions (FHLB) and to the mortgage instrument (FNMA) and by reducing the risk of mortgage investment (FHA). The goal of these policies was to improve the efficiency of the mortgage market so that it could attract a competitive market share of existing savings. The large and continued accumulation of mortgages under federal auspices since 1966 suggests that the intent of policy has shifted to diverting a greater than competitive market share of savings to housing in an attempt to achieve the legislated housing goal, embodied in the Housing and Urban Development Act of 1968, of adding 26 million new or rehabilitated housing units to the nation's housing stock by 1978.[14]

The impact of agency activities on home mortgages flows and residential construction expenditures is the subject of much debate. At one extreme are those who contend that, because credit rationing is so pervasive in the home mortgage market, agency mortgage purchases induce a like increase in household mortgage supply and housing expenditures. At the other extreme are those who contend that because funds flow freely from one market to another, the increase in agency mortgage market support will have no impact either on these quantities or on relative interest rates. At issue is the extent to which issues of securities by agencies to finance purchases of home mortgages ultimately induce other sectors to invest less, freeing up resources for housing production.

The prospects of other sectors sharply reducing their ultimate credit demands in response to small increases in borrowing rates are slim. Governments continue to borrow to finance operating deficits, for example. While business firms do shift their borrowing pattern somewhat to minimize total borrowing costs, their total borrowing is reduced by much less than the agency security issues. The extent to which agency intermediation ''crowds out'' other borrowers depends on the relative elasticities of the supply of mortgages vis-à-vis the supply of other securities. Empirical estimates indicate that the corporate demand for funds is much less elastic than household demand. State and local government demand appears to be moderately less elastic, while U.S. government borrowing is totally inelastic with respect to interest rates. These relative elasticities suggest that agency mortgage market purchases will result in only marginal increases in the total supply of mortgage credit, primarily at the expense of state and local governments.

This hypothesis is consistent with the results of simulations of a flow-of-funds model reported by Hendershott and Villani.[15] These results imply that, for every $1 billion infusion of mortgage credit by agencies, $850 million "leaks" from the mortgage market. Through a series of complex portfolio adjustments by many investors, the financial system channels these funds to the market for agency securities. This decrease of $150 million in the borrowing by other sectors is achieved only by a substantial increase in the borrowing rates of these sectors.

What do these results imply for the net impact of direct federal credit market intervention on the mortgage and housing stock during the past decade? Net federal support for the home mortgage market increased by over $42 billion between 1965 to the end of 1975. This accumulation is estimated to have increased the stock of home mortgages by just less than $7 billion (.15 times $42 billion). Given a loan-to-value ratio of .75, the stock of housing increased by about $10 billion as a result of the federal support. And if the loan-to-value ratio increases, as might be expected, the increase is even less. To put this impact in better perspective, the household housing stock has recently been valued at nearly a trillion dollars by the Department of Commerce.[16] Thus, agency activity increased the housing stock by about 1 percent in the past decade.

The finding that agencies had a relatively small impact on the total quantity of mortgage credit suggests that other mortgage investors must have left the market. Not surprisingly, it was less restricted investors, such as life insurance companies (LICS), private pension funds (PPFS), and mutual savings banks (MSBS), that shifted into other assets. These portfolio shifts are illustrated in Figure 1 which contains the shares of home mortgages held by various institutions. The share held by LICS and PPFS has fallen throughout the past two decades, but the decline during the last decade was significantly more precipitous. The decline during the earlier decade is primarily attributable to the more rapid asset growth of SLAS, a captive of the mortgage market. Portfolio shifting accounted for a smaller share; the percentage of total LIC and PPF assets invested in home mortgages fell only slightly from 18 percent in 1956 to about 14 percent in 1966. During the decade the two institutions accumulated $15 billion in home mortgages.

With the accelerated growth of agencies (and mortgage pools) beginning in 1966, LICS and PPFS literally abandoned the home mortgage market. During the 1966-1975 decade their aggregate holdings fell back to the 1955 level. The switch in mortgage holdings from LICS and PPFS to agencies is illustrated vividly in Figure 1. The combined share of the federally sponsored credit agencies, including the pools, and the private discretionary investors remained roughly constant at 17 percent of the market between 1965 and 1975, but the relative share of agencies has increased sharply from 2 percent to 12 percent.

The other discretionary sector whose behavior changed sharply around the middle 1960s is mutual savings banks. During the 1956-1965 period over 70 percent of the increase in their assets was in the form of home mortgages; during the 1966-1975 decade this percentage fell to 32 percent.

FIGURE 1
Relative Shares of Home Mortgages Outstanding Held by Various
Sectors, 1957 to 1975

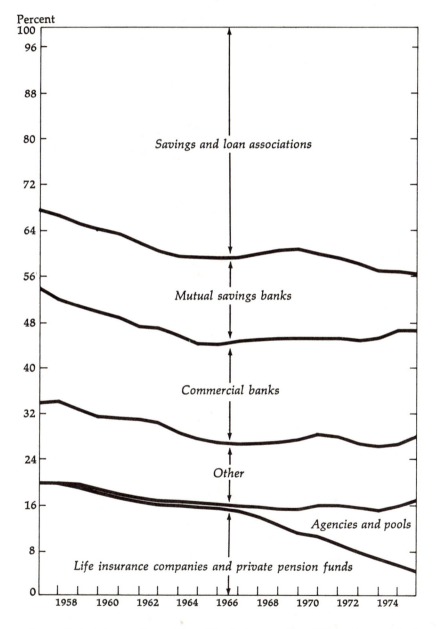

FIGURE 2
Observed and Adjusted Spreads Between Home Mortgage
and Corporate Bond Rates
(percentage points)

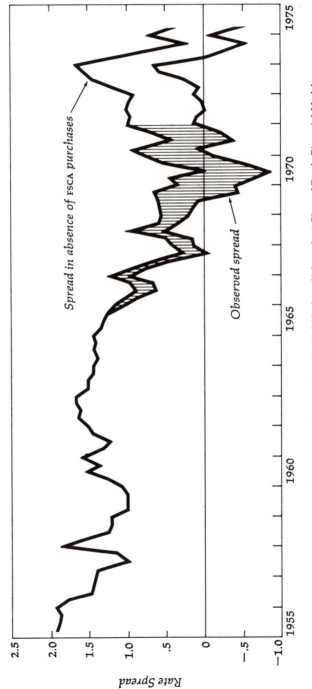

Source: Reproduced from Patric H. Hendershott, *Understanding Capital Markets, Volume 1 : A Flow-of-Funds Financial Model* (Lexington, Mass.: Lexington Books, 1977), p. 242.

The relative shift of discretionary investors out of home mortgages was a rational response to a decline in the relative yield on mortgages induced by the agency purchases. The impact of agencies on the home mortgage rate can be illustrated with reference to the spread between the home mortgage rate and the corporate bond rate plotted in Figure 2.The average spread, which oscillated around 1.33 percentage points during the 1956-1965 period, fell to zero by 1971, and has since fluctuated around this low level. The historical spread was due to the servicing costs and default-risk and marketability premiums built into home mortgage rates. Timothy Q. Cook considered numerous possible explanations for the fall in the rate spread, including changes in the risk, marketability, and servicing costs.[17] He concludes that increased mortgage purchases of sponsored agencies were probably the principal cause.

The Hendershott and Villani model simulations support Cook's hypothesis. Agency mortgage purchases are calculated as having reduced the spread between the yields on home mortgages and corporate bonds by 87 basis points, or approximately two-thirds of the observed decline. This impact on the interest rate differential is indicated in Figure 2 by the hatched area. In the absence of the activities of the agencies, the mortgage rate would have been at the upper bound of the area; the observed rate is the lower bound. While the estimated impact of the agencies on the home mortgage rate may be on the high side, it seems clear that the agencies have reduced the home mortgage rate by at least a half percentage point from what it would have been in the absence of the expansion in their activities.

SUMMARY

Federal participation in the home mortgage market has grown substantially during the past decade. The percentage of the stock of home mortgages effectively held by the federal government and its sponsored agencies rose from 5 percent in 1965 to 15 percent in 1975. Federal supply of home mortgage credit takes three general forms: (1) direct mortgage purchases by FNMA, FHLMC, and GNMA; (2) indirect purchases of SLAS financed by advances (loans) from the FHLBS; and (3) indirect purchases of institutions other than SLAS induced by the federal guaranteeing of mortgage pools. In the second half of the 1960s, the increased federal role was due to growth in FNMA; in the 1970s the mortgage pools have constituted the primary federal impetus. Advances have exhibited a strong cyclical movement around a trend approximating the growth rate of total home mortgage debt.

The growth of the sponsored agencies, particularly FNMA, is not called for in their charters. The primary cause of the growth appears to be the monetary reward to be gained. Because FNMA can borrow at virtually the risk-free Treasury rate, borrowing and investing in mortgages is profitable. It is profitable both for FNMA shareholders and for mortgage bankers who originate and service most of the mortgages FNMA purchases. One interpretation of the recent buildup of FHLMC's holdings (and the upward trend in the level of advances) is that SLAS, too, decided to participate in this sure thing. The implicit profits of FHLMC indirectly accrue to them, and they also sell the mortgages to FHLMC, earning the origination and servicing fees. The reason why these organizations are allowed to violate the intent, if not the exact wording, of their charter and are allowed to use their special status as federal agencies to reap profits for themselves and their constituencies is uncertain. However, a likely explanation, or at least a prerequisite to the continuation, of these activities is the prohousing bias of the relevant congressional committees—Banking, Housing, and Urban Affairs in the Senate and Banking, Finance, and Urban Affairs in the House. This same bias would explain why the extraordinary growth in the mortgage pools has not been questioned.

The most obvious impact of the agencies has been the reduction in the home mortgage rate relative to other rates and the consequent shift of discretionary investors—life insurance companies, pension funds, and mutual savings banks to some extent—out of the home mortgage market. Given this shift, the increase in total mortgage credit has been far less than the increase in that supplied by the agencies (one estimate is only 15 percent). While there has almost certainly been some positive stimulus to housing, the magnitude has apparently not been large. In our view, . . . the primary impact of the creeping federalization of the home mortgage market has been a gain (lower mortgage rate) for homeowners who would have purchased their homes in the absence of the agency actions and a loss (lower deposit rate) for depositors. On the other hand, the cyclical lending of FHLBS to SLAS has obviously played an important and necessary (in our regulated financial system) role for housing.

NOTES

1. The rise in advances in 1966 was limited by liquidity problems within the FHLB system. The system solved this problem by borrowing longer term in sufficient quantities to enable accumulation of short-term asset holdings. These holdings can be drawn down to make advances when the demand for such funds rises.
2. Net advances were 5.1 percent of SLA assets at the end of 1965 and 4.8 percent at the end of 1976. The peak of this ratio, 9.4 percent, occurred at the end of 1974.
3. FHLMC actually issues securities; GNMA simply guarantees the mortgage pools themselves. The securities/pools are issued in denominations of $25,000. The rationale for the high denomination is probably the same as that for the minimum $10,000 denomination in which Treasury bills are sold—to prohibit depositors with limited financial wealth from shifting out of deposits.
4. A more conservative estimate is obtained by assuming that only three-quarters of net advances and mortgage pools other than those held by SLAS constitute support of the home mortgage market. The ratio of direct plus 75 percent of indirect support to total mortgage debt also tripled between 1965 and 1975, rising from .045 to .135.
5. For a full discussion of the growth in federal support of this market, see Leo Grebler, "The Role of the Public Sector in Residential Financing," *Resources for Housing*, Proceedings of the First Annual Conference, FHLB of San Francisco, 1975, pp. 67-116.
6. National Housing Act, section 304(a)(1); 12 U.S.C. 1719 (a)(1).

7. Department of Housing and Urban Development, Summary of Budget Authorizations and Expenditures for Fiscal Year 1972, Office of the Secretary, January 1971.
8. National Housing Act, Title III—National Mortgage Associations, Public Law 479, 73rd Congress, 48 Stat. 1246, 12 U.S.C. 1701.
9. "FNMA's Financial Goals," Office of Corporate Planning, April 12, 1976, unpublished report of the FNMA.
10. FNMA is also only one of two (the other is FHLBS) privately owned corporations that benefit from a "Treasury Backstop Authority" which authorizes the secretary of the Treasury to purchase up to $2¼ billion of FNMA obligations at any one time.
11. A full discussion of FHA ceiling rates, "points," and their impact is given in chapter 4 of *Regulation and Reform of the Housing Finance System*.
12. For a discussion of the operation of this market, see Richard Sandor, "Trading Mortgage Interest-Rate Futures," FHLB *Journal*, September 1975, pp. 2-9.
13. *Savings and Loan Fact Book*, United States League of Savings Associations, Chicago, 1976, p. 94.
14. Housing and Urban Development Act of 1968, Public Law 90-448, 82 Stat. 476, 601 12 U.S.C. 1701 and 42 U.S.C. 1441a.
15. Patric H. Hendershott and Kevin E. Villani, "The Federally Sponsored Credit Agencies, Their Behavior and Impact," in R. Buckley, J. Tuccillo, and K. Villani, eds., *Capital Markets and the Housing Sector: Perspectives on Financial Reform* (Cambridge, Mass.: Ballinger Publishing Company, 1977), pp. 291-309.
16. John C. Musgrave, "Fixed Nonresidential Business and Residential Capital in the United States, 1925-75," *Survey of Current Business*, April 1976, Table 6, p. 51.
17. Timothy Q. Cook, "The Residential Mortgage Market in Recent Years," *Economic Review*, FRB of Richmond, September/October 1974, pp. 3-18.

8

The Evolution of Housing and Its Social Compact

George Sternlieb and James W. Hughes

The United States is in the process of dismantling the very apparatus that has woven together our social and political fabric since the Great Depression. The 1980 Census—indicating that 64.4 percent of the nation's households own their own homes—may well mark the high point of an incredible ascension which moved the America of 1930—a land primarily of renters—to one of owners— and owners of a product which is the envy of the rest of the world.

Housing is not merely a refuge from the elements; it is an essential tool binding together an America of enormously varied humanity. Home ownership glues people to the system. There is an implicit promise that if we maintain the work and thrift habits of yore, we can enjoy the central material symbols of belonging—and chief among them is the real potential of home ownership.

We have reached a historic turning point in home ownership. According to the statistical evidence, home ownership is now beginning to decline, a decline that is the deliberate result of an implicit public policy assault. The seemingly immortal housing boom of the post-World War II era was abruptly terminated in 1978-79 in an attempt to cope with the fiscal excesses accumulated over the preceding decade. Housing was removed from its sheltered credit market standing, seriously threatening the capacity for future home ownership. But we are not

From *Urban Land*, Vol. 41, No. 12, 17-20. Reprinted with permission from *Urban Land*, December, 1982, published by the Urban Land Institute, 1090 Vermont Avenue, N.W., Washington, D.C. 20005.

merely altering the shape of the shelter industry; rather, we are threatening the harmony which has characterized the last half-century.

In 1931, President Hoover established a planning committee on housing. In his charge, he stressed that "nothing contributes more to happiness or sound social stability than . . . homes." Even before the convening of the committee, Hoover announced his intention to recommend to the Congress what he called " . . . a system of home loan discount banks." But it was not until 1933, when the Home Owners Loan Act was passed, that the Federal Home Loan Bank System was established.

The system, in a synopsis by Milton Semer, was:

> . . .conceived broadly and simply . . . to have a dual function: first, to provide a means for accumulating long-term savings of individuals and families, encouraging such savings; and second, plowing the capital thus accumulated back into housing in the form of first mortgage loans for the building or purchase of homes. The instrumentalities were not conceived of as banks in the ordinary sense and were clearly distinguished from commercial institutions. Underlying this approach were two closely related propositions: first, the encouragement of long-term savings and habits of thrift was in the best interests of people and stability generally, especially home ownership, and second, that long-term individual savings were a particularly appropriate source of funds for home mortgage investment. They were thus distinguished from the more volatile flow of funds into and out of the general investment markets.

The concepts of stability and trust permeated the structure and terminology of these financial institutions. The matrix of enabling legislation which emerged thus had as its central instrument specialized lending institutions for housing, and this marked the true emergence of the thrift industry.

Generous tax-exemption provisions were provided for these institutions in return for their concentration on housing. This certification provided assurance to depositors. At the same time, the FHA-insured mortgages revitalized confidence both on the part of depositors and lenders. The development of the long-term self-amortizing loan swept the nation and became the standard not only for government-insured mortgages but also for uninsured ones.

In the heart of the economic darkness that was the Great Depression, both Republicans and Democrats alike moved to strengthen and revitalize a concept as old as America—the ownership of real property—merely shifting it from the rural scene to the urban and suburban one. We supplemented the vision of the independent farmer, viewed by Jefferson as the backbone of the nation, with a reality of the homeowner whose acreage may have been relatively minute, but whose sense of dignity and honor was equally enhanced by the new shelter emphasis.

Recovering from the Depression was a long and painful process. The new housing tools provided a source of inspiration not only to those who could take advantage of them but also to others who could hope and aspire to a future which would include a home of their own. And the trauma of World War II generated a remarkably homogeneous set of shared values about the future to come.

The enormous buildup of home-front capital also enabled the era of the American dream house to take place. G.I. and defense-worker savings combined with the dreams and aspirations of home ownership, long frustrated by the economic constraints of the 1930s and war, set the stage for America's "golden housing era."

But this could not have reached reality without the basic financial infrastructure which had been set in place in the 1930s. The specialized housing lending institutions, fortified increasingly by the development of secondary financial markets which provided them with greater liquidity, and the long-term fixed-rate self-amortizing mortgage, were key to this process.

The America of the late 1940s and 1950s believed in housing, believed in growth, believed in development. Without this credo, there could not have been the emergence of the large-scale homebuilders and land developers who overcame the housing shortages bedeviling the rest of the world—and provided housing which most Americans could afford.

Between 1950 and 1970, the nation's overall housing inventory increased by 50 percent—21 million units—while median family incomes virtually doubled in real terms (see Figure 1). The positive relationship between housing cost burdens and growing affluence permitted home ownership rates to soar beyond 62 percent (see Figure 2). And the nation's minorities also shared in these gains. Between 1940 and 1970, the home ownership rates of black and "other" households surged from 24 percent to 42 percent. The housing momentum of America was unprecedented.

The advances registered in the 20 years prior to 1970 served only as a prelude to the frantic activity of the 1970s. Between 1970 and 1980, we added almost 20 million units to the nation's shelter stock, replicating in one decade the achievements of the previous two. The 1970s turned out to be the most prolific housing decade ever. Not only were unsurpassed quantities of housing delivered to America's citizenry, but also the quality of the product reached levels inconceivable to consumers of an earlier generation.

By 1973, the year of the oil embargo, the long-sustained march of ever-increasing affluence for the American family halted. As shown in Figure 1, median family income in constant dollars peaked in 1973. By 1981, the median family income in America was almost $2,300 below the 1973 high.

Housing production accelerated, however. Land costs moved from 12 percent of total house costs to 20 and 30 percent and even more. It was not that Americans had run out of land, but rather that restrictive zoning practices made developable land a relatively scarce commodity. When the increases in raw land were compounded by the rise in locally mandated requirements for infrastructure, with sewer hookup charges in some jurisdictions moving into the $3,000 to $5,000 range, accompanied by requirements for land dedication to service future generations, the results added to the inflation in housing prices.

Figure 1
Median Family Income: 1950 to 1981
(Current and Constant 1981 Dollars)

	Current Dollars	Constant 1981 Dollars
1950	$3,310	$12,549
1955	4,418	15,003
1960	5,620	17,259
1965	6,957	20,054
1970	9,867	23,111
1973	12,051	24,663
1980	21,023	23,204
1981	22,388	22,388
Gains in Real Income (Constant 1981 Dollars)		
1950 to 1960	$4,710	37.5%
1960 to 1970	5,852	33.9
1970 to 1973	1,552	6.7
1973 to 1981	−2,275	−9.2

Source: U.S. Bureau of the Census, Current Population Reports, Series P-60, No. 134, *Money Income and Poverty Status of Families and Persons in the United States: 1981* (Advance Data From the March 1982 *Current Population Survey*). U.S.Government Printing Office, Washington, D.C., 1982.

Lagging real incomes, a sagging dollar in the international arena, unprecedented inflation with deepening personal tax bites and accelerating housing prices reinforced the classic belief of housing as a safe haven. And consumers rather than government adopted this notion with a vengeance. Housing was seen as a rare refuge in an increasingly uncertain and hostile environment. Driven to this sanctuary, people perjured themselves in filling out mortgage applications and were willing to pay exorbitant shares of their income to board the housing train. Housing in America became much more important, as a form of investment, of forced savings (and tax savings), and more as a refuge from inflation than as a refuge from the elements.

What permitted a scared America to achieve such sanctuary was the continued availability of New Deal-originated mortgage instruments—designed for stable noninflationary economic environments—extended into a period characterized by strikingly new terms. They made housing borrowing an unprecedented bargain and fed an insatiable housing demand, which in itself directly served to escalate the upward surge in housing costs.

Much bemoaned but unacted upon during this time was the increasing failure of the industry to provide new products for first-time homebuyers. Only those with a "trade-in" could afford the market. At the same time, housing and the old financial order were subjected to additional stresses; the house became a vehicle for maintaining consumption patterns in the face of stagnating incomes. Home ownership became not only the symbol of the good life, it became a means for financing its continuance. Who needed a formal savings account when the house had become the chief repository of personal stored wealth? The consumption ethic conquered the habits of thrift assiduously cultivated in the original social housing compact. Government policy made losers of savers and winners of speculators.

The thrift industry also was suffering. While disintermediation—the flow of savings out of thrift institutions into more rewarding havens—was far from a novelty, it was a built-in regulator of the total economic system. As funds flowed out of the thrifts, housing and related industries in turn would be slowed, thus braking the economy. Thrift institutions, attempting to stabilize their annual operating statements, had long argued for a broadening of their deposit-gathering capacities. The Carter administration invented the certificate of deposit. This destroyed the wall that had been erected between general market interest rates and the specific functioning of the housing market as we had known it for decades past. Within very short order, the thrift institutions lending money came not from the conventional sources of the past but rather from CDs and a range of other money-market types of borrowing. We had traded low-cost funds for low-cost housing for money availability at a high cost. Instead of stemming inflation, we fed it.

The Federal Reserve, with its October 1979 switch to monetarism, signaled the explicit retreat from the "excesses" of the recent past. The federal government attempted to curb the housing demand hysteria that it created and for which it was responsible. Too much capital for housing and "reindustrialization" were the new catch phrases voiced in a variety of quarters. Housing's priority status within the nation's credit markets was terminated. We moved toward a nondifferentiated, homogeneous financial market.

The transition was not gradual and orderly. Mortgage costs soared with long-term interest rates moving up to the 18 percent level. Fewer and fewer potential buyers could qualify for a loan at these levels, regardless of their desperation. Annual average housing starts during 1981 and 1982 were only half the two million annual starts achieved in both 1977 and 1978.

When current housing mechanisms are examined, there is a dreadful feeling of déjà vu. In essence we have spent the last four years reinventing just those perils and shortcomings of the market which were thought long cured. Before the Home Owners' Loan Act of 1933, for example, it was customary for a homebuyer to obtain two or three separate mortgage loans. This was necessitated by the low level of coverage of first mortgages—they were relatively short term, many running for five years or less. They were not amortized and the balloon payments fell due at the end of the short term of the mortgage. Homeowner aspirants of today find such strictures commonplace.

The peaks and troughs of annual housing starts are far from a novelty. Our current situation is much more consequential. It is not an acute attack which will pass in a year or two, but it gives every evidence of being a long-term chronic wasting disease. We have changed the shape of the housing delivery system by submerging its financial requirements.

The issue of inflation is used practically as a catch-all explanation of all of the ills on the domestic scene. And, certainly this is the case in terms of housing. Without minimizing inflationary stresses the disease is in the process of being cured. It would be the height of foolishness to fail to couple the recuperation with appropriate structural rebuilding. But this certainly is not taking place.

The full measure and future implications of this reality are just beginning to be felt. As yet the owners in residency—particularly if they are long term—are living so cheaply as to be relatively unaffected. The newcomers to the scene, however, arrive at the station just as the housing train has departed. Certainly there are substitutions in consumer behavior that are and will continue to take place but they are much more limited. And hedonistic expenditure does not provide a surrogate for housing. It does not require an overly active imagination to forecast a rising tide of discontent, and the questioning of a system which cannot provide the trophies of hard work and a disciplined approach to living.

The recognition of the fragmentation of America has been widespread. The ravages of sustained inflation and income stagnation have, from a marketing perspective, diminished the vast middle market. In its stead, consumer segmentation has become the new religion: the isolation of affluent elite enclaves. Lost in the shuffle is the broad middle.

In most of the world the predominant need is for housing as shelter—as protection against the elements and as a means of providing basic physical security. Most Americans, however, are fortunate enough to have a society in which housing standards have risen to the point where they serve much more significantly as focal points for the good life, as prestige, and as measures of success.

We still have not sketched out a road map which takes the patterns of shelter purchasing, of lifestyle, of symbol and reality, from those which evolved historically to the requirements and limitations of the future. The failure to generate policy within a more adequate fuller range of priorities is evident—and will be even more costly tomorrow unless a more creative conceptual apparatus is created.

The ameliorative measures in housing do not require a wholesale return to the patterning of yesterday. There are immediate approaches which could produce significant results. It should be noted in this context that the bulk of the so-called "new creative mortgages" avoid the realities. Most of them presume a continuance of inflation which will support relatively low payment levels at the beginning of their tenure, and much higher ones later on.

Figure 2
Home Ownership Rates: 1920 to 1980*

	Total	White	Black and Other
1920	45.6%	48.2%	23.9%
1930	47.8	50.2	25.2
1940	43.6	45.7	23.6
1950	55.0	57.0	34.9
1960	61.9	64.4	38.4
1970	62.9	65.4	42.0
1973	64.4	67.1	43.4
1979	65.4	68.4	44.5
1980	64.4	N.A.	N.A.

*Percent of total households who are owners.
Source: U.S. Department of Commerce, Bureau of the Census, *Statistical Abstract of the United States: 1981* (Washington, D.C., 1981).

All the forms of renegotiated-term mortgages suffer from the lack of projectability that they impose upon the borrower. In the midst of much beating of the breast that the long-term mortgage is dead, there are opportunities to revive it. These could include such elements as permitting individual retirement accounts to be used for first-time housing purchases without penalty. This type of approach has become a very fruitful staple in many of the industrialized nations.

The working couple, putting $4,000 a year in their IRA, achieves a reduction of taxes on this sum plus exemption on the earnings of the principal. This is an enormously potent locomotive which should be attached to the housing train. It should further be noted that this vehicle could be structured so that the rates of return are fully compatible with the requirements of a mortgage—thus avoiding the wait for return of mortgage interest rates to the single-digit level.

Within the context of a need for a half-step housing mechanism, given the reduced shelter buying power of Americans, further attention to the possibilities of rental/condominium conversion is clearly warranted. And here, certainly, is an area in which the Administration's commitment to reducing government infringement would pay great dividends—given local strictures that have risen on condo conversion. The inexpensive condo must be joined by modest cost, one-family housing in order to balance the reduced housing buying power that has characterized post-1973 Americans.

Systems that do not deliver the goods invite alternatives that promise more. Americans have a marvelous capacity to rally around the flag at a time of stress. It is time now, however, to structure tomorrow. The time for belaboring past sins must give way to more positive assertion of priorities.

9

Housing Finance in the 1980s:
Economic Factors Indicate Future Directions

Kent W. Colton

In the 1930s, the system of housing finance in the United States was in shambles. The country was in the middle of a serious depression, and, in 1931, housing starts dropped disastrously to 100,000. Further, owners of existing housing faced distress since homes at that time were financed almost exclusively through the use of short-term mortgages with a balloon payment that was due at the end of the mortgage term. With money extremely scarce, home owners were unable to pay off or refinance the balloon loan, and financial institutions faced numerous defaulted, non-yielding mortgages.

The country survived the crisis of the 1930s through a combination of ingenuity and public and private cooperation. The mortgage instrument was restructured and now very few home buyers can remember anything but the standard rate fixed payment mortgage. Also out of that crisis came the Federal Home Loan Bank System, the National Housing Act of 1934, the Federal Housing Administration and an initial commitment to government assistance in the area of housing.

As the 1980s begin, the country faces another era of rapid change in the system of housing finance. Twenty years from now, one will find the changes in this period to be as significant as those in the 1930s, and perhaps as traumatic. Al-

From *Journal of Housing*, Vol. 43 (January 1981), pp. 15-20. Reprinted by permission of the *Journal of Housing*.

ready, significant alteration has been seen, but the revolution is not over, and the future will once again depend on the ability to adapt.

In order to review housing finance in the 1980s, one must examine the problem and identify the nature and process of change. Implications of these changes for housing related financial institutions, housing in general, and multi-family and assisted housing in particular then can be analyzed.

WHAT IS THE PROBLEM?

The United States has a unique system of housing finance and financial institutions. Composed of over 14,000 commercial banks, 4,000 savings and loan associations, almost 500 mutual savings banks, and over 21,000 credit unions, these institutions—both federally and state chartered—form a crazy-quilt that has done a remarkable job of serving the financial needs of the country over the last 40 years.

However, during the past decade and a half, the residential construction industry has experienced three major housing cycles, and the country is now in the process of a fourth. Such cycles are costly, not only to home buyers who cannot obtain financing, but they also lead to increased unemployment, an imbalance in building materials, and added inflationary pressures. Although the housing finance system has not caused such problems, it has aggravated the situation. When periods of high interest rates occurred, by law and by regulation, mortgage oriented "thrift" institutions have been restricted—on the asset side of their balance sheets—primarily to long-term mortgages. Thus, as rates rose, the interest the institutions could earn on their portfolios has been relatively fixed.

On the liability side, thrift institutions have been limited in the types of deposits they could accept. Starting in 1966, Regulation Q ceilings were applied to thrift institutions in order to keep the cost of deposits down and to avoid excessive competition, especially with commercial banks. Such ceilings reduced competition to thrift institutions from commercial banks for deposit funds, but they were ineffective in preventing competition from other financial markets. This led to disintermediation and a lack of mortgage money during past periods of tight credit.

Problems concerning the volatility of savings deposits influence all financial institutions, but they are acutely applicable to thrift institutions because of their restricted mix of assets and liabilities. For example, the share of mortgages held by savings and loan firms increased from 29.7 percent in 1946 to 45-47 percent in more recent years. However, as savings and loans have become more important in mortgage lending, they also have accounted for a larger share of the fluctuations during periods of tight credit and disintermediation. Although savings and loans financed around 40-50 percent of the residential mortgages over the last decade, they accounted for a much larger share of the volatility in the flow of money for housing. Although the savings and loan share of net increases in home lending climbed to as high as 60 percent in the early 1970s, during times of tight credit in late 1974—the very time when mortgage flows were critical in reducing cyclical fluctuations—the percent of savings and loan investment in the mortgage market dropped sharply to around 30 percent. The same phenomenon is occurring during this current cycle. Savings and loan mortgage lending climbed to between 50 and 60 percent of the dollars loaned during the rebound of 1976 and 1977, but in 1979 and 1980 the percentage dropped significantly. In the first quarter of 1980, savings and loans provided only 25 percent of the home mortgage lending. The savings and loan industry has suffered from volatility, and the home buyer and the housing industry have been hurt in the process.

CHANGE AND REFORM

In order to address these problems, a number of proposals have been made for the comprehensive reform of financial institutions. The recent dialogue began more than a decade ago with the President's Commission on Financial Structure and Regulation, commonly referred to as the Hunt Commission. Since that time, there has been a wide range of special studies and proposed legislation. Some of these include the financial institutions act passed by the Senate in 1975, the House of Representatives' study on Financial Institutions and the Nation's Economy, the Regulation Q Task Force established by the Carter Administration, the checking account equity act passed by the House in 1979, and, finally, in March of 1980, the passage of the depository institutions deregulation and monetary control act.

The passage of this act undoubtedly brings the most far-reaching changes that have been seen concerning financial institutions and systems of housing finance since the 1930s. Amazingly consistent with the ideas that have been discussed throughout the decade, the provisions in the new bill generally focus on six areas: broadening the deposit/liability powers of thrift institutions, broadening the investment/asset powers of thrift institutions, expanding the number of alternative mortgage instruments, removing or providing greater flexibility for deposit rate ceilings, the override of state usury ceilings, and reserve requirements for all depository institutions. (See Exhibit 1.)

When Congress finally acted, a substantial reform law was passed, and the changes listed above obviously mean a major alteration in the financial structure and system of housing finance. However, in order to understand the forces that impact the future, it is important to ask why Congress took so long to pass the legislation, and what forces finally brought about financial institution reform.

PASSAGE OF DIDMCA

Congress took over a decade to pass financial institution reform primarily because of the divergent views and approaches found among the interests involved

Exhibit 1

Alternative Proposals for Change at the Congressional Level

	Hunt Commission	FIA (Senate)	FRA-FINE (House)	Consumer Checking Account Equity Act (House)	Deposit Institution Deregulation Act (Senate)	House/Senate Compromise Regarding 1979 Court Decision	Depository Institutions Deregulation and Monetary Control Act of 1980
Broaden deposit liability powers	X	X	X	X[3]	X	X[6]	X
Broaden investment asset powers	X	X	X		X		X
Expand the number of alternative mortgage instruments	X		X[1]		X[4]		X[4]
Remove deposit rate ceilings	X	X			X		X[8]
Tax credit and other housing incentives	X	X	X[2]		X[5]	X[7]	X[9]
Results	Basis for discussion, but many reforms have not been enacted.	Passed Senate Dec. 1975 but never considered in House.	Split into three separate bills, but none passed.	Passed House Sept., 1979; stalemate conference with Senate.	Passed Senate Nov., 1979; stalemate conference with House.	Authorized court banned items, but only until March 31, 1980.	Passed by the House and Senate and signed into law at the end of March 1980.

Notes:

1. Called for flexibility in deposit rate ceilings, but tied the ceiling to the amount of assets in housing.
2. Included special tax and other incentives for financial institutions to invest in low- and moderate-income housing.
3. Broadened powers somewhat but only NOW accounts, share drafts, remote service units (RSUs) and automatic transfers.
4. Includes same mortgage lending powers for S&L's as for commercal banks. Would therefore legalize a full range of alternative mortgage instruments, although authorizing regulations would still be necessary.
5. No HMC, but preempts state usury ceilings.
6. Only authorizes share drafts, RSUs, and automatic transfer.
7. Preempts state usury ceilings but only until March 31, 1980.
8. Phases out Regulation Q rate ceilings over six years, subject to the actions of a Depository Institutions Deregulation Committee.
9. Preempts state usury ceilings, but provides affected states the right to override the preemption.

in the reform process. At least six factors interact and create change in the area of housing finance: (1) the federal government, especially the executive branch and the Congress; (2) regulatory agencies, including regulators at both the state and federal level; (3) concerned industries, including not only financial institutions, but also all of the housing oriented interests such as home builders, realtors, housing officials, and housing manufacturers; (4) technological innovations; (5) public consumer pressures; and (6) economic and market conditions such as rising inflation and interest rates.

Competition among one of these factors—the concerned industries—has been the major cause for the decade of congressional inaction. As the competing interests battled within the framework of financial reform, each group was able to show strength in working against various dimensions of reform. The result was the neutralizing of the overall influence of the housing related interests.

In addition to the failure of the concerned housing related industries to move towards reform, there also has been a paralysis at the federal government level, especially in Congress. Throughout the decade of the 1970s, the House and Senate took very different positions on financial reform. In fact, it is quite likely that nothing would have happened without action by the federal courts that ruled that automatic transfers, remote service units, and share drafts were illegal. This focussed attention and required compromise, and without such judicial action, the legislative reform might still be pending.

In view of the absence of a positive push for comprehensive reform from the concerned industries and the federal government during the decade of the 1970s, change primarily has been left to the other four factors—economic and market forces, technology, consumer pressure, and piecemeal regulatory revision. Still, the impact of these factors has been significant; in fact, they have provided the primary force in achieving financial reform.

THE FORCES BEHIND FINANCIAL REFORM

After examining the congressional impasse for the past decade, there may be a temptation to conclude that little reform occurred until March 1980. This is far from true. Although national legislation was slow in coming, a significant "silent revolution" has been under way for some time. It began somewhat slowly in the early 1970s, but by the end of the decade it was moving rapidly, providing a sharply different environment for the activities of financial institutions in the 1980s.

The list of reforms is extensive, but a few of them include: (1) money markets and other rate sensitive deposit certificates, now 50 percent of all deposits in federally chartered savings and loan institutions, an astounding growth from nothing just two and a half years ago; (2) expanded depository powers, most notably negotiable orders of withdrawal; (3) alternative mortgage instruments, including variable rate, graduated payment, reverse annuity, renegotiable rate, shared appreciation, and graduated payment adjustable mortgages; (4) mortgage backed securities and expanded secondary markets, a significant source of funds for single- and multi-family housing; (5) state housing finance agencies and mortgage revenue bonds; and (6) electronic fund transfer systems, a technological innovation.

By the time Congress passed DIDMCA in March 1980, the federal government was no longer the most important factor in the process of change. Indeed, the action by Congress and pressures from the concerned industry had been superceded by the "silent revolution" and the other factors involved in the change process—the market place, consumer pressure, regulatory action, and the technology. Whether one wanted the new bill or not, by the time it passed, it didn't matter; Congress was only legitimizing what was already happening.

IMPLICATIONS FOR THE FUTURE

In the years to come, there undoubtedly will be a number of important and even profound changes. First, the liability structure for savings and loans has been substantially altered; this movement can be expected to continue and it will place increasing pressure on the profits of thrift institutions and on mortgage rates.

Second, the negative earnings that a number of institutions are experiencing—in 1980, the average return on assets was the lowest on record—and the dependence on the money market certificate will heighten the need for further flexibility on the asset side of the thrift portfolio. The standard payment fixed term mortgage may survive, but only along with a wide range of other alternatives. As these new alternatives develop, one must focus on the needs of both the borrower and the lender.

Third, there will be a continued emphasis among thrift institutions on the secondary market as a means of providing housing finance. In fact, the secondary market probably will be providing 40 to 50 percent of all conventional mortgage money within five to 10 years.

Fourth and finally, some thrift institutions will face severe solvency problems in the next decade because of the stock of assets they have that are frozen in low-yielding mortgages issued in the 1960s and 1970s. Government assistance may be required to avoid bankruptcy by allowing thrift institutions to sell some of their older, low-yielding mortgages at a discount to federal credit agencies such as FNMA or GNMA with subsidies provided to help absorb part of the losses.

IMPACT ON HOUSING

There are at least three areas of concern regarding the impact of change on the housing market: the influence of reform on mortgage rates, the influence on the overall size of the housing stock, and the impact on housing cycles and the stability of the flow of money for housing.

The first two areas are closely related. As mortgage rates vary, they will influence the demand for housing and the overall level of home building. To some extent the impacts of financial reform will be offsetting. On the one hand, greater flexibility concerning deposit rate ceilings will enhance the ability of thrift institutions to compete for funds during periods of tight credit and thus avoid some of the drastic impacts of disintermediation. For example, in the first part of 1979, the money market certificate had an important impact on stemming disintermediation and providing money for housing. Some have estimated that MMCs helped to fund 300,000 housing starts in the first half of 1979—homes that otherwise would not have been built. On the other hand, increases in deposit rates and changes in the liability structure of thrift institutions also will alter profit margins and will apply strong pressure to raise mortgage rates. In other words, if the cost of money for a savings and loan institution is higher because depositors are no longer subsidizing home buyers, then the rate for mortgages is likely to be higher, especially in today's market. The bottom line, then, may be more money available for housing during periods of tight credit, but at a higher rate.

The influence concerning the impact on the third area—housing cycles and the stability of the flow of money—is somewhat clearer, but still imprecise. Flexible deposit rate ceilings will allow thrift institutions to compete more effectively for deposits during periods of tight credit; expanded liability powers will provide thrifts new sources of money; and broader investment powers will enable thrift institutions to offer alternative mortgage instruments and shorter-term assets that will allow a return that will match more effectively the changing costs of funds. Since the flow of funds for housing from savings and loan firms is so volatile, all of these features should help to stabilize the flow of dollars, even during periods of tight credit.

Once again, however, there are offsetting factors. Broader investment powers will mean that thrift institutions will be allowed to purchase non-housing assets, and this will provide some drain on the percentage of housing investment, although a larger base of deposits may compensate for this drain. More important, given dramatic rises in interest rates, cycles in the housing industry are to a large extent inherent in the nature of houses. Houses are the epitome of long-life durable goods. When interest rates rise, the purchase of such goods is easily postponed. If inflation continues to fluctuate and monetary policy continues to bear a major burden for stabilization policy, then continued periods of tight money, high interest rates, and associated declines in housing production can be expected. The result may be smaller cyclical fluctuations, but with an overall lower level of housing production. In other words, the easing of housing cycles over time may mean more money during the troughs, but it may also mean less housing during peak times of easy credit.

MULTI-FAMILY AND ASSISTED HOUSING

It is possible that some shift from single-family to multi-family housing production will occur. Over the last decade there has been a marked decrease in the
proportion of renter occupied housing to single-family homes. People have
realized that single-family home ownership is heavily subsidized by the federal
government through various tax benefits, and an increased preference for home
ownership, not only as a consumption item, but as an investment has resulted.
From 1950 to 1980, the percentage of housing units occupied by renters fell from
45 percent to about 34 percent of the total housing stock. Further, in recent years,
multi-family housing starts have declined relative to single-family starts, with a
large share of those multi-family starts either provided through federally subsidized programs or absorbed in the market for condominium ownership. In
1978, for example, 587,000 multi-family units were started, but only 190,000
were private rental units with the balance either subsidized or for-sale housing.

As noted earlier, financial reform probably will put additional pressure on the
cost of single-family houses through continued pressure on mortgage rates, thus
adding to the trend of the last few years where costs for single-family homes have
risen faster than the rate of inflation. Using 1967 as a base, the consumer price
index increased from 100 in 1967 to 207.1 in February 1979. The cost of home
ownership, however, has increased at a faster rate, with a comparative rise to
245.7 during this same period. In contrast, rental costs have risen only to 170.8,
considerably less than the price rise of the CPI, and far below the rise in price of
single-family home ownership. Eventually, some consumers will realize this dis-
crepancy and there will be a greater demand for multi-family housing over the
next decade. This demand will be further heightened by the demographics of the
baby boom which will continue at least through 1990. Some of this demand will
be eased through a change in lifestyle over the decade of the 1980s, such as
doubling up among some households, the production of smaller and comparatively less costly homes, and a shift in preference by some to condominiums as
compared to single-family homes. Still, it seems that there may be increasing
pressure for some people to rent as they are "priced out" of the home ownership
market and as the demand for housing rises throughout the 1980s. As this demand increases, the cost of renting housing units should rise along with the production of multi-family housing. Changes in housing finance will not cause such
an increased demand or rise in rents directly, but they will add to the trends that
already are likely.

The shift to multi-family housing will not be too dramatic. Regarding nonsubsidized multi-family housing, the economics for development are extremely difficult. The same pressures that will cause the mortgage rate for single-family
homes to rise also will influence the financing of multi-family housing. Without
substantial increases in rents or additional tax benefits (such as improved acceler-

ated depreciation for multi-family housing), it is unlikely that dramatic increases in production will occur. Ultimately, the demographics may force an increase, but this shift will be a marginal, as opposed to a dramatic, rise.

The level of production of government assisted multi-family housing will depend on two factors—public priorities and the costs. The tools for financing multi-family housing are already in place through such programs as Section 8, tandem plans, mortgage-backed securities, and state and local issues of tax-exempt bonds. How much money Congress is willing to appropriate to facilitate such financing will depend on its priorities. Realizing that there will be great pressure to hold down federal expenditures over the next few years, subsidized housing programs undoubtedly will be competing with other demands on government funds. This will limit the resources available. The Government Accounting Office completed a report September 30, 1980, evaluating alternatives for financing low- and moderate-income rental housing. The report, along with the response from HUD, raised a number of questions. Although the final answer is not clear, it is important to determine which financing mechanism within the new system of housing finance will be the most cost-effective in providing assistance for low- and moderate-income housing.

Finally, if more multi-family and government assisted housing is to be developed in the future, attention to new sources of funds and, perhaps, shifts in tax policy will be needed. The use of mortgage revenue bonds to provide low- and moderate-income housing is one creative response that has occurred over the last few years. It should continue. Congress has passed legislation restricting the use of tax-exempt, single-family and multi-family mortgage revenue bonds as a part of the recent budget reconciliation package. The new bill places a limit of 9 percent of the preceding three years of activity or $200 million, whichever is greater, on the level of mortgage revenue activity that any state can undertake between now and the end of 1983. Limitations to provide bounds on the use of mortgage-revenue bonds are needed. It is essential, however, that such financing mechanisms be available in the future, not only through 1983, but beyond. Further, faster tax write-offs for low- and moderate-income rental housing, perhaps through a 20-year write-off, or less, rather than the typical 30- or 40-year write-off should be considered. The greatest impact of changes in the tax laws, however, would come from a decrease in the benefits for single-family home ownership. Some have proposed to cap single-family tax credits at some level, for example, $2,000, or to provide a limit of 25 percent of annual mortgage and property taxes as a tax deduction. Proposals that tinker with the home ownership deduction are still almost unthinkable at present, but they may become necessary in the future.

CONCLUSION

History is replete with examples of institutions unresponsive to the need to change being replaced by new ones. The system of housing finance and financial institutions faces major questions over the next decade. This clearly is a time of transition, and the future will hinge on the capacity to respond. DIDMCA did not pass because it was good for housing, per se. It passed because of the silent revolution and economic pressures. It is the opinion of this author that without this reform the system of housing finance would not have survived and the upheaval would have eventually been worse. Now that the change is occurring, it might not be ideal, but all must learn to manage the revolution that is under way. Thrift institutions must become "one-stop family financial centers," providing a wide range of consumer and housing services. In turn, the government should closely monitor the financial position of thrift institutions during this time of change. The housing finance system of the future undoubtedly will be very different and all will need to adapt.

With change comes new opportunities, coupled naturally with risks and potential difficulties. The question is whether we can adapt in such a way as to avoid major disruptions. As the poet Emerson once noted, "This time like all times is a good one, if we but know what to do with it."

10

Rationale of the Present Tax Benefits for Homeowners

Richard E. Slitor

INTRODUCTION

This article examines the rationale for the present Federal income tax benefits for homeowners, against a background of current tax reform literature which is preoccupied quite narrowly with the equity aspects of the present longstanding rules. This treatment involves the exclusion of the imputed rental value of an owner-occupied residence from gross income coupled with homeowners' deductions for mortgage interest and local property taxes. After reviewing the case for and against the present tax treatment, the study proceeds to examine quantitatively the impact of the homeowner exclusions and deductions; the role of property taxes in the housing consumer's choice between homeownership and tenancy; the economic equity and administrative considerations relevant to policy decisions affecting the inclusion or exclusion of imputed rental value of owner-occupied homes in the income tax base; the effects of tax incentives for investors in rental housing on housing supply and its distribution among different classifications of units; and the probable effects of housing-related aspects of the current tax reform proposals presented by the Treasury Department before the House Ways and Means Committee April 30, 1973.

From the U.S. Department of Housing and Urban Development. *Housing in the Seventies: Working Papers. II. National Housing Policy Review*. Washington, D.C.: U.S. Government Printing Office, 1976. pp. 907-19.

RATIONALE AND BENEFICIAL EXTERNALITIES OF TAX BENEFITS FOR HOMEOWNERS

The Federal income tax (and the typical State income tax structure, which follows the Federal pattern) provides important tax benefits for both rental and owner-occupied housing. In the case of homeowners, who receive the greatest direct benefits, the tax advantages comprise the exemption from income tax of the net imputed rental value, together with the deductibility of mortgage interest and property tax payments. Smaller benefits accrue to renters in the form of more abundant rental housing supplies and therefore lower rents reflecting the accelerated tax depreciation allowances available to rental housing investors. On net balance, however, the direct tax benefits for homeowners outweigh the indirect benefits to tenants, creating the issue—which has agitated tax reform literature particularly in the past decade—known as the discrimination in favor of the homeowner and against the tenant.

It is now almost standard procedure for experts and scholars in the field of tax reform to characterize the homeowner's tax benefits as ''massive tax subsidies,'' which (1) violate principles of tax equity and economic neutrality; (2) cost taxpayers generally substantial annual erosion of the public revenues; (3) favor taxpayers in positions to own their homes, particularly if they are in the affluent tax brackets where the incremental tax saving per dollar of exclusions or deductions may range as high as 70 percent under the existing structure of Federal individual income tax rates; (4) affect resource allocation by stimulating overexpansion of the housing stock and additional housing consumption as against other forms of consumption, including luxury features such as swimming pools, tennis courts, barbecue patios, etc.; and (5) contribute to serious national problems at least partially associated with overexpansive housing outlays, such as urban sprawl.

The tax reform school goes to great lengths to demonstrate the obvious and intended thrust of the tax laws in encouraging and rendering financial assistance to homeownership. In contrast with this penchant for detailed exposition of the nature and distribution of homeowner tax benefits, this school shows a curious obtuseness in understanding or articulating fairly the social objectives and externalities that tend to justify the pro-homeownership features of the income tax law.

One of the most recent and otherwise professionally competent studies of the income tax benefits for housing concludes on this note:

> With respect to any conceivable policy objective, the pattern of tax benefits seems to be capricious and without rationale. Apart from the alleged, but unsubstantiated, benefits accruing to the community when households come to own their own homes, there appears to be no reason for subsidizing homeownership rather than other investments or the consumption of owned rather than rented housing services or of other commodities.[1]

The argument is then carried further, almost in legal brief fashion, to say that even if it were acknowledged that "homeownership benefits society by making homeowners more stable or less antisocial than they otherwise would have been, the pattern of tax benefits is ill suited to the objective."

The "ill-suitedness" is attributed to the fact that large benefits go to above-average income families and negligible aid to low income households who generally have not received any of the "salutary discipline of property management."[2]

In a footnote addendum to these observations, the same author states that in his opinion "no study has shown both of the following: (a) that the beneficial effects of housing are due to housing itself rather than adequate income, i.e., that the composition, rather than the level, of consumption matters; (b) that correlations between homeownership and socially or personally desirable characteristics (or the absence of antisocial characteristics) are not the joint results of other psychological, sociological or economic characteristics. The issue of which way causation runs also is frequently troublesome."[3]

There is, nevertheless, an important and not usually very systematically stated rationale for the present income tax treatment in its encouragement to homeowners. This rationale goes beyond ameliorating slum conditions and combating social environments which are detrimental to human health and development and which foster crime, delinquency, and vandalism. It also goes beyond the notion that homeownership is a good thing because (1) it helps to foster a sense of stability and identity with a community, and (2) owing to the reliance of municipalities on property taxes, direct payments of property taxes (undisguised as part of rental payments) are likely to make them more responsible citizens and better judges of the proper scale of local expenditures.[4]

The most persuasive rationale for encouraging homeownership through the income tax system and indeed other aspects of national policy consists of both (1) the elemental considerations of building family economic security in a troubled and insecure world which have always prompted prudent individuals to strive to own their own homes, and (2) a variety of more sophisticated points based on the favorable externalities of homeownership which are important to national policy and may not be reflected in the interplay of supply and demand for different types of housing and tenure arrangements in the marketplace.

The tax reform school, along with their high motives and purist standards with respect to comprehensiveness, uniformity, and neutrality of the income tax base seem to have a basic hostility towards homeownership. In this regard they seem to be advocates of a viewpoint which probably has less merit than that of those social observers and environmentalists who are hostile to the automobile as a feature of middle class suburban living and commuting.

The most relevant and persuasive externalities favoring homeownership relate quite directly to the cost and conditions of housing consumption.

Tenancy is perhaps the most expensive form of housing consumption because it affords very little if any incentive to careful use and day-to-day maintenance. It opens the door to hard, indifferent use bordering on vandalism by tenants in many situations. By contrast, owner-occupancy encourages better maintenance, both through reduction of unnecessarily hard use and saving of damage and repair costs and through creation of effective incentives for the occupier to support efficient long-range upkeep of the property. If all American automobile consumption were converted to a rental basis, one can be confident that the social costs of this important part of our standard of living would rise enormously unless an elaborate and administratively costly system of rewards and penalties were introduced to motivate owner-like utilization. This merely illustrates how housing consumption costs, representing a still larger share of family budgets, would rise if everyone went on a tenancy basis and how they are reduced by increasing the proportion of owner-occupancy.

Homeownership helps reduce the cost of housing in another important way. The expense of rented quarters includes a substantial rate of return on risk capital in an inherently capital-intensive activity. The homeowner can in effect earn this return on his own commitment rather than have to pay it to a landlord investor. Since the risks of landlord investment are greater than those of an owner-occupier, and the inevitable overhead of rental management adds to costs in the case of tenant occupancy, there is a further saving on this score in owner-occupancy. It seems doubtful that even large landlord operations could secure lower mortgage interest or related financing costs which would compensate for the higher equity return and management costs involved in landlord ownership.

The whole problem of landlord-tenant relations is one which is handled with great difficulty in the prevailing judicial system. In general, the growing permissiveness of the courts with respect to tenant obligations tends to increase rental costs. At best, the additional social costs of adjudication between landlord and tenant are an appreciable factor in the social economies of homeownership.

Homeownership provides various opportunities for do-it-yourself projects which permit use of the spare time of the owner and his family in creating wealth and income. While this may be taken into account by potential homebuyers weighing the tenure decision and while some "home workshop" and gardening activities are possible for tenants, there remains a substantial balance of superiority in favor of homeownership in this regard. This is true particularly with respect to possible home improvements as well as repair and maintenance, which the tenant would not undertake in order to benefit the landlord. Moreover, the social benefits from eliciting this kind of spare time activity, which add to wealth and reduce the burden on social resources available for home repair and improvement, outweigh those received by the homebuyer. He may tend to think only of the net gain over and above the cost of his effort, while the gain from the social viewpoint is substantially the gross contribution of do-it-yourself efforts.

Inflation hedging through homeownership is an important consideration motivating the prudent householder weighing a housing tenure decision. However, in an economy which has not yet mastered the technical and political arts of reasonable price stabilization in the various situations that confront it, it is also probably desirable for society to have a substantial part of the population partially inflation-hedged. Hardship and social instability due to expropriation by inflation are reduced, pressure for compensating escalation is moderated, and the area of surveillance under possible rent control is narrowed. This area of homeowner externalities is controversial and not fully explored. Nevertheless, it should be considered as one of the desirable society-stabilizing aspects of homeownership which helps favorable income tax treatment.

Homeownership—at least with a substantial equity—also provides an important form of basic economic security to workers. The individual who owns his home is better able to ride out periods of unemployment and reduced earnings.[5] It is true that loss of equity in a mortgaged home may constitute a hazard of unemployment. But this hazard is reduced as a sizable equity is established, particularly in view of the various forms of social insurance which, along with even mortgaged homeownership, exist to help tide over periods of economic stress.

Home purchase under the modern level payment mortgage plan involves a form of systematic, mandatory current saving once the initial commitment is made. Homeownership encourages saving in this way as well as providing the inducement to accumulate the original downpayment. The form of saving involved is in effect invested in a highly secure asset which provides a basic element of economic security for the homeowner and his family. Is this a desirable social result which can be counted as a favorable externality of the home purchase decision? Does not the tenant help support saving via mortgage repayment at the landlord level? Does the curtailment of mortgage principal really represent net saving in view of the fact that housing is a form of consumption represented by the depreciation of the housing asset? In general, the answers to this series of questions suggest that home purchase savings (1) help secure a broader distribution of wealth and (2) augment investment in an asset (even though like other physical assets it is subject to depreciation) essential to the well-being and economic security of homeowning families. This overall result is one which most people would regard as a favorable externality.

The question of work force mobility is sometimes raised by those who see an unfavorable social externality in widespread homeownership. They argue that tenancy is conducive to mobility while homeownership ties the worker to his property, creating additional economic impediments to geographical movement in response to economic changes. Since homes may be bought and sold, and the tax laws permit tax-free turnover of residential investments where the owner has to move in order to accept employment at a new location, the barriers to employee movement because of homeownership are moderate indeed. Some employers, of course, pay the employee's costs of moving, including possible losses on disposition of a home; under these circumstances, homeownership can hardly

Table 1
Estimated Federal Income Tax Expenditures, Calendar Years 1967-72
(in millions of dollars)

	Housing and Community Development					
	1967	**1968**	**1969**	**1970**	**1971**	**1972**
Deductibility of interest on mortgage on owner-occupied homes	$1,900	$2,200	$2,600	$2,800	$2,400	$3,500
Deductibility of property taxes on owner-occupied homes	1,800	2,350	2,800	2,900	2,700	3,250
Total	3,700	4,500	5,400	5,700	5,100	6,750

Source: "Estimates of Federal Tax Expenditures," House Committee on Ways and Means, prepared by the Staffs of the Treasury Department and Joint Committee on Internal Revenue Taxation, June 1, 1972, U.S. Government Printing Office, Washington, D.C., 1973, Table 1, pp. 4-5.

be termed a mobility barrier. On the whole, the mobility consideration can hardly be regarded as a substantial offset to the various favorable externalities of owning rather than renting one's residence.

HOMEOWNER TAX BENEFITS AND THE TAX EXPENDITURE DOCTRINE

The income tax benefits for homeowners have inevitably become enmeshed in the whole discussion of so-called "tax expenditures" and the "tax expenditure budget." The continuing examination of Federal subsidy programs has included subsidy-like programs that do not involve direct cash disbursements but provide comparable benefits such as those which take the form of tax reduction.

The tax expenditure budget concept was originally explained in the Annual Report of the Secretary of the Treasury for fiscal year 1968.[6] Its basic thrust is that a fully revealing picture of the national budget with respect to expenditures and receipts would include the revenue cost of the various tax incentive concessions as budget expenditure items, presumably balanced on the receipts side by corresponding tax collections which would materialize if the tax concessions in question were abolished. Exponents of the tax expenditure budget stress the weaknesses of the backdoor or hidden budget approach to national policy objectives: (1) Its tendency to erode the tax base and confuse tax equity standards and the standards guiding public expenditures to secure desired actions or economic responses, (2) its failure to proceed through normal legislative channels whereby specialized committees can pass on the merit of expenditures in their field of jurisdiction, and (3) its tendency to permit tax expenditures to evade the annual budget review process and become embedded in the tax laws, persisting after the

Table 2
Estimated Distribution of Homeowner Tax Preferences of Individuals by Adjusted
Gross Income Class, Calendar Year 1972
(in millions of dollars except adjusted gross income class)

Adjusted gross income class	Deductibility of interest on mortgages on owner-occupied homes	Deductibility of property taxes on owner-occupied homes	Total
$ 0- 3,000	(1)	$ 5	$ 5
3,000- 5,000	$ 15	25	40
5,000- 7,000	85	95	180
7,000- 10,000	310	240	550
10,000- 15,000	845	590	1,435
15,000- 20,000	835	640	1,475
20,000- 50,000	1,160	1,135	2,295
50,000-100,000	195	340	535
100,000 and over	55	180	235
Total	3,500	3,250	6,750

(1) Less than $.5 million.
Source: "Estimates of Federal Tax Expenditures," previously cited, Table 2, 8-9.

needs which called them into being have been met or after the favorable benefit-cost ratio which initially supported them has deteriorated.[7]

The tax benefits for homeowners, or more specifically the deductions for mortgage interest and property taxes on owner-occupied homes, have been the subject of periodic estimates of revenue cost along with other items deemed to merit inclusion in the Federal income tax expenditures (or subsidies) periodically prepared for the Joint Economic Committee or for the House Ways and Means Committee by the Congressional Committee and Treasury Staffs.

Excerpts from the most recent set of estimates show the homeowner tax benefit items in recent years (and their distribution by income level in 1972) in Table 1.

Tax expenditure analyses are primarily statistical quantification of the money involved in tax concessions for various types of income, spending, or economic activity, designed to provide systematic information on the hidden or indirect expenditures. As such, they provide information useful in appraising the cost of such concessions in relation to their benefits to the economy. Like related analyses of the erosion of the tax base relative to a comprehensive measure of taxable income capacity, the tax expenditure studies tend to support attacks on the equity and economic efficiency of the various tax incentives or subsidies embedded in the income tax structure. Thus, the $6,750 million estimated tax benefits for homeowners in 1972 tend to be cast in the image of a bonanza of shocking magnitude, two-thirds of which goes to homeowners of adjusted gross income classes above $15,000 (see Table 2). To see this amount in perspective, it represents about 7 percent of total individual income taxes, 3 percent of total Federal receipts, and .6 percent of gross national product. Moreover, the estimates do not adequately make clear how effectively they take account of the fact that part of the itemized homeowner deductions merely overlaps the standard deduction which taxpayers could take anyway, regardless of homeownership, and which have been compensated by a general increase in tax rates to recoup the revenue.

While tax expenditure data developed from official sources in recent years have not included the amount attributable to the exclusion of net imputed rent over and above the two deduction items, Goode's estimates of about a decade ago show that in 1960 the ''net vent'' item (over and above mortgage interest and property taxes) would have been slightly greater than the mortgage interest item.[8]

The significance and interrelationships of the three major income tax advantages of homeowners will be analyzed qualitatively and quantitatively in a subsequent section of this report.

Interplay of Property Tax and Income Tax

This study will examine the burden of the local property tax, the interplay of the property tax and income tax provisions, and the net combined impact on housing costs in the aggregate and by income level.

Until recently very few analysts in the field of housing economics have been prepared to recognize the obvious fact that the property tax, which accounts for the great bulk of local government tax revenue and about 40 percent of combined State-local government tax revenue, is tantamount to an excise tax on basic housing consumption of some 25 to 35 percent in most populous areas of the country.

The income tax advantages of homeownership compensate to a considerable extent for the burden of local property taxes, but the offset is uneven and there remains a heavy net additional load on low income housing consumers, including homeowners and renters.

The deductibility of property tax for Federal income tax purposes is not unique; most other State and local taxes are deductible by the Federal income taxpayer. It is difficult therefore to attribute the sharp increases in property tax levels in recent years, chiefly to the fact that local tax authorities count on the deductibility feature to ease the impact of the levies they impose to provide local governmental services. It is not plausible, however, to assert that there is no interconnection, particularly in areas where the taxing authorities are aware that many of their homeowners are in affluent Federal (and State) income tax brackets.

This general topic, including the economic and locational impacts of the property tax–income tax complex on housing stocks and consumption, will receive specialized attention in a subsequent section.

Scope of this Article

It is apparent that taxes constitute a substantial part of the cost of housing. It will also be evident from the discussion which follows that the formulation of tax requirements by the various levels of government not only affects the distribution of that cost among housing consumers but also has major impacts on housing tenure, supply and quality, locational development, land use patterns, and the phenomenon of urban sprawl, as well as the processes of central city blight and deterioration. These impacts will be examined in the following sections.

A major concern of the paper will be the role of the present exclusion of imputed rental income along with the homeowner income tax deductions in the evolving dialogue and legislation on tax reform. This concern necessarily focuses on the economic, equity, and administrative aspects of present treatment and proposals for revision—particularly those directed at the inclusion of imputed rental income in the personal income tax base.

IMPACT OF THE HOMEOWNER DEDUCTIONS

This section examines a range of major economic impacts of the existing homeowner tax benefits on housing markets, including related capital market effects and locational effects.

In general, the existing tax benefits for homeowners tend to:

- Increase the demand for owner-occupied relative to rental housing units, thus raising the proportion of total housing units which are owner-occupied.
- Raise the value of owner-occupied units and decrease the rentals of rental units which are at least partially competitive with owner-occupied housing.
- Stimulate housing, consumption, the upgrading of the housing stock, and the more expansive use of land, contributing to decentralization and urban sprawl trends.
- Exert upward pressure on the interest rate structure due to the stimulus to a capital-intensive form of consumption.
- Expand the homebuilding industry and the factors of production it utilizes in constructing owner-occupied units.
- Develop larger and more specialized home mortgage markets and the financial institutions—such as the building and loan associations—which supply housing finance.

These points are developed in more detail under the following headings.

Homeownership v. Tenancy

There is clear evidence that the income tax has affected the choice between

Table 3
Percent of Owner Occupancy, Total, and by Race and Residence, by Decennial Years 1900-70 (in percent)

Year	Total	White	Negro and other	Non-farm	Farm
1900	46.7%	49.8%	23.6%	36.9%	64.4%
1910	45.9	NA	NA	38.6	62.8
1920	45.6	48.2	29.9	40.8	58.1
1930	47.8	50.2	25.2	46.0	53.9
1940	43.6	45.7	23.6	41.1	53.2
1950	55.0	57.0	34.9	53.4	65.7
1960	61.9	64.4	38.4	61.0	73.8
1970	62.9	65.4	42.0	62.0	80.5

Source: Compiled from *Statistical Abstract of the United States 1972*, U.S. Department of Commerce, Bureau of the Census, U.S. Government Printing Office, Washington, D.C., 1973, Table 1155, p. 687.

homeownership and renting so as to increase the proportion of owner-occupied housing units. At least one expert observer is of the opinion that the home-owner tax benefits have had more influence on the tenure decision (owning as against renting) than on the total amount of housing consumption—based on the assumed principle that the "price differential that will induce a shift from renting to owning is doubtless much smaller than that required to divert expenditure from other goods and services to housing."[9]

The impact of the income tax-related reduction in housing costs (estimated at 12 to 30 percent in a substantial range of incomes covering most moderate and affluent income brackets) on homeownership trends is clearly suggested by the data in Table 3.

As the data show, the rise in owner occupancy developed as a clear trend only after 1940, the approximate beginning of the substantial mass income tax introduced in the World War II period. In the 3 decades since 1940, total owner occupancy has risen roughly 20 percentage points to nearly 63 percent. In the 4 preceding decades, the percentage of owner occupancy actually declined by about 4 percentage points. Comparable trends are shown for white and Negro housing, and for nonfarm and farm. While various nontax factors may have encouraged homeownership in the period since 1940—such as greater affluence, the automobile and the suburban trend, and modernized and government-assisted mortgage financing—it seems unmistakable that the important tax savings under the higher and more pervasive individual income tax of the World War II and postwar periods have been a major factor.

A distribution of housing unit tenure percentages by income class would probably show a higher percentage of owner occupancy the higher the income, and a greater post-1940 rise in owner occupancy in those income brackets impacted most heavily by the expansion and steepening of the income tax.

The rise in the percentages of owner-occupied housing units since 1940 has been matched, of course, by an opposite trend in their complements, the percentages of rental occupancy. Thus while both owner-occupied and renter-occupied housing units have increased in absolute numbers, the percentage decline in tenancy has moderated the absolute increase in the number of rental units. The trend towards homeownership and away from rental occupancy is all the more impressive because it has occurred during a period of increasing urbanization of population, and large metropolitan areas tend to have a lower percentage of owner occupancy than farm and smaller communities.

Demand for Owner-Occupied and Rental Housing Units

The tax benefits for homeowners have increased the demand for owner-occupied housing by amounts which have been roughly quantified. While these benefits have diverted demand from rental housing, the rental sector itself has enjoyed the tax benefits of accelerated depreciation and the whole real estate tax shelter for rental housing investors, who have themselves tended to stimulate rental housing demand, although relatively less than has occurred in the owner-occupied sector.

The tax benefits of homeownership have been estimated on the average to be equivalent to a reduction in the basic cost of housing consumption of about 13.75 percent. With a price elasticity of demand for owner-occupied housing of about −1.5, this results in an increase in housing demand and consumption in the owner-occupied sector (roughly two-thirds of the existing stock and a higher proportion of the current demand) of about 20.625 percent.[10] The benefits are greater the higher the individual's applicable tax bracket. For middle income taxpayers with applicable bracket rates in the 32 to 45 percent range (taxable income in the range of $20,000 to $40,000, married persons filing joint returns), the tax benefits—even assuming homeowner deductions of 62.5 percent of basic housing consumption—would be 20 to 28 percent of basic housing costs. Again, with a price elasticity of −1.5, this would increase demand and consumption for owner-occupied housing by some 30 to 42 percent in the moderately affluent-middle bracket range just designated.

The elasticity of demand measure used in the above estimates is important. While the older literature on housing demand tended to place price elasticity of demand at near unity (−1), more recent estimates place it higher, near −1.5. (A corresponding estimate of income elasticity for owner-occupied housing demand is 1.427, with a slightly lower figure, apparently 1.338, for rental housing).[11]

While demand for rental housing tends to be reduced by the cross-elasticity response to tax-related cost reductions for owned homes, this effect is partially offset by the pass-through to renters of the accelerated depreciation tax benefits for investors in rental housing. The tax benefits from the excess of accelerated (chiefly 150 percent and 200 percent declining balance formulas) over straight-line depreciation are estimated to range between 7 and 10 percent of the gross rental value of rental housing property. With a −1.5 price elasticity of demand, the resulting increase in demand and consumption in the rental housing sector is estimated at roughly 10 to 15 percent.[12]

The rise in housing consumption as a percentage of total personal consumption expenditures in the post-World War II period tends to confirm the estimates of increased demand for housing based on tax benefit and elasticity of demand data.

Goode has indicated that although the influence of the favorable tax treatment cannot be isolated, it has probably been one of the factors responsible for the rapid increase in consumer expenditures for housing since World War II.[13]

Goode's data follow.

Housing Expenditures as Percentage of Total Private Consumption

Year	Current Prices	Constant (1954) prices
1909	19.3%	—
1919	13.3	—
1929	14.4	10.0%
1950	10.9	11.4
1960	12.8	12.7

On the basis of these 1919–1960 data, Goode observed that in current prices housing expenditures (space rental value of tenant-occupied and owner-occupied dwellings) were still a smaller fraction of total personal consumption in 1960 than in 1929 and prior years; but in constant prices housing consumption expenditures represented a much larger percentage of total consumption than in 1929. Goode regarded the constant price estimates as "suspect" in view of the surprisingly small increase shown by the implicit price deflator for housing expenditures from 1929 to 1960.[14] A larger increase would have resulted in a greater rise in constant-price housing expenditures relative to total private consumption.

More recent data on housing and other personal expenditures in current dollars show housing at 14.9 percent of total private consumption in 1971, exactly equal to the 1929 percentage but 4 percentage points or 36.7 percent higher than in 1949 and 1.2 percentage points or 8.8 percent higher than in 1939. The data are summarized below.

Based on 1960 data, Laidler has estimated the "overinvestment" in owner-occupied housing stock as a result of the exclusion of imputed rental value (along with the homeowner deductions for mortgage interest and property taxes) at about $60.7 billion in relation to a total owner-occupied housing stock of $355.4 billion, or at an overall ratio of about 17 percent, including lower income brackets where no overinvestment occurred due to tax benefits. In the income classes affected, the overinvestment was estimated in a range of 20 to 35 percent.[15]

An opponent of homeowner tax benefits, Laidler estimated the "welfare loss"

Housing and Other Personal Consumption Expenditures
(Dollar Amounts in billions)

	1929	1939	1949	1959	1969	1971
Total personal consumption expenditures	$77.2	$66.8	$176.8	$311.2	$579.5	$664.9
Housing expenditures:						
Amount	$11.5	$ 9.1	$ 19.3	$ 43.7	$ 84.1	$ 99.2
Percentage of total	14.9%	13.7%	10.9%	14.0%	14.5%	14.9%

Note: Percentages calculated from unrounded figures.

Source: Compiled from *Facts and Figures on Government Finance*, 17th Biennial Edition, 1973, Tax Foundation, Inc., Table 37, p. 53.

due to the calculated "overinvestment" in owner-occupied housing, which presumably flowed from the overallocation of capital resources (and related services supplied by the public and private sectors) to owner-occupied housing, at a surprisingly low $500 million per year, or roughly $2.50 per capita. This somewhat wan end product was made to look more impressive by the suggestion that it be interpreted as representing the "dollar value of extra resources the government could take away from the public if it were to abolish the subsidy and seek to leave consumers at the same level of economic welfare that they enjoy at present."[16]

For purposes of the present analysis, the most impressive fact would seem to be that the homeowner tax benefits are estimated to have increased the owner-occupied housing stock as of 1960 by about 20.6 percent relative to a tax-neutral position, 17.1 percent of the existing stock, or about $61 billion. At current 1973 levels, the net addition to the owner-occupied housing stock attributable to these income tax benefits would be in the order of $76 billion.[17]

Rental housing stocks may also be considered to have been increased by the reductions in rentals (7 to 10 percent of gross rental value) and accompanying 10 to 15 percent increase in demand. If rental housing stocks may be estimated at about one-half the owner-occupied stocks, and the increase due to accelerated depreciation tax benefits at about 12.5 percent (midpoint of the 10 to 15 percent range indicated above), the addition to rental housing stocks attributable to depreciation tax benefits may be estimated to be in the vicinity of $23 billion at 1973 levels. . . .

The econometric analyses on which the above estimates are based do not seem to take clearly into account the effects of cross-elasticity of demand between owner-occupied and rental housing. Since the two alternative forms of housing tenure are in a sense substitute or rival forms of housing services, a decline in the price of one tends to increase its use, thus decreasing the marginal utility and curtailing the demand for the other form of housing.

The two forms of tax benefit, one for owner-occupied and the other for rental housing, increase the overall housing demand and consumption. The increase between the two sectors is not proportional because owner-occupied housing derives a greater tax benefit, one which is extended to the consumer with greater certainty than the investor-oriented benefit in the rental field. Moreover, the increase in owner-occupied demand by itself is not likely to be as great as if there were not appreciable tax benefits for rental housing too.

Similarly, the depreciation benefits for rental housing do not increase the consumption for rental housing as much as they would in isolation, so to speak, or in the absence of the large, more direct and certain benefits for homeowners.

In short, the two types of tax benefit increase housing consumption, not by as much as if all housing received the homeowner-type benefits but by more than the amount of increase if all housing received benefits only at the level of the rental housing benefits. The reallocation of housing demand from rental to owner-occupied units is less than if only homeowner tax benefits were provided.

Locational Effects

The locational effects of homeowner tax benefits have been substantial. Generally speaking, the homeowner provisions have tended to (and still do):

- Contribute to the formation of the suburban areas of the large metropolitan complexes, typically the more affluent and rapidly growing sections of the country;
- Encourage expansive land use, thus furthering decentralization, urban sprawl, and low-density as against high-density residential development;
- Facilitate the middle class exodus from the central city to suburban and exurban residential developments;
- Stimulate the condominium form of tenure which combines the tax benefits of homeownership and the convenience and economy of high-rise multiple unit housing in urban, suburban-fringe, retirement, and resort areas;
- Afford relatively little tax savings to the rural areas, particularly the less affluent parts of rural and small-community America, where—even though homeownership percentages are high—housing is likely to be older, rental values very moderate, money incomes low, and applicable tax rates determining the benefit from home-owner deductions and exclusions also low;
- Pour relatively small tax benefits into the central cities where, unlike the suburbs, rented units still constitute the predominant (over half) form of tenure and the income tax brackets of the owner-occupants tend to be lower.

It is difficult to quantify the effects of the tax benefits for homeowners with regard to these various locational developments. The predominant locational influence is, of course, the decentralization of metropolitan areas, urban sprawl, and resulting agglomeration of megalopolitan areas in which the suburban or exurban fringe of the city merges into that of another. The homeowner tax treatment has contributed to this in certain interrelated ways:

- It has facilitated and encouraged middle class flight to the suburbs by helping finance the additional housing costs;
- It has stimulated additional housing consumption and this has included more spacious lots and acreage than would otherwise be desired or practicable, along with roomier, more rambling home construction, including the appurtenances of garages, parking areas, swimming pools, patios, etc.

It seems fair to say that the additional and more expansive housing construction in the suburbs stimulated by the homeowner tax benefits has contributed 20 to 30 percent to the area expansion of the communities embraced within the definition of standard metropolitan statistical areas.

The diversion of capital and managerial or promotional resources to suburban construction has probably contributed further to the neglect by the private sector of low and moderate income residential development in the central cities, already unattractive because of the lower incomes and greater risk and difficulties in the central city areas.

Prices and Values of Owner-Occupied and Rental Housing Units

The additional consumption of housing services due to homeowner tax benefits has probably raised housing construction costs, these higher factor costs generally affecting owner-occupied and rental housing alike. However, the additional pressure on land or site values has probably resulted in a relatively greater increase in the cost and price of the typical owner-occupied unit consisting of a separate single family house with an appropriate parcel of land. This increase in site values has been less important for the multiple unit high rise. Thus rental housing has been impacted to a lesser extent. In the owner-occupied field, techniques of land economization have thus developed, including the condominium apartment and cluster developments with suburban "townhouses."

The rise in value of owner-occupied homes, supported by the homeowner tax advantages along with the inflation-hedging and land speculation incidental to housing consumption, has been so substantial in recent years that realistic rental values now fall appreciably short of the 10 to 12 percent of fair market value of property that Aaron suggests is the real estate market rule of thumb for single family houses.[18] Laidler uses a figure of 11 percent in his estimates of homeowner tax subsidies.[19] It is almost a matter of common observation that in many suburban areas gross rental of as much as 9 percent of market value of homes intended to be owner-occupied are out of the question. Only a moderate depression of the rental market in some areas may force rentals of single family houses intended for owner occupancy as low as 7.5 percent of market value of

Table 4
Consumer Price Indexes, by Commodity Groups, Selected Years 1960-71
(1967 = 100)

Year	Housing (shelter)	Rent	Homeownership Cost*
1960	88.7	91.7	86.3
1964	92.9	95.9	90.8
1965	94.5	96.9	92.7
1966	97.2	98.2	96.3
1968	104.2	102.4	105.7
1969	109.8	105.7	116.0
1970	116.3	110.1	128.5
1971	121.3	115.2	133.7

*Includes home purchase, mortgage interest, taxes, insurance, and maintenance and repairs.
Source: Statistical Abstract of the United States 1972, Table 565, p. 348.

the property. The tax benefits of homeownership along with other factors have become capitalized in property values, presumably chiefly the site value, making it necessary to utilize these properties on an owner-occupied basis unless the owner is prepared to accept a temporary loss with some consolation in the form of favorable tax depreciation deductible from the rental income.

Anyone prepared to pay the costs of renting a substantial suburban home finds it necessary to be an owner or to negotiate a lower rent which in effect puts him in an economic position comparable to owner-occupancy.

One specific cost effect of the homeowner tax benefits is their impact on the price of capital—mortgage interest rates in the first instance but indirectly on the whole structure of interest rates in capital markets. The greater demand for housing—which is a capital-intensive form of consumer service—will thus raise capital costs for rental housing consumers and all consumers in proportion to the services of capital embodied in their consumption. Savers and capital investors will of course benefit from the higher interest rates generally engendered by the pressure of the capital-intensive demands of homeowners. This matter will be reviewed in the more specialized context of mortgage and capital market effects later in this chapter.

Effects on Homebuilding Industry

The pressure of additional demand for housing spurred by the homeowner tax deductions and exclusions has been reflected in homebuilding costs, construction methods, site values, and techniques for economization of scarce resources.

Between 1947 and 1959, the residential nonfarm structures component of gross private domestic investment increased from $10.4 billion to $24.8 billion, or by 138.5 percent; in the same period, total gross private domestic investments grew from $34 billion to $75.3 billion, or 121.5 percent. Gross national product

Table 5
Index of Union Wage Rates, Selected Trades, 1945-1971
(1967 = 100)

	1945	1950	1955	1960	1970	1971
Building trades	30.7	47.0	60.0	75.4	128.8	144.0
Printing trades	33.5	56.9	69.0	80.6	121.2	133.6
Motor truck drivers and helpers	28.6	44.8	59.4	75.4	122.5	137.8
Local transit operators	29.7	47.2	59.8	73.9	125.2	135.8

Source: Compiled from data in *Statistical Abstract of the United States 1972,* Table 375, p. 234.

rose from $231.3 billion to $483.7 billion, an increase of 109.1 percent in the 1947-59 period. Nonresidential structures increased from $23.4 billion to $45.1 billion or 92.7 percent over the same period.[20]

This brief recital of basic data on residential construction growth in a key period of postwar development suggests clearly the differentially higher rate of expansion of housing investment as compared with other forms of investment and the GNP as a whole. While various factors were at work producing this result, it seems difficult to escape the conclusion that homeowner tax benefits (along with depreciation tax stimulation for rental housing) accounted to a considerable extent for the higher growth rate for housing investment.

Costs

The inevitable result of this pressure has been rising costs, chiefly due to labor and land, although building materials have not lagged far behind.

Homeownership housing costs have risen more rapidly than other living costs and other types of housing costs (computed of course without regard to income tax benefits). Table 4 shows this effect in the past decade or so.

Union wage rates have risen more rapidly in the building trades than in comparable selected trades, but the differential increase has occurred only in the recent period. (See Table 5.)

Analysis of price and cost indexes for construction show the role of union wage scales on raising building costs. The fact that small residential building costs have risen less rapidly than the composite for apartments, hotels, office buildings or for commercial and industrial buildings may indicate the greater degree of unionization outside the small residential structure field. Nevertheless, the pressure of the homeowner tax deductions may communicate itself throughout the construction sector, contributing indirectly to the strength of the unionization movement in the apartment and commercial and industrial building sector.

As Table 6 shows, the price index for new one-family homes sold increased from 94 to 123 between 1965 and 1971, an increase of 29 index points or a price

Table 6
Price and Cost Indexes for Construction and Selected Components: 1950 to 1971
(1957-59 = 100 except as otherwise indicated)

	1950	1955	1960	1965	1968	1969	(1967 = 100)		
							1969	1970	1971
Price index for new one-family homes sold (1967=100)	NA	NA	NA	94.0	106.0	115.0	115.0	118.0	123.0
Wholesale prices of construction materials (1967=100)	78.9	90.4	95.5	95.8	105.6	111.9	111.9	112.5	119.5
Union hourly wage scales in the building trades (1967=100)	47.0	60.0	75.4	90.9	106.6	115.4	115.4	128.8	144.0
Construction cost indexes, E.H. Boeckh and Associates: small residential structures	80.3	92.4	104.2	115.2	136.7	148.0	116.2	122.4	132.8
apartments, hotels, and office buildings (composite)	75.8	90.4	105.0	118.5	139.9	151.8	116.1	124.4	135.0
commercial and factory buildings (composite)	74.0	89.5	104.7	117.2	139.1	149.1	114.5	123.1	133.9

Source: Compiled from *Statistical Abstract of the United States 1972,* Table 1136, p. 677.

rise of about 30.9 percent. In the same period, consumer prices generally increased about 25.4 percent, wholesale prices, about 17.9 percent. Again, the differentially higher rise in single family homes as compared with the consumer and wholesale price indexes generally suggests the economic pressure of additional housing demand based in part on income tax advantages.

The same type of differential appears from a comparison of indexes of shelter costs under rental as against owner-occupied tenure.

The comparison above may bring out the higher site value element which enters to a greater extent into homeownership costs (until such time as the high rise condominium dominates the market).

Comparison of Indexes of Shelter Costs

			Increase	
Shelter	**1960**	**1971**	**Index points**	**Percent**
Rent	91.7	115.2	23.5	25.6
Homeownership costs	86.3	133.7	47.4	54.9

Source: Computed from Statistical Abstract of the United States 1972, previously cited, Table 565, p. 348.

Rise of the Mobile Home Industry

One of the major responses of the homebuilding industry to the pressure of demand, partly attributable to tax factors, on housing resources—especially labor and land—is the expansion of the mobile home industry.

In 1965, shipments of mobile homes amounted to 216,000 units, or 14.7 percent of the 1,473,000 conventional private housing starts and 12.8 percent of the 1,689,000 combined total of housing starts and mobile home units. By 1971, mobile home shipments had risen to 497,000 units, 24.2 percent of the 2,052,000 private housing starts and 19.5 percent of the 2,549,000 combined total of housing starts and mobile home units.

Mobile home construction offers various advantages, primarily greater efficiency of construction on a mass production basis under factory conditions rather than onsite construction, affected by weather and utilizing traditional methods involving waste motion, etc. The mobile home itself may be located on a very small plot of ground with relatively little cost for sewer, water, and utility connections. Nevertheless, a major influence stimulating this move toward production of more economical—if slightly inferior and less esthetic by traditional standards—housing is the increase in labor and site value costs, due in part to increased housing demand flowing from the homeowner tax deductions.

Land Development

In the first two decades of postwar housing experience under the mass income tax, expansive land use, assisted by tax savings to homeowners, led to suburban and exurban development with junior estates, equestrian pursuits, and living patterns modeled after the 19th century gentry of Britain and Europe. This phase now seems to be approaching a turning point.

Expansive use of land spurred in part by the homeowner tax advantages, along with population growth and concentration of population in large metropolitan aggregates, has had the expected results: Land scarcity and higher land prices. Sprawl, fringe development, leapfrog development, and other techniques to cope with rising land values, reached limits. (In some cases, presumably temporary, the shortage has been aggravated by limitations on new water and sewer connections; this enhances the value of existing lots in use or approved for utility services. The latter type of shortage is not due to land shortage per se, although less expansive use of land would reduce the cost of sewer and water networks).

The scarcity of land for homebuilding purposes has elicited several discernible adaptations by the homebuilding industry:

1. Cluster or townhouse suburban housing development.
2. High-rise, garden-type, or similar land-economizing condominium development.
3. Reduction in the size of building lots.

Specific quantitative measures of these responses of the homebuilding industry to land scarcity and higher site values are not readily available. They are, however, noticeable. In the new equilibrium which is developing, the high land prices still tend to "capitalize" the tax savings for homeowners acquiring and using the land. The net land costs to homeowners, after their homeowner tax savings, are in line with their lower marginal utility, reflecting their more expansive use of land and with the higher marginal utility to renters who do not enjoy such tax benefits and rationally must use land more sparingly. In short, homeownership supports a more land-intensive form of housing than tenancy; this remains true even after the various forms of land economization that have developed in response to higher residential land prices.

Impact on the Mortgage Market and Capital Markets Generally

Although housing construction is a labor-intensive form of production, the provision of housing services by the completed residential property is in effect a highly capital-intensive form of production of consumer services.

The tax benefits for homeowners by stimulating additional housing have made extra, tax-related demands upon capital suppliers. Initially, the impact of these added demands is on the home mortgage money supply, but pressure on this market raises mortgage interest rates and draws in capital from other sectors of the capital market, realigning interest rates, albeit at a higher overall average level. In the process, interest rates became higher because capital supplies became tighter in the other interrelated capital market sectors from which the tax-pressurized home mortgage market draws its needed savings supplies.

The impact of the higher interest rates is felt particularly by consumers of products and services which, like housing, involve a capital-intensive production process. These consumers are not able to cushion the higher interest rates traceable to additional home mortgage financing by tax deductions.

Government may respond to the higher interest rates in home mortgage markets with various measures to increase the funds available for home mortgage purposes. To the extent the government's additional efforts merely provide additional funds for homebuyers via the budget or via budget-financed subsidies to mortgage finance institutions, the taxpaying population generally, including homeowners, shares the cost via the tax system or, in the absence of adequate taxation and related stabilization measures, via the inequitable form of burden-sharing provided by price inflation.[21]

NOTES

1. Henry Aaron, "Income Taxes and Housing," *The American Economic Review*, Vol. LX, No. 5 (December 1970), p. 803.
2. Ibid.
3. Ibid., n. 33.
4. Dan Throop Smith, *Federal Tax Reform*, McGraw-Hill, New York, 1961, pp. 91-92.
5. From the social viewpoint, the capital invested in owner-occupied homes is less likely to become "unemployed," in contrast with the vacancy potential of rental housing. This helps stabilize an element in the GNP.
6. For a brief review of the literature on the subject, see *The Economics of Federal Subsidy Programs*, Joint Economic Committee, Congress of the United States, Jan. 11, 1972, U.S. Government Printing Office, Washington, D.C., 1972, p. 30, n.1.
7. For a review of the merits of the tax incentive, backdoor spending or tax expenditure approach to policy objectives versus the direct expenditure method, with particular reference to housing programs, see Richard E. Slitor, *The Federal Income Tax in Relation to Housing*, National Commission on Urban Problems, Research Report No. 5, U.S. Government Printing Office, Washington, D.C., 1968, Chapter V, pp. 86-100; and Richard E. Slitor, "Tax Incentives and Urban Blight," in *Tax Incentives, Tax Institute of America Symposiums*, Heath Lexington Books.
8. As of 1960, Goode estimated that the combined revenue loss from exclusion of new rent and deduction of mortgage interest and property taxes on nonfarm owner-occupied dwellings was $3.8 billion, of which $1.2 billion was due to the net rent and $2.6 billion to the two deductions. Richard Goode, *The Individual Income Tax*, Studies of Government Finance, The Brookings Institution, Washington, D.C., 1964, pp. 120-124. Goode's discussion specifically recognizes that his estimates do not allow for the use of the standard deduction by some homeowners. However, it does not mention the significance of the fact that even for taxpayers claiming the itemized deductions, the itemized amount is not a clear gain to the taxpayer since he could have taken the standard deduction anyway. He observes, however, that the standard deduction presumably would be reduced if itemized.
9. Richard Goode, *The Individual Income Tax*, Studies of Government Finance, The Brookings Institution, Washington, D.C., 1964, pp. 125-126.

10. See Henry Aaron, "Income Taxes and Housing," *The American Economic Review*, Vol. LX, No. 5 (December 1970), pp. 602-603. This estimate assumes an overall mean marginal tax rate among homeowners of 22 percent and exclusion of imputed rent plus deductions of mortgage interest and property tax expenses equal to 62.5 percent of gross rental value.

11. See David Laidler, "Income Tax Incentives for Owner-Occupied Housing," in *The Taxation of Income From Capital*, Arnold C. Harberger and Martin J. Bailey, Editors, Studies of Government Finance, The Brookings Institution, Washington, D.C., 1969, pp. 51-52, 58, and Table 4, p. 71.

12. These figures are based on independent estimates by the author but are closely in line with the middle of the range of estimates developed by Aaron, "Income Taxes and Housing," previously cited, Table 10, p. 802. It should be noted that the applicable tax rate appropriately assumed in calculating investors' tax benefits in connection with rental housing is substantially higher than that appropriate for the typical homeowner, probably in the 40 to 70 percent range. Certain higher estimates by Sunley are discussed later.

13. *The Individual Income Tax*, previously cited, p. 125.

14. Source: Estimates for 1909 and 1919 from J. Frederick Dewhurst and Associates, *America's Needs and Resources*, New York: Twentieth Century Fund, 1955, p. 206. Figures for later years derived from estimates of the Office of Business Economics, U.S. Department of Commerce: *U.S. Income and Output*, 1958, and *Survey of Current Business*, July 1963. The constant-price estimate for 1929 (*U.S. Income and Output*, p. 5) in 1957 prices.

15. "Income Tax Incentives for Owner-Occupied Housing," previously cited, Table 2, p. 60.

16. "Income Tax Incentives for Housing," previously cited, p. 64.

17. Estimate based on extrapolation of the additional housing in proportion to the growth of the total housing stock at the average annual rate prevailing in the 1960-70 decade, shown in *Statistical Abstract of the United States*, 1972, previously cited, section 33, p. 846.

18. See "Income Taxes and Housing," previously cited, p. 799.

19. "Income Tax Incentives for Owner-Occupied Housing," previously cited, p. 61.

20. 1971 *Business Statistics*, Biennial Supplement to the Survey of Current Business, U.S. Department of Commerce, Office of Business Economics, pp. 191-192.

21. For a somewhat truncated version of this standard analysis, see Aaron, "Income Taxes and Housing," previously cited, p. 803.

III
Direct Federal Housing Assistance

11

Historical Overview of Direct
Federal Housing Assistance

J. Paul Mitchell

PUBLIC HOUSING

Public housing is housing owned and operated by a government agency. Public ownership removes the need for a positive return on the capital invested and allows the borrowing of capital at interest rates lower than those required for private investment. While both these advantages permit lower rents, neither involves an outright public subsidy of lower income households. An additional potential source for lower rents, involving an outright public subsidy, is for government to rent such housing at levels below actual cost and make up the deficit from general revenues (taxes).

Public housing in the United States is still based on the landmark Wagner Housing Act of 1937. A century of housing reform gradually turned toward government ownership as the solution to the dreadful slum conditions of industrial cities. A few public housing projects had been built during World War I, but they had been turned over to private ownership at the end of the war. Housing had been added to the list of federal public works projects designed to provide employment as the Great Depression deepened in the early 1930s. The 1937 act created the mechanism—federal funding for projects owned and operated by specially created local housing authorities—which continues today. The first wave of public housing construction was ended by World War II, when resources were diverted and temporary housing was constructed near war industries plants.

Public housing languished until another landmark, the Housing Act of 1949, combined it with slum clearance to produce urban renewal. Urban renewal's large clearance programs included very little public housing to replace demolished units. Indeed, public housing languished once again during the 1950s; those projects built were generally on a huge scale. Until the 1980s the volume of construction has waxed and waned, depending upon the particular administration's social philosophy and spending priorities. Changes have been made in the method of determining rent, income eligibility, and the level of federal subsidy. Special elderly housing has appeared. Large-scale projects have been discouraged in favor of a scattered-site approach. Non-profit organizations and private developers and landlords have been enlisted in various ways to provide low-cost housing for low- and moderate-income households.

Through all its changes and despite numerous attacks, public housing remains. Yet the wisdom of providing public housing continues to be suspect, and the commitment to public housing as the preferred solution to the problem of inadequate housing is not now, and never has been, strong. It has been attacked, on the one hand, as blatant socialism and, for the past 20 years, on the other hand, even by some of its former supporters, as counterproductive and inefficient, and charged with merely creating new slums.

According to Charles Abrams, "The slum exists because no nation is able to produce adequate housing at a cost that workers can afford. It is the shelter that the industrial age provides for its rank and file."[1]

Abrams's pessimistic observation certainly applies to the burgeoning industrial centers of nineteenth century United States. Whether they came from Ireland, Poland, or Nebraska, a steady stream of job seekers crowded into shacks and tenements hastily thrown together. Although they might look good to twentieth century street people in Calcutta, these accommodations were nonetheless squalid. High rents and low wages forced crowding. Shoddy construction resulted in flats without light, fresh air, or protection from the elements. Primitive technology and explosive growth created neighborhoods with few amenities; many were liberally strewn with garbage, and animal and human refuse.

Slums were thus easily, and appropriately, identified with ill-health, disease, and early death. Just as important, they were offensive to the eyes and noses of the upper classes. Slums were associated with a host of social pathologies— crime, vice, personal disorders. Such a degraded environment seemed a serious threat to the physical, social, and moral well-being of its residents. Concern over the dangers of slums was compounded by the fact that most slum dwellers, especially in northeastern and north central cities, were immigrants or children of immigrants. Cultural and physical differences, amid the festering slum environment, threatened not only the erosion of traditional American values but even the destruction of social order. Efforts to remedy the ills of unhealthful and unsafe housing, and programs to provide public or publicly assisted housing, have been concerned with both the plight of the poor slum dweller and the spectre of social disorder.

A host of remedies for slums and bad housing was proposed between 1830 and 1930. One approach is typified by the New York Association for Improving the Condition of the Poor (AICP), formed in 1843 and lasting well into the twentieth century. Its socially prominent members were primarily concerned with the moral uplift of the impoverished. The AICP appealed to the conscience of the wealthy; it sought to channel their charitable contributions to projects that would help the "deserving poor" rise above their dismal surroundings and to avoid charity that only encouraged the indolent poor. Reporter Jacob Riis represented the journalistic crusaders' zealous attack on slums through relentless publicity and frank exposure. *How the Other Half Lives: Studies Among the Tenements of New York* (1890) was the first of several hard-hitting books Riis wrote, and it remains a classic description in human terms of slum living. Carroll D. Wright, much less flamboyantly, sought to stimulate and inform the battle by amassing data measuring the extent and qualities of poor housing. As U.S. Commissioner of Labor he produced *The Slums of Baltimore, Chicago, New York, and Philadelphia* (1894), an overwhelming statistical indictment of big city living conditions. Jane Addams, from Hull House in Chicago, developed the neighborhood settlement house as a cultural oasis and source of hope through communal self-affirming activities. Henry George advocated the single tax as the most effective way to eliminate slums; if the public would tax the entire unearned increment added to the value of land by urban growth, there would be no speculative real estate profits and, hence, no slum lords. Socialists insisted that bad housing was the direct inevitable result of low wages. The only way to eliminate slums was to pay workers a living wage, which would only be possible if the economic system were changed so workers themselves owned the means of production.

Public housing as a solution grew from two major housing reform movements. One was the model tenement movement, which sought enlightened investors who would build decent housing designed to provide adequate shelter and adequate profits. The second was the effort to regulate housing by setting minimum legal standards and thereby prohibiting the worst types of housing.

The model tenement idea was based on the conviction that capitalists could and would combine philanthropy and profits. As a movement, it lasted from the 1850s to the 1910s. Its advocates and practitioners were genuinely interested in helping the poor, not by charity, but by offering them an environment conducive to the development of sound moral principles. Model tenements were supposed to be well-designed and soundly constructed; they were to be profitable, but reasonably rather than speculatively, so that the sturdy working classes could afford the rents. They would prove that business principles and morality were compatible and thus attract emulators. Eventually, they hoped, working class housing would be provided by the intelligent and wealthy classes, rather than short-sighted, ultimately irresponsible speculators who were currently setting standards.

From time to time there were some model tenement successes which pointed the way for improved apartment design—more open spaces, better interior arrangements, larger plots, more interesting details. But as is often the case, its few outstanding examples—the Octavia Hill Association of Philadelphia, Alfred T. White's apartments in New York City, and the Pullman community outside Chicago—are noteworthy because of their scarcity. The movement ultimately failed because the concept of limited dividends did not attract sufficient wealthy investors to the risky enterprise of renting housing to poor tenants. It was based on the misapprehension that apartment owners either were, or would be, extremely wealthy individuals who could afford to indulge altruism. In the actual case, real estate, then as now, constituted a major perceived means to wealth. Slum housing in particular, usually small and cheap, attracted marginal owners who often lived on the same property with their tenants. Slum owners, in short, had neither the financial security nor the paternalistic motives required for a limited dividend approach. The model tenement movement failed to change that.

Housing reform through restrictive legislation offered an altogether different avenue to slum improvement. It attacked bad housing directly by legal proscription: investors and builders would not be allowed to construct unsafe and unhealthy houses, and landlords would be required to improve existing units. New York City enacted a law directly applicable to dwellings in 1867; subsequent laws were enacted in cities throughout the country, the most famous being the New York Tenement House Law of 1901. Such laws usually required plumbing, light, and direct access and set minimum standards for space, window area, public space, construction materials, and the like. If appeals to altruism could not induce landlords to provide decent accommodations, then standards would be imposed by law.

Restrictive legislation's greatest success has been in banning the construction of new units inherently substandard and in establishing standards. Housing reformers were, however, disappointed by the enforcement of such laws. Enforcement was hampered by the sheer size of the task—there were too many dwellings and not enough inspectors. The temptations offered inspectors by landlords for overlooking violations also hampered enforcement, as did the tendency in some cities for the entire process to become involved in the unsavory side of political manipulation. But just as significant a shortcoming grew from the cruel fact that zealous enforcement of codes required improvements whose cost landlords inevitably passed on to tenants. And finally, restrictive laws could not ensure the provision of dwellings. Investors could not be forced to build; particularly, they could not be forced to build housing that would rent at prices affordable to the working poor.

Both the model tenement and restrictive legislation movements enjoyed modest success, and both contributed to the overall improvement of housing standards. Nevertheless, each of these movements fell short. Neither could eliminate the slum nor provide adequate housing for the poor.

By 1930 two things seemed clear to housing activists. First, substantial improvements in urban housing conditions necessitated massive capital investment.

Second, private enterprise simply had not provided an ample supply of decent housing affordable to low-income residents. These two conclusions were strengthened by the conviction that better housing required the elimination of existing bad housing.

Attention gradually turned toward the public sector. Both model tenement advocate Alfred T. White and tenement house law crusader Lawrence Veiller had vehemently denounced the idea of public ownership or direct governmental provision of housing. But the failure of private enterprise led 1930s housers to conclude that some public inducement, some government subsidy, was needed. For some, public subsidy was merely a pragmatic response to the high costs of land and construction in cities. For others, public participation was a moral duty, the proper response of an industrial society with a conscience to the problems created by social inequities.

Granting a need for public subsidy, was public ownership of housing advisable? Committed housing reformers were not of one mind. James Ford, for example, in his monumental, two-volume *Slums and Housing* (1936), raised the objection that public ownership of housing would extract the money to rehouse a limited number of slum families from taxpayers whose own incomes would be only slightly higher. He also warned that "the very safeguards designed to prevent waste of public capital" seriously handicapped government's actions as compared with actions by the private sector. Ford recommended that the federal government help pay for the elimination of substandard housing and that state or local government retain ownership of the cleared lands but lease them to private capital for housing construction. Ford argued that land was a "proper field for public ownership." Land management was a legal, rather than business, problem; accounting would be simple; and public interest in land management was paramount. He expected that government would take an immediate financial loss in order "to make the land available at a price inviting to private capital." But he believed that thus encouraged, and under careful government standards and supervision, slum rebuilding could be handled by the private sector.

While James Ford wanted government only to own the land on which private enterprise built and managed low-income housing, others believed that the entire operation should be owned and operated by the public. The precedent for this approach was twofold: 1) the government-owned housing in Europe, especially England; and 2) the municipally owned utilities in American cities. Such housing reformers as Catherine Bauer, Edith Elmer Wood, Langdon Post, Mary Simkhovitch, and Msgr. John A. Ryan argued, in speeches, magazines and journals, and anywhere else they could get a hearing, that government had a moral duty to provide housing. They contended that only through government ownership would housing be treated as a public utility rather than as a source of wealth. Only public ownership could eliminate the inherent contradiction between the need for profit and the need for low-cost housing, a contradiction which doomed private enterprise to failure.

Housing reformers of whatever persuasion emphasized the need for large-scale slum clearance and rehousing. For them, the small size of individual lots was it-self a major contributor to substandard housing and slum neighborhoods. Be-cause so much of the bad housing environment was really a neighborhood effect, reformers believed that piecemeal reconstruction or rehabilitation would soon be overwhelmed. The massive scale of slum clearance and the anticipated rehousing projects also argued for public ownership and operation.

The Great Depression provided the historical occasion and circumstance for the beginning of public housing. There had been modest public housing efforts under state and local auspices during the 1920s, most particularly in New York under the leadership of Governor Al Smith. But the onslaught of the Depression, with unemployment nationally at 25 percent and much higher in many cities, exhausted state and local governmental resources. Demands for public action therefore came to focus on the federal government. Slum clearance, construction employment, and adequate housing for the working classes thus all melded into a demand for action.

The early public works phase of public housing experienced the same prob-lems as other public works projects: cautious administration, bureaucratic delays, and a tentative philosophic commitment. A program designed to put construction workers back to work, and which was centrally controlled, seemed inherently antithetical to sensitive treatment of local housing needs. Pressure continued from housing reformers to launch a federally funded housing program which would be designed to provide low-cost housing and to operate it with the needs of its low-income tenants uppermost.

Opposition to such a program was strong, particularly from the private housing sector. But opposition also came from those, including public servants, with negative attitudes toward the poor. Even Congressmen who favored a more ac-tive housing role for government had deep reservations about public ownership of housing and fears of the long-range consequences of providing a direct sub-sidy.

Such opposition and reservations were reflected in three major concerns: 1) not to create a permanent dependent class as clients; 2) not to house public clients luxuriously; and 3) not to infringe upon the private sector. The first concern led to the idea that tenants should pay their own way, i.e., that rents should be set at levels that would make the projects self-liquidating. It also resulted in setting upper income limits so that, as tenants' incomes improved, they would have to move out. One last measure stemming from the fear that public housing might create a permanent dependent class was the initial practice by most local housing authorities of not admitting persons who were receiving public relief. The second concern led to stringent cost limitations and to economy measures that sometimes resulted in inadequate design and provisions (e.g. highrise buildings with too few elevators making stops at only every other floor). The desire not to compete di-rectly with private enterprise reinforced the policy of firm upper income limits for eligibility. It also tied public housing to slum clearance. In the 1930s there were high vacancy rates in most cities and rental units were boarded up and involved in tax delinquency sales. As a result, housing was available and rentals were relatively low. But the volume of construction, repair, and maintenance had diminished to such an extent that the quality and quantity of adequate housing had declined. In such conditions added housing competition from the government seemingly posed an undue threat to the free market. If slum clearance could be linked to public housing, then at least the total supply of housing units would not be increased. Since slum clearance would remove some of the worst existing housing, reformers were also inclined to bless this union.

After two years of intense debate, the Housing Act of 1937 was finally enacted, thereby creating the framework for the United States's public housing system. The U.S. Housing Authority controlled the funds which it was authorized to borrow because it retained the contractual right to approve the plans, site, and cost of a project. But the initiative for conceiving, planning, and building a public housing project rested with local authorities, as did the actual administration of projects once completed. Local control was vested in local housing authorities, created under their respective state laws, acting as independent agencies appointed by and responsible to local elected officials. This combination of federal funds and general policies, on one hand, and decentralized implementation and particular decisionmaking, on the other, was intended to apply federal resources in a locally sensitive manner. The structure has essentially remained, albeit while federal oversight has shifted from one agency to another; the major change has been in the gradual increase in federal regulations which spell out policies and administrative procedures in finer and finer detail.

Public housing projects were usually centrally located on sites in transitional areas of marginal housing and mixed uses. The feeling that this was a significant social experiment often resulted in careful preparation, design, and planning. Sturdy physical facilities coupled with the provision of social services helped make these projects a success. Four to five decades later many of these early projects still provide solid shelter and often remain the best public housing local authorities have to offer. But fewer than 40,000 units were completed before World War II intervened.

As World War II heated up after 1939, the conditions under which public housing had been launched changed. Industrial output climbed steadily and unemployment declined dramatically. By mid-1940 the country's new housing problem was one closely tied to the needs of war industries: thousands of newcomers poured into Detroit, Newport News, and other war material production centers. Severe local housing shortages threatened to choke off the production of ships, guns, and tanks. From then until the war's end in 1945 a fierce struggle was waged over the nation's public housing policy, and the program so bravely launched in 1937 slowed to a near halt.

The battle over defense housing was waged over two issues, both elements of the basic question of whether there ought to be public housing at all. One fight was a bureaucratic contest over whether defense housing should be administered by the U.S. Housing Authority as part of the nation's public housing program or by more particularistic agencies called into being to coordinate the government's war efforts. The other controversy raged over whether wartime housing for industrial workers should be built solely as temporary shelter, to be demolished or sold to private owners at war's end, or as permanent housing for the nation's lower income workers.

The Lanham Act, in October, 1940, embodied the idea that defense housing should be temporary and in no way threaten the private housing sector. Under its provisions about 945,000 housing units were constructed, almost all of shoddy materials, and designed to be demolished as soon after the war as possible. In 1945 Congress authorized that Lanham Act housing be made available to distressed families of servicemen and to veterans and their families. These barracks-like projects with paper-thin walls remained to help ease the transition to peacetime: the demand for autos and consumer goods kept the wheels of industry turning once tank and gun production ceased, and the return of 12 million veterans kept the pressure on tight housing markets. In many communities Lanham Act housing served as the spawning grounds for the famous Baby Boom. But shoddy construction and cramped quarters hastened the deterioration of the Bonny Hames and Victory Apartments. As veterans and blue collar workers could afford to, they moved out. Gradually these rabbit warrens emptied and were torn down, amid expressions of good riddance rather than lament. War housing added nothing to, indeed subtracted much from, the design and implementation of a coherent national public housing program. The opponents of public housing had clearly won the war within the war.

In spite of the acute housing shortage of the immediate postwar years, virtually no public housing was constructed. The private housing market, however, boomed, partially fueled by the FHA and VA loan programs. Congressional debates, as well as public discussion of the issue, indicated that public housing, far from being accepted as an integral part of a national housing strategy, was still fighting for its very survival. Indeed, it survived only by strengthening, even making primary, its link to slum clearance and the revitalization of city centers.

The Housing Act of 1949 was the result of this protracted debate. It promulgated the goal of a decent home and a suitable living environment for every American family, a goal which has remained both so heralded and so elusive. Under its terms, Congress authorized the construction of 810,000 units over the next six years, which would bring the total to one million public housing units by 1955. The Housing Act of 1949 also provided the mechanism and funding for large-scale redevelopment projects, ostensibly for slum clearance operating in tandem with the construction of public housing. Redevelopment used the model of federal funding and local decision-making provided in the 1937 housing act. Local renewal authorities, appointed by and responsible to locally elected officials, would initiate and administer the development of renewal projects. They would assemble large parcels of land, clear them of existing outmoded structures, replan infrastructure, and then sell the land to private developers. Assembling and preparing centrally located land was extremely expensive in relation to vacant or underdeveloped land on the urban periphery. In order to be competitive, therefore, this cleared land would have to be sold at a loss to private developers; federal funds would make up two-thirds of the difference between cost and sale price.

Time proved there was more interest in renewal for commercial purposes than in additional public housing. Even the initial promise that public housing would replace inadequate shelter demolished for renewal went unfulfilled. In the six years following the Housing Act of 1949 only 192,000 units were completed and, after twelve years, only 289,000. It was not until 1972 that the 810,000 units authorized in 1949 had been made available for occupancy. The 135,000 annual rate envisioned in 1949 has never been reached. The peak year was 1971 when 91,500 new public housing units were opened; however, in 1976 and 1977 the Nixon moratorium reduced the annual total to less than 7,000, the lowest figures to date. Public housing thus did not receive the commitment of funds necessary to make it a significant vehicle for realizing the goal of a decent home in a suitable environment for every American family.

Public housing changed as economic and social conditions changed. The working class for whom public housing had been built originally was, after World War II, being housed in little, single-family dwellings on the outskirts of cities and towns, aided by higher wages, mortgage insurance, and more liberal home-lending terms. Large-scale, multifamily housing no longer fit the American dream of ideal shelter and neighborhoods. The income ceilings placed on public housing tenants drove out those whose incomes rose. And financial constraints, along with the desire to avoid housing poor people in a style even remotely luxurious, stripped later projects of design amenities and social services. Consequently, public housing acquired an institutional look and often provided a living environment far short of the model communities its initial backers had envisioned. As a result, by the 1960s, public housing's clientele had shifted from the upwardly mobile working poor to a more or less permanently dependent group, the hard-core poor whose minority status, lack of education or training, and/or family conditions relegated them to housing of last resort. Even the group whose needs were most catered to after 1959, the elderly, were a permanent dependent group: they were not likely to get younger, find better-paying jobs, or attain greater wealth.

Along with the change in public housing's clients came a shift in the method of determining rents. Initially rents had been set at levels which would enable the local housing authority to cover its operating costs. But costs rose faster than tenants' incomes, which put a real squeeze on their meager budgets. Tenant protests were especially potent when directed against a public landlord; the image of a cold-hearted government extracting over 50 percent of a poverty-stricken family's income for rent in a spare highrise tenement was political dynamite. The federal response came in a series of amendments enacted from 1969 to 1971, collectively called the Brooke Amendments (after their sponsor Senator Edward Brooke of Massachusetts). The effect of the Brooke Amendments was to shift the basis for determining rent levels from operating costs to tenants' incomes. The upper limit for public housing rents was set at 25 percent of tenant income, from which allowances for dependents and certain types of income were excluded. Rents thus varied from almost zero to above cost levels, with enormous concentrations at the lower end of the scale.

The impact of this new rental policy was financial relief for hard-pressed tenants, but it came at the expense of financial disaster for local housing authorities. Incomes simply did not cover expenses. The Housing and Community Development Act of 1974 offered a small measure of relief by setting a minimum rent of either 5 percent of family income or the portion of a tenant's welfare income earmarked for housing. Still, the gap between rent receipts and operating costs remained wide and had to be made up by increasing federal subsidies in the form of heftier annual contributions. In 1982 Congress sought to reduce direct federal subsidy payments by gradually raising the rent ceiling to 30 percent of tenant income.

Throughout its half-century of existence public housing has failed to capture the public's fancy. On the national level it has always encountered fierce opposition from well-organized lobbying groups. Organizations such as the National Association of Real Estate Boards and the United States Savings League have consistently attacked public housing as a socialistic program which threatens private enterprise with unfair competition from the public sector. Local realtors and others who comprise these associations actively disseminated nationally prepared anti-public housing propaganda in their own communities, especially during the 1940s and 1950s. They were effective, particularly in some smaller cities, in preventing or delaying the formation of local housing authorities.

Still, on the local level, opposition has been less ideological than particularistic and site specific. This is because public housing stops being abstract and becomes a very tangible physical presence on the neighborhood level: "Don't build it in *my* neighborhood!" From an individual's perspective public housing is usually seen as a drab, institutional, unsightly project out of scale with the neighborhood, inhabited by people who are, by definition, undesirable—low-class, uncaring, of the wrong race, with bad attitudes, and a host of social pathologies that will ruin the neighborhood. Of course a public housing project, its opponents contend, will destroy property values. This image of public housing as a sort of colony of society's outcasts and failures has militated against the creation of a broadly based constituency at the same time it has so often forced the location of public housing in areas no one else wants. The public clamor for public housing has never materialized.

Finally, public housing has lost much of its support from those sympathetic to the need for direct housing subsidies. As all too many projects seemed merely to recreate the slums they were supposed to replace, and at an inordinately high price, serious doubts have been expressed from all quarters as to the appropriateness of public housing as a solution. In their efforts to reconstruct entire communities and build better neighborhoods, early reformers had envisioned building on a grand scale, but this created institutional agglomerations of hard-core poverty cases and problem families. Too often public housing seemed to depress, rather than uplift, the human spirit. By the late 1960s critics were even suggesting that the slow pace of new public housing was a blessing in disguise. At the same time, public housing served only a very small proportion (something around 5 percent) of those eligible because, as a capital investment program, it was so expensive. On the grounds of both horizontal equity and cost-effectiveness public housing was vulnerable. Nevertheless, it is important to remember that most local housing authorities have had to deal with waiting lists of prospective tenants.

ALTERNATIVES TO PUBLIC HOUSING

The persistent unpopularity of, and reluctant commitment to, public housing have prompted a continuing search for alternatives. Not surprisingly, efforts to enlist the private sector have predominated, despite the fact that the very existence of public housing testifies to the failure of the private market to provide decent housing for low-income persons. That the private sector does things better remains an article of faith. Therefore, if the problem is that little or no profit can be made by providing decent housing for the poor, the task of government should be to make such enterprise profitable by some form of subsidy to private investors, who will then step forward with their superior expertise and do the job faster, cheaper, and better.

There have been other less ideological and more pragmatic reasons advanced for efforts to replace public with private housing:

1. Public housing represents an enormous capital investment; if this capital investment were private, public housing assistance dollars would stretch further and cover more needy households.
2. Public housing involves a long-term ownership commitment to a tangible physical product; private ownership, with guarantees of public subsidy for shorter time periods, would be more flexible and allow adjustments to changing needs and/or conditions.
3. As people moved away from central cities, there remained a large stock of available adequate housing; it seemed foolish and wasteful for the public to construct new units when there were surplus privately owned units.
4. Public housing in large projects created large concentrations of disadvantaged households with attendant social problems; privately owned units

would be inherently more decentralized and offer superior living environments without the stigma of project residence. This scattered-site approach—economic and social integration—had become one of the major goals of all federal housing programs after the late 1960s.

The effort to enlist the private sector took several major forms. One form was to encourage religious, charitable, and other eleemosynary organizations to commit their financial and human resources to low-income housing projects. Another was to induce private investors and developers to form limited dividend corporations which would develop low-income housing (comparable to the model tenement movement). The most basic form, however, was to subsidize some part of the process in order to make low-income housing profitable and thereby attract basic profit seekers.

PROGRAMS

Programs to provide alternatives have proliferated during the past quarter century. The following are among the most significant programs directed toward achieving the ends discussed previously.

Elderly Housing

Housing subsidies for low-income people who are elderly have been politically more popular than subsidies for families. This has been true both on the national and on the local levels. Elderly tenants tend to cause little damage, pay their rent on time, and make few demands on neighbors and neighborhoods. There is relatively little stigma attached to retirees, widows, and widowers with low incomes; moreover, everyone hopes eventually to be old. Furthermore, high-density apartments are well-suited to elderly clients. Consequently, much of the public housing built since the late 1950s has been elderly housing—in some years two-thirds of new authorizations. Section 202 of the 1959 Housing Act authorized low-cost, direct federal loans to private nonprofit sponsors for new or rehabilitated rental housing structures for the elderly. The 1961 Housing Act authorized the subsidy of operating costs (for the first time ever) of public housing units occupied by elderly tenants. The Section 8 rent supplement program of the Housing and Community Development Act of 1974 (see below) began with a heavy imbalance of elderly over family new construction units. In general, low-income elderly have fared better than low-income family households in direct subsidy programs.

Below-Market Interest Rates

The 1961 Housing Act, Section 221 (d) (3), introduced a subsidized, below-market rate mortgage insurance program under which private investors—profit-making or nonprofit-making—would provide rental housing for moderate-income families ineligible for public housing but unable to afford decent shelter in the open market. Since the Federal National Mortgage Association would buy the mortgages made by private lenders, 221 (d) (3) was in effect a direct loan program. As interest rates rose during the 1960s, the gap widened, and the program's cost increased. Moreover, for budget accounting purposes the entire mortgage value was recorded as an outlay in each project's initial year; this made the program seem extremely expensive and opened it to adverse criticism. Such criticism hit home because rents needed to meet expenses were still too high for low-income tenants, and most 221 (d) (3) projects were built for households at the top of the income eligibility scale. Finally, only about 10,000 units were built in each of the program's first seven years.

Still, the housing industry liked the below-market interest-rate idea. So did Congress and both the Douglas and Kaiser Commissions which reported the results of their studies in 1968. Rising interest rates meant that interest constituted an ever larger proportion of total housing costs, which in turn offered an appealing target for federal efforts to make housing more affordable.

The Housing Act of 1968 constituted a landmark: it established numerical goals for housing production during the succeeding decade. There were two driving forces behind this effort to increase housing production: 1) the postwar "Baby Boom" generation was then entering its prime family-formation years; and 2) the 1949 goal of a decent home in a suitable living environment required substantial replacement of existing inadequate housing. Accordingly, in 1968 Congress enacted the Kaiser Commission's recommended 10-year goal of 26 million new and rehabilitated housing units, including 6 million units for lower-income households.

Subsidized interest rates were to be the major vehicle for stimulating lower income housing construction. Section 235 provided a subsidy for low-income homeowners by making up the difference between mortgage payments at 1 percent interest and the market rate. Section 236 provided the same subsidy for owners of multifamily rental units. This Section 236 superseded Section 221 (d) (3); it differed from Section 221 (d) (3) by paying the subsidy to the project owner annually rather than buying the mortgage in its entirety at the outset. Both programs stimulated the volume of housing construction: 1971, 1972 and 1973 were peak years with total starts in excess of 2 million each. But, again, rising interest rates boosted program cost, the Section 235 homeownership program was vulnerable to abuse by contractors, and the burdens of homeownership caused many lower-income families to abandon homes in which they had little equity. Consequently both interest-rate subsidy programs fell victim to the Nixon moratorium in 1973 and were not revived.

Housing Allowances
(Rent Certificates and Housing Vouchers)

Housing allowances are payments made directly to eligible households to help cover housing costs in privately owned units of their own choosing. The idea first was discussed in terms of "rent certificates" during the debates over public housing in the 1930s, again during the postwar housing policy debates from 1944 to 1949, and by the President's Advisory Committee on Government Housing Policies and Programs in 1953. Its proponents, including the National Association of Real Estate Boards, were ardent champions of private enterprise who argued that the private housing market, using existing units, could provide housing at lower cost and more efficiently than could public housing projects. Rent certificates would simply increase effective demand and thereby restore incentive to an otherwise unprofitable field. In the 1930s rent certificates were rejected as too much like a dole and, hence, degrading to recipients, and as too scattered to effect significant improvement in the housing stock of urban slums. In the 1940s and 1950s such proposals were rejected, even by conservatives such as Senator Robert A. Taft, because (1) they would cost more than public housing, (2) the program's scale would become unwieldy, (3) a government program would discourage rather than entice private enterprise, and (4) new low-rent housing would not be expanded, and substandard housing would not be eliminated.

Housing allowances resurfaced after more than a decade, this time as "rent supplements" and "leased housing" in the Housing Act of 1965. Under the 1965 rent supplement program, payments would be made to the private owners of newly constructed or substantially rehabilitated housing so that low-income households could live there. Such payments were limited to the difference between the unit's fair market rent and one-fourth of the tenant's income; as income increased, subsidy payments would be reduced, but tenants who could eventually pay full rent unassisted would not be evicted.

The 1965 Housing Act, under its Section 23 leased housing program, further tapped the private housing supply by authorizing local housing authorities to lease existing private housing units and in effect sublet them to low-income families eligible for regular public housing. Again, the tenants paid a portion of their income for rent and the government paid the difference. As with the rent supplement program, Section 23 leased housing stopped short of being a true housing allowance in that local housing authorities located the housing, the subsidies went directly to landlords rather than households, and the subsidies were tied to particular housing units rather than to eligible households.

By the late 1960s there was heightened interest in a true housing allowance strategy. To the usual bias in favor of private ownership was added a new argument: improvements in the nation's housing stock had sharply reduced the proportion of inadequate housing units. To many students of housing there seemed to be an ample supply of decent shelter—it was simply too expensive for low-income households. There remained substantial disagreement on this issue, but a significant body of housing experts thus redefined the nation's housing problem as an income-distribution problem. Accordingly, solutions proposed were designed to reduce the financial burden of low-income households who were forced to pay inordinate portions of their meager incomes for rent. In 1968 the President's Committee on Urban Housing, or Kaiser Committee, recommended that housing allowances, not tied to specific units, be tried on an experimental basis. Given a large supply of vacant housing in many cities, housing allowances using existing privately owned units seemed to offer lower subsidy costs than newly constructed public housing requiring large capital investment. But serious doubts were raised about its potential inflationary impact.

Authorized by the Housing Act of 1970, HUD began the groundwork for a major social experiment launched in 1973, and eventually extending to 12 cities —the Experimental Housing Allowance Program (EHAP). Housing allowances—the difference between the fair market rent (FMR) of a standard unit and 25 percent of the assisted household's income—were paid to participating households, who were then free to find their own housing. The amount of their subsidy was determined by their income and housing needs, not by the actual rent they paid. They had an incentive to find lower rents because they could keep whatever savings they could realize. EHAP was designed to find out the impact of housing allowances on 1) the quantity of housing services consumed by low-income households, 2) the supply of new or rehabilitated housing, 3) possible housing inflation, 4) household mobility, and 5) neighborhood upgrading, among others. EHAP has been written about exhaustively. Its results were not predictable and by no means conclusive; they have been read by both opponents and proponents of housing allowances as bolstering their respective contentions.

President Nixon believed that housing allowances were more flexible, deconcentrated, and efficient than public housing. He even seriously considered what some housing experts were advocating during his first term, namely, that housing allowances become an entitlement program. His administration looked to EHAP for guidance, intending to make housing allowances the foundation for a new housing policy after the moratorium. President Nixon's task force, the National Housing Policy Review, recommended that federal housing policy focus on the demand side—that subsidies should go directly to those who needed them rather than to the owners of specific units.

The Housing and Community Development Act of 1974 represented the next step in the direction of housing allowances. Its Section 8 was designed to deal with the great variety in quality of housing stock, vacancy rates, and rent and income levels observable in different cities. Section 8 was based on private ownership and management of assisted housing units, and set locally determined fair market rent (FMR) levels for acceptable units of varying sizes and characteristics. It provided a subsidy equal to the difference between the actual rent paid and 15 to 25 percent (depending on income level) of a participating household's income. The local housing authorities received the federal monies and administered the program, including quality determination, contract-letting for construction, and actual rent payments, which went directly to landlords.

Section 8 had two different thrusts represented by three major subprograms.

The first thrust was a construction strategy in which subsidies were tied to specific housing units. Section 8 New Construction resembled public housing, except that private owners were required to make the capital investment. When a project was approved, its sponsor was guaranteed the FMR on all occupied units for a long period, usually twenty years. Tenants would receive individually determined rent supplements. This subprogram was designed to retain private ownership and encourage private investment by removing the risk from low-income housing development. Section 8 New Construction was aimed primarily at tighter housing markets; however, developers in such markets were reluctant to undertake the extra paperwork and delays inherent in public programs and were insufficiently attracted by financial inducements to abandon more lucrative market-rate construction. Section 8 Substantial Rehabilitation provided financial subsidies to landlords who needed to make major improvements to bring their units up to standards. It was aimed particularly at housing markets with sufficient housing quantity but deficient housing quality.

Section 8's second thrust was a demand strategy in which subsidies were tied to eligible households. The Section 8 Existing program provided for the use of existing adequate housing. Holders of a Section 8 certificate could find their own housing anywhere in that housing authority's jurisdiction, limited only by the FMR ceiling; they could even remain in their current housing, if it met quality and FMR standards, and receive a subsidy if rent exceeded 25 percent of their income. The Section 8 Existing program got off to a fast start. It was particularly effective in localities characterized by an ample supply of adequate housing and higher vacancy rates. While the amount of individual subsidies was determined by rents paid, and while households had little or no incentive to rent at lower rates, this subprogram was tied to individual households rather than specific housing units.

For nearly a decade Section 8 remained the basic alternative to public housing. The number of assistance commitments made each year declined from 517,000 in 1976, to 206,000 in 1980, and to 112,000 in 1982. A 60 to 40 percent division between the Existing and the two Construction subprograms in 1976 became a 40 to 60 division during the last half of the Carter administration which favored supply over demand subsidies. At the end of 1980 Section 8 and public housing were each assisting about 1.2 million households. And after just ten years, Section 8 New Construction and Substantial Rehabilitation had produced more units than had public housing in over forty-five years.

HOUSING ASSISTANCE PRESENTLY: FORWARD OR BACKWARD?

The Reagan administration has assigned a low priority to housing. Indeed, its major housing assistance goal has been to reduce costs. The Reagan administration therefore not only requested no new funds for housing construction, under either public housing or Section 8, but "deobligated" units for which funds had been previously appropriated. The Housing and Urban-Rural Recovery Act of 1983 finally eliminated the Section 8 New Construction and Substantial Rehabilitation subprograms entirely. That same act provided for a modest rental rehabilitation and development grant program with standards which insure that such housing will be provided in areas where the poor are already heavily concentrated.

In 1981 President Reagan appointed a Commission on Housing to review existing housing programs. By this time EHAP had been completed, and its results had been voluminously published and debated. The Reagan Commission's Report (1982) recommended a number of policy changes, of which two will be noted. Regarding public housing, the Commission deplored the erosion of local control, as federal regulations over the years had prescribed rigid, detailed procedures for everything from accounting to evictions. The report noted distress at the dramatic increase in federal subsidies since 1969, coupled with the deteriorated financial condition of numerous local housing authorities. Federal restrictions added to the cost squeeze as much as the low income of public housing tenants. The report emphasized two considerations. First, a number of low-income households had special difficulty finding adequate, affordable housing in the free market (these included large families, minorities, and single-parent families); such households truly relied on public housing as housing of last resort. Second, there was substantial variation among local housing authorities, and even among different projects run by a single local housing authority; this called for project-by-project determinations rather than the traditional lock-step, single-policy solution. Accordingly, the Reagan Commission's report proposed five options for public housing, to be implemented on a project-by-project basis:

Option 1. Retain the project under public ownership for occupancy by households with incomes below 50 percent of the median income, paying only a modest portion of their incomes for rent.

Option 2. Sell the project or convert to homeownership.

Option 3. Deprogram the project; sell or demolish, at a loss, a project whose social, financial, and physical viability is so poor that it cannot be maintained at reasonable cost.

Option 4. Free up project rents, allowing the local housing authority to charge rents covering operating costs and continuing only federal debt service subsidy.

Option 5. Develop an alternative tailored to the unique circumstances of the project.

The Commission report contended that this range of options was akin to the "common sense approach in the world of private real estate, and it would offer Federal and local governments a fresh opportunity to consider the best interests of all parties, especially public housing tenants.'' Though this report has not been fully implemented, the administration has used the budget process and administrative regulations to alter operating and maintenance payments to local housing authorities, virtually to stop new construction, and to raise the payment ceiling for tenants to 30 percent of their income, with a minimum of 10 percent.

The Reagan Commission concentrated the main thrust of its direct housing subsidy policy recommendations in a system of direct payments to low-income renters, which it called a Housing Payments Program. The amount of these direct payments would be determined by the income of individual households and local fair market rents, not by actual rents paid. Housing payments would not be tied to specific housing units; rather, they would enable subsidized households to shop for housing in the private market with an augmented income but with the freedom to pay more or less than the standard rent. The 1983 act actually established a version of this recommendation under the label of housing vouchers. However, it was only a voucher demonstration program, limited to very low-income households whose incomes were less than 50 percent of the area's median. It provided funds for only 15,000 families and required substantially all of these funds to be used with the rental rehabilitation and development grant program. Thus, even the few households involved would not be able to shop widely for housing, one of the key features of a true housing allowance program.

In the area of housing assistance, the Reagan administration has tried to shrink and to replace the accumulated programs of the past half-century with cheaper options. To a considerable degree it has succeeded.

READING SELECTIONS

In Chapter 12 Lawrence Friedman describes the negative approach to housing reform. He moves from the tenement house laws of the late nineteenth century through the housing codes of the mid-twentieth century. Friedman notes the environmental determinism of early housing reformers who believed that as bad housing made bad people so would good housing improve not only the physical but also the moral and intellectual well-being of former slum dwellers. Legislating against inadequate housing, Friedman concludes, is an inherently limited approach to the problem of bad housing.

Robert M. Fisher, in Chapter 13, traces the origins of federally aided public housing from the tentative housing projects built during World War I. He sees an even more direct descent from the public works projects developed by various federal agencies to provide employment and stimulate materials production during the Great Depression. Such programs set the stage for the permanent low-income public housing created by the Housing Act of 1937.

Chapter 14 contains excerpts from hearings before the U.S. Senate Committee on Education and Labor; the work from these hearings evolved into the Housing Act of 1937. Senator Robert Wagner of New York, the bill's major sponsor, clearly emphasizes the job creation and slum clearance dimension of his proposal. Senator Wagner was clearly aware of political realities, and undoubtedly these appeals enabled the program to see the light of day. The commitment to public housing on its own merits was tenuous from the start. Mayor Neville Miller of Louisville expresses the sentiments of big city mayors who welcomed public housing as a vehicle for improving public health and social control in slum neighborhoods.

In "The Origins and Legacy of Urban Renewal," Chapter 15, Marc A. Weiss takes issue with the idea that public housing and slum clearance were equals in the Housing Act of 1949. According to this older conventional view, the Eisenhower administration's strong opposition to public housing effectively undermined a well-intended program and allowed slum clearance (urban renewal) to muscle public housing aside. But Weiss argues that from its legislative inception the program was designed to provide public assistance for downtown commercial redevelopment; public housing, he insists, was added only to give urban renewal respectability and attract the political support of housing reformers. Thus, the program was flawed both conceptually and politically. Weiss contends that housing reformers were simply flimflammed into supporting a program actually antithetical to their interests.

In Chapter 16, "The Dreary Deadlock of Public Housing," Catherine Bauer summarizes the criticism of public housing after its first twenty years. One of the most prominent experts, Bauer wonders why this particular reform movement had not yet been accepted, and why it was still dragging along, "not dead but never more than half alive." She found a simple answer: the usual public housing project was alien to the American housing ideal. She argues that since conditions had changed—the horrible early industrial tenements were disappearing, and the Great Depression was over—the time was ripe for a fresh start and new public housing formulae.

Chapter 17, by Eugene J. Meehan, is a review of the changes made in public housing from 1949 to 1974. Meehan has studied public housing at the community level, particularly in St. Louis, site of the notorious Pruitt-Igoe projects demolished in 1972. His commentary is chiefly concerned with the impacts of program changes both on project administration and on tenants. Meehan also notes the growing importance of leased housing as a form of housing subsidy.

In 1967 President Johnson appointed the National Commission on Urban Problems and gave the mandate to recommend ways in which federal, local, and private efforts "can be marshaled to increase the supply of low cost decent housing." The Douglas Commission (its Chair was Senator Paul Douglas of Illinois) submitted a lengthy report, *Building the American City*. Included in this report was the selection of Chapter 18, "Publicly Assisted and Subsidized Housing," which summarizes and reviews the performance of federal efforts, other than public housing, to 1967. This selection also contains some of the arguments which have continued to rage over the relative merits of a "shallow subsidy'' which would reach large numbers of the moderately poor versus a ''deep subsidy'' which would provide greater assistance to fewer recipients who would be among the very poor.

''Interest Rate Subsidies,'' Chapter 19, is a selection from the voluminous study, *Housing in the Seventies*, commissioned by President Nixon when he declared his moratorium on housing assistance in 1973. Of the confusing array of housing assistance programs, Sections 235 and 236 were among the most controversial. On the basis of this review, both programs were terminated.

Chapter 20, ''Housing Allowances: An Experiment That Worked,'' by Bernard J. Frieden, summarizes results from the Experimental Housing Allowance Program (EHAP). He notes the debate over alternative direct housing subsidy strategies and the light shed by EHAP on several of the outstanding points of contention. He concludes that housing subsidy clients did not react as expected and that federal policymakers should pay heed to the wishes of their clients, who may not really want ''better'' housing than they have.

The final selection, Chapter 21, is a review article by Chester Hartman, a persistent critic of housing allowances and demand subsidies. Hartman contends that because ''housing markets are not at all like the free markets of textbook economics,'' attempts to make subsidies replicate the marketplace are misguided at best. He deplores housing allowances as part of a 1980s shift toward undoing the results of a half-century of housing reform.

NOTE

1. Charles Abrams, *Man's Struggle for Shelter in an Urbanizing World* (Cambridge, Massachusetts: The M.I.T. Press, 1964), p. 5.

12

Housing Reform: Negative Style

Lawrence M. Friedman

PUBLIC RESTRICTIONS ON SLUM HOUSING: TENEMENT HOUSE LAWS AND THEIR DESCENDANTS

The negative approach to slum reform, using restrictive housing laws, is the oldest and most persistent of the housing solutions. Constant criticism of its efficacy and adequacy has not succeeded in ending reliance upon it. Public housing and urban renewal have not ousted this ancient rival; rather they have assimilated restrictive measures into themselves and assigned them a major role in the design of their programs.

Building restrictions are of ancient lineage and appeared quite early in American history. In New York, for example, pre-Revolutionary laws tried to prevent people from keeping hay, straw, pitch, tar, and turpentine where the danger of fire was great; a law of 1766 created a fire zone where houses had to be made of stone or brick and roofed with tile or slate.[1] These and later restrictions were not confined to slum areas. The New York tenement house law of 1867 was a different kind of law. It applied only to dwellings. It set up minimum standards that had to be observed by "tenements," which it defined as

From Lawrence M. Friedman, *Government and Slum Housing: A Century of Frustration*. (Chicago), 25-55, © 1968 by Rand McNally & Co. Reprinted by permission of Rand McNally & Co.

> every house, building, or portion thereof which is rented, leased, let or hired out to be occupied, or is occupied as the home or residence of more than three families living independently of another, and doing their cooking upon the premises, or by more than two families upon a floor, so living and cooking, but having a common right in the halls, stairways, yards, waterclosets or privies.[2]

This definition covered virtually all the houses in the slum areas and virtually none of the houses of the well-to-do. The age of the apartment house and the apartment hotel had not yet arrived; the vast majority of the rich lived not in apartments, but in private houses which were excluded from the act.[3]

The New York law of 1867 is, if not the ancestor of all succeeding tenement and housing codes, quite close to the evolutionary root.[4] It exerted a powerful, direct impact on much later legislation, e.g., the Massachusetts tenement house law of 1868[5] and the Milwaukee housing ordinance of 1905.[6] Whether or not later legislatures helped themselves to the language of the 1867 act or of some other model is irrelevant. The tenement law idea spread not by textual persuasion but through the spread of circumstances similar to those which led to the passage of the original act or acts. (Reform movements, of course, are as much a circumstance as the condition of plumbing is.) There has been, in fact, a great deal of borrowing in housing legislation. Detail varies greatly over time, if only because codes more or less must keep up with technological and social change in housing standards. But the basic idea of restrictive housing legislation is much the same now as it was in 1867.

The 1867 law was divided into 19 sections. It ordered tenement and lodging houses to be equipped with ventilators, fire escapes, "good and sufficient water-closets or privies" (§5), "proper and suitable conveniences or receptacles for receiving garbage and other refuse matters" (§8), and adequate chimneys. Another provision declared that "the roof of every such house" had to be kept in good repair ... so as not to leak" (§4); another restricted the habitation of cellars. Some provisions applied only to buildings erected after the effective date of the act, e.g., provisions relating to ceiling height and window area (§14). The law concerned itself primarily with gross physical characteristics of tenement buildings. But some attempt was made to cut down overcrowding on lots with one building already on them (§14). Thus, in embryo at least, the law of 1867 had some slight regard for slums as social settings, as well as aggregations of brick and stone.

Primarily, however, the law of 1867, like later laws, assumed that a slum was a physical entity, whatever else it was; control of physical abuses was *per se* a contribution to solving the evils of the slums. No one has expressed this view better than Jacob Riis. Describing the destruction of the so-called "Mulberry Bend," a notorious block in New York, Riis asked the rhetorical question: "Are we better off for scattering the poison and the poverty of the Bend?" His answer was a resounding, "Yes."

It is not scattered. The greater and by far the worst part of it is destroyed with the slum. Such a slum as this is itself the poison. It taints whatever it touches. Wickedness and vice gravitate towards it and are tenfold aggravated, until crime is born spontaneously of its corruption. Its poverty is hopeless, its vice bestiality, its crime desperation. Recovery is impossible under its blight. Rescue and repression are alike powerless to reach it. There *is* a connection between the rottenness of the house and that of the tenant that is patent and positive. Weakness characterizes the slum criminal, rather than wickedness. Chameleon-like, he takes the color of his surroundings. It is not where they shall go, but that they shall not go there at any rate, that is the important thing. In this much are we, are they, better off, that there will never be another Mulberry Bend for them to go to. In its place will come trees and grass and flowers; for its dark hovels light and sunshine and air.[7]

The prediction, of course, has not been borne out—a fact that casts doubt on the assumptions that underlay it.

New York was the pioneer in tenement house legislation. This fact should not surprise us. Tenement house legislation concerned the urban poor; the largest city in the country was in New York State—New York City had more foreign-born, more poor people, and more crowded slums than any other city.[8] Slum conditions at the time of the law of 1867 were appalling. New York City had grown like a weed since the turn of the century. Many of the immigrant poor and the poorer workmen lived in converted houses from which the rich had run; thousands of others lived in cellars, in rear apartments thrown up on the back of small lots, and in specially built "tenant-houses." In the slums, conditions of overcrowding, filth, misery, and degradation were indescribable. A legislative report of 1857 spoke of the

hideous squalor and deadly effluvia; the dim, undrained courts oozing with pollution; the dark, narrow stairways, decayed with age, reeking with filth, overrun with vermin; the rotted floors, ceilings begrimed, and often too low to permit you to stand upright; the windows stuffed with rags . . . the gaunt, shivering forms and wild ghastly faces, in these black and beetling abodes.[9]

The characteristic Manhattan tenement was taller than the characteristic home of the poor in other cities, if only because New York is a long, narrow island, where space is at a premium. Chicago, by way of contrast, spread out in all directions, developing slums of small frame houses, "shambling, dilapidated," but in "striking contrast to the closely built, tall brick buildings that extend in deadly uniformity . . . in New York's poverty areas."[10] Yet the law of 1867 was not a *welfare* response to New York's especially blatant and obnoxious conditions. It was in an important sense a law to reduce social costs. The 1867 legislation was a by-product of one of New York's recurrent cholera epidemics which ravaged the city just after the end of the Civil War. In 1866, the Metropolitan Board of Health was created for the city, and this agency was the prime beneficiary of the law of 1867; it was granted major administrative powers under the act.[11]

The act of 1867 was a failure in several senses. Few states or municipalities followed its example, at least before 1900. Moreover, the law was not well-enforced. Certainly, it failed to check the growth of the slums. Conditions became or seemed to become worse than ever. By 1900, the city was more crowded, the poor suffered more, and the moral and physical stench from the slums was more offensive than ever to the respectable members of the community. Articulate men of the age were obsessed with fear—fear that the American dream was being destroyed, that the American social system was decaying, that the country was undergoing radical changes for the worse. Prominent New Yorkers could easily hold to these opinions. Political corruption, crime, drunkenness, and juvenile delinquency were, if not more prevalent, more socially visible than before. The gentler classes trembled at the crowds of immigrants pouring into the cities and worried about the lawlessness of strikers, about the concentration of wealth, and about the spread of radicalism—worried, in general, whether America could survive the passing of the symbolic frontier. Whether the problems of the times were as new or as serious as people thought is irrelevant. The sense of crisis was crucial.[12]

In this age of upheaval, the disease of the slums was perceived as a disease of the whole body politic. The sense of the social costs of the slums was dramatically heightened; it affected even stalwart conservatives. Justice Peckham of New York, whose chief claim to fame is his bitter hostility to social legislation as a New York and federal judge, conceded the need for a war on the slums. In his view, the evils of the slums endangered society and called for legal action: fires, disease, "tendencies to immorality and crime where there is a very close packing of human beings of the lower order in intelligence and morals . . . must arouse the attention of the legislator."[13] The sense of social cost set the reform conscience free from the crippling effects of a moralizing attitude toward the poor. The careers of a band of vigorous, reform-minded men and women coincided happily with a point of history in which a heightened sense of the social costs of the slums made tenement house legislation finally possible on a grander scale than before. This took place from 1900 to the present.

The conditions laid bare by men such as Jacob Riis, by the writers in the popular press, and by various state and local investigating bodies were in fact not new; but they were still appalling. The New York Tenement House Committee of 1894 found that "only 306 persons out of a total of 255,033, whose living conditions were carefully examined by its investigating staff, had access to bathtubs in their homes." In 3,984 tenements, with a population of 121,323, there were only 51 private toilets; others had to content themselves with access to toilets in yards, basements, or halls.[14] Most of these were unspeakably filthy: "Foul, malodorous privy vaults, filled to the yard level and, in many cases, overflowing into the yards and draining into adjacent cellars, the floors and even the walls covered with an accumulation of fecal matter." This was the story in New Jersey.[15] Every other sanitary sin was found in the tenements: broken pipes with sewer gas escaping, heaps of trash and broken bottles, garbage strewn everywhere: But there were worse things about the tenements. In the tall, densely-massed tenements, suffering men and women were crowded into tiny rooms; no sunlight penetrated into the blackness. Life on the teeming streets showed the horrified eye of the beholder every kind of crime, immorality, and corruption. Hunger and disease prowled the dirty corridors. This, as Jacob Riis described it, was "how the other half lives."[16]

Riis was a journalist; other reformers worked within government for passage of tenement house laws. One critical aim of the reformers was to arouse the sleeping public—to show the world how bad conditions were, how much society itself was a victim of the slums. They wrote government reports and studies as well as articles in the press and magazines. A federal study of the slums was published as early as 1894.[17]

No housing reformer used publicity more astutely than Lawrence Veiller of New York. He, more than anyone else, was responsible for the New York Tenement House Law of 1901. He had been active in the Tenement House Committee of New York's Charity Organization Society; and in 1899 he set out before the public at the Sherry Building on Fifth Avenue a "tenement house exhibition" with maps and photographs of the horrors of the slums.[18] He induced the legislature to create a Tenement House Commission in 1900, which he dominated. The Commission produced a monumental study, a vivid yet dispassionate document of life in the lower depths. Photographs of conditions in the tenement were included in the study for those who would not read or for whom the written work was too pale. The technique was a fruitful one. Wisconsin, too, had a tenement house study preceding its law of 1907; its Commission also produced a report, complete with photographs, to shock the conscience and stir the Assembly.[19]

The public opinion that was mobilized was a narrow and select one; its extent must not be exaggerated. Newspapers made comments, a few key citizens were aroused, and a few key legislators were persuaded or embarrassed.[20] What may be more critical in explaining the "success" of the tenement house movement in the age of Veiller was the nature of the economic opposition. Tenement house reform did not evoke opposition from any major, powerful economic group. To be sure, builders and owners of tenements opposed the passage of the law of 1901; but most of these were small men, not great landlords.[21]

We might know more about the dynamics of housing legislation if we knew more about the tenement house business. What is known, though spotty and speculative, suggests that the lords of the land were not big business. Many small tenements were owned by men and women of the same ethnic background and originally of the same social class as their tenants. Perhaps this was less true of New York City than elsewhere. The tall tenements of New York took considerable capital to build. But the physical nature of tenement houses in other cities suggests a good deal about the nature of their ownership. In cities outside New York, most tenements were small frame houses, rear shanties, or the discarded mansions of the rich, broken up into tiny segments. In Chicago at the turn of the century, the slums consisted of "dilapidated frame structures" and small brick or wooden houses:

> Sometimes an entire block will be covered by cottages and two-storied houses. Many of these are little, unpainted tenements, rickety and awry from age and poor building. In the rear, one often sees an irregular line of closely packed shanties, chicken-coops to all appearances, dilapidated sheds of almost piano-box size, with stove pipes extending a foot above the top.[22]

In Washington, D.C., the characteristic slum house was the alley house, put up for Negroes in the period starting with the Civil War. The alley house had no sewers, no water mains, no indoor plumbing, "no pavement, no lights, no provision for the removal of garbage."[23] It was bare shelter, little else. Life in these shanty-towns was grim and unyielding; but it was not a life dominated by baronial overlords. No class of big tenement house owners corresponded to the big businessmen, manufacturers, and bankers of the day. To a striking degree, the slum landlord was himself a product of the slums. He was often an uneducated, half-impoverished man of immigrant stock. As we shall see, some of his sins can be ascribed to his environment—legal, social, and moral—as much as the sins of his tenants can.

The New York law of 1901 was the most elaborate tenement house act yet-passed. It was a considerable advance on its predecessor, the much amended law of 1867.[24] Superior sophistication in draftsmanship and experience with the failings of the older act account for much of this technical advance. Credit must also be given to the political skill of Lawrence Veiller who fought for the bill and prevented its dilution in Albany. The new law ran to more than one hundred sections. Once again, a sharp distinction was made between existing tenements and tenements to be constructed or converted in the future. Out of this distinction grew the expressions "old-law" and "new-law" tenements which passed into the language of New Yorkers. The main emphasis of the New York law was on the physical condition of the tenements. But the social needs of life were not totally neglected; light, air, and space were as important to the draftsmen as plumbing and fire protection and not merely for reasons of health. The morality of slum life was also carefully considered by the draftsmen. The act provided, for example, that

> In every apartment of three or more rooms in a tenement house hereafter erected, access to every room, including the bath rooms and water closet compartments, shall be had without passing through any bedroom.

> No room in any tenement house shall be so overcrowded that there shall be afforded less than four hundred cubic feet of air to each adult, and two hundred cubic feet of air to each child under twelve years of age....[25]

The privacy provision is a good example of middle-class morality imposed upon the slums. Lack of privacy was and is a characteristic of slum life; but the clause in question had a special kind of privacy in mind.[26] It reflects a climate of opinion which saw moral degradation as one of the chief evils of the slums—the temptations to which small children were exposed, the absence of sexual restraint, and the fact that innocents were forced to live in close proximity to prostitutes. The New York Tenement House Department solemnly reported that when "dissolute women enter a tenement house their first effort is to make friends with the children. Children have been lured into their rooms, where they beheld sights from which they should be protected." The Tenement House Law of 1901 provided "severe and drastic measures so as to drive these women out of the tenement houses where respectable working men and their families lived." The law did not "seek to regulate the evil of prostitution generally, but solely to remove such contaminating influences from the tenement house dwelling, believing that such conditions should not exist in the homes of the poor."[27] The aim of the privacy provision was to reshape the moral environment of the areas where poor people lived. Characteristically, for its period, it attempted to mold social reality through manipulating housing design. The provision against overcrowding was a less obvious example of the same impulse and the same solution. Overcrowding is a social and moral evil as well as a sanitary sin.

Nonetheless, the physical emphasis was primary. The provision on overcrowding, for example, reflected strong views on the noxiousness of dark and uncirculated air, as much as anything else. Moreover, nonphysical reforms were pursued through physical means. From a mid-twentieth-century viewpoint, the idea of improving moral conditions through changes in housing design and construction seems curiously archaic. Many housing experts, though not all, think that public housing and its problems teach us the futility of social reform through better plumbing and more space. We shall return to this problem again. In Veiller's day, we should remember, the path to reform lay precisely in the direction of stressing physical improvement. The argument that reformers had to make was that the poor were no different from the rich in innate morality and sense. "The rich and the poor," wrote Veiller, "are indeed alike in all essential particulars."[28] The point was to demonstrate that reform would not be wasted on the poor. Were poor people dirty? It was because they had no bathtubs. Public baths, when provided, were heavily used by the multitudes.

> Few people realize the efforts made by most of the tenement house population to keep clean under the most adverse conditions. When all the water that can be obtained must be carried up several flights of stairs, cleanliness is indeed a virtue.

As conditions changed, so did people's habits, Veiller argued. "We all live up to our environment, more or less, like the beggar in the bed of the king."[29] In 1900, to argue that the poor suffered from special disabilities of mind, family, personality, and social organization was to argue for doing nothing about the slums. Two generations later, the same arguments implied not less but more government intervention.

An important feature of the 1901 law was its meticulous attention to problems of administration and enforcement of the law. The law of 1867 had created a flexible, discretionary system with great power lodged in the Metropolitan Board of Health, which was created just prior to the law. The system of administration was a natural outcome of the background of the act. Fear of a cholera epidemic radiating out of the slums led to creation of the Board and passage of the act. The 1901 law sharply limited areas of formal discretion; it attempted to lay down rules which were objective, clear, and therefore easily enforceable. Administrative discretion was limited, so that city departments could concentrate on enforcement rather than interstitial decision-making, free from the temptations to laxity inherent in discretionary systems.[30] A "total window area in a water-closet [of] . . . not . . . less than three square feet"[31] cannot be mistaken, and anyone can tell by the use of a tape-measure whether a water-closet violates this law. The New York act also called for a system of building permits and a registry of all tenement houses. Veiller wanted as little as possible left either to politics, to chance, or to the human failing of administrators.

The New York law was followed by tenement house laws in a number of other states: New Jersey, Connecticut, Wisconsin, and Indiana.[32] Most of these laws adhered closely to the main outlines of New York's statute. Wisconsin was exceptional. Here, for complex reasons—perhaps a mere blunder—the tenement house law provided for no special administrative machinery. General law enforcement officers, local city officials, and state factory inspectors would presumably carry out the act. No permit or registry system was established. Yet the act had the broadest coverage of any state statute. New York's law was confined to "first class cities" (New York City and Buffalo were the only members of this class); and Connecticut's law was restricted to cities of more than 20,000 population.[33] Wisconsin's law was unlimited. This was another blunder. Weak administration and excessively bold coverage were a fatal combination. The law, passed in 1907, lasted one year only. It was declared unconstitutional in 1908 in the case of *Bonnet* v. *Vallier*.[34] But the Wisconsin court went out of its way to express approval of the general aims of tenement house legislation. The court confined its critique of the act to particular aspects of this particular law; it did not cast doubt on the general legality of housing reform. The court's opinion was frank; tenement house legislation was a good thing, but only for major metropolitan areas. The 1907 law was "unreasonable" in its scope and detail. Indeed, the court suggested what the "reasonable" contents of a new law might be, almost inviting passage of a better act. This hint bore fruit in 1909.[35]

The Wisconsin decision stands alone. Courts have sustained state tenement house laws against constitutional attack whenever the problem has arisen.[36] This is a particularly significant fact in that the tenement house laws were passed at a time when social and economic legislation was unusually vulnerable to judicial review. Yet the number of cases was small, and the results (except perhaps in the Wisconsin case) no comfort to opponents of the laws. Perhaps the invisibility of the slum owner, the fact that he was typically a small businessman, often of immigrant stock, allowed the courts to see these statutes as entirely wholesome, not as interferences with the free market or as disturbances to the American system. No such difficult choices faced the courts as in labor cases, where bloodshed and violence stalked the streets outside the courtroom. In the tenement house cases, the social costs of slum housing could be reckoned without strong countervailing arguments or interests.

Even *Bonnet* v. *Vallier* was in a sense no anomaly. The court constantly stressed that the Wisconsin law was inappropriate except in crowded urban centers. The notion that tenement house legislation could be applied to honest small-town Americans was offensive to the court. The tenement house laws met with approval only as measures imposed upon the lawless, filthy, un-American urban slums. In 1912, in *Grimmer* v. *Tenement House Department of New York*[37] the highest court of New York held that the New York tenement house law did not apply to an "apartment house with certain hotel features," in other words, to the kind of building usually called an apartment hotel. The New York statute defined a tenement house as one occupied by three or more families living independently and doing their cooking on the premises. It did not distinguish between apartments for the rich and for the poor. Grimmer's apartment hotel literally fit the statutory definition. The court's strictly legal arguments for exempting the apartment hotel have something of a specious ring. Most likely the court simply could not see why a building should be subjected to regulation as a tenement when it had "parquet floors of oak," entrance halls "covered with imported Vienna marble," floors of "white Italian marble," ceilings and cornices "decorated in metal," servants' quarters, and many baths, gas ranges and sinks. The spirit of the legislation did not apply to buildings whose tenants were of an "independent" class, "able to exact proper living conditions without the help of such drastic provisions as are found in the Tenement House Act."

In the early part of the twentieth century, what could be called a national housing-reform movement came into being.[38] In 1910, Lawrence Veiller helped found a National Housing Association, with the support of the Russell Sage Foundation. He extended his influence by publishing a number of books and pamphlets on housing; in 1910 he published a *Model Tenement House Law* and in 1914 a *Model Housing Law*. Both of these bore the imprint of the Russell Sage Foundation. These model laws were useful as sources of textual inspiration. It was necessary to avoid slavish imitation of New York's laws which Veiller thought unsuitable elsewhere.[39] Veiller traveled frequently to cities and states which were considering housing legislation to exert influence and pressure. His energies helped achieve a substantial spread of the housing law idea. Kentucky, Indiana, Massachusetts, Pennsylvania, and California enacted state housing laws by 1917; Michigan, Minnesota, and Iowa by 1919.

By 1920, about twenty cities had enacted new housing codes while twenty more had inserted housing provisions in their building and health ordinances. Virtually all of these cities—which include Syracuse, St. Paul, Grand Rapids, Duluth, Berkeley, Cleveland, Columbus, Lansing, Portland, Oregon, and Salem, Massachusetts—adapted their codes from the New York law or Veiller's model laws.[40]

Successful enactment of tenement house reform was due to a number of factors: (a) a heightened perception of the problem of urban slums; (b) a corps of dedicated and organized reform workers committed to housing reform; (c) the absence of strong ideological opposition; and (d) the absence of strong economic opposition. These four factors were interrelated. The judicial history of the laws indicates, for example, that judges were able to see, grasp, and advance the objectives of the movement; validity failed where judges saw no true need for reform (*Bonnet, Grimmer*). Tenement house legislation was in a classical tradition of American reform; unlike public housing, it was not socialistic; it required no direct government intervention, only regulation, and it was therefore moderate in scope (Veiller himself was bitterly opposed to public housing).[41] The laws were framed or construed to apply only to the urban poor who, arguably, were beyond the help of the market system. The absence of strong economic opposition probably played a key role in ensuring the passage of these laws. Many slum landlords themselves lived in the slums; others were one generation or less away from slum life; in neither case was the landlord a member of polite business society. It was relatively easy to override or ignore the opposition of unorganized small businessmen of this kind.

The Slumlord: Rise of a Scapegoat

The point about the slum landlord is worth dwelling on. The tenement house movement helped fix him in his permanent position as an American devil and scapegoat. Albion Fellows Bacon, who led a movement for housing reform in Indiana, cried out that "to collect rent from our old death-traps of tenements is really to take blood money."[42] Jacob Riis agreed; he blamed much of the problem of the slums on "human greed"; a man "has no right to slowly kill his neighbors, or his tenants, by making a death-trap of his house."[43] Moreover, "reform by law must aim at making it unprofitable to own a bad tenement."[44] This was an early sounding of the cry to "take the profit out of the slums," a cry that has echoed down to the present day. A belief that landlords were greedy villains was a necessity for the housing reformers. Since reform laws imposed costs on landlords without reimbursing them in any way, and since no one expected or wanted rents to rise, it was morally necessary to believe that rents were exorbitant and that costs could be absorbed without giving up a fair return. It was convenient, therefore, to assume that landlords were a class of evil men, overcharging ignorant tenants and callous to the point of criminality. The fact that tenement house owners were not respectable old-American businessmen, by and large, made it easier to adhere to this notion. Successful management of small slum houses may demand that the owner live in the house; this was too high a price to pay for anyone with alternative avenues of profitable investment. Simple economics then suggests that only slumdwellers could afford to own at least some of the slums. In fact, the evidence shows that many slum landlords did live in the slums. A study of Jersey City housing, published in 1903, found 111 resident owners of 539 tenements studied—more than one out of five. ''As a number of these landlords own two or more houses, while a number of other houses are owned by landlords in neighboring streets, the actual number of houses managed by owners practically resident is considerably greater.''[45] Of course, most landlords were absentees. Some people grew rich on the slums and moved elsewhere. Slums were owned by the Astors and by Trinity Church. But slum ownership, by and large, was and is more local, more decentralized, and more widespread than most other forms of enterprise. A study of some 300 properties in a Los Angeles slum found that one-third of the properties were owned by occupants; and another third were owned by people in the same postal zone.[46] A Milwaukee study showed a somewhat similar pattern.[47] New York City of course is more concentrated in ownership. Milwaukee and Los Angeles may deviate somewhat from the ownership pattern in older large cities. But it is clear that the business of low-income residential property is not highly concentrated; there is no equivalent of General Motors or the A & P among slumlords.

In any event, nothing impeded the progress of the notion that slum money was tainted money; and belief in the evils of slum ownership became a self-fullfilling prophecy. Bad reputation is a cost to a man, even if it cannot be measured exactly and valued in dollars. The business of selling illegal property or services, such as drugs or gambling, necessarily demands exorbitant profits; investors must be attracted by high returns into occupations of great risk and small prestige. Slum ownership has something of the same quality. As tenement house legislation became more stringent in its demands, slum ownership became virtually as legally perilous as running a brothel. If tenement house rules are too strict, in the economic sense, they cannot be obeyed without loss of profit. When the rules are overstrict, corruption sets in; landlords will ''purchase . . . code revision through payments to building inspectors.''[48] The codes will, moreover, be variably enforced. Laxity and corruption will alternate with periods of severe crackdown—perhaps following a disastrous fire or a scandal. But variable enforcement is merely another aspect of the high risk of slum ownership. Unpredictable enforcement makes one's livelihood a gamble; the pay-off cannot completely avoid the risk of exposure and punishment. These risks, like the bad reputation of the landlord, are real costs to an owner, and ownership of slum property will in time come to reside in those men who can take the heat. At least this is a plausible hypothesis. More precise work on the economics and sociology of slum ownership might shed more light on the question of who owns the slums and how much they earn from this source.

Whatever the facts, the persistent model of the evil slumlord characterizes—and probably hampers—housing movements to this day. (The converse notion—that good houses, well-run by respectable businessmen, would return fair profits—lies at the base of the model tenement house movement, which will be discussed below.) Not that the notion of the evil slumlord is completely untrue. It can be assumed that over the years a filtering-down process of landlords has occurred. The process is difficult to document, particularly for past generations; but it seems clear that it has taken place. The costs, risks, pains, and annoyances of slum ownership are too much for the "reputable" man. During the New York wave of rent strikes, a lawyer who represented a client with a building in the rent strike area claimed that eleven real estate firms refused to take over the management. The president of the New York Real Estate Board claims that owners "who once maintained well-kept tenements . . . have left the business," selling out to "quick-profit speculators."[49] Many of the worst landlords are those at the very end of the filtering-down process. This seems apparent from frequent articles in the newspapers on the difficulty of locating and pinning down slum landlords. One tenement house, which was in the news in New York in 1965 and which had been declared unfit for human habitation, was fined twelve times for code violations. The violations were charged to three different men, Gluck, Haver, and Samuel Braun. The tenants "believed the owner was Seymour Gelfand, but they sent their rent to Arthur J. Clyne." Gelfand said he had merely been "escrow agent for Joseph Braun and Harry Holtzman who are not the owners either"; the building belonged to the 454 West Realty Corporation "whose last known address was a post office box. The city believes Mr. Holtzman holds the four mortgages on the building."[50]

These shadowy figures may be the landlords who "milk" their buildings; as the buildings sink toward utter ruin, the property rights are traded among a group of owners, some of them totally unscrupulous, others apparently mentally deranged. New York's "slum queen," Mrs. Auguste Redman, made 125 court appearances in the four years ending in 1961, was fined thousands of dollars, given two years probation, then finally sent to jail. The probation department recommended "commission to Bellevue hospital for psychiatric observation."[51] These dead-end landlords hide or run until the building no longer pays, either because its ruin is complete, because vandals have gutted it, or because its cumulative illegality finally becomes so gross that the building is fined to death, demolished by court order, or otherwise extirpated by law.[52] Thus, there is an important group of slum properties—those nearly at the end of their rope—which are not exorbitantly profitable; they are not profitable at all. In the slums, buildings may return big profits, small profits, or no profits, depending upon where they are situated in the life-cycle of a house, who the owner is, and the general state of the neighborhood. At least this is a plausible guess.[53] That some slum buildings are losers is plainly established. Woody Klein studied a particularly noxious building in New York: 311 East 100th Street. It was a dead loss to the owners.[54] David Satter reports that the worst buildings in Chicago's Lawndale district are unprofitable.[55] The worst buildings, then, are dead-end buildings owned by dead-end slumlords; neither is able to make even a dishonest dollar.

Legislative programs (some intentionally, some not) are calculated to make the small landlord fade away. In 1936, in the midst of the depression, enforcement of new amendments to New York's housing laws seemed to threaten certain city landlords with ruin. An Association of Harlem and Bronx Property Owners was formed; it fought unsuccessfully in court and legislature for relief.[56] But in 1935, a law was passed which suspended enforcement of the Multiple Dwelling Law against an owner who, together with the owners of two-thirds of the property in an area designated by the local housing authority or state board as "suitable . . . for housing," agreed to convey his houses and lots "to a limited dividend housing corporation organized under the state housing law" (or to the housing authority itself) for clearance and rebuilding.[57] Another law suspending enforcement made a somewhat different point. In 1936, the state amended the Multiple Dwelling Act, excusing civil and criminal penalties for six months to owners who acquired ownership of tenements by foreclosure.[58] Savings banks had chosen to evict 4,000 families from noncomplying tenements on which they had foreclosed, rather than "take the risks of prosecution." The law was passed to give them and their tenants relief. Depression conditions created this crisis; but law, policy, and politics sharply distinguished between the individual owner (the classical landlord) and the reputable, corporate owner. As we shall see, the same distinction has been made in more recent programs.[59]

From Tenement House Laws to Housing Codes

The rush to enact restrictive housing laws and ordinances slowed down in the 1920's and decidedly so in the 1930's. A good deal of disillusionment had set in on the part of those who had actively backed tenement house laws. In the first place, the laws were hard to administer and enforce. The story is best known for New York. Constant complaints were heard that the staff was too small to do its job. This was to be expected. Reform movements that are oriented toward the passage of legislation measure enactment as success. Some relaxation of passion is afterwards hard to avoid. It is hard to maintain the same high pitch of enthusiasm for problems of administration, appropriation, and staff as for the enactment crusade.

Administration and enforcement are problems for all government agencies and programs. Yet tenement house laws seemed unusually "impractical" and unusually difficult to enforce. Complaints of poor enforcement come from many jurisdictions and are curiously similar. Perhaps the tenement house laws were unenforceable even under favorable circumstances. The New York law of 1901 was well drafted and particularly cunning in its administrative provisions. Why then was enforcement imperfect? One conventional answer blames feeble enforcement on inadequate staff. But perhaps some defects in these laws made a comparatively large staff necessary.

The very fact that slum landlords formed a diffuse class of small businessmen was a stumbling block for enforcement. It meant that regulation had to be imposed; compliance with forms, formalities, and complex regulation was not a standard business habit. Moreover, some provisions of the tenement house laws imposed costs on landlords or tenants without providing any means of meeting these additional costs. Provisions against overcrowding, for example, if vigorously enforced, would have compelled large slum families either to rent more space at a higher rent, move into larger but poorer housing, or split up their household groups.

Blanket prohibitions on overcrowding, then as now, were also hard to enforce because no attempt was made to understand the causes of overcrowding and to provide alternative solutions. For example, during the age of heavy immigration, many small landlords took in lodgers. This was a serious source of overcrowding. Yet the lodger system served a real function in "slums of hope." It helped the immigrant to adjust to an alien culture. Men lodged with their relatives or with fellow-countrymen who spoke their language. True, conditions were sometimes virtually intolerable. Some lodging houses were squalid dormitories for transients and immigrants. In a Milwaukee building in 1903, seventeen Hungarians lived in four rooms; when the building was inspected in the afternoon, some of the lodgers who worked on night shifts were asleep. The inspector thought it "quite probable that the same beds [were] occupied at night by another set of men who worked during the day." But many of these men were residents in this country only temporarily; some expected to lead the life of a lodger only long enough to earn money to bring their families over; others wanted to save every penny possible and return home with substantial savings.[60] Landlords, in turn, often took in lodgers to help eke out low family incomes. In short, the lodging houses served important functions. Reformers quite properly objected to conditions in the lodging houses. But what were the alternatives?

Other provisions of the tenement house laws interfered with customary practice. One section of the New York law of 1901 prohibited the encumbering of fire escapes. But tenants were used to treating fire escapes as part of their home; they resented any efforts to make them change. The provisions could not be made to work. Sometimes the fire escapes were cleared off for the inspector, but encumbered again moments later. Moreover, city judges would not cooperate in punishing offenders. In 1906, a concerted effort to clear up the fire-escape problem failed because city "magistrates were apparently loath to impose fines on immigrants and workers for violations which they considered relatively trivial."[61]

Like the slum landlord, the "lax judge" has been a constant character in the drama of slum housing and another scapegoat of reform. In 1966, too, there was an outcry against him. In New York, the Community Service Society attributes the failures of code enforcement at least partly to the New York City Housing Court. At fault is the "court's failure to comply strictly with criminal procedure" and its "view that most defendants are not 'criminals' in the usual sense of the word." The Society has suggested that the court tighten its procedures and that it impose heavier fines and even jail sentences on offenders.[62] But the persistence of the lax judge—like the persistence of the evil slum landlord—invites a more-or-less sociological explanation. It seems apparent that the housing-case judge sees his role differently from that of the administrator. The judge has before him a series of concrete instances—specific individuals charged with specific acts. He does not necessarily feel that his duty requires him to advance at all costs the policies of the housing code; his role is that of the judge who dispenses justice in the particular case.[63] The landlord and the tenant in the fire-escape cases are individuals confronting the power of the government. Then, too, lower court judges may be drawn from the same economic and social strata of society as the landlords. They may be upwardly mobile men of immigrant stock, like the landlords. They may thus tend to see the landlord's point of view.[64] Campaigns against the landlord, moreover, are often responses to political pressures of the moment; but political pressures may have less effect on judges than on other elected office-holders. Especially is this true when the importance of any particular decision in a housing case is virtually nil. For these and other reasons, the lax judge has remained a problem of the housing laws.

Were the tenement house laws really successful? Did they have an impact on life in the slums? In certain gross respects, measurable change took place during the age of the tenement house laws. By 1915, in New York, "windows had been installed in 300,000 interior rooms of old-law tenements and several thousand school sinks had been replaced by water closets."[65] The death toll from slum fires had been greatly reduced; the filth had been, if not eliminated, substantially reduced. Hunger and disease had perceptibly abated. Yet the reformers remained dissatisfied; and what is more, their dissatisfaction took the form of psychological abandonment of their own device—the tenement house laws. In 1936, Edith Abbott wrote: "Gradually it became clear . . . that the housing problem was almost as immovable as the Sphinx." She agreed that the tenements of Chicago were improving; but she refused to credit the change to "any important improvements in the tenement house ordinances of Chicago, nor to the enforcement of these ordinances." Change had been brought about by technological progress which affected the environment of the poor. Nowadays every urban evil under the sun is blamed on the automobile, but to Edith Abbott the automobile was a blessing. It rid the slums of the horse, and along with it, "the filthy stables and the dreadful manure heaps."[66]

The sources of dissatisfaction with the tenement house laws were various and in some ways puzzling. But the fact of disillusionment was clear. Disillusionment, whether or not justified, removed an important prop from the political and social underpinnings of the tenement house movement. Some housing reformers turned their attention to an ancient colleague, and rival, of the tenement house movement: the model tenement house. As we shall see, this movement was never crowned with full success. Some housing experts began to turn to a more radical solution: government-built houses for the poor. Indeed, the tenement-house laws themselves were adduced as causes for the breakdown in any private solution. Reformers, through experience, had learned that "private builders are not in business for pleasure"; when regulatory measures extract the profit from housing the low-income groups, this market is abandoned: "Now that building codes and other building ordinances are in effect, it is unlikely that private enterprise will ever again undertake to house the lower income groups in new dwellings."[67] "The best restrictive legislation," wrote Edith Elmer Wood, "is only negative. It will prevent the bad. It will not produce the good. Especially, it will not produce it at a given rental. And rental is a despot. A high standard of restrictive legislation will not be enacted, or if enacted, will not be enforced, when its enforcement will leave a considerable number of people homeless."[68] During the First World War, the federal government took small steps to ease the shortage of houses for war-workers.[69] The program was hastily dismantled after the war, and the public housing movement was swept aside in the rush to "normalcy." Nonetheless, the cutting edge of the reform brigade had shifted away from tenement house regulation toward public housing. During the 1920's, a few concrete steps were taken in the states toward support of positive housing programs; in the 1930's the New Deal housing and resettlement programs suggested that the day was near when a profound housing solution was at last possible. The Wagner-Steagell Housing Act was passed in 1937. The housing-code movement continued to sleep.

But the public housing program in turn lost its glamour, as we shall later explore in more detail. The housing code came back into its own after the Second World War with the rise of urban renewal. The Housing Act of 1949 created federal urban redevelopment. This Act required the federal government in deciding whether or not to extend slum clearance and redevelopment aid to particular cities to consider whether "appropriate local public bodies" in such cities had undertaken "positive programs . . . for preventing the spread or recurrence . . . of slums and blighted areas through the adoption, improvement, and modernization of local codes and regulations relating to land use and adequate standards of health, sanitation, and safety for dwelling accommodations."[70] The roots of this requirement lie deep in the nature of urban redevelopment—a program which, as we shall see, has closer allegiances to business and political goals and to the social cost concept than to welfare. The new emphasis on housing codes was only part of a new emphasis on central city planning. It thus differed profoundly from the impetus behind the original tenement house laws. The resulting housing codes were, however, in many ways similar to the older tenement laws.

The code requirement has gradually become more explicit. The Housing Act of 1954 broadened the attack on blight by adding the concept of "urban renewal" to the older concept of "redevelopment." Renewal made use of a whole range of techniques; no longer was federal aid confined to bulldozing and rebuilding from scratch. The law now demanded from each city a "workable program" before federal renewal gold could flow in. The statute specifically mentioned a housing code as a possible element of a "workable program." The Housing and Home Finance Agency (HHFA) made the requirement mandatory; finally, in 1964, the statute was amended to reflect this fact.[71] Consequently, there has been a great rush to enact housing codes.[72] Many major cities had long had housing codes; but the rest, and many smaller communities as well, are quickly falling into line. "Up to 1955, only 56 communities had housing codes. By July 1961, the number had increased to 493, and by July 1963 to 736."[73]

It is clear why the cities have adopted the codes; they must do so or forfeit federal money. Buy why has the federal government forced the codes on the cities? One reason may lie in the increased acceptability, sophistication, and presumed utility of land-use controls of which housing codes are only one example. There are other reasons, too. The costs of urban renewal are vast; billions of dollars will be needed to reconstitute the cities. Federal subsidy is available to help do the job of clearing the worst of the slums; but costs would be reduced and the federal dollar could go further if marginal areas were upgraded through the use of lesser measures. "Over the long pull," it might be possible to "establish healthy cities with reduced requirements for... Federal aid."[74] The use of housing codes is one such technique. It may prevent or arrest blight in neighborhoods near the slums or with spots of blight scattered here and there. Countless millions of renewal dollars might be saved in the long run.

The new emphasis on housing codes is thus in part a tool for a kind of cut-rate urban renewal.[75] Through land-use techniques and housing codes neighborhoods can be preserved and even upgraded; the creation of new Georgetowns and Oldtowns can be stimulated. Deterioration can be arrested. The use of housing codes to create or help create what are in effect new neighborhoods resembles the positive aspects of many housing programs as much as or more than it resembles the negative regulatory use to which, historically, these codes have been put. The historic regulatory use, to be sure, remains. The codes, it is felt, help quarantine neighborhoods against the creeping diseases of the cities. In theory the codes, if rigorously enforced, would mitigate the horrors of all but the very worst slums. The main thrust of the program, however, is to fight blight; and the main justification for the use of the codes is based on a social-cost approach which sees in blight a source of economic and social injury to the community. The welfare elements in the program (e.g., relocation requirements) have been distinctly secondary, both in the governing statutes and in their administration. Because code enforcement is relatively cheap and is useful as a conservation device, code enforcement stands in better odor today than at any time since the days of Veiller. Indeed, the Housing Act of 1964 authorized a new type of renewal project—the code-enforcement project—"to be comprised wholly or substantially of a program of code enforcement" but financed by the federal government.[76] And the 1965 act expressed a Congressional finding that there is a "need to study housing and building codes" (along with zoning, tax policies, and development standards) to determine how, with government aid, "local property owners and private enterprise'' can ''serve a greater share of the total housing and building need.'' Accordingly, HHFA was directed to study local ''housing and building laws, standards, codes, and regulations,'' with an eye to making them simpler in structure and easier to enforce.[77]

Explicit theories voiced in the literature to justify use of the codes break no new ground. Joseph Guandolo, then Associate General Counsel of HHFA, wrote in 1956 that

> Slums and blight are brought about by owners of property who are unable or unwilling to maintain or improve their property at decent levels, by unconscionable, profiteering landlords squeezing bootleg profits out of wretched housing, and occasionally by tenants who are indifferent to their squalid environments. But ... the ultimate causation factor is the local government itself [which] ... fails to enforce effectively ... adequate police power measures to control bad housing, improper environments and overcrowding.[78]

The reader will note the historic emphasis on the evil landlord and the faith in the efficacy of controls if enforcement problems could only be somehow surmounted. Petulant complaints against local government have, if anything, increased with the passage of time. The entrance of the professional city planner onto the arena has, to be sure, made a difference in the rhetoric of housing; the planner has placed his stamp quite notably upon the vocabulary of social costs. Planlessness and chaos are now among the leading evils, along with the more conventional sorts. We can see this planners' influence in many statutory definitions of a ''blighted area.'' The Wisconsin Blight Elimination and Slum Clearance Act, for example, after reciting the usual symptoms of blight, adds these as telltale signs of decay:

> predominance of defective or inadequate street layout, faulty lot layout in relation to size, adequacy, accessibility or usefulness, ... diversity of ownership, tax or special assessment delinquency exceeding the fair value of the land, defective or unusual conditions of title....[79]

Some of these signs no doubt refer to the consequences of ''premature subdivision,'' that is, arrested developments on the fringe of the cities.[80] Both in and out of town, however, the definition of blight owes much to the principles and ideals of experts in urban design and land-use controls.

The contents of modern housing codes, however, do not differ essentially from those of the tenement house laws. This fact may be somewhat obscured by the manner in which, in some cities, ''housing-code'' elements are lumped together with elements of building codes, plumbing codes, electrical codes, and the like. We can analytically reserve the term housing code for ordinances and statutes which set up standards for ''minimum facilities and equipment which are required in each dwelling unit'' for ''maintenance of the dwelling unit and of facilities and equipment'' and for ''conditions of occupancy of the dwelling unit.''[81] In fact, there were never any pure housing codes; the tenement house laws typically contained fire and safety provisions as well. Building codes can and do overlap with housing codes. A provision for a minimum number of windows in a dwelling might be contained in either sort of code. Minimum plumbing standards could be in either, or in a plumbing code. But peculiar to a housing code are standards applicable only to dwellings *qua* dwellings (e.g., forbidding habitation in cellars, even though these cellars were built in perfect conformity to the building code), relating to the maintenance rather than to the erection of the building (e.g., insisting that the roof not leak), or to the social conditions or behavior of the tenants (e.g., forbidding overcrowding).

Since the days of Veiller, there has been, naturally, considerable upgrading of standards. As before, codes seek if possible to set up hard and fast standards which can be objectively measured and thus, in theory at least, easily enforced. Some standards can be policed through the use of building or occupancy permits. The Milwaukee Housing Code asks that ''every habitable room shall have at least one window facing directly to the outdoors. The minimum total window area, measured between stops, for every habitable room shall be 10 percent of the floor area of such room.'' But other sections of the same code set up maintenance standards incapable even in theory of precise enforcement by objective standards or regulation through building or occupancy permits. Thus, ''every interior partition, wall, floor, and ceiling shall be capable of affording privacy . . . and maintained so as to permit them to be kept in a reasonably good state of maintenance and repair.'' And the Milwaukee Code directs many of its sections against tenants. For example, ''every occupant of a dwelling or dwelling unit shall dispose of all his rubbish in a clean and sanitary manner by placing it in . . . rubbish containers.''[82] Such provisions are as little likely to be enforced as the provision against obstruction of fire escapes in the New York law of 1901. Probably some of these provisions were inserted to provide a kind of balance between landlord and tenant—to show that tenants, too, have duties and responsibilities under the law.

The provisions of the codes are arrived at through a process part political, part idealistic, and part economic. The influence of tenants, owners, reformers, bankers, and politicians may be felt to a greater or lesser degree. The codes must be politically palatable. They must attempt to strike some sort of balance between laxity and stringency. As Warren Lehman has pointed out, standards which are too low simply ''clutter up the books''; standards which are too high can be ''used as weapons . . . by prospective purchasers to soften sellers . . . by building contractors and suppliers as a means of drumming up business . . . as weapons to assure party regularity,'' or ''simply for graft.'' The too-harsh code also leads to the vice of ''unequal enforcement.''[83] Not everyone would agree that unequal enforcement is necessarily evil; it has been recommended and used in programs of selective neighborhood conservation and rehabilitation, as in St. Louis.[84] But graft, corruption, and venality are hardly commendable under any theory.

Perhaps some of the fault lies in the moralizing tendency of tenement house laws and housing codes and in the use of evil landlords and lax politicians and judges as scapegoats. These may be more than labels. They may be, as we have argued, self-fulfilling prophecies.[85]

Recent programs call for a vast increase in the pace of enforcement of housing codes. The federal code-enforcement program has been slow in getting started; at this writing, it is still too early to judge its total impact.[86] So far, tenement house laws and housing codes have neither cleared the slums nor convinced housing experts that they can do so. Enforcement has been a persistent headache. The perception of failure of housing codes has called for and will call for alternative solutions. Some of these solutions ask for more public effort; others for more voluntary means. Some programs, too, have attempted to mix private and public efforts, achieving slum reform by mobilizing more or less nongovernmental groups to take advantage of the restrictive codes and other housing laws.

NOTES

1. Joseph D. McGoldrick, Seymour Graubard, and Raymond J. Horowitz, *Building Regulation in New York City* (New York: Commonwealth Fund, 1944), pp. 34-35.
2. Law N.Y. 1867, ch. 908, §17. The act also applied to lodging-houses, defined as "any house or building, or portion thereof, in which persons are harbored or received, or lodged for hire for a single night, or for less than a week at one time, or any part of which is let for any person to sleep in for any term less than a week."
3. See James Ford, *et al., Slums and Housing*, I (Cambridge, Mass.: Harvard Univ. Press, 1936), pp. 867, 869. On the rise of the apartment hotel, see *Grimmer* v. *Tenement House Department*, 204 N.Y. 370, 97 N.E. 884 (1912). The account in McGoldrick, Graubard, and Horowitz, p. 7, claims that the apartment hotel was invented in 1919 as an evasion of the Tenement House Law. But the Grimmer case proved that the device was older. On the rise of the apartment house, see Christopher Tunnard and Henry Reed, *American Skyline* (Boston: Houghton Mifflin, 1956), pp. 122-24.
4. Modern housing codes are mostly municipal ordinances. Some states have or have had statutory codes. The housing codes may exist by themselves, or they may be mixed in with building codes, plumbing codes, or the like. The word "tenement" has unfortunate connotations; New York's present state law uses the phrase "multiple dwelling," which is more neutral in tone.
   The New York Multiple Dwelling Law was passed in 1929. It applied to cities of more than 800,000 population, though smaller municipalities could elect its provisions (N.Y. Mult. Dwelling Law, §3(2)). A tenement house law remained on the books in New York state, but it applied only to the city of Buffalo. That city elected to come under the Multiple Dwelling Law in 1949. The Tenement House Law then became a dead letter. It was repealed in 1952 (Laws N.Y. 1952, ch. 798). In 1950 the Multiple Dwelling Law was amended to make its provisions mandatory for cities with more than 500,000 population, i.e., Buffalo and New York City (N.Y. Mult. Dwelling Law, §3(1)). Useful information on the background of the Multiple Dwelling Law is given by MacNeil Mitchell, "Historical Development of the Multiple Dwelling Law," *Consolidated Laws of New York Annotated*, Vol. 35-A (1946), pp. ix-xxi.
5. Laws Mass. 1868, ch. 281.
6. Lawrence M. Friedman and Michael J. Spector, "Tenement House Legislation in Wisconsin: Reform and Reaction," *American Journal of Legal History*, 9 (1965), 41, 52-53.
7. Jacob A. Riis, "The Clearing of Mulberry Bend," *Review of Reviews*, 12 (1895), 172, 177; see Ernest Flagg, "The New York Tenement-House Evil and Its Cure," *Scribner's Magazine*, 16 (1894), 108, blaming much of the vice in New York's tenements on the standard 25' × 100' lot.
8. Perhaps the character of the city's elite is an alternative or better explanation for the timing of tenement house reform. Both New York City and Boston were pioneers in tenement house reform; both cities had well-established leisure classes with strong senses of social obligation.

Frontier Chicago had a quite different kind of "society." I am indebted to Martha Derthick for this suggestion.

9. Quoted in Ford, *et al.*, I, p. 134.
10. Edith Abbott, *et al.*, *The Tenements of Chicago 1908-1935* (Chicago: Univ. Of Chicago Press, 1936), p. 170.
11. Charles E. Rosenberg, *The Cholera Years* (Chicago: Univ. of Chicago Press, 1962), pp. 192-234; Roy Lubove, *The Progressives and the Slums: Tenement House Reform in New York City 1890-1917* (Pittsburgh: Univ. of Pittsburgh Press, 1963), pp. 1-28.
12. See, in general, Richard Hofstadter, *The Age of Reform* (New York: Alfred Knopf, 1955).
13. J. Peckham, in *Health Department* v. *Rector, etc., of Trinity Church*, 145 N.Y. 32, 50 (1895).
14. Quoted in Lubove, pp. 91, 92. In 1892, in the one-third square mile adjacent to Chicago's Hull-House, there were only three bathtubs. Jane Addams, *Twenty Years at Hull-House* (New York: New American Library, 1961), p. 221.
15. Board of Tenement House Supervisors of New Jersey, *First Report* (Executive Document No. 26, 1904), p. 35.
16. Many articles in popular magazines and the press between 1885 and 1910 graphically described these conditions. See, for example, Edward T. Devine, "Housing Conditions in the Principal Cities of New York," *Charities*, 7 (1901), 491; Edessa Kunz, "The Housing Problem in Wisconsin," *Charities and the Commons*, 18 (1907), 251; Alice Rollins, "The Tenement-House Problem," *Forum*, 5 (1888), 207. Not all painted a totally black picture of the tenements. See, for example, William T. Elsing, "Life in New York Tenement-Houses as Seen by a City Missionary," *Scribner's Magazine*, 11 (1892), 697.
17. Carroll D. Wright, *The Slums of Baltimore, Chicago, New York, and Philadelphia* (Washington, D.C.: House of Representatives, Executive Document No. 527, 7th Special Report, U.S. Commissioner of Labor, 1894).
18. Lawrence Veiller, "The Tenement-House Exhibition of 1899," *Charities Review*, 10 (1900), 19.
19. Robert W. DeForest and Lawrence Veiller (eds.), *The Tenement House Problem*, 2 vols. (New York: Macmillan, 1903); Bureau of Labor and Industrial Statistics of Wisconsin, "The Housing Problem in Wisconsin," *Twelfth Biennial Report*, Part IV (1905-1906). This study was authorized by Laws Wis. 1903, ch. 203. For other reports, see Edith Elmer Wood, *The Housing of the Unskilled Wage Earner* (New York: Macmillan, 1919), pp. 46-59.
20. See Friedman and Spector, p. 41, for the state of public opinion in Wisconsin.
21. Some landlords—New York's Trinity Church, for example—were particularly vulnerable to public opinion. The first attacks on Trinity as a landlord came in the decade of the 1890's. The church's image was not helped by its losing struggle against the Board of Health, which insisted that water be furnished to tenants in upper stories of tenements. See *Health Department* v. *Rector, etc., of Trinity Church*, 145 N.Y. 32 (1895). Major reforms were undertaken in 1909 and 1910. See *Report as to the Sanitary Conditions of the Tenements of Trinity Church* (New York: Trinity Church, 1895); Charles T. Bridgeman, *The Parish of Trinity Church in the City of New York*, VI (New York: Trinity Church. 1962), pp. 116-28; *Yearbook and Register of the Parish of Trinity Church* (New York: 1909), pp. 386-402; Robert H. Bremner, *From the Depths: The Discovery of Poverty in the United States* (New York: New York Univ. Press, 1964), pp. 116, 208.
22. "Chicago's Housing Conditions," *Charities Review*, 10 (1901), 292.
23. Wood, p. 47.
24. Amended in Laws N.Y. 1879, ch. 504; Laws N.Y. 1880, ch. 399; Laws N.Y. 1884, ch. 272; Laws N.Y. 1884, ch. 448; Laws N.Y. 1887, ch. 84; Laws N.Y. 1887, ch. 288; Laws N.Y. 1888, ch. 422; Laws N.Y. 1889, ch. 211; Laws N.Y. 1890, ch. 486; Laws N.Y. 1891, ch. 39; Laws N.Y. 1891, ch. 204; Laws N.Y. 1892, ch. 329, ch. 655, ch. 673; Laws N.Y. 1893, ch. 173; Laws N.Y. 1894, ch. 247; Laws N.Y. 1896, ch. 991; Laws N.Y. 1900, ch. 279.
25. Laws N.Y. 1901, ch. 334, §75, §112.
26. Veiller inserted a similar provision in his model housing law and remarked that, "This provision is made especially necessary in the case of tenement houses, because of the practice of tenants taking lodgers and boarders into their apartments." Lawrence Veiller, *A Model Housing Law* (2nd ed.; New York: Russell Sage Foundation, 1920), p. 146. Edith Elmer Wood called the privacy provision "a safeguard of far-reaching sociological importance," Wood, p. 68.
27. Quoted in Tenement House Department of the City of New York, *First Report*, I (1902-3), pp. 93, 94.

28. Lawrence Veiller, *Housing Reform* (New York: Russell Sage Foundation, 1910), p. 16.
29. Ibid., pp. 17, 18.
30. The New Jersey Board found this a positive virtue despite "criticism" of the board's lack of "discretion": "the absence of general clauses in the law" prevents "the use of influence to obtain special favors and concessions, relieves the Board of much useless argument and protects . . . the public . . . from loose administration." Board of Tenement House Supervisors of New Jersey, p. 64.
31. Laws N.Y. 1901, ch. 334, §69.
32. Laws N.J. 1904, p. 96; Laws Conn. 1905, ch. 178; Laws Wis. 1907, ch. 269; Laws Ind. 1909, ch. 47. None of these acts was a verbatim copy of the New York law. The New York law was used as a draft or model from which the draftsmen worked. Thus, the Connecticut law was much shorter than the New York model. It omitted the fire protection sections. It changed many of the specific dimensions required, e.g., minimum room heights were 8 feet 6 inches in Connecticut, and 9 feet in New York. There were also differences in definitions, in the scope of the law, and in administrative provisions.

    Laws Pa. 1895, No. 110, p. 178, naturally owed nothing to the New York law. The Pennsylvania act seems to have had little or no influence outside of the state.
33. Laws Conn. 1905, ch. 178. Smaller cities could choose to come under the act if they wished. The act originally applied to the cities of Hartford, New Haven, Waterbury, New Britain, and Meriden. After the 1910 census Danbury, Stamford, and Norwich were added. Bureau of Labor Statistics of Connecticut, *24th Report* (1910), p. 203.
34. 136 Wis. 193, 116 N.W. 885 (1908).
35. Laws Wis. 1909, ch. 394, ch. 592.
36. In New York, see *Tenement House Department of the City of New York* v. *Moeschen*, 179 N.Y. 325, 72 N.E. 231 (1904), *aff'd per curiam*, 203 U.S. 583, 51 L. Ed. 328 (1906); *Adler* v. *Deegan*, 251 N.Y. 467, 167 N.E. 705 (1929) (Multiple Dwelling Law).
37. 204 N.Y. 370, 97 N.E. 884 (1912).
38. Lubove, p. 143ff.
39. Lawrence Veiller, *A Model Tenement House Law* (New York: Russell Sage Foundation, 1910), p. 2; Veiller, *A Model Housing Law*, 2nd ed., p. v.
40. Lubove, p. 146; see also Wood, p. 60-90.
41. Lubove, pp. 179-81.
42. Albion Fellows Bacon, *What Bad Housing Means to the Community* (Boston: American Unitarian Association, n.d.), p. 14.
43. Jacob Riis, *How the Other Half Lives* (New York: Hill & Wang, 1957), p. 205.
44. Ibid., p. 217.
45. Mary B. Sayles, *Housing Conditions in Jersey City* (Philadelphia: Supplement to Annals of American Academy of Political and Social Science, 1903), p. 51. Approximately similar findings for Chicago are in Abbott, *et al.*, pp. 363-400. The 1894 federal report on Chicago, Baltimore, Philadelphia, and New York found considerable variations in tenure. In Baltimore 80.44 percent of the families in tenements were renters, in Chicago 89.77 percent, in New York 99.15 percent, and in Philadelphia 92.45 percent. Wright, pp. 584-94.
46. Letter from Professor Fred E. Case, Graduate School of Business Administration, University of California, Los Angeles, March 15, 1966.
47. Eugene Edward Molitor, *The Significance of Slum Ownership to the Urban Planning Function: A Case Study in Milwaukee* (Unpublished master's thesis, University of Wisconsin, Madison, 1961).
48. Warren Lehman, "Building Codes, Housing Codes and the Conservation of Chicago's Housing Supply," *University of Chicago Law Review*, 31 (1963), 180, 189.
49. *New York Times*, Feb. 22, 1964, p. 28, col. 5.
50. *New York Times*, Jan. 23, 1965, p. 38, col. 1. Gelfand said, "the city had been informed that the owners were not in the position to remove the violations, and intended to 'walk away from it.' No one paid any rent, he said." This then was a building at the end of its tether. See "Slum-Makers are Shadowmen," *Journal of Housing*, 14 (1957), 232 (cited hereafter as *JH*). See also the case studies of landlords hauled into New York's Housing Court, in Community Service Society of New York, *Code Enforcement for Multiple Dwellings in New York City*, Part II, "Enforcement Through Criminal Court Action" (1965), pp. 33-50.

51. See "Courts Beginning to Get Tough in Code Violation Cases in Cities Everywhere," *JH*, 18 (1961), 163.

52. Demolition is discussed at pp. 68-72 of Friedman, *Government and Slum Housing: A Century of Frustration* (Chicago: Rand McNally & Co., 1968).

53. Not enough is known about the economics of slum ownership. See Arthur D. Sporn, "Empirical Studies in the Economics of Slum Ownership," *Land Economics*, 36 (1960), 333, which found wide varation in profitability. For another discussion, see Alvin L. Schorr, *Slums and Social Insecurity* (London: Thomas Nelson, 1964), pp. 69-74. Since the text was written, an important new study has shed great light on the problem. George Sternlieb, *The Tenement Landlord* (New Brunswick: Rutgers Univ. Press, 1966).

54. Woody Klein, *Let in the Sun* (New York: Macmillan, 1964), pp. 141-68, 273-74.

55. David Satter, "West Side Story," *New Republic*, 155 (July 2, 1966), p. 15.

56. Mabel L. Walker, *Urban Blight and Slums* (Cambridge, Mass.: Harvard Univ. Press, 1938), pp. 147-50.

57. Laws N.Y. 1935, ch. 863. Regardless of ownership, enforcement was not suspended as to conditions "dangerous to the life or health of any occupant."

58. Laws N.Y. 1936, ch. 809, amending Multiple Dwelling Law §304.

59. See Friedman, *op. cit.*, p. 176. Recently, however, the law has specially favored owners who are below the poverty line themselves.

60. Kunz, p. 297. On the lodging house problem, see also *Abbott, et al.*, pp. 341-62.

61. Lubove, pp. 161, 164. There were difficulties with the analogous provisions in New Jersey; tenants resented giving up the use of fire escapes for storage. Board of Tenement House Supervisors of New Jersey, *Second Report* (Legislative Document No. 24, 1905), p. 35.

62. "Slumlords' Fines Called Too Low," *New York Times*, Jan. 27, 1965, p. 23, col. 1. The recommendations were based on the Society's interesting and thorough 1965 study, *Code Enforcement for Multiple Dwellings in New York City*, the second part of which dealt with enforcement through criminal court action. For other complaints about low fines, lax judges, or the slow pace of judicial enforcement, see "The Slum Operators: A Day in Court," *Chicago Daily News*, May 22, 1963, p. 1., col. 1; *New York Times*, Dec. 6, 1963, p. 38, col. 1; "[New York City Buildings Commissioner Charles G.] Moerdler Scores Judges on Housing," *New York Times*, April 9, 1966, p. 26, col. 2.

63. See "Slum Violations Get Easier Fines," *New York Times*, Aug. 19, 1965, p. 33, col. 1.

64. Early in 1966, a considerable fuss in New York City was made over the fact that in-laws of Charles Moerdler, the Building Commissioner, owned slum houses with code violations. Moerdler insisted that he was capable of treating his relatives impartially, and the tempest subsided. No one was really surprised that a man like Moerdler might have relatives who owned slum property (with or without violations). But it would have been inconceivable for his relatives to be dope peddlers, prostitutes, common thieves, or even ex-convicts. *New York Times*, March 13, 1966, p. 1, col. 7.

65. Lubove, p. 165, quoting from the eighth report of the New York Tenement House Department.

66. Abbott, *et al.*, pp. 476-77.

67. Michael W. Straus and Talbot Wegg, *Housing Comes of Age* (New York: Oxford Univ. Press, 1938), p. 19. Straus and Wegg held out two hopes: innovations in building techniques, or "some subsidy."

There is a certain inconsistency between the two sources of disillusionment: that the codes were ineffective, and that they were so effective that they choked off low-income housing construction. In a sense, however, both statements can be true at once. "Reputable" low-income housing had become more difficult and expensive. The *laissez faire* housing of the nineteenth century was now formally illegal; businessmen would not and could not any longer put up great numbers of new buildings that would house the very poor, meet code standards, and still return good profits. Additions to the stock of low-income housing would of course continue to occur as long as poor people existed. But some of the increase would come through illegal means, and the new supply would tend to corrupt and disrupt the administration of existing housing laws.

68. Wood, p. 20.

69. Friedman, *op. cit.*, pp. 95-96.

70. 63 Stat. 414, §101(a) (1949).

71. Friedman, *op. cit.*, p. 162.

72. On legal problems arising under the codes, see Joseph Guandolo, "Housing Codes in Urban Re-

newal," *George Washington Law Review*, 25 (1956), 1; Note, "Municipal Housing Codes," *Harvard Law Review*, 69 (1956), 1115; Note, "Administration and Enforcement of the Philadelphia Housing Code," *University of Pennsylvania Law Review*, 106 (1958), 437. A comprehensive and excellent survey is to be found in "Enforcement of Municipal Housing Codes," *Harvard Law Review*, 78 (1965), 801.

73. HHFA, *17th Annual Report* (1963), p. 387; see, for example, the history of code adoption in Birmingham, Alabama, *JH*, 18 (1961), 71. In Buffalo, HHFA "ruled the city's old Multiple Dwelling Law inadequate and cut off aid''; the city then passed an "adequate code." *New York Times*, July 29, 1965, p. 58, col. 1.

74. The President's Advisory Committee on Government Housing Policies and Programs, *Report* (December, 1953), p. 112.

75. Housing codes can of course be used as part of a broader approach; F. Stuart Chapin, Jr., has suggested uniting zoning, subdivision control, building, housing, fire, and other codes into a single "urban development code" to "function as a positive influence in shaping growth." "Taking Stock of Techniques for Shaping Urban Growth," *Journal of the American Institute of Planners*, 29, No. 2 (May, 1963), 76, 85.

76. 78 Stat. 785 (1964); Melvin Stein, "The Housing Act of 1964: Urban Renewal," *New York Law Forum*, 11 (1965), 1, 3-5; *JH*, 22 (1965), 207. The "workable program" provision is also discussed in Friedman, *op. cit.*, p. 162.

77. P.L. 89-117, §301(a) (1965).

78. Guandolo, p. 3.

79. Wis. Stat. §66.431(4) (e).

80. Described in Philip H. Cornick, *Premature Subdivision and Its Consequences* (New York: Inst. of Public Administration, 1938).

81. Gilbert Barnhart, *Local Development and Enforcement of Housing Codes* (Washington, D.C.: Housing and Home Finance Agency, 1953), p. 6.

82. Milwaukee, *Code of Ordinances*, ch. 75, §75-6(1), §75-7(5), §75-9(2). Comment, "Federal Aids for Enforcement of Housing Codes," *New York University Law Review*, 40 (1965), 948.

83. Lehman, pp. 180, 188-91.

84. William W. Nash, *Residential Rehabilitation: Private Profits and Public Purposes* (New York: McGraw-Hill, 1959), pp. 96-104. On selective enforcement in Milwaukee, see William L. Slayton, "Urban Renewal Short of Clearance," in Coleman Woodbury (ed.), *Urban Redevelopment: Problems and Practices* (Chicago: Univ. of Chicago Press, 1953), pp. 313, 319-22, 345-53.

85. For the phrase and concept, see Robert K. Merton, *Social Theory and Social Structure* (Glencoe, Ill.: Free Press, 1957), p. 421ff.

86. At the end of April, 1966, programs calling for the expenditure of $5,268,534 had been approved by HUD; applications for six times this amount were pending. See "First Rehabilitation Loans, Grants Approved in East, Midwest, West Regions of HUD," *JH*, 23 (1966), 253.

13

Origins of Federally Aided Public Housing

Robert M. Fisher

> *The Congress shall have power to . . . provide for the common defense and*
> *general welfare of the United States: . . . [and] to make all laws which shall*
> *be necessary and proper for carrying into execution the foregoing powers*
> *and all other powers vested by this Constitution in the Government of the*
> *United States or in any department, or officer thereof.*
> —UNITED STATES CONSTITUTION, ART. 1, SEC. 8.

Up to World War I federal housing activities followed precedents laid down early in the nation's history. Dwellings were provided for certain employees of the United States, such as military personnel and selected civilian government workers and their families. Prior to 1918 this traditional pattern was never altered by congressional legislation.

A noncongressional presidential commission had suggested several years earlier, however, that the scope of the federal housing program should be enlarged. In 1908 President Theodore Roosevelt appointed an advisory committee to study slum problems in the District of Columbia. A year later the President's Homes Commission recommended, among other things:

> If the government can build prisons for the criminals, almshouses for the poor, asylums for the afflicted, and public schools, libraries, etc., on which millions of dollars have been spent, it would seem that in common sense and in logic there can

From Robert M. Fisher, *Twenty Years of Public Housing* (New York), 73-91, © 1959 by Robert Moore Fisher. Reprinted by permission of Harper & Row, Publishers, Inc.

be no condemnation for an application of the same solicitude to the aid of those who are in a condition of semiparalysis, owing to economic conditions. A little government aid extended to these unfortunates in the form of a loan to build them habitable dwellings would tend immensely toward their uplifting and improvement. . . .

All unsightly and insanitary property should be condemned and purchased by the government, improved in a uniform manner, and inexpensive and healthful habitations erected for the poor, who could rent or purchase these homes on installment plans, at low rates of interest.[1]

These novel ideas failed to move Congress to action. And until World War I, the government continued to follow its traditional role of building residential accommodations exclusively for federal employees.

WORLD WAR I EXPERIENCES

Federal housing activities broadened considerably during the emergency period of World War I. They were justified in terms of a so-called critical shortage of dwellings for workers in shipyards and defense industries. To meet this situation, the government kept within its traditional role by constructing housing for federal employees—in this case civilian workers in United States arsenals and navy yards, and their families. But for the first time it went further to build dwellings for employees of private defense plants. It also extended loans to limited-dividend housing corporations.

The government's wartime housing operations were administered by the Emergency Fleet Corporation for workers in merchant shipyards and by the United States Housing Corporation for other employees in defense industries.[2] The two agencies, among other things, were involved in the completion of about 15,183 family dwellings and 14,745 accommodations for single persons. These totals approximate the 21,848 low-rent public-housing units initiated some fifteen years later by the Housing Division of the Public Works Administration. But they fall well below the total of 627,000 units completed during World War II and administered by the Federal Works Administrator or his successors under the terms of the Lanham Act, as amended.

The United States Shipping Board
Emergency Fleet Corporation

Under authority of the Shipping Act of 1916, the United States Shipping Board Emergency Fleet Corporation was organized on April 16, 1917, to acquire, maintain, and operate merchant vessels in the commerce of the United States. It was later empowered in 1918 to buy or sell land and dwellings for the use of employees (and their families) of shipyards in which merchant ships were being built for the United States. The Emergency Fleet Corporation could also "make loans to persons, firms, or corporations in such manner upon such terms and security, and for such time not exceeding ten years, as it may determine to provide houses and facilities'' for shipyard workers. Its authority was to end with the termination of the war.[3]

In its operations, the Emergency Fleet Corporation extended housing loans to realty companies incorporated by shipbuilders. (It also loaned money to private transit companies to improve passenger transportation facilities to shipyards, requisitioned several hundred old houses, and helped to adjust cases of alleged rent profiteering.) Ten-year loans at 5 percent annual interest were secured by blanket mortgages on the property of the realty companies. These companies were expected to build houses and other quarters on their own land and repay the federal loans after any excessive war expenses up to 30 percent of development costs had been written off. They were obliged to limit dividends paid on their stock to 5 percent until the loans were repaid and to 6 percent afterward.

As the Shipping Board pointed out in its *Second Annual Report, 1918*, to keep control over its investment and

> . . .to avoid paternalism and the placing of the government in the role of landlord, the Emergency Fleet Corporation assumed the position of mortgagee or banker lending government funds on safe security, the main consideration being the forwarding of the construction program. . . . But its interest being broader than that of a mere mortgagee or banker, the Fleet Corporation had under its mortgage reserved the power to exercise control over the rentals, sales, and management of the project.

It also supervised the layout, architecture, and construction of the projects. This was perhaps the first example of the degree to which federal controls may accompany the extension of government credit for private housing activities.

By the middle of 1919, 28 projects financed largely by Emergency Fleet Corporation loans had been completed. In 15 states and 23 cities, the projects included:

> . . .8,336 houses and 849 apartments, making a total of 9,185 dwelling units for employees with families. In addition, accommodation was provided in dormitories, boarding houses and hotels for 7,564 single employees. . . . The Fleet Corporation spent a total of $67.3 million on housing and in addition loaned $2.2 million to municipalities and utility companies.[4]

After the war ended, the realty companies defaulted on their mortgage loans. In June, 1920, Congress directed the Emergency Fleet Corporation to dispose of the projects acquired on mortgage foreclosure. Four years later nearly all of them had been sold or transferred to other agencies at a net loss to the Federal government of about $42 million.

The United States Housing Corporation

On July 9, 1918, the Bureau of Industrial Housing and Transportation of the Department of Labor incorporated the United States Housing Corporation

(USHC) under the laws of the State of New York.[5] By delegation of authority, USHC was authorized by Congress to provide "housing, local transportation and other general community utilities for such industrial workers as are engaged in arsenals and navy yards of the United States and in industries connected with and essential to the national defense, and their families. . . ."[6]

For this purpose, the United States Housing Corporation could make loans to builders or construct and manage facilities itself, provided "That in no case . . . shall rents be furnished free, but the rental charges shall be reasonable and just as between the employees and the government." Furthermore, Congress specified that "houses erected by the government under the authority of this Act shall be of only a temporary character except where the interests of the government will be best subserved by the erection of buildings of a permanent character. . . ." Upon congressional approval, "such property shall be sold as soon after the conclusion of the war as it can be advantageously done. . . ."

The United States Housing Corporation generally followed a policy of constructing housing facilities itself, in contrast to the policy of the Emergency Fleet Corporation of making loans to shipbuilders. One observer has noted:

> This policy [of the United States Housing Corporation] was a radical departure from American practice. The Federal government, it is true, owned residential property in its parks, reservations, navy yards and arsenals. But there was no precedent for extensive building of private dwellings or complete communities for the use of the industrial population.[7]

By the fall of 1919, the United States Housing Corporation had expended $52,373,000 for 55 projects. It finished 27 developments located in 16 states and the District of Columbia. Accommodations were provided for an estimated 5,998 families and 7,181 single persons. In July, 1919, Congress directed that the properties should be sold at their fair market value. A net loss of about $26 million was realized on the entire operation.

According to one writer:

> The greatest single contribution of the government efforts [by USHC] consisted of a demonstration of the advantages to be gained by the correlation in a single enterprise of all the factors that affect the quality of housing. Operating for the most part on a large scale, the directors of these developments were able to unite the services of city planner, architect, landscape designer, engineer, and builder, and to fuse their efforts into a single result. The result was attractive, unified, consistent, and effective. It has consequently exerted a widespread and profound influence upon the thought and practice of the country, particularly among those whose professional activities are involved.[8]

But the government's wartime housing activities failed to convince Congress of the necessity for a permanent federal program. In calling for the postwar sale of publicly owned facilities, Congress reaffirmed its faith in the ability of private enterprise to meet all housing needs. This attitude was reflected during hearings held by the Senate Select Committee on Reconstruction and Production during 1921. The so-called Calder Report issued by the Committee under its chairman, Senator William M. Calder (New York), stated:

> The committee is of the opinion that it is in the interest of public welfare that the Federal, State, or municipal governments, should not participate directly in the housing business, but that they should rather take such action as may be necessary to insure continuity of operation and an adequate supply of fuel, transportation, credit, and raw materials, and should also make most readily available to those engaged in the industry information as to the best practices and methods. Much can be accomplished through cooperation when the American people better understand that ample transportation, an uninterrupted supply of fuel, and a normal use of credit for both capital and consumable commodities are essential to continuous employment of labor and to the permanent reduction of prices.[9]

Further government housing action thus awaited the advent of another emergency. Nevertheless, two important precedents had been set by the wartime programs: federal housing loans to limited-dividend corporations established by shipbuilders and direct public construction of housing projects for private employees of defense industries. During the Depression of the 1930s, the government followed these precedents in broadening its housing policies. With the different character of the times, however, the emphasis shifted from providing accommodations at going rentals for war workers to developing housing at below-market rents for low-income families regardless of their source of employment.

EXPERIMENTS IN THE EARLY 1930s

The onset of the Great Depression brought a severe drop in housing construction as well as in other economic activities. The unfavorable outlook led President Herbert Hoover to call a privately financed conference of housing experts in Washington, D.C., in December, 1931, to review the situation. Thirty-one committees of the President's Conference on Home Building and Home Ownership produced eleven volumes of reports and recommendations.

With regard to the role of public housing, the Committee on Large-Scale Operations made the following observations:

> Government participation in housing has long been a recognized and accepted form of procedure in the United States. In almost every organized urban community, the local government establishes building codes, maintains a system of building inspection, and throws the safeguards of the law about property in land and investments in building loans.
>
> But governmental participation in housing now goes far beyond its traditional regulatory character. In various states and at various times the government has: (1) provided tax exemption for certain fixed periods, (2) publicly financed utility installations, (3) provided access to new housing by publicly financed systems of

transportation, (4) granted the right of eminent domain to condemn property, (5) extended tax exemption privileges to housing corporations which limit their dividends or their rents, or both.

The object of such action has been to stimulate housing construction for the lower-income groups. Unfortunately this aid has not always been accompanied by correct technical restrictions and adequate supervision. In several instances the policies pursued have been subject to serious question. As large-scale operation attempts to reach the marginal groups with family incomes insufficient to provide a decent modern home, governmental action must take on a more positive character. . . .

The committee has taken into account the housing experience of European countries. Their governments have been forced to participate in low-cost housing for various reasons to a much greater degree than we hope will be necessary in the United States. *This committee is firmly of the opinion that private initiative taken by private capital is essential, at the present time, for the successful planning and operation of large-scale projects. Still, if we do not accept this challenge, the alternative may have to be government housing.*[10]

But Congress soon went far beyond these recommendations. Before long the Federal government itself assumed the role of promoting or developing low-rent housing through such agencies as the Reconstruction Finance Corporation, the Housing Division of the Public Works Administration, and the United States Housing Authority. Within five years federal low-rent housing measures evolved from the temporary Emergency Relief and Construction Act of 1932 to the permanent United States Housing Act of 1937.

The Reconstruction Finance Corporation: 1932-1933

The Reconstruction Finance Corporation was authorized by the Emergency Relief and Construction Act of 1932 to advance funds to limited-dividend corporations for housing. It could

> . . .make loans to corporations formed wholly for the purpose of providing housing for families of low income, or for reconstruction of slum areas, which are regulated by State or municipal law as to rents, charges, capital structure, rate of return, and areas and methods of operation, to aid in financing projects undertaken by such corporations as are self-liquidating in character. . . .[11]

This law followed the precedent established during World War I by the Emergency Fleet Corporation of making housing loans to limited-dividend corporations. But it placed the regulation of the corporation in the states or municipalities rather than in the federal agency which extended the loans. And it permitted occupancy in the projects by any eligible tenants regardless of their source of employment. No writedown of capital costs, however, was allowed.

When the 1932 Act was approved, only New York State was qualified to benefit from it. In 1926 the Legislature had passed a law establishing a State Housing Board under whose supervision 11 limited-dividend housing projects had been completed. This law served as a model for a number of other states which enacted legislation in 1932 and 1933 making limited-dividend corporations eligible to receive federal loans for low-rent housing.

Within a year after its creation, the Reconstruction Finance Corporation's limited-dividend lending powers were transferred to the Housing Division of the Public Works Administration. Up to that time, RFC had agreed to make one loan of $155,000 to finance rural homes in Ford County, Kansas. It had also agreed to advance $8,059,000 to the Fred F. French Company of New York City to finance the construction of Knickerbocker Village. This 1,593-unit project was built at the former location of the "Lung Block" on the Lower East Side of Manhattan. Approximately 1,085 substandard apartments were demolished on the site.

The Housing Division of the PWA: 1933-1937

The scope of federal low-rent housing activities was considerably broadened in 1933 under the terms of the National Industrial Recovery Act. This Act authorized the President to create a Federal Emergency Administration of Public Works (the PWA) headed by an Administrator. Title II specified:

> *Sec. 202.* The Administrator, under the direction of the President, shall prepare a comprehensive program of public works which shall include among other things the following: . . . (d) construction, reconstruction, alteration, or repair under public regulation or control of low-cost housing and slum-clearance projects. . . .
> *Sec. 203.* (a) With a view to increasing employment quickly (while reasonably securing any loans made by the United States) the President is authorized and empowered, through the Administrator or through such other agencies as he may designate or create, (1) to construct, finance, or aid in the construction or financing of any public-works project included in the program prepared pursuant to section 202; (2) upon such terms as the President shall prescribe, to make grants to States, municipalities, or other public bodies for the construction, repair, or improvement of any such project, but no such grant shall be in excess of 30 per centum of the cost of the labor and materials employed upon such project; (3) to acquire by purchase, or by the exercise of the power of eminent domain, any real or personal property in connection with the construction of any such project, and to sell any security acquired or any property so constructed or acquired or to lease any such property with or without the privilege of purchase. . . .[12]

To carry out these statutory provisions, the PWA Administrator, Harold L. Ickes, who was also Secretary of the Interior, established a Housing Division on June 23, 1933. A year earlier the Reconstruction Finance Corporation had been authorized to extend loans to private limited-dividend corporations regulated by state or municipal law to finance the reconstruction of slum areas or the construction of new housing for low-income families. The Housing Division could do much more. It could lend money to any limited-dividend corporation regulated by federal, state, or local law to finance the construction or rehabilitation of low-cost housing and slum-clearance projects. It could also make 30 percent grants and 70 percent loans to public bodies for the same purpose. Or it could buy, condemn, sell, or lease property in developing new projects itself.

According to a report by Administrator Ickes:

> In undertaking a public-housing program, the five principal objectives and policies of the Housing Division were: First, to deal with the unemployment situation by giving employment to workers, especially those in the building and heavy-industry trades. Second, to furnish decent, sanitary dwellings to those whose incomes are so low that private capital is unable to provide adequate housing within their means. Third, to eradicate and rehabilitate slum areas. Fourth, to demonstrate to private builders, planners, and the public at large the practicability of large-scale community planning. Fifth, to encourage the enactment of necessary state-enabling housing legislation so as to make possible an early decentralization of the construction and operation of public-housing projects.[13]

Loans To Limited-Dividend Corporations

On July 8, 1933, the PWA Housing Division announced that it would follow a policy of advancing loans to housing corporations that limited annual dividends to 6 percent. This program had been taken over from the Reconstruction Finance Corporation under Title III of the National Industrial Recovery Act. Amortized loans were available at 4 percent annual interest for 25- to 35-year terms. They covered up to 85 percent of estimated project costs and were secured by a first mortgage.

By the end of 1933 the Housing Division received over 500 applications from 197 cities in 39 states for limited-dividend housing loans. Only a few requests met PWA requirements. In all the Housing Division made 7 loans with a total allotment of about $10.6 million. An estimated 3,123 dwelling units were built, mainly on vacant sites.

The Housing Division reserved the power to supervise the development and the management of the dwellings closely. Until the mortgages were fully repaid, it could regulate rental and tenant selection, control fiscal policies, and require adequate maintenance of the properties. But despite the supposed advantages of public supervision and financing, the 7 limited-dividend projects began operations by charging average gross rents of $10.38 per room per month. In the opinion of Harold A. Gray, director of the PWA Housing Division, these rents were so high that they excluded many low-income families for whom the dwellings were intended. While testifying before the Senate Education and Labor Committee in 1937, Mr. Gray maintained that some other method of financing was needed:

> The experience of the Housing Division of the PWA with the seven housing projects financed with money loaned to private limited-dividend corporations shows the need for subsidies to assure the low-rent character of housing projects. Although the money was loaned at a lower rate of interest than could be obtained from private sources and some savings were also effected by means of careful planning,

none of these limited-dividend projects received grants or subsidies and they are therefore comparable [in this respect] to housing facilities constructed by any responsible private individual or corporation. The results have shown that the projects cannot be operated and the debt liquidated unless rentals are charged which are more than can be paid by persons of truly low incomes.[14]

The unexpectedly small number of eligible applications for limited-dividend projects as well as the relatively high rents scheduled for completed projects led the Housing Division to suspend its program on February 23, 1934. Within the previous nineteen months, little construction activity had been stimulated by federal low-rent housing activities. Only 8 urban loans had been allotted by the Reconstruction Finance Corporation or the PWA. They totaled $18.6 million and helped to finance the construction of about 4,716 dwellings. Three projects in New York City received more than four-fifths of all the funds and dwellings involved.

Direct Construction of Projects

As the PWA Administrator explained, the next step led to construction of projects directly by the government:

> Due to the general absence in February 1934 of adequate state laws authorizing local public bodies to engage in housing activities, the Housing Division turned to the only method then available to it for undertaking projects to relieve unemployment and to meet the housing needs of the low-income groups, namely, direct federal construction. Pursuant to this federal housing program, the Housing Division initiated federal housing projects throughout the country.[15]

Within three and one-half years, the Housing Division undertook 51 projects in 36 cities within 20 states, the District of Columbia, Puerto Rico, and the Virgin Islands. Some 21,848 units were started with over $36 million in funds provided under the National Industrial Recovery Act and the Emergency Relief Appropriation Act of 1935.[16] Total development costs, including site acquisition and demolition, averaged about $6,200 per unit.

Although launched as an unemployment relief measure, the PWA Housing Division building program was set back both in 1934 and in 1935 when funds were transferred to other agencies for more direct relief purposes. Aside from their political aspects, these transfers implied that housing did not provide employment opportunities so quickly as some other relief activities. This implication was later confirmed by studies made by the Bureau of Labor Statistics of 47 PWA housing projects built in the continental United States.

According to the studies, the length of time required to complete a project varied from 12 to 32 months and averaged 21.7 months. The peak in man-hours-worked-per-month, however, occurred well after construction began in each case. "Employment at the construction site was generally low during the first 6 months, rose rapidly to a peak at the end of about 1 year, decreased gradually for approximately 4 months, and then declined rapidly for about the sixteenth or seventeenth month.''[17] It was estimated that for every manhour worked on a project site, an average of 1.32 man-hours were required for off-site labor. Of total development costs, about 38 percent went for on-site payrolls, 44 percent for materials, and 18 percent for other expenses and profit.

Early in the PWA building program, projects were constructed mainly on slum-clearance sites acquired by the Housing Division through purchase or condemnation, as authorized by the National Industrial Recovery Act. But in 1935 a court decision in the case of *United States* v. *Certain Lands in the City of Louisville* (Kentucky) held that the Federal government could not exercise the power of eminent domain for slum-clearance and low-cost housing.[18] This decision led the Housing Division to build most of its later projects on vacant lands. Even so, more than 10,000 substandard units were demolished during the entire Housing Division program.

Forty-nine PWA-built projects and 21,639 dwelling units were subsequently kept in the low-rent program. According to USHA's *Annual Report, 1939*, about 70 percent of the dwellings were located in the North and 30 percent in the South census regions. Four states claimed half the units—New York (3,344), Ohio (3,152), Illinois (2,414), and Tennessee (1,794). Of the 49 projects, 17 were inhabited exclusively by white tenants, 15 by nonwhites, and 17 had mixed occupancy. All projects contained two-or-more-family structures rather than single-family houses.

The larger cities got the bulk of the program. More than three-quarters of all units were built in cities of 250,000 or more inhabitants in 1940. Projects ranged in size from 1,622 units in Williamsburg (initially named Ten Eyck) Houses, New York City, to 50 in Highland Homes, Wayne, Pennsylvania. The average size was 442 units—25 percent less than the average of 588 units for the 8 limited-dividend projects.

The first project—604 units in Techwood Homes, Atlanta, Georgia—was opened for occupancy on August 15, 1936. This and other projects completed within the next 14 months were initially operated under the provisions of the George-Healey Act of 1936.[19] The Act waived federal civil and criminal jurisdiction over the housing projects, authorized payments in lieu of taxes, prescribed rental calculations, and fixed tenant eligibility requirements. Most of these provisions were later modified and incorporated in the permanent United States Housing Act of 1937.

Because PWA-built projects were then federally owned, they were exempt from ordinary real estate taxes. To compensate for this fact, the George-Healey Act authorized the PWA Administrator to enter into an agreement for "the payment by the United States of sums in lieu of taxes" upon the request of any state or locality where a project was located. Payments were to be made out of receipts derived from project operations. They were to be "based upon the cost of the public or municipal services to be supplied for the benefit of such project or the persons residing on or occupying such premises, but taking into consideration the benefits to be derived by such state or subdivision from such project.''

In operating the projects, the George Healey Act provided that the PWA Administrator should

> . . .fix the rentals at an amount at least sufficient to pay (1) all necessary and proper administrative expenses of the project; (2) such sums as will suffice to repay, within a period not exceeding sixty years, at least 55 per centum of the initial cost of the project, together with interest at such rate as he deems advisable.

The provisions for a 45 percent grant and a 60-year maximum period in which to repay the 55 percent of the capital cost resulted in lower rents than had previously been obtained. On a weighted basis, monthly gross rents per dwelling unit averaged $27.30 for 18 continental projects operated under the George-Healey Act in mid-1938. This figure was about 38 percent below the average weighted monthly gross rent of $43.92 per unit being charged on 6 PWA limited-dividend projects at the time.

As for tenant eligibility requirements, the George-Healey Act specified that dwellings

> . . .shall be available only to families who lack sufficient income, without the benefit of financial assistance, to enable them to live in decent, safe, and sanitary dwellings and under other than overcrowded housing conditions: *Provided*, That no family shall be accepted as a tenant in any such project whose aggregate income exceeds five times the rental [including utilities] of the quarters to be furnished such family.

Additional standards and regulations were established under administrative interpretations of the Act. Occupancy was further restricted to (1) actual families, excluding lodgers or unattached individuals; (2) maximum densities, so that no more than five persons, say, might occupy a four-room unit; (3) families formerly living in substandard dwellings and unable to obtain adequate housing within their means; (4) responsible tenants, chosen in order that ''every family accepted for consideration is capable of paying the rent and has a satisfactory character.''[20]

Meanwhile, the Housing Division encouraged state legislatures to enact laws enabling local authorities to develop and administer new public-housing projects and manage PWA-built units. This policy was promoted by a desire to decentralize the program. Decentralization was prompted by the provisions of the Federal law as well as by two leading court decisions.

In 1935 the Louisville case had denied federal use of the power of eminent domain to acquire sites for public housing. But shortly afterward a New York court held in *New York City Housing Authority* v. *Muller* that local authorities could employ the power of eminent domain for this purpose. Further acquisition of slum sites for public housing thus depended upon a greater degree of local participation in the program than had previously taken place.

With the encouragement of the Housing Division, New Jersey and Ohio passed the required enabling legislation in 1933. By the end of the year, three local authorities had been established—the first in September 1933 as the Cleveland Metropolitan Housing Authority. Four years later, a total of 30 states, the District of Columbia, and Hawaii had passed enabling legislation. Nearly 50 local authorities had been set up.[21]

From June 1933 to September 1937 then, the temporary PWA public-housing program laid the basis for the permanent low-rent program. It helped to focus attention on substandard housing problems and the use of federal funds to deal with them. It built up the first large inventory of low-rent public-housing projects. It operated these projects according to principles later adapted to the program under the United States Housing Act of 1937. Finally, the PWA Housing Division stimulated the passage of enabling legislation in a majority of the states. Local authorities created under it were ready to participate in a decentralized program allegedly stressing local initiation, financing, construction, and management of the projects.

SUMMARY

A permanent federal housing program for government employees—especially military personnel and certain civilian workers—has long been in operation. Steps to broaden this program by including other types of tenants were taken in two major stages. Each was justified in terms of a temporary, emergency situation.

The initial stage occurred during World War I. It terminated at the end of the war after setting precedents involving large-scale federal construction of dwellings for nongovernment employees and federal loans to private limited-dividend corporations. The second stage took place during the Great Depression. It eventually led to the permanent low-rent program administered under the provisions of the United States Housing Act of 1937.

In the early 1930s federal low-rent housing policy turned first to extending 25- to 35-year loans to limited-dividend corporations to build housing for tenants regardless of their source of employment. Approximately 4,700 units were built in 8 projects aided by federal loans of less than $4,000 per unit. More than 1,000 substandard dwellings were demolished.

Since few eligible applications for loans were submitted, government policy turned to promoting the direct development and administration of projects by the PWA Housing Division. Construction was financed by emergency appropriations designed to relieve unemployment as well as supply housing. Accommodations were let at rents calculated to return 55 percent of the capital investment, with interest, to the government over a period of up to 60 years.

Under the PWA program, about 21,800 dwellings were started in 51 projects and 10,000 substandard units demolished. The total federal grant involved in developing these public-housing accommodations would have amounted to nearly $2,800 per unit if the program had run for 60 years—or an average of almost $47 annually per unit.

According to the National Resources Planning Board's report in 1940 on *Housing, the Continuing Problem*, this PWA Housing Division program represented

> ...the first real attempt to correlate slum clearance and the construction of new dwellings and was the first intensive public housing program in this country. It stimulated the States to enact enabling laws; it gave impetus and direction to the long-existent demand for a Nation-wide housing program; and it provided a practical and legal background for the development of such a program.

The PWA Housing Division experiences thus set the stage for the United States Housing Act of 1937. This act permitted a further reduction in rentals by authorizing the government to make yearly grants, called annual contributions, to local authorities over periods of up to 60 years. In most cases, maximum annual contributions were sufficient to pay all (or nearly all) principal and interest payments on funds borrowed to finance the development of the projects. Since no return was required on the capital investment, local authorities could theoretically reduce rents to levels adequate to cover operating expenses alone.

NOTES

1. U.S., Congress, Senate, *Reports of the President's Homes Commission*, 60th Cong., 2d Sess., 1909, Senate Doc. no. 644, p. 320. In 1921, Congress appropriated funds for research in construction within what became the Division of Building and Housing in the National Bureau of Standards. (Public Law 18, 67th Cong., c. 23, 1st Sess., approved June 16, 1921, H.R. 6300, 42 Stat. 29.)
2. The following discussion is based largely on Miles L. Colean, *Housing for Defense, A Review of the Role of Housing in Relation to America's Defense and a Program for Action* (New York: Twentieth Century Fund, 1940), chap. 1.
3. Public Law 102, 65th Cong., c. 19, 2d Sess., approved Mar. 1, 1918, S. 3389, 40 Stat. 438.
4. Miles L. Colean, *op. cit.*, p. 14; list of projects, p. 155.
5. The President was authorized to create such a corporation by Public Law 164, 65th Cong., c. 92, 2nd Sess., approved June 4, 1918. H.R. 12280, 40 Stat. 594. This authority was delegated to the Bureau of Industrial Housing and Transportation of the Department of Labor.
6. Public Law 149, 65th Cong., c. 74, 2d Sess., approved May 16, 1918, H.R. 10265, 40 Stat. 550.
7. Miles L. Colean, *op. cit.*, p. 19. The Housing Corporation also made vacancy surveys, maintained registry and placement services, discouraged rent profiteering, and helped improve transportation facilities to defense plants.
8. Ernest M. Fisher, "Housing Legislation and Housing Policy in the United States," *Michigan Law Review*, vol. 31, no. 3, January 1933, p. 325.
9. U.S. Congress, Senate, Select Committee on Reconstruction and Production, *Reconstruction and Production*, 66th Cong., 3d Sess., 1921, report no. 829, p. 5.
10. "Large-Scale Housing," Final Report of the Committee on Large-Scale Operations, 1932, in John M. Gries and James Ford (eds.). *The President's Conference on Home Building and Home*

Ownership (Washington: The President's Conference on Home Building and Home Ownership, 1932), vol. 3, pp. 18, 19, 24.

11. Emergency Relief and Construction Act of 1932, Public Law 302, 72d Cong., c. 520, 1st Sess., approved July 21, 1932. H.R. 9642, 47 Stat. 709 at 711, Title II, Sec. 201 (a) 2.

12. Public Law 67, 73d Cong., c. 90, 1st Sess., approved June 16, 1933, H.R. 5755, 48 Stat. 195 at 201, 202.

13. "Report by Harold L. Ickes, Administrator of Federal Emergency Administration of Public Works. Dated April 1, 1937, Relating to Activities of Housing Division of Federal Emergency Administration of Public Works," U.S. Congress, Senate, Committee on Education and Labor, *Hearings, To Create a United States Housing Authority*, 75th Cong., 1st Sess., 1937, p. 20. The following discussion is based mainly on the report of Administrator Ickes, cited hereafter as Ickes Report.

14. Senate Education and Labor Committee, *1937 Hearings, To Create a United States Housing Authority*, p. 14.

15. "Ickes Report," p. 21.

16. The Emergency Relief Appropriation Act of 1935, Pub. Res. No. 11, 74th Cong., c. 48, 1st Sess., Approved Apr. 8, 1935, H.J. Res. 117, 49 Stat. 115.

17. Herman B. Byer and Clarence A. Trump, "Labor and Unit Costs in PWA Low-Rent Housing," *Monthly Labor Review*, vol. 49, no. 3, September 1939, p. 582.

18. 9 F. Supp. 137 (W.D. 1935), aff'd. 78F. (2d) 684 (C.C.A. 6th Cir. 1935), dismissed on motion of Solicitor General, 294 U.S. 735, 55 Sup. Ct. 548, 79 L. Ed. 1263 (1936).

19. Public Law 837, 74th Cong., c. 860, 2d Sess., approved June 29, 1936, S. 3247, 49 Stat. 2025. The sponsors of the Act were Senator Walter F. George (Georgia) and Congressman Arthur D. Healey (Massachusetts). The provisions of the Act applied only to projects owned by the United States.

20. "Ickes Report," pp. 36-37.

21. *Annual Report of the United States Housing Authority for the Fiscal Year 1939*, p. 36. There has often been a substantial difference between the number of local authorities in existence and the number with active low-rent programs.

14

Excerpts from Legislative Hearings for the Housing Act of 1936

U.S. Senate, Committee on Education and Labor

STATEMENT OF THE HONORABLE ROBERT F. WAGNER, UNITED STATES SENATOR FROM THE STATE OF NEW YORK

Mr. Wagner.... It is not necessary to prove here that millions of people in America live in homes that are injurious to their health and not conducive to their safety; for you have all known and felt these conditions in every city and rural area of your respective States. Nor do I need to elaborate upon the fact that bad housing leaves its permanent scars upon the minds and bodies of the young, and thus is transmitted as a social liability from generation to generation.

I intended to confine my discussion to the economic problems raised by the legislation proposed, using the word "economic" in its more restrictive sense....

The central problem confronting the American Nation today is not the depression which is being left behind, but rather the character of the recovery that is now under way.... [Employment has not picked up, despite the upturn in profits. The real reason is that, over the long term, increasing productivity means that men will be displaced by machinery.]

The opportunities for large-scale re-employment today are not to be found in the consumer goods industries. ...

When we get to the bottom of the problem, we find a lag in home construction. Only one-fifth as many dwellings were built last year as 10 years ago....

For these reasons, Mr. Chairman and members of the committee, the whole country awaits the time when the sound of the rivet and the saw are joined more loudly in the chorus of economic recovery. When we consider the long-time deficit that has accumulated, the existence of unhealthful quarters that must be replaced, and normal growth in the future, it is very conservatively estimated that the country needs at least 10,000,000 new family units during the next 10 years. A building program of this magnitude will absorb both the unemployment in the durable goods industries, and the overflow of the technologically unemployed from other fields. Ministering to a widespread and basic market, housing will provide the most stabilizing and stimulating influence that can be devised.

The Government's Role in Housing

I take it we are all in agreement that a building program of this magnitude must be predominantly the task of private industry. But nonetheless the Government has an inescapable supplementary role to play, a role justified by the success that has met our recent efforts in connected but nonetheless distinct fields.

The major housing activities of the Government to date have been set in the context of the emergency needs of early 1933. It was then imperative to save home owners from eviction, to repair dwellings that had become dilapidated or decayed, and to rescue the investors in real estate from complete ruin. To these tasks the Home Owners' Loan Corporation and the Farm Credit Administration have applied themselves assiduously and successfully. Ninety-five percent of the loans made by these organizations have been used to repay business and banking debts, and it may be said that they have contributed mightily toward saving our financial system from disintegration. But today the problem before the Nation is positive rather than negative. Instead of saving old homes, new ones must be built. Rather than refinancing old investments, areas must be developed for the operation of new capital.

It is true that some agencies of the Government have been designed to stimulate new construction. The Reconstruction Finance Corporation is empowered to issue building loans by private enterprise. But such undertakings can do no more than to facilitate the financing of homes for people who can afford homes and who have credit standing. This kind of assistance, if taken alone, may promote another short-lived building boom for the well-to-do, but it can never clear the slums. It may restore the residential industry to its 1926 status as an uneven luxury trade, but it can never create the solid foundation for permanent economic stability. A foundation must be at the bottom and not at the top. In housing, this means provision for the large market at the bottom of the economic structure who need housing most.

At the present time, about 18,000,000 families in America, or 60 percent of the Nation, have incomes of not more than $1,000 a year. This means they can spend only $200 to $250 a year for rent. But taking the country as a whole, at least $315 per year is necessary to provide a family of five with 3½ rooms of decent and sanitary quarters, at an average rate of $7.50 per room per month. The provision of safe and sanitary housing for low-income groups is thus a distinct and separate problem in its own right. By universal admission, it cannot be mixed, either administratively or substantively, with reorganizing the mortgage market, or stimulating the flow of credit into profit-seeking construction for the well-to-do. By universal admission, it requires partial public financial support to remedy a threatening social and economic evil.

Provisions of the Bill

The bill now before this committee is directed toward the problem created by low incomes, which, as we all recognize, affects directly the welfare and even the safety of every economic group. . . .

The kind of slum clearance embraced in this bill does not mean pure destruction. It may be limited to the repair or renovation of buildings upon existing slum sites. It may mean the clearing away of the slum site and the building of better quarters on the same spot. In some cases, it may mean the construction of low-rent homes upon cheaper and economically more desirable land. But in all cases, it places the emphasis rightfully upon stimulation of the building industry, upon re-employment, and upon creating safer and more sanitary homes for the slum dwellers and others of very low income. . . .

I want to emphasize the public policy behind this Federal financial assistance. The most important consideration is, that public housing projects should not be brought into competition with private industry. It is the meager character of the assistance to date that has made it impractical to rent the present public housing projects except to people of moderate means. This has brought on the very type of competition with private industry that should be avoided, and in addition has carried us directly into a kind of housing that has no just claim on public funds. For example, the only so-called low-rent housing project of the Federal Housing Administration rents for $12.50 per room per month, bringing it within the reach only of families with incomes well over $2,500 a year. To reach those who are really entitled to public assistance, and to get into the field where private enterprise really cannot operate, is the objective of this bill.

In addition to these provisions, the bill contains other safeguards against competition with private industry. Every housing project that receives a penny of Federal assistance, either loan or grant, will be available only to those families of low income who cannot purchase safe and sanitary quarters elsewhere. If there is competition, it will be only with the miserable conditions of slums and blighted areas.

Encouragement of Private Investment

. . . If enterprise does its part, every dollar of Federal grant should be matched by $48 of private expenditure for home building, with its connected economic improvement. . . .

Financial Provisions

The financial provisions in this bill are modest. . . .

STATEMENT OF HON. NEVILLE MILLER, MAYOR
LOUISVILLE, KENTUCKY

. . . Mr. Miller. . . . I would like to first present a resolution which was passed at the annual meeting of the United States Conference of Mayors, November 20, 1935: . . .

Federal Housing Program

Whereas, there has been a great deal of public attention to the question of a public housing program though relatively little has been accomplished on such a program, and

Whereas an extensive housing plan on a Nation-wide scale would give strength and stability to the economic structure of the Nation, and

Whereas numerous surveys and studies of housing conditions throughout the country indicate the growing shortage and congestion in housing facilities, and

Whereas the disgraceful conditions in city slums and country hovels have a directly detrimental effect on the social well-being of these areas and the surrounding communities, and

Whereas it is obvious that the Federal Government must assume the financing of such self-liquidating projects through loans or investments and low interest rates; Now, therefore, be it

Resolved, That the United States Conference of Mayors does hereby urge upon Congress and the President the vital importance of this problem and the need for a well-coordinated and extensive housing program for the so-called low-income group, where desired and the need exists, and

Further, that the United States Conference of Mayors lend its assistance to the preparation and realization of such a program which will be substantially financed by the Federal Government though in the interest of economy and efficiency the responsibility for the administration of the specific projects of the program be in the hands of the local authorities where so desired.

I also have here, which I would like to file, a group of telegrams received by the United States Conference of Mayors during this past week from various mayors of various cities around the country, all in support of the Federal housing bill, as follows:

[Mr. Miller then read telegrams from the Mayors of New York City, Detroit (MI), Milwaukee (WI), Memphis (TN), Omaha (NE), Dayton (OH), Tulsa (OK), El Paso (TX), Tampa (FL), Racine (WI), Augusta (GA), Madison (WI), Bethlehem (PA), Evansville (IN), and Stamford (CN).]

As far as the housing bill affects Louisville, I want to say we are very much in favor of it and hope it will pass.

I have brought here, which I would like to file for the purpose of the record, which will explain better than I can say in words, the facts I wish to show, in five maps of the city of Louisville. [Maps not included.]

On these maps, for instance, on the first map we have spotted tuberculosis cases in 1933; on the second map we have spotted the major and minor crimes for the year 1933; on the third map we have spotted the location of residence of the cases which were treated at the city hospital during the year 1933; on the fourth map we have spotted the residence of the cases handled by the municipal relief bureau, which is the city bureau to take care of the relief problem, for the year 1933; and on the fifth map we have spotted a combination of crime, disease, relief, city hospital cases for that year.

All of these maps will show that there is a very definite district in the city of Louisville which would be the ideal place for a slum clearance and housing project, and that from the standpoint of the city administration in both health and crime, if this territory could be cleaned out and improved it would be of a great benefit to the city. . . .

The great trouble which I think all cities are having, and which is true in Louisville and all other cities, is that due to the automobile and other factors, there is a tendency to move out of what might be called the old residential district in the city, to the outlying areas.

In Louisville, within the last 20 years' space, that district in Louisville has perhaps decreased in population by at least 25 percent. That territory is still there, and it is serviced by sewers, by streets, and by all of the public utilities, and the cost for keeping up those services [has] to be maintained.

On the other hand, the people moving out of those districts go to the outlying territories where they have no sewers and have none of the other services. . . .

If we could rehabilitate that area which is perfectly good from location and all other standards, we would really bring back to the city a territory which would be much more sizeable and beneficial from many standpoints, which today looks like it is soon going to become a blighted area between the business area and the residential district.

All diseases, juvenile delinquency, and crime [are] higher in this area than any other part of the city, and I think from the city's standpoint that is one of the most important things which we have to consider at the present time.

We have made a study of four districts in that area, for instance, at the city hospital, in reference to narcotic, insane, major and minor crimes, illiteracy, dependency, family service, public health, nursing, and municipal relief, and find on those total services, the total cost to the city of Louisville is approximately 2½ million dollars, of which four small areas contribute $176,000; or putting it perhaps in a more concrete manner, the taxes raised from those four small areas are $52,304 and the cost for those services alone mentioned, is $176,544, or an excess over the tax receipts of $124,240.

The cost for those services over the city as a whole is $8.30 per person, and the cost in district no. 1 for those services per person is $34.20, or over 4 times the average cost to the city; in district no. 2 it is $20.85; in district no. 3 it is $23; in district no. 4 it is $18.75, all compared with the cost over the entire city of $8.30.

We have taken also some lots through those various areas as a comparison of the social cost to the assessment and the tax value. The most striking loss is a lot in district no. 2, which is down in the colored district, where the assessed value is $450, the city receives $4.95 in taxes and the social cost was $1,330, or 296 times what was received in taxes.

Selecting various other lots, five lots in district no. 1 ran 20.5 times the taxes, and others ran 6.5 times the taxes and 41.5 times the taxes; and, taking certain lots in the other districts, they will show approximately the same as a whole.

There is a high lot in district no. 3, where the total tax received is $31.68 and the social cost is $1,538.06, making 106 times the taxes received, and that will be true right straight through.

In studying it from the question of tuberculosis, there is in the city as a whole one case to every 463 people in the city; in district no. 1 there is one case to every 226; and in the four districts as a whole there is one case to every 156 people in those four districts as compared to one case for every 463 people in the city as a whole.

Of course district nos. 1 and 2 are down in the colored belt where the tuberculosis rate is higher than in other places.

I have a table [Table not included] here which I would be glad to file, which shows the ratio of the tuberculosis cases is three to one as compared with the rest of the city, for these four districts.

It also shows that the tuberculosis deaths is two to one; that the city hospital cases are 1.8; major crimes 4.6 times the average; and minor crimes, 3.8 times; delinquency and dependent children 2.4 times; family service is 1.5 times; municipal relief is 2.5 times.

This table will show all of those averages, and that they run more than twice the average in the rest of the city.

As to housing as it affects Louisville we have made a study of the possibility of getting some housing in some other way than by the Federal Government, and we find it is absolutely impossible to get any private industry to build any houses for this low-income group, for the simple reason that they cannot pay sufficient rental.

Also, to really meet this problem we would have to have power to condemn property, and it would have to be done on a large-scale operation. If it cannot be done on a large-scale operation, the surrounding territory would so influence the neighborhood that I am afraid any investment put in there would be lost. . . .

[There simply has been virtually no construction of housing for low-income families in recent years. Whatever house construction there has been has been beyond the means of the residents of the slum clearance area residents.]

There are two other phases I would like to mention, as affecting the city of Louisville, and I think all cities, and that is, we are very much in favor of two particular items in this bill. One is the item where the civil and criminal jurisdiction is returned to the city on this character of property.

Under the present law the city lacks such jurisdiction of property owned by the

Federal Government, and I think for the proper administration of the city it is absolutely necessary that the city laws be extended to this class of dwelling houses.

The other item is the question of taxes. This bill provides there may be entered into an agreement with the city to pay an annual sum in lieu of taxes. There has been some hesitancy on the part of a good many cities in going into these housing projects for the reason the city cannot afford to lose or to carry these large areas within the city without receiving some return in the form of taxes or payments.

There is one other thing I would like to say, and that is in regard to the present situation in Louisville due to the fact that we have had some publicity, as the Louisville case was the case which was taken to the Supreme Court of the United States. The project was a slum clearance project, and was first started in 1933, and was well under way and would perhaps have been largely completed by this time if it had not been for certain political influence which came into play for the express purpose of preventing this housing project being carried through. It was taken into court, which stopped that project. Since then we have had two low-cost housing projects started and they are now partially complete. Both of those two projects were on property which was purchased without condemnation proceedings. . . .

Both of those are housing projects, and while they fulfill one need, they do not fill what is perhaps the greatest need from the city's standpoint, and that is rehabilitation of the territory which is already serviced with utilities, streets, and sewers, and I think I can say from the standpoint of the city as a whole there is a great deal of interest still in the old project; and I think the public as a whole, the business interests, and the social interests, are all very anxious to see that old project, which is in the slum area, carried out, and we hope that this bill will give us the right to join with the Federal Government. . . .

. . . I am quite sure Louisville will be very anxious and will cooperate in every way in setting up as many housing projects as are feasible in the city. . . .

15

The Origins and Legacy of Urban Renewal

Marc A. Weiss

"I just hope that we'll be very careful that you don't use the words 'urban renewal' too often. That has a bad connotation." This was Senator Hubert Humphrey's response in the summer of 1977, to a suggestion that the federal urban renewal program, which had terminated at the end of 1974, should be revived.[1] A decade of riots and protest in ghetto communities, much of it aimed at the unpopular "Negro removal" program, had the former vice-president and his colleagues on the defensive. And with good reason. Urban renewal agencies in many cities demolished whole communities inhabited by low income people in order to provide land for the private development of office buildings, sports arenas, hotels, trade centers, and high income luxury dwellings.

The National Commission on Urban Problems, appointed by President Johnson in response to urban disorder and headed by former Senator Paul Douglas, documented the negative impacts of urban renewal on low income neighborhoods. As of June 30, 1967, approximately 400,000 residential units had been

Special thanks to Ann Markusen and Roger Montgomery for extensive, enthusiastic assistance in the research and writing of this paper. Thanks also to Martin Gellen; Michael Teitz; T.J. Kent, Jr.; G. William Domhoff; John Mollenkopf; Amy Glasmeier; Seymour Adler; Madeline Landau; Richard Walker; Peter Marouse; and the Institute of Urban and Regional Development, University of California, Berkeley, for ideas, assistance, and encouragement. Part of this research was undertaken with financial assistance from Judith de Neufville, and I thank her both for this and for her helpful criticism.

From Pierre Clavel, John Forester, and William W. Goldsmith, eds. *Urban and Regional Planning in an Age of Austerity* (New York, 1980), 53-80, by permission of Pergamon Press Inc.

demolished in urban renewal areas, while only 10,760 low-rent public housing units had been built on these sites.[2]

The Douglas Commission argued, however, that the unhappy consequences of urban renewal for low and moderate income city residents were not what Congress had in mind when it created the federal program in 1949. Since the policy goal of the 1949 Housing Act was "a decent home and a suitable living environment for every American family," the Douglas Commission concluded that the urban renewal program was a "failure" because "too many local and Federal officials in it and too many of their allies and supporters either did not understand its major purposes or did not take them seriously."[3]

Given that the 1949 Housing Act was the product of a Democratic president and a Democratic Congress, it is not surprising that the Democratic oriented Douglas Commission should wish to shift the blame elsewhere. During the past 30 years many people have propounded or accepted the view that urban renewal was "a slum clearance program with the avowed purpose of improving living conditions for slum residents," and thus that the program had failed.[4] Nothing could be further from the truth. The fact is that if one traces the history of Title I of the 1949 Housing Act back to its origins in the early 1930s there is a remarkable continuity between the vision of the program's original proponents and the ultimate results.

Urban renewal owes its origins to the downtown merchants, banks, large corporations, newspaper publishers, realtors, and other institutions with substantial business and property interests in the central part of the city. Through the Central Business District Council of the Urban Land Institute and local chambers of commerce, these influential groups and individuals refined, packaged, and sold their proposal. The state and local laws passed in the 1940s and 50s and the federal law passed in 1949 fulfilled the goal that this powerful coalition had set for itself. Most of the actual renewal projects were based directly on plans and priorities that had been thought out many years earlier.

From the beginning city planners were urban renewal allies with downtown businessmen. While their aims for the city were somewhat different, they discovered that their relationship was mutually beneficial and it prospered accordingly. Urban renewal has been an important reason for the growth of the city planning profession, so it is only fitting that city planners today are confronting the many problems left in its wake.

Public housers are a different story altogether. Initially they were on opposite sides of the barricades from the central business district boosters. The key backers of replanning and redevelopment were the staunchest foes of public housing. The housers resented the persistent attacks they received from what they called "the reactionary lobby," but by the mid-1940s the public housers began to view urban renewal as the silver lining to their political cloud. Slums could not be cleared without adequate relocation housing, they reasoned, and in a time of severe shortages public housing would be needed for lower income people. Fortified by this logic, they energetically supported urban renewal and helped lobby it through Congress and state and local legislative bodies. But when it came time for the public housers to claim their reward for "good behavior," the central district businessmen were still firmly in command. The more progressive minded housers were completely shut out of the shaping and operation of urban renewal. They were condemned to watch from the sidelines, their active role confined to writing critical reports.

Poor people and minorities learned that they could not count on the paternalism of the public housers to save them from the bulldozers. Eventually they rioted, organized, and won some rights and benefits that contributed to urban renewal's formal demise in the mid-1970s (only to be reincarnated as Community Development Block Grants and Urban Development Action Grants).

It is hoped that planner/houser-activists of the current generation have learned a lesson from this modern tragedy: if a program has serious conceptual problems, it may be better to oppose it altogether instead of reluctantly supporting it and hoping it will magically transform itself "sometime in the future." At the very least, adopting this opposition strategy gives one the satisfaction of being able to say "I told you so," when failure results. At most, it helps lay the essential ground work for building powerful coalitions and mass movements that can achieve long-term progressive structural change.

MYTH #1. URBAN RENEWAL WAS DESIGNED TO HELP SLUM RESIDENTS

The Genesis of "District Replanning"

Urban renewal was discussed seriously as a public issue in the early 1930s after the collapse of the urban real estate boom of the 1920s and the onset of the Great Depression. At that time urban renewal, then termed "district replanning," was heralded as the solution to the problem of "blight." A blighted area was not necessarily the same thing as a slum. A "slum" was a social concept: low income people living in generally crowded, unsanitary, and crime-ridden conditions.

Blight, on the other hand, was an economic concept. Basically it meant declining property values. In the 1920s and 30s, the market for developed land in the inner city was shrinking due to the movement of middle income people and industry to peripheral areas.[5] Downtown property owners, including major financial institutions such as banks and insurance companies, industrial corporations with downtown office headquarters, commercial land developers, hotel owners, department store and retail store owners, newspaper publishers, major realtors and realty management companies, and trustees of private hospitals and universities feared that property values would plummet and their businesses would suffer.

This coalition of powerful interests turned to the government for assistance. They wanted to initiate large-scale efforts to replan and rebuild the blighted areas bordering the central business district for profitable commercial use and high-income residential developments surrounded by parks, good transportation access, and attractive public facilities.

District replanning was first spelled out in detail at President Hoover's Conference on Home Building and Home Ownership in 1932. Interestingly enough, the coalition behind district replanning did not include the construction industry.

The Committee on Blighted Areas and Slums defined a blighted area as an "economic liability to the community" and a slum as a "social liability."[6] It also noted that due to extremely high densities slums are often economically profitable and therefore not technically blighted, but argued that slums should be cleared anyway because "they are not infrequently found to exist on highly accessible, and thus potentially very valuable, urban land."[7] Since, in the midst of the Depression, committee members assumed that business could not extend across all blighted areas, they argued that slum clearance "contemplates the use of former slum sites for the housing of higher income groups."[8] This would be accomplished principally through wholesale demolition of the existing structures, followed by large-scale rebuilding operations.

To accomplish such rebuilding, sizable tracts of land had to be assembled within a reasonable amount of time and at a price that would make the subsequent development profitable. Here there were a number of obstacles. Most developers simply did not have the capital necessary for such large-scale operations. The major banks and insurance companies had the capital, but the land developers they financed found it extremely difficult to assemble complete land parcels that would span an area large enough to cordon off the new development from undesirable slum dwellers and from noisy and unsightly commercial and industrial land uses. Two principal problems faced the would-be large-scale operator: 1) the asking price for the land was often more than they wished to pay; 2) they occasionally faced "holdouts," where, for one reason or another, they could not obtain a particular parcel at all. Their solution was for local governments to use eminent domain powers to acquire land and then resell it to private corporations at a discounted price, with accompanying tax abatements.

The first part of this solution, the use of eminent domain, had already been tried in New York City. In the late 1920s a group of area banks promoted a district replanning scheme for Manhattan's Lower East Side.[9] The city used a provision of the state constitution permitting it to take land for public works projects and sell or lease the excess to private developers.[10] The land was taken, the tenants evicted, and the buildings razed. But the effort collapsed because the city was forced by the court condemnation proceedings to pay such high prices for the slum property that "the private builders who had previously expressed interest now expressed only dismay."[11] The area was later turned into a park. From this experience downtown corporate institutions resolved to fight not only for the public sector to use its legal powers to help replan the district, but to use its taxing powers to pay for a substantial portion of the costs.

As to the legality of the district replanning approach, the Committee on Blighted Areas and Slums took the position that "the elimination of slums is a public purpose."[12] It conceded that local governments could also eliminate slums by strictly enforcing housing codes and demolishing slum dwellings as fire or health hazards, but committee members disliked this method because "the land remains in the hands of the original owners."[13] They preferred district replanning, since government would transfer land ownership to new large-scale developers.

While elimination of slums was the public purpose of district replanning, the committee members did not seem concerned that once slum dwellers were cleared from the "potentially very valuable land" they would continue to live in slum housing somewhere else. The President's Conference final report emphatically opposed providing any public assistance or requiring rebuilders to provide private assistance to slum dwellers displaced by district replanning:

> We do not concur in the argument that the slum must be allowed to exist because there are persons dwelling in them who could not afford to dwell in better surroundings. It is our view that the slums must, nevertheless, be removed for the benefit of the community. We are confident that a large portion of the group displaced by slum clearance will be able to find suitable accommodations elsewhere.[14]

Another vital element in the district replanning scheme, was that private enterprise must be provided with "the benefits of up-to-date city planning."[15] In other words, in order for the property values and development opportunities to be upgraded, the local government was expected to pay for the supporting infrastructure that would accompany private rebuilding. This would include new street systems and transportation facilities, schools, parks, playgrounds, public buildings, and utilities such as water and sewer lines. Equally important, the downtown landowners insisted that the local government use its regulatory powers and city planning apparatus to guarantee that undesirable land uses be kept out of the district through zoning ordinances, density and lot coverage restrictions, and building and housing codes, all tied together by a master plan for the area. Thus the public sector was being called upon to protect and enhance the value of the current and future investments of the large-scale rebuilders and their downtown allies. This use of government to rationalize and stabilize corporate expansion, generally on behalf of the larger economic interests at the expense of smaller ones, was already well established by the Progressive Era, of which "up-to-date city planning" was a part.[16]

By 1932 the basic plan for what was later called urban renewal was already clearly spelled out. Very little changed over the years except that the federal government ended up playing a much larger role than anticipated in the early 1930s. In fact, the federal government eventually picked up the tab for two-thirds, three-fourths, or more of the costs to local government of land acquisition, clearance, site preparation, improvements, and city planning. The heavy federal subsidies solved the problem of high land costs by allowing the local government to resell the land to private developers at a considerable discount. This enabled local governments to resuscitate the moribund urban land market by moving in and purchasing large chunks of land for renewal purposes, without passing on the considerable costs to the large-scale rebuilders. The downtown property lobby did not propose this federal solution in 1932 because they did not think that such massive federal expenditures were feasible. The New Deal, of course, changed their perceptions of the political potential of the U.S. Treasury.

The Selling of District Replanning

Planners' efforts to popularize the concept and refine the principles of district replanning in the 1930s, were backed up by the more powerful lobbying efforts of the big urban realtors. This effort was led by the National Association of Real Estate Boards (NAREB).[17] In 1935 NAREB's executive secretary, Herbert U. Nelson, unveiled a plan for neighborhood protection and improvement districts that would enable 75 percent of the property owners in a district to form a public corporation which, if approved by the city council, could condemn land and levy taxes within its district in order to facilitate "improvement."[18] Such an arrangement certainly accorded with Mr. Nelson's own philosophy, as outlined in the letter to the president of NAREB in 1949:

> I do not believe in democracy. I think it stinks. I believe in a republic operated by elected representatives who are permitted to do the job, as the board of directors should. I don't think anybody but direct taxpayers should be allowed to vote. I don't believe women should be allowed to vote at all. Ever since they started our public affairs have been in a worse mess than ever.[19]

The Neighborhood Improvement plan made limited headway in a few state legislatures, and the following year Nelson began to expand NAREB's efforts by setting up the Urban Land Institute (ULI) as a research arm of NAREB. During the next few years NAREB, their colleagues in the United States Savings and Loan League (USSLL), the U.S. Chamber of Commerce, and other builder and business groups, along with their allies in the Federal Housing Administration (FHA), were preoccupied with the battle against public housing. Only after they had successfully blocked any further public housing appropriations in Congress in 1939 did they turn their attention back to district replanning.

In 1940 the Urban Land Institute, reconstituted as "an independent agency for research and education in the field of real estate" and an "advisory service to aid cities in replanning and rebuilding,"[20] and with a Board of Trustees including Herbert U. Nelson and leaders of a number of large corporations, undertook as its first major project a nation-wide study of the problem of decentralization.[21]

During the next two years the ULI published studies on Boston, Cincinnati, Detroit, Louisville, Milwaukee, New York City, and Philadelphia, each one recommending some plan whereby the city could condemn land in the blighted areas near the central business district and then sell or lease the land to private developers for replanning and rebuilding.[22] In a major ULI board meeting in January of 1942 the ULI adopted a postwar replanning program.[23] The plan, not too different from what was adopted by Congress seven years later, called for local redevelopment commissions (created under state enabling legislation) to use federal funds to acquire land in blighted areas and then sell or lease the land to private businesses for redevelopment. It also recommended that the federal government provide grants to local planning agencies ''for the purpose of preparing master plans for metropolitan areas and replanning blighted areas,'' a proposal not enacted until 1954. Having promulgated the plan, the ULI, NAREB, and allied parties began a concerted effort to win passage of the program at the federal, state, and local levels.[24]

ULI's model for the proposed federal urban land agency was the FHA. NAREB had been one of the FHA's biggest boosters since its inception in 1934.[25] Its members appreciated the close and mutually supportive relationship between FHA officials and private realtors, lenders, and builders. The FHA field directors, in particular, were extremely close to private sector groups. FHA personnel came mostly from building, lending, and realty businesses.[26] Thus it is not surprising that the FHA produced its own report in 1941, *A Handbook on Urban Redevelopment for Cities in the United States*,[27] or that three years later Seward Mott who, as Director of the FHA Land Planning Division, had been involved in the preparation of the 1941 *Handbook*, became the Director of the ULI.

By 1943 the ULI had prepared federal legislation for a neighborhood development act sponsored by Senator Robert Wagner of New York. The planners prepared their own bill, the Federal Urban Redevelopment Act, which was introduced by Senator Elbert Thomas of Utah. This bill was the communal brainchild of Alvin Hansen, a New Deal economist then working for the Federal Reserve Board, Alfred Bettman, one of the leading planning and zoning attorneys in the U.S., and Guy Greer, an editor of *Fortune* magazine. The Hansen-Bettman-Greer proposal grew out of discussions within the National Resources Planning Board, the American Institute of Planners and The National Planning Association.[28] The planners, as Catherine Bauer later recalled, ''saw redevelopment as the means toward more rational and efficient organization of central areas, by removing wasteful or inappropriate land uses and facilitating new development in conformance with some kind of plan for the area.''[29]

Planners' enthusiasm for large-scale redevelopment envisioned greater public sector powers over future land use. This was the principal difference between the two bills. Under the Thomas bill the local redevelopment agency could only lease the land to private developers, retaining title and therefore control in the agency's hands. Also, the federal subsidy would be in the form of long-term, low-interest loans and annual contributions to help amortize the redevelopment agency debt (similar to the federal public housing program). The annual contributions would give the federal government some continuing control over the redevelopment process. The ULI opposed the leasing only provision and the annual contributions. They wanted the local government to be able to sell the land to private developers. They also wanted the federal government to make large one-time capital grants to the local redevelopment agency and then keep its nose out of the whole business. In Title 1 of the 1949 Housing Act, ULI beat the planners on both points.

Winning at the State and Local Level

The Wagner and Thomas bills were essentially shelved by Congress until after World War II. ULI, impatient to get on with the job of urban redevelopment, began to focus more of its efforts on state government. Corporate leaders in the various downtowns across the country started hiring planners to draw up plans for postwar redevelopment. Fearful that federal redevelopment efforts might be linked to a revived public housing program after the war, ULI and its lobbying partners decided to exert more leverage on state and local governments as a way of bypassing federal control. They reasoned that if their own program was already firmly in place at the state and local level, it would be easier to exert pressure on Congress, the president, and the federal bureaucracy for ULI-preferred solutions.

When Seward Mott became director of ULI in 1944 he immediately began lobbying aggressively in state legislatures for the ULI redevelopment program. (In 1946 ULI created a special Central Business District Council to work with local business groups promoting urban redevelopment legislation.)[30] This program was spelled out in a document entitled "Principles to be Incorporated in State Redevelopment Enabling Acts,"[31] which grouped the various state laws and bills into three categories: Type 1, which ten states had already passed, Type 2, which had been passed by the Arkansas and Tennessee legislatures, and Type 3, favored by the ULI. Under Type 1, either the private corporation or the municipality assembles the land under eminent domain powers and then the corporation clears the site and redevelops it. ULI disliked these laws because they generally did not allow for reuses other than for housing, and they were not sufficiently comprehensive in their approach to large-scale planning and coordination of transportation and public facilities with the redevelopment project. What ULI liked was the fact that a Type 1 redevelopment corporation law "provides an excellent channel for the investment in housing of the huge sums in the coffers of the insurance companies and similar large financial institutions."[32] The Principles concluded that "This legislation has been fairly easy to pass and is considered by many an opening wedge toward the further consideration of the whole problem."[33]

Type 2 included laws that "make the public housing authority the redevelopment agency. They usually require the rehousing of displaced tenants, and greatly broaden the power of the public housing authority." ULI was unalterably opposed to this approach because: 1) the emphasis was on housing for low-income tenants rather than "for the benefit of the city as a whole"; 2) placing redevelopment in the hands of the public housing authority "would tend to discourage the participation of private enterprise"; 3) a greater role should be given to the local planning commission; and 4) redevelopment "should not be under the control of any special interest" such as public housing officials—rather it should be in the hands of civic leaders and private enterprise redevelopers.[34]

ULI's preferred redevelopment legislation (Type 3) was eventually adopted by the majority of the states, many of them before 1949. Type 3 laws authorized the creation of a local urban redevelopment agency, "a department of the local government composed of representative citizens,"[35] completely separate from the public housing authority, and under local, not federal control. The reuse of the cleared land in the blighted area could be for any purpose "in accordance with a comprehensive plan and with the objective of securing the highest and best use of the area."[36] This meant profitable development of any variety, not necessarily residential.

Two principles that ULI held dear were that "there should be no restrictions on the profits or dividends derived from private redevelopment projects," and "the redevelopment agency should not be required to provide for the rehousing of displaced tenants."[37] The first of these was generally accepted by state legislatures and the federal government. The second principle was violated by the federal statute, which placed a moral if not a financial responsibility on the local redevelopment agency for relocation. As the subsequent history of the program demonstrated, however, federal, state, and local officials honored this requirement more in the breach than in the observance.[38]

That ULI should have typified Type 1 as a law benefiting large insurance companies grew directly out of an experience in New York. The state of New York had passed an Urban Redevelopment Corporation Law in 1941, but no redevelopment took place until 1943, when the Metropolitan Life Insurance Company forced the legislature to change the law by removing restrictions on profits and dividends as well as removing any responsibility on the part of the redeveloper for relocating displaced tenants. In addition, Metropolitan Life was granted a 25-year property tax abatement. This tax abatement ultimately proved so costly to New York City that it would have saved $11 million by simply giving the land to Metropolitan.[39] The net result of this 1943 New York law was Metropolitan Life's Stuyvesant Town, where 10,000 low income people were driven from their homes in an 18-block area of Manhattan to make way for an expensive apartment complex for 24,000 people. Stuyvesant Town was restricted to whites only and, of the 10,000 people displaced by the project, only 300 could afford to live in the new complex.[40]

ULI objected to the New York law because housing was the only permitted reuse, and because there was no provision for comprehensive planning for streets, parks, schools, and other amenities that would enhance the property values in the surrounding area. ULI wanted open ended reuse combined with significant planning, infrastructure, and financial support from the public sector. Their model was Pennsylvania's Type 3 law and its application in Pittsburgh.

Pennsylvania passed a redevelopment enabling law in 1945 at the urging of Richard King Mellon, head of a corporate empire that included Gulf Oil and Alcoa. Mellon had hired Robert Moses and a number of other planners and lawyers to come up with a comprehensive plan to boost property values in the central business district—the Golden Triangle. With the cooperation of Pittsburgh's Democratic Mayor, David Lawrence, Mellon enlisted the other major corporate leaders behind his strategy. The strategy involved creation of an independent redevelopment agency based on the ULI Principles, the recruiting of Equitable Life Insurance to construct an office complex (the first *commercial* redevelopment project), the construction of two new parkways, a state park, a convention center, a sports stadium and arena, luxury apartments, and more high-rise office buildings.[41]

The Pittsburgh plan, hailed by the media as a "Renaissance," set the tone for central city redevelopment across the country and became the model for downtown business interests and planners before the 1949 Housing Act ever reached President Truman's desk. This ULI model was the one that prevailed: a federal FHA-type agency to financially assist locally controlled Pittsburgh-style urban renewal in every city in the United States.[42]

Winning at the Federal Level

The story of the passage of the 1949 Housing Act has been recounted in detail elsewhere.[43] Essentially, the Act was a triumph for the ULI. Its one minor setback was an inconvenient but relatively painless provision that required land use in the project area to be "predominantly residential" either before or after redevelopment. The "before" allowed housing to be torn down and replaced by commercial or industrial facilities. Despite this rather large loophole, defenders of Myth #1 insist that the predominantly residential requirement proves that the consensus of Congressional opinion was that urban renewal's primary purpose was to provide more low-income housing. This is simply untrue.

The predominantly residential requirement was included in the 1949 Act mainly at the insistence of conservative Ohio Senator Robert Taft. Taft was the key Republican backer of the Housing Act and it could not have passed without his support. Taft was basically opposed to the ULI-FHA-Pittsburgh model of publicly-funded urban redevelopment, and argued that the only type of redevelopment program that the federal government should pay for was construction of low income housing. Here are his statements during 1945 hearings on housing and redevelopment:

> But why we should undertake to relieve cities just because they don't look nice and because they don't have the real-estate values that somebody once thought they had, I don't understand that. Some people made plenty of money out of that real estate at one time. What is the justification for our going into that thing beyond the housing question? As long as it is just housing I can understand it.
>
> I like the idea, myself, of tying it up to housing, as compared to the more ambitious plans that are being presented both by the Bettman-Hansen group and the real-estate boards . . .
>
> I think a limited redevelopment in the hands of public housing authorities is a more defensible program than one of having the Federal Government interest itself in rebuilding the whole city.[44]

What is important about Senator Taft's position is that not one single witness supported it, not even the various representatives from the public housing lobby, because of a previous compromise they had made to back the realtor's program in exchange for new public housing authorization. Taft's efforts to block ULI redevelopment failed, and all that survived was the toothless "predominantly residential" language, which did not require construction after clearance to be either residential or for low and moderate income people, nor did it require that low income housing be built elsewhere for displaced slum dwellers.

MYTH #2. URBAN RENEWAL WAS AN OFFSHOOT OF THE PUBLIC HOUSING MOVEMENT

Urban scholars and planning professionals often portray urban renewal as simply an extension of the goals and methods of the public housing movement.[45] However, public housing activists and urban renewal lobbyists were bitter foes in the 1930s, each representing a different constituency and pursuing different interests. Proponents of urban renewal such as ULI and NAREB led the fight against the public housing program. Conversely, public housing advocates such as Catherine Bauer and Nathan Straus strongly opposed ULI's redevelopment proposals.

Public housing's primary supporter was organized labor. During the Depression the building trades' unions were desperate for public works projects. With so many people unemployed and overcrowded into poor housing, construction and industrial unions put their political strength behind the public housing program. Labor, in particular, the building trades, showed great enthusiasm, for obvious reasons. Senator Wagner read into the Congressional Record a resolution of the American Federation of Hosiery Workers that pointedly mentioned labor's "double interest in the construction of low-rent dwellings." Labor was "representative both of the unemployed building and material workers and of low-income families in need of better housing.'' In the climate of the New Deal, a program aimed at rehousing the ''submerged middle class'' was seen as politically acceptable.[46]

Downtown property interests, while strongly opposing the federally financed public housing program, fought to assure that, in carrying out the program, local public housing authorities purchased inner-city, blighted land to bail property owners out of the moribund market. ''The importance of the public housing program of the 1930s in bolstering blighted area land prices is often overlooked or brushed aside by housing enthusiasts.''[47] The prospect of the federal government as a major central-city land purchaser helped whet the appetite of certain business interests for a large-scale redevelopment program. Construction of public housing on cheap vacant land on the periphery of the city was anathema to realtors, home builders, financial institutions, and their chief government ally—the FHA.[48]

Ironically, while most public housers considered themselves distinct rivals of the NAREB and its supporters, the creation of the United States Housing Authority in 1937 ultimately played a vital role in paving the way for the federal urban renewal program by clearing away the legal, political, and institutional roadblocks. By the end of the 1930s nearly every state had passed enabling legislation that was upheld in state courts verifying the constitutionality of the use of eminent domain to clear slums and blighted areas. It is extremely important to note that the public purpose of the rehousing program was considered to be slum clearance; in other words, the legal justification for the public housing program was to alleviate the threat to the community's health, safety, morals, aesthetic sensibility, and general welfare caused by the existence of slum housing. The valid public purpose was to *eliminate* bad housing, not to build good housing or to subsidize disadvantaged people's incomes. How the land was reused and what became of the former residents was incidental to the main goal.

Public housing also created the political infrastructure that made urban renewal possible. Not only was its legality generally established by the late 1930s, but in most large and many smaller cities housing authorities had demonstrated the viability of using federal monies to execute a locally controlled urban development program. Public housing had created employment for contractors, construction suppliers, building trades workers, architects, landscapers, planners, engineers, social welfare workers, and public officials. (This latter group had its own professional organization, the National Association of Housing Officials, later renamed the National Association of Housing and Redevelopment Officials, which demonstrates the relationship.) When appropriations for construction of new public housing were voted down by Congress in 1939,[49] this disparate group focused on redevelopment for a major federally funded urban public works program. The realtors and financial institutions who had fought against public housing began to push for urban redevelopment much more vigorously after 1939, as soon as the threat of an expanded low-rent housing program had been squelched.

Public housing and urban renewal are completely different programs. The former is redistributive to low income people whereas the latter is redistributive to upper income people. The base of support for the two programs in the 1930s and early 40s was extremely different. At the same time, however, public housing blazed the trail for redevelopment in three ways: 1) politically, by popularizing the idea of intergovernmental public action to clear slums; 2) legally, by establishing the public purpose of clearing slums and blighted areas in state legislatures and the courts; and 3) organizationally, by creating a federal-local infrastructure of interest groups and professionals ready and willing to embrace the new program.

MYTH #3. ALL THE PROBLEMS OF URBAN RENEWAL CAN BE BLAMED ON THE REPUBLICAN PARTY

Publication of the Douglas Commission Report in the late 1960s offered Democratic politicians and urban planners a safe haven from the heavy criticism they received about urban renewal. It did this by blaming the evils of urban renewal on the 1954 Housing Act, passed by a Republican Congress under a Republican President, rather than on the original 1949 Act, passed by a Democratic Congress under a Democratic president[50] (the 1954 Act changed "urban redevelopment" to "urban renewal," but this was very little more than a cosmetic name change; for background, see Colean (1953) and President's Advisory Committee, 1953). There is absolutely no basis for this particular brand of partisan, political buckpassing.

The Douglas Commission attacked the Republicans for doing two things: emasculating the public housing program and eroding the predominantly residential requirement. A careful look at the record demonstrates that neither of these charges is true. The emasculation of public housing and the trivialization of the "predominantly residential" rule had taken place in the Truman Administration, much earlier than 1954.

Richard Davies has pointed out about President Truman that "he gave every appearance of staunch liberalism in his housing policies, but in the day-to-day conduct of his housing agency he closely adhered to the real estate lobby's position."[51] The real estate, builder, and financial lobby made a concerted effort throughout the struggle over the 1949 Housing Act to defeat the public housing program and to insure that urban redevelopment would be separated from public housing agency control both nationally and locally. The ULI and colleagues pressed for the new urban redevelopment program to be operated by the FHA, because of FHA's close ties to and supportive relationship with realtors, builders, and lenders. At one point early in 1949, after Truman's come-from-behind reelection and the Democratic Congressional victory, NAREB and other lobbyists supported an abortive effort to separate urban redevelopment from the Housing Act altogether.[52] Such a separation would have made clear the true nature of urban renewal according to the ULI-Pittsburgh model.

Once the Housing Act passed, however, ULI lobbyists were not disappointed by the results. Urban redevelopment was kept entirely separate from the Public Housing Administration and was lodged directly in the Office of the Administrator of the Housing and Home Finance Agency (HHFA), Raymond Foley. Foley, who had served for two years as head of FHA and 11 years as FHA Field Director in Michigan, was well favored by NAREB and friends.[53] Foley's choice to head the new Division of Slum Clearance and Urban Redevelopment (DSCUR), Nathaniel Keith, staffed the division with professionals from FHA and other business-oriented agencies.[54]

No sooner did the DSCUR program get started than Keith, under prompting from Truman and Foley, began issuing regulations and making statements that discouraged redevelopment agencies from using projects for low-rent housing and encouraged redevelopment for high-rent residential, commercial, or industrial purposes.[55] Truman slashed public housing drastically as soon as the Korean War broke out in June 1950.[56] Within less than a year after the passage of the 1949 Act, "the language of the housing reformers" within HHFA was replaced by "the vocabulary of the real estate and mortgage finance industries."[57]

Given that public housing was "emasculated" both at the federal level and in local communities in 1950, the Douglas Commission's complaint against President Eisenhower is relatively groundless. As to their discussion of the "predominantly residential" rule, I have already demonstrated that its origins can be traced to Senator Taft and not to liberal Democrats or housing activists. Furthermore, the rule, aside from helping to give redevelopment some legal and moral legitimacy by linking it to the issue of slum housing, has always been relatively meaningless because it still allowed redevelopers to tear down low-rent dwellings and replace them with high-rise office buildings. The Douglas Commission conceded that this was "technically true" (National Commission, 1969, p. 157), but they claimed that Congress envisioned redevelopment primarily as a low-rent housing program, based on some ambiguous wording in a Senate committee report but *not* in the 1949 Housing Act. Had the Congress been serious about such matters they would have included strict and enforceable legal safeguards in the legislation itself. According to the Douglas Commission, such an approach was rejected by Congressional urban renewal advocates because "clamping down conditions and requirements . . . would have amounted to a strait jacket on local action or would have killed the program."[58] On this point the Douglas Commission was in complete agreement with the realtor-developer-financier lobby, which had argued from the very beginning for maximum flexibility in the urban renewal program.

Despite this rather large gap between legislative language and political rhetoric, the Douglas Commission still insisted that the so-called "skid-row amendment" to the 1954 Housing Act somehow perverted the original spirit and intent of the 1949 redevelopment program. This amendment exempted 10% of urban renewal funds from the "predominantly residential" requirement and was passed with bipartisan support (Senator Taft had died the year before). The rationale behind the amendment was that there were nonresidential areas around central business districts, universities, hospitals, and other institutional settings that certain city interests wished to clear and redevelop for nonresidential purposes. In 1959, under a Democratic Congress, the exemption was extended to 20 percent plus colleges and universities, and in the New Frontier-Great Society years it was further extended to 35%, plus hospitals, medical schools, nursing schools, and several other special exemptions.

Long before this wave of exemptions advocated principally by liberal Democrats, the Democratic officials who ran HHFA and DSCUR from 1949 to 1953 paid only lip service to their "predominantly residential" requirements. The classic case of abuse was the Columbus Circle Slum Clearance Project in New York City, crafted by Robert Moses and approved by DSCUR during the Truman Administration. Columbus Circle at 57th and Broadway was a valuable commercial site in the early 1950s when Moses induced the New York City Planning Commission and DSCUR to approve it as a Slum Clearance Project. This designation was based on the argument that a small number of aging tenements at the far end of the project's carefully drawn boundaries, constituting less than 1 percent of the total property value of the project area, were "substandard" and "insanitary."[59]

The redevelopment plan for the two-block area called for the construction of a commercial exhibition hall (the New York Coliseum) occupying 53 percent of the site and a luxury high-rise housing development occupying the other 47 percent. Since the "predominantly residential" rule was defined by DSCUR as being at least 50 percent of the total square footage of the project area, Moses needed to tip the balance by 3 percent. He announced that the tenants of the new apartment building could park their cars in the Coliseum's underground garage if their own parking lot was full. The New York City Planning Commission and DSCUR than designated 18,000 square feet of the Coliseum's underground garage as "residential," which made the entire Project "predominantly residential" in its reuse.[60]

The Columbus Circle charade prompted Congressman John Phillips of California, a Republican, to introduce an amendment to the 1954 Housing Act limiting redevelopment funds solely to residential reuse. Big city Democrats generally denounced the measure as limiting the flexibility of the urban renewal program. Business interests such as the owners of the *New York Times* lobbied heavily against the measure and defeated it in the Senate.

The New York courts had already ruled that under the 1949 Housing Act federal and local government agencies could define "substandard" dwellings and "predominantly residential" any way they wished. One judge's dissenting opinion, however, pointed out that the New York City Planning Commission and HHFA had completely ignored the physical condition of the numerous commercial structures in their determination of the area as blighted and suggested that the sole reason for including the few tenements in the project area may have been "merely to lend color to the acquisition of land for a coliseum under the guise of a slum clearance project." [61]

Such was the record of the early implementation of urban development under the Democratic Administration. And yet when Charles Abrams criticized HHFA Administrator Foley's handling of the new program, Foley was vigorously defended by none other than Senator Paul Douglas himself. In 1952 Douglas told the National Housing Conference that Foley was "acting in complete accordance with the intent of Congress." So pleased was Douglas with Foley's behavior, in fact, that the Senator proclaimed: "I feel like conferring upon him the Congressional Medal of Honor." [62]

The Role of City Planners in Urban Renewal

Since urban renewal was so clearly harmful to low and moderate income people even in its earlier incarnations as urban redevelopment and district replanning, why did so many planners enthusiastically support and participate in creating, selling, and implementing this program? The obvious answer is that in many ways city planning had its principal base of support among the various business groups that were most actively involved in pushing for urban renewal.

The growth of the city planning profession is inextricably linked to urban renewal. "Up-to-date city planning" was an integral part of the renewal package from the very beginning. The Urban Land Institute and the downtown lobby fought for comprehensive planning as an important element in their efforts to bolster central business district property values. Planners worked hard at ironing out the details of urban redevelopment legislation and at making the program academically, professionally, and politically respectable. It is hardly coincidential that the original name for the program was "district replanning."

Planners participated in these efforts because they saw urban renewal as their best chance to redesign and rebuild the city according to a more rational land use pattern. [63] Many planners, such as Seward Mott or Alfred Bettman, worked closely with the downtown corporate coalition because they shared the same values about what was best for the city. Others worked with the downtown business leaders simply because they were a politically powerful group that supported city planning. Alan Altshuler has documented how in Minneapolis the "planning activity was sustained mainly by the support of the Downtown Council." [64] Leaders of several large corporations wanted urban renewal, and the Minneapolis city planning department expanded to accommodate them. Studies of Pittsburgh [65] and New Haven [66] also detail the role of planners in designing urban renewal strategies at the behest of powerful downtown businessmen. The alliance that city planners made with local business leaders, whether out of shared values or political realism, has been a continuing part of the urban renewal saga. In 1942, for example, the National Resources Planning Board (NRPB) decided to promote

a scheme they called "progressive planning." The head of its urban section decided to initiate several demonstration projects, during which an NRPB planner
would move into a medium-sized community and, backed by technical assistance
from the NRPB and other federal agencies, involve local residents in preparing a
comprehensive physical, social, and economic plan. The NRPB wanted to use
these demonstration projects to test their model for federal urban redevelopment.[67]

NRPB's approach in Corpus Christi, Texas was to turn to the most powerful
elements of the community for support:

> . . .the mayor, the president of the largest bank, the head of Southern Alkali Cor-
> poration, representatives of the extractive industries (oil, gas, and fishing), and real
> estate board, and the Junior Assistance Club, who were interested in redeveloping
> the central part of the city and preserving land values, each pledged the support of
> his particular constituency. The NRPB's agents, in turn, were sensitive to the inter-
> ests of those whom it relied upon for assistance.[68]

Apparently the NRPB's definition of progressive planning did not include participation by other groups in Corpus Christi. Funigiello points out that "the needs
of other segments of the community (Chicanos, blacks, the unorganized and in-
articulate) seem to have been ignored with impunity," leading to "the now familiar practice of demolishing inner-city ghettos, uprooting ethnic minorities,
and replacing them with high-rent commercial and residential dwellings occupied
by well-to-do-whites."[69]

Many city planners' jobs have directly depended on urban renewal activities.
When Congress passed the 1949 Housing Act there were only 600 planners in the
country.[70] By the 1960s there were thousands of city planners, thanks largely to
the federal government's 701 Planning Grants to local government, initiated in
1954 to facilitate workable urban renewal programs. For example, the Douglas
Commission notes that "some smaller cities and urban counties have been
stimulated by the availability of urban renewal funds to develop a capability for
comprehensive urban planning which they previously lacked" (*National Commission*, 1969, p. 163). This is equally true for larger cities, particularly during
the 1950s. While the new generation of planners was being trained to implement
renewal techniques, the old-timers, such as Harland Bartholomew and Ladislas
Segoe, had more business than they could handle traveling from city to city in the
1940s and 50s consulting on downtown renewal plans.

The planners' only other option for survival would have been to build an alternative coalition for city planning based on different values and different people's
needs. The best example of this type of effort was the public housing movement
in the mid-1930s.[71] Labor unions and unemployed workers' groups constituted
an important part of the coalition supporting this program. A number of planners
worked on various aspects of public housing. Had they been able to sustain this
alliance, their livelihoods would have been dependent on a different set of inter-

ests than those of the large corporations and central city bankers and realtors. But NAREB, ULI, and other corporate lobbyists succeeded in defeating the public housing movement in 1939 and again in 1950, after which the movements dissipated and the program dwindled. Most planners interested in city rebuilding chose to work for corporate expansion—many of them willingly, others more reluctantly. Dissenters turned to community organizing or teaching.

The Role of Public Housers in Urban Renewal

When the ULI, NAREB, and their allies began pushing for urban redevelopment as a better slum clearance program than public housing, many public housing supporters were distinctly hostile to what they saw as an attack on their program.[72] Catherine Bauer, whose *Modern Housing*[73] had been a manifesto for the public housing movement in the 1930s, denounced the ULI approach in characteristically strong language:

> In the sacred name of "master plans," "bold reconstruction," "saving cities," and whatnot, it is proposed to bail out with Federal subsidy the owners of slum and blighted property—not in order to rehouse their present tenants properly, but to stimulate another wave of speculative overbuilding for the well-to-do and thus, it is naively hoped, to turn the tide of decentralization and preserve downtown property values based on high densities and even higher hopes.[74]

Yet in 1946 Catherine Bauer wrote that she "had no objection to bailing the boys out" provided "we get more workable cities" in return.[75] Bauer remained skeptical of urban renewal because she did not feel that urban decentralization could or should be reversed. But most of the others in the public housing lobby became strong supporters of redevelopment legislation. After 1939, they hoped to strike a deal with the realtors in order to save public housing. "The realtors could have their 'urban land Triple-A' (a reference to Agricultural Adjustment Act, which was interpreted here to be a "bail-out" for farmers) if the low-income segment of the population received public housing."[76]

At the end of World War II the prospects of high unemployment and a severe housing shortage began to worry many Americans. Public housing activists felt that such a situation would force Congress to revive the public housing program. In order to achieve the broadest possible base of political support for their program, it was included in the massive Wagner-Ellender-Taft Housing Bill. Public housers lobbied vigorously for passage of the entire bill. The legislation contained many provisions that were strongly backed by the builder-realtor-financier-FHA lobby and that helped underwrite the great postwar suburban expansion. The bill also included the urban redevelopment title. Public housing activists reasoned that, given the housing shortage, slums and blighted areas could not possibly be rebuilt without new public housing for the residents who would be displaced. Supporting redevelopment, they thought, was one way of getting more support for their own program.[77]

But there were also other reasons that public housers lobbied for urban redevelopment, in addition to the political bargain that was struck over the inclusion of public housing in the overall Wagner-Ellender-Taft Bill. Many hoped that local redevelopment agencies would sell or lease cleared land at cut-rate prices to local housing authorities. They hoped in vain, however, because the HHFA and the local agencies wanted redevelopment for private enterprise, and had no interest in using cleared land for public housing.[78] Had subsidized land costs been the sole aim of the public housers, however, they could just as easily have fought for this subsidy as a direct part of the public housing program rather than pinning their hopes on an entirely separate redevelopment program. Senator Taft suggested such an approach during the 1945 Senate hearings, but the public housers were already committed to their compromise strategy.[79]

Public housers also supported redevelopment because many of them believed in comprehensive city planning and wanted to see public housing interspersed with middle income housing, parks, recreation areas, schools, and retail stores, instead of being isolated in large projects.[80] City planners, however, were more interested in ULI-type concerns than in public housing.[81]

Finally, most housing reformers were middle class people who placed a high value on the elimination of slums as an end in itself. Their concern with tearing down unsightly buildings often took precedence over their concern for the welfare of the people who lived in them.[82] This attitude on the part of many constituent groups in the public housing movement made it possible for them to be pleased with a program that would clear slums, regardless of the ultimate fate of the anonymous slum dwellers.

The paternalistic attitude held by housing reformers led to a serious conflict of interest between the leaders of the public housing movement and the people for whom they were allegedly speaking. Public officials, writers, lawyers, and union leaders were not the ones who would be displaced by the federal bulldozer. While they may have been disturbed by the "relocation problem," many argued in 1949 and even later that urban renewal's contributions to civic welfare outweighed its deficiencies.[83]

As the price for its support of urban redevelopment, the public housing lobby successfully included in the 1949 act a requirement that those displaced by slum clearance be relocated in "decent, safe, and sanitary dwellings" at affordable rents and in convenient locations. The price, however, was never paid, for the provision was ever enforced by the HHFA, and local redevelopment agencies simply ignored it.[84] Public housers gave their vital support to urban renewal, and without them the legislation might never have passed.[85] Yet they simply did not have the power to force the federal, state, or local governments to meet their terms. NAREB, ULI, and their allies exerted enough power to block public housing after the passage of the 1949 act.[86] The large downtown corporations also exerted a vast amount of power, ensuring that the urban renewal program they had been fighting for since the early 1930s was implemented to their satisfaction.

Thus the public housers were placed in the position of having helped to pass a program that failed miserably for them. Urban renewal did not build low-rent housing—it destroyed it.[87] It is a sad commentary that public housers and planners, by their support of urban renewal, lent public legitimacy to this destruction. It was clear too, that the downtown corporate coalition understood the value of this added legitimacy. For example, Richard King Mellon's lawyer asked Pittsburgh's Democratic Mayor to head the new redevelopment agency because "If we condemned people's properties, it was better for the Mayor with his popular following to be responsible, rather than someone with the Mellon or U.S. Steel nameplate."[88]

Even if more relocation housing had been available, however, this still might not have mitigated the effects of urban renewal's destructiveness on people's lives.[89] In most cases the residents of blighted areas wanted to stay where they were. To be rehoused in a public housing project provided little consolation. Besides, politicians and businessmen often deliberately used relocation housing to increase racial segregation.[90]

Since the days of "district replanning" in the 1930s, when the committee on Blighted Areas and Slums recommended that slum dwellers be removed from "potentially very valuable urban land"[91] many public housing advocates have all too willingly agreed with the ULI position that "Slum sites are most often desirable for private housing for higher income families."[92]

LESSON #1: POOR PEOPLE MUST SPEAK FOR THEMSELVES

The lesson of urban renewal is that poor people must be politically well-organized and must speak for themselves. They cannot rely on middle class organizations and individuals who represent different interests to speak for them. Had the slum dwellers been highly organized in the 1940s, they would surely have fought against urban renewal. Such opposition might have forced other elements of the public housing coalition to shift their position. This shift might possibly have defeated urban renewal or brought about some useful reforms. It took another twenty years before the urban riots of the 1960s forced Congress to pass legislation providing modest financial assistance to people who would be displaced by future urban renewal projects. Congress also amended the renewal laws to provide for some degree of citizen participation by community organizations fighting redevelopment. Both of these reforms were hard-earned victories of a mass political movement.

In the case of welfare reform in the late 1960s and early 70s, poor people did defend their own interests rather than relying on other voices to speak for them, with surprisingly good results. President Nixon's proposed Family Assistance Plan (FAP) was supported by many liberal politicians and social work professionals as a "foot-in-the-door." Liberal professionals and the organizations they represented argued that despite its drawbacks, FAP was a positive measure that should be passed and then improved at a later date. This was precisely the position that the public housers took during the urban redevelopment debate in the late 1940s.

However, an organization of welfare recipients—the National Welfare Rights Organization (NWRO)—strongly opposed FAP because it would take away many of their hard-won rights and benefits. The NWRO did not agree with the liberal foot-in-the-door theory. They saw it more as a "foot-in-the-rear." Welfare rights members preferred no reform to the Nixon reform. Many leaders of the social welfare lobby labeled NWRO's position unreasonable and extremist. But the ghetto riots had given poor people some political leverage. NWRO convinced a few key Senate liberals to withdraw support for the FAP, contributing to its defeat.[93]

In San Francisco a plan was prepared in the mid-1940s to redevelop a large area near the downtown. This area—termed the Western Addition—had experienced a rapid influx of blacks during World War II. It was a low-rent district that also contained a large number of Japanese-Americans who had resettled there after their release from the U.S. internment camps. San Francisco's civic leaders wanted to clear the area and rebuild it with middle and upper income housing that would be attractive to suburban commuters.[94] Local residents turned out at a public hearing in 1948 to oppose the designation of their neighborhood as a redevelopment district,[95] but this protest went unheeded and, over the next 25 years, thousands of Western Addition residents were displaced.[96] By the 1960s the community was considerably angrier and better organized—enough to initiate a lawsuit temporarily halting the displacement process. By this action the community gained a substantial amount of publicly assisted housing within the project area.[97]

The experience of massive displacement in the Western Addition, combined with the potential effectiveness of community protest, prompted a group of tenants and property owners in San Francisco's South of Market redevelopment area to launch their own movement against the bulldozers. Retired merchant seamen and longshoremen living in the project area, with their trade union backgrounds to guide them, built a protest organization called Tenants and Owners Opposed to Redevelopment (TOOR) in the late 1960s. TOOR used a lawsuit to block the proposed Yerba Buena project for several years and eventually won their demand for publicly assisted relocation housing located in the South of Market area, with TOOR as the developer.[98]

LESSON #2: A BAD BARGAIN IS WORSE THAN NO BARGAIN

In neither the Western Addition nor the South of Market case, however, were the protesters able to stop the redevelopment agency from taking away their community. This confirms the wisdom of the NWRO strategy to stop potentially regressive measures *before* they turn into repressive public agencies with large budgets. Whether urban renewal actually could have been stopped is questionable, given its powerful base of support. But at the very least, if the organized poor and housing reformers had banded together and pursued an opposition strategy, the mythological excuses enunciated by the Douglas Commission and its supporters would not have held up for so long. Such opposition would have made clear who was for redevelopment and who was against it.

The emerging progressive coalitions of the 1980s must be based solidly within community and labor organizations. Planners, housers, and other professionals will then be in a better position to choose sides and avoid the compromises of the 1949 Housing Act that (according to Professor Donald Foley) Catherine Bauer later characterized as "a sellout." We would all do well to heed the advice offered by a black community spokesman at the 1948 San Francisco redevelopment hearings:

> You will recall that during the fight in the State Legislature this association, with these other organizations, asked that certain definite guarantees be written into the law to protect the rights of minority citizens, and to guarantee that public housing would be available so that persons of low income groups could enjoy the privileges enjoyed by others. We lost at this period of the game. Everyone said, "This is not the time to talk about such projects."
>
> We came to the San Francisco City Planning Commission, presented our problems, and once again were told "This is not the time."
>
> Now, the association, as it looks upon the law as written, and as it is to be implemented, feels that the difference between the proponents and the opponents is this: Some people say, "Let's go into this thing and revise it after we take this step." Experience has taught minority peoples that if we don't start out right we might not end up right.[99]

NOTES

1. U.S. Congress, Joint Economic Committee, *Financing Municipal Needs*, 1977, p. 77.
2. National Commission on Urban Problems, *Building the American City*, 1969, p. 163.
3. Ibid.
4. Frieden and Kaplan, 1975, p. 23.
5. Hoyt, 1933, p. 279-367; Walker, *Urban Blight and Slums*, 1938; Urban Land Institute, *Decentralization*, 1940B; National Resources Planning Board, *Better Cities*, 1942A, p. 19; Ludlow, "Land Values and Density," 1945, p. 5.
6. President's Conference on Home Building and Home Ownership, *Slums, Large Scale Housing and Decentralization*, 1932, p. 1.
7. Ibid., p. 9.
8. Ibid.
9. Ibid., p. 4.
10. Jackson, *A Place Called Home*, 1976, p. 188.
11. Caro, *Power Broker*, 1974, p. 375.
12. President's Conference, 1932, p. 9.
13. Ibid., p. 9.
14. Ibid., p. 10.
15. Ibid.
16. Kolko, *The Triumph of Conservatism*, 1963; Weinstein, *The Corporate Ideal*, 1968; Scott, *American City Planning*, 1969; Fitch, "Planning New York," 1976.

17. Gelfand, *A Nation of Cities*, 1975, p. 112.
18. Walker, *Urban Blight and Slums*, 1938, pp. 227-231; National Resources Committee, *Urban Land and Planning Policies*, 1939, p. 279.
19. U.S. House of Representatives, *Hearings Part 2*, 1950, p. 25.
20. Urban Land Institute, *The Urban Land Institute*, 1940A.
21. In 1940 the ULI released the results of a survey of 512 appraisers from 221 cities entitled *Decentralization: What Is It Doing To Our Cities?* (ULI, 1940B). At the same time it commissioned detailed studies by local realtors and financiers of the problems of decentralization in 13 American cities. A large portion of the money for these studies came from the Estate of Marshall Field, the largest property owner in downtown Chicago (*Business Week*, January 18, 1941, p. 61), through its trustee, George Richardson, who was also a ULI Board member, and who had been a member of President Hoover's Committee on Blighted Areas and Slums and Committee on Large-Scale Operations.
22. Urban Land Institute, *Proposals for Downtown Boston*, 1940C; *Decentralization in New York City*, 1941A; *Proposals for Downtown Cincinnati*, 1941B; *Proposals for Downtown Milwaukee*, 1941C; *Proposals for Downtown Philadelphia*, 1941D; *Proposals for Downtown Detroit*, 1942A; *Proposals for Downtown Louisville*, 1942B.
23. Urban Land Institute, "Urban Land Institute Adopts Huge Post-War City Replanning Program," 1942C, p. 1.
24. Urban Land Institute, *Outline for a Legislative Program*, 1942D.
25. U.S. House of Representatives, *Hearings, Part 2*, 1950, pp. 19-22.
26. Wheaton, "The Evolution of Federal Housing Programs," 1953, pp. 356-8, 431.
27. Federal Housing Authority, *A Handbook on Urban Redevelopment*, 1941.
28. Greer and Hansen, 1941; National Resources Planning Board, *Better Cities*, 1942A; *National Resources Development*, 1942B.
29. Bauer, "Redevelopment: A Misfit in the Fifties," 1953, p. 9.
30. Urban Land Institute, *The City Fights Back*, 1954, pp. 9-15.
31. Urban Land Institute, *Technical Bulletin No. 2*, 1945A.
32. Ibid., p. 2.
33. Ibid.
34. Ibid.
35. Urban Land Institute, *Statement by Seward Mott*, 1945B, p. 3.
36. Urban Land Institute, *Technical Bulletin*, p. 3.
37. Ibid., p. 4.
38. Hartman, "The Housing of Relocated Families," 1964.
39. Abrams, *The Future of Housing*, 1946, p. 380.
40. Burdell, "Rehousing Needs," 1945; Strauss, *The Seven Myths of Housing*, 1944, pp. 179-80; Gelfand, p. 124.
41. Lubove, *Twentieth Century Pittsburgh*, 1969, pp. 87-141; Urban Land Institute, *City Fights Back*, 1954, pp. 185-95; Lowe, *Cities in a Race With Time*, pp. 110-63.
42. Domhoff, *Who Really Rules?*, 1978; Hartman, *Yerba Buena*, 1974; Mollenkopf, "The Postwar Politics," 1978; Edel, "Urban Renewal," 1971; California State Commission, *Blighted!*, 1946; Urban Land Institute, *The City Fights Back*, 1954 and *Nine Cities*, 1969; Mowitz and Wright, *Profile of a Metropolis*, 1962, pp. 1-140; Caro, *Power Broker*, Lowe, *Cities in a Race with Time*, 1967.
43. Gelfand, *A Nation of Cities*, 1975; Wheaton, *Evolution of Federal Housing Programs*, 1953; Keith, *Politics and the Housing Crisis*, 1973; Davies, *Housing Reform*, 1966; Feinstein, "Policy Development," 1974; Foard and Fefferman, "Federal Urban Renewal Legislation," 1960.
44. U.S. Senate, *Hearings Pursuant to S. Res. 102*, 1945, pp. 1558, 1699, 1792.
45. Bellush and Hausknecht, *Urban Renewal*, 1967.
46. Friedman, *Government and Slum Housing*, 1968, pp. 99-117; Woodyatt, "The Origin and Evolution," 1968.
47. Ludlow, "Land Values," 1945, pp. 5-6.
48. Strauss, *Seven Myths of Housing*, pp. 47-93.
49. Woodyatt, "Origin and Evolution," pp. 193-229.
50. National Commission, *Building the American City*, 1969, pp. 156-7.
51. Davies, *Housing Reform*, 1966, p. 135.

52 Wheaton, "The Evolution of Federal Housing Programs," 1953, p. 432; Keith, *Politics and the Housing Crisis*, 1973, pp. 89-90; Gelfand, *A Nation of Cities*, 1975, pp. 149-50.

53. Davies, *Housing Reform*, 1966, pp. 60-62.

54. Feinstein, "Policy Development in a Federal Program," 1974, p. 82.

55. Feinstein, Ibid., pp. 81-107.

56. Davies, op. cit., 1966, pp. 130-131.

57. Feinstein, op. cit., 1974, p. 89.

58. National Commission, *Building*, op. cit., 1969, p. 153.

59. Feinstein, op. cit., 1974, p. 260.

60. Feinstein, op. cit., 1974, p. 232.

61. Feinstein, op. cit., 1974, p. 263.

62. Feinstein, op. cit., 1974, p. 263.

63. Sanders and Rabuck, *New City Patterns*, 1946.

64. Altshuler, *The City Planning Process*, 1965, p. 295.

65. Lubove, *Twentieth Century Pittsburgh*, 1969.

66. Domhoff, *Who Really Rules?*

67. National Resources Planning Board, 1943A. *National Resources Development Report, Part 1*, 1943A, pp. 31-6; and *National Resources Development Report, Part 2*, 1943B, pp. 102-5; Funigiello, *The Challenge to Urban Liberalism*, 1978, pp. 163-86.

68. Funigiello, *Challenge to Urban Liberalism*, p. 182.

69. Ibid.

70. Feinstein, "Policy Development," 1974, p. 67.

71. Woodyatt, "Origin and Evolution," 1968.

72. Strauss, *Seven Myths of Housing*, 1944, pp. 69-93; Gelfand, *A Nation of Cities*, 1975, pp. 117-8.

73. Bauer, *Modern Housing*, 1934.

74. Funigiello, loc. cit. *Challenge to Urban Liberalism*, 1978.

75. Gelfand, *A Nation of Cities*, 1975, pp. 136, 204-5.

76. Ibid., p. 128.

77. Bauer, "Is Urban Redevelopment Possible?", 1946 and "Redevelopment and Public Housing," 1950; Vinton, "A New Look," 1949; Meyerson and Banfield, *Politics, Planning and the Public Interest*, 1955, p. 19.

78. Feinstein, "Policy Development," 1974, pp. 87-92.

79. U.S. Senate *Hearings on Housing*, p. 1699.

80. Ibid., pp. 1738-41; Abrams, *The Future of Housing*, 1946, pp. 378-9.

81. Vinton, "A New Look," 1949.

82. Friedman, *Government and Slum Housing*, 1968; Meyerson and Banfield, *Politics, Planning and the Public Interest*, 1955, p. 18.

83. Keith, *Politics and the Housing Crisis since 1930*, 1973; Abrams, *The City is the Frontier*, 1965.

84. Hartman, "The Housing of Relocated Families," 1964 and *Yerba Buena*, 1974; Caro, *The Power Broker*, 1974, pp. 961-83.

85. Bauer, "Is Urban Redevelopment Possible?", p. 66.

86. Feinstein, pp. 87-8; Davies, pp. 126-32; Meyerson and Banfield, *Politics, Planning and the Public Interest*, 1955.

87. National Commission, *Building the American City*, 1969, p. 163.

88. Lowe, *Cities in a Race with Time*, p. 134.

89. Gans, "The Human Implications," 1959; Fried, "Grieving for a Lost Home," 1963.

90. Lowi, *The End of Liberalism*, 1967, pp. 25-65; Bowly, *The Poorhouse*, 1978, pp. 111-32.

91. President's Conference, 1932, p. 9.

92. Abrams, 1946, p. 379.

93. *The Welfare Fighter*, October 1972; Kotz and Kotz, *A Passion for Equality*, 1977, pp. 261-78; Moynihan, *The Politics of Guaranteed Income*, pp. 532-3.

94. San Francisco City Planning Commission, *Western Addition District*, 1947A and *New City*, 1947B.

95. City and Council of San Francisco, *Public Hearing*, 1948.

96. Hartman, 1974, p. 100.

97. Mollenkopf, "Community Organizations," 1973.

98. Hartman, *Yerba Buena*, 1974.

99. City and Council of San Francisco, p. 27.

16

The Dreary Deadlock of Public Housing

Catherine Bauer

Low-rent public housing has not followed the normal pattern for reform movements in modern democratic countries. Every social experiment starts off as an abstract idea, frequently in an atmosphere of violent theoretical debate. But after it has been tried out for a while, one of two things usually happens. Either it dies off, an acknowledged failure, or it "takes" and is accepted as an integral part of the ordinary scheme of things. The original theories, meantime, become modified and adapted to actual conditions. In the U.S., public attitudes about social security, collective bargaining and national economic controls have all followed the classic steps outlined years ago by George Bernard Shaw: 1) it's impossible; 2) it's against the Bible; 3) it's too expensive; and 4) we knew it all the time. But public housing, after more than two decades, still drags along in a kind of limbo, continuously controversial, not dead but never more than half alive.

No obituary is yet in order for the U.S. Housing Act of 1937 "as successively [but only in minor respects] amended." It is more a case of premature ossification. The bare bones of oversimplified New Deal theory have never been decently covered with the solid flesh of present-day reality. Even among public housing's most tireless defenders, many would welcome a fresh start if they did not fear that in the process any program at all might get lost.

If the dreary deadlock is to be broken, it is first necessary to figure out what

From *Architectural Forum*, Vol. 106, No. 5 (New York, 1957), 138-42, 219, 221, by permission of Billboard Publications, Inc., 1515 Broadway, New York, New York 10036.

really ails the program. If it is purely a matter of selfish reactionary obstruction, we who want to rehouse slum-dwellers will just have to go on fighting until we win. But if there are inner weaknesses as well, it is high time we faced up to them.

IS THE REAL ESTATE LOBBY TO BLAME?

Unquestionably private builders, lenders and property owners have been increasing in political power ever since the mid-thirties, when Uncle Sam rescued them from ruin. And it is equally obvious that they have been all-out in their opposition to public housing.

In general, however, their tactics have been so arrogant, and most of their claims so wild, that they have often tended to backfire. In recent years, moreover, some of the National Association of Real Estate Boards' allies (notably the National Association of Home Builders) have become more sophisticated about the slum problem, and highly vocal about the need to remedy it. The current slogans are "renewal" and "rehabilitation." But generally it becomes clearer that Operation Fix-Up is no cure-all, and that outright clearance and redevelopment bring relocation problems that cannot be glossed over. The great national spread of antislum propaganda by ACTION (The American Council to Improve Our Neighborhoods) probably tends to favor the cause of public housing, however inadvertently.

The most serious effect of all the controversy has been more subtle. Public housing officials, federal and local, have been kept continuously on the defensive, and the neuroses that come from chronic fright and insecurity are translated into excessive caution, administrative rigidity and lack of creative initiative. Everybody tends to sit tight, clinging desperately to the beleaguered formula, instead of trying to improve it in the light of experience and public attitudes. Sporadic efforts to broaden or modify the program have usually met with as much opposition from professional public housers as from opponents of public housing. Moreover, the hostility has probably tightened management controls, making "project" housing more and more institutional.

But even so, despite the millions they have spent in a vain effort to kill it, the real estate interests can hardly be held wholly responsible for the program's failure to take hold.

SOLID SUPPORT IS LACKING

If the public housing program in its present form had managed to achieve real popularity with the general run of ordinary citizens and their leaders, and above all with the people who live in slum and blighted areas, the real estate opposition would by now have lost its political force. The idea of public housing would be taken for granted, like old-age pensions of FHA mortgage insurance.

But this has not happened. The program has never called forth the kind of pervasive and persuasive popular support that oils the wheels of change in democratic countries. The lot of public housing tenants has undoubtedly been improved in many ways. But the fact remains that only a small proportion of the people eligible for occupancy (by legal definition, low-income families living in substandard homes) actually apply for low-rent dwellings in public housing projects. And of those who do, most appear to be desperate for shelter of any kind: minority families about to be thrown on the street by clearance operations, "problem" families sent by welfare agencies, and so on.

Moreover, general local support by civic-minded groups, such as one might reasonably have expected for such a program, has seldom developed. The U.S. Housing Act has been kept alive by the earnest annual efforts of the Washington offices of national labor, welfare, veteran, municipal, civic and religious organizations, held together by the National Housing Conference and sparked by the genius and devotion of its executive vice president, Lee Johnson. But despite considerable prodding, the local branches and members of these organizations have on the whole been apathetic, sometimes lending their names in a crisis but rarely showing much continuing interest. Where there are established citizens' housing organizations, they tend to be kept going by a few devoted individuals with little general backing.

WHY ISN'T THE PROGRAM POPULAR?

This question has never been seriously investigated, but in general terms, the answer seems quite clear. Life in the usual public housing project just is not the way most American families want to live. Nor does it reflect our accepted values as to the way people should live.

In part the weaknesses are inherent in the physical design. As Architect Henry Whitney said in the first (and still one of the best) critiques by an experienced housing official: "The typical publicly subsidized dwelling is deficient in interior space, in outdoor privacy, and in true American residential character.... Families with children generally want to live in individual homes.... A yard, a porch or a terrace is almost universally desired." While everybody who had any choice was moving into a one-story home, the housing authorities were busily erecting high-density, high-rise apartments, with no private outdoor space whatever. Significantly, perhaps, public housing is most accepted in the one American city where apartment living is also most taken for granted—New York. But even there, opinion surveys show that most tenants would prefer ground-level living if they could get it.

There are also more subtle social reasons for the lack of enthusiastic acceptance. Public housing projects tend to be very large and highly standardized in their design. Visually they may be no more monotonous than a typical suburban tract, but their density makes them seem much more institutional, like veterans' hospitals or old-fashioned orphan asylums. The fact that they are usually designed as islands—"community units" turning their backs to the surrounding neighborhood which looks entirely different—only adds to this institutional quality. Any charity stigma that attaches to subsidized housing is thus reinforced. Each project proclaims, visually, that it serves the "lowest income group."

The resulting degree of rigid social segregation is difficult to align with traditional American ideas. And in addition, if a tenant manages to increase his income beyond a certain point, out he goes, a restriction which also results in the continuous loss of natural leadership among the tenants themselves, and a trend toward problem families as the permanent core of occupants.

On the other side of the ledger has been the considerable success of nondiscrimination and mixed racial occupancy in northern public housing projects. But even this great gain is being lost. Owing to the preponderance of minority families in the lowest income group, and in the areas slated for clearance and relocation, the proportion of minority occupancy tends to rise above the line where mixture is successful, and more and more projects become virtually all-Negro.

And finally, there is the question of management policy and practice in itself. Because of legal requirements, high densities, problem families and sensitivity to continuous political attack, local authority landlordship tends to be rigid and heavy-handed, with all kinds of rules and regulations unknown in ordinary private rental management and unthinkable in a pattern of individual ownership. Sometimes special welfare services are provided which, under these peculiar conditions, may be admirable and necessary. But even at its best, this type of concern by one's landlord seems paternalistic in American terms, and hardly adds to the popularity of project living for normal families.

These are the issues that keep coming up in critical analyses by housers, in conversations with all kinds of people all over the country, and in the few random studies by social scientists. And alongside these criticisms is the patent fact that, with all its drawbacks, the program is so expensive. I doubt that the fact of subsidy in itself is very important in the general public reaction, or in any stigma that may attach to public housing occupancy at present. With all their profound and well-justified faith in private enterprise, Americans have never been purists in the matter of accepting public aid where necessary to achieve something they want. The idea of subsidy is part of the American system, whether for shipping or public education, irrigation projects, redevelopment schemes or housing. Had we not enjoyed a steadily rising market, the FHA-VA system of mortgage aid would have cost the taxpayers far more than the most tremendous public housing program ever envisioned. And certainly no stigma attached to accepting the costly aid of HOLC. But subsidies must look reasonably sensible in terms of value received. And the fact that high-rise apartments (which no one likes very much anyway), erected by local housing authorities, tend to cost more than the price of a modest FHA-insured tract house, even allowing for a substantial speculative profit, just does not look sensible on the face of it. So the unattractive aspects of the program cannot even be justified on the grounds of economy.

And finally, with all the hullabaloo and all the expense, the program still does not meet even the most obvious immediate need of families displaced by clearance or renewal operations, let alone the need in outlying areas for families whom FHA cannot serve. The legal income limits are so low and the other limitations so rigorous, including the territorial jurisdiction of municipal housing authorities, that only a small portion of the need can be met through public housing aid.

PREMISES: TRUE OR FALSE?

How do the assumptions that shaped the public housing program stand up today under quite different economic conditions and in the light of more than twenty years of experience?

Clearly the basic premises are as sound today as they were then. Even after a long period of high prosperity, there are just about as many insanitary, congested and dilapidated homes in the U.S. as there were in the middle of the depression—probably with more people living in them! And today almost everyone recognizes their existence, and admits that these conditions must somehow be remedied. It is also as true as ever (if more reluctantly recognized) that you cannot get rid of slums just by tearing them down, or fixing them up. Somewhere, in reasonably suitable location, there must be better homes available to the slum occupants, at prices they can afford to pay. And although prosperity, FHA, VA and more efficient homebuilding techniques have expanded the effective market for new private housing, it is still true that practically no slum dwellers can afford new, privately built homes, and the few who can are often minority families who would not be accepted. There is some "filtering up," now that the postwar shortage at middle and upper price levels has been relieved. And if there were no vast backlog of outright slums, and little or no urban growth, and no racial discrimination, then a strong program of enforcement and rehabilitation might actually do the job of housing low-income families adequately. But the situation is far different. Millions of existing slum dwellings should be torn down as soon as possible; millions of additional low-income families are certain to migrate to urban centers (a large proportion of them Negroes). And in the light of this, how can filtration possibly be expected to solve the slum problem, now or in a thousand years! Even a slight stepping-up of the process, if it is not merely to produce a lot of new slums by stuffing several families into a dwelling intended for one, would mean a rate of devaluating decent older property that would disrupt the real estate market more than any amount of public housing. FHA financing, also, is geared to steady or rising values for the life of the house, not a reduction in monthly payments that would permit it to "filter down," however gradually.

Apparently it is still as true as it ever was that we need some new housing within reach of families now outside the effective private market. Prosperity only makes the continuance of slum living conditions less excusable, the need for effective solutions more urgent. And the rising significance of the racial aspects of the housing problem adds to the urgency. So does the relocation problem growing from the desire to revitalize central blighted areas and from the tremendous displacement of homes for freeways and other public works.

The basic problem we tried to tackle in the U.S. Housing Act is still with us. What was wrong with our efforts to solve it?

In the light of 1957 conditions, it now seems there were two fundamental fallacies in the original approach, one a matter of basic policy formulation and administration, the other a matter of physical planning and design. The 1937 approach was natural, valid and even necessary at the time, and it represented progress in relation to what had gone before. But it jelled too soon, became too rigid, without allowing for flexible adaptation to American values and conditions.

TWO-HEADED HOUSING POLICY

The most questionable assumption was the notion that slum rehousing should be established permanently as an independent program, with its own separate legislation and administrative machinery at both federal and local levels, quite apart from other housing policies and the overall housing picture. This insured the segregation of the low-income slum-dweller, and fortified his isolation as a special charity case by permitting only public initiative and public landlordship, with narrow rules of eligibility, for any form of subsidized housing that might be needed. This also contributed to the segregation of upper-income families in FHA schemes, and to that lily-white suburbia that now presents such a critical problem. And it is just as much public housing's responsibility as the National Association of Home Builders that there is such a vast gap between the two narrow, entirely separate types of federal housing policy, with no real responsibility at any level of government to determine overall housing needs—whether on a national basis or at any given community—and to see that policies are adjusted to meet those needs.

This came about because federal housing aids were all initiated on an ad hoc emergency basis during the depression, with little thought for long-term needs or goals. But depression-mindedness continued too long: it was a fallacious element in much postwar planning, particularly housing. Vested interests grew up and were institutionalized around each separate fragmentary program, with the result that all three major groups—lenders, builders and public housers—have been about equally opposed to the kind of coordination that would permit more flexibility and realism in meeting the full range of local needs.

Similarly, while the early crusade on behalf of local initiative and responsibility was fine, and the establishment of local housing authorities (or something of the kind) was a necessary step, their permanent role should never have been defined and jelled so narrowly. We now have a proliferation of special-purpose local agencies concerned with slums and housing, with no responsibility anywhere to view the housing picture as a whole, least of all at the metropolitan level where this is most essential. The result is a few expensive, high-density, over-controlled municipal projects, mostly on central sites, and a vast chaotic flood of middle-class individual homes in the suburbs. With all our complicated housing machinery we cannot solve either the relocation problem in central areas or the equally urgent problem of balanced development out on the fringe.

Viewed in retrospect, it would have been worthwhile, for the sake of better integrated, more flexible tools, to make some real concessions. Not the principle of subsidy, for this is absolutely essential to any solution of the slum problem. But if necessary, public landlordship might have been given up and in any case it should have been possible to subsidize various forms of private housing enterprise, including suburban tracts for individual ownership, in order to meet a wider range of need and popular desire (and, incidentally, to bring some private building interests over to advocacy of public housing).

MISAPPLIED "COMMUNITY PLANNING"

Having established machinery that could only produce a type of residential development quite alien to any American ideal of community, we then proceeded to dramatize this extreme form of paternalistic class-segregation architecturally, in the name of "modern community planning."

The basic ideas that stemmed from the British garden city planners, and were rationalized by the Bauhaus school of modern architects, contributed vital concepts to American housing. The reaction against chaotic individualism and the wasteful crudity of the ubiquitous gridiron street pattern was long overdue. But in grasping for modern principles of large-scale community design, we embraced too wholeheartedly functionalist and collectivist architectural theories that tended to ignore certain subtler esthetic values and basic social needs. To experiment in this direction was healthy and necessary. The mistake, again, was to jell both policy and practice in rigid formulas that prevented further experimentation to adapt and humanize these principles in suitable terms for the American scene.

The public housing project therefore continues to be laid out as a "community unit," as large as possible and entirely divorced from its neighborhood surroundings, even though this only dramatizes the segregation of charity-case families. Standardization is emphasized rather than alleviated in project design, as a glorification of efficient production methods and an expression of the goal of "decent, safe and sanitary" housing for all. But the bleak symbols of productive efficiency and "minimum standards" are hardly an adequate or satisfactory expression of the values associated with American home life. And all this is, in addition, often embodied in the skyscraper, whose refined technology gladdens the hearts of technocratic architectural sculptors but pushes its occupants into a highly organized, beehive type of community life for which most American families have no desire and little aptitude.

There is no room in such schemes for individual deviation, for personal initiative and responsibility, for outdoor freedom and privacy, for the type of small-scale business enterprise that plays such an important social role in most slum areas. Management domination is built in, a necessary corollary of architectural form.

HOW TO REFORM THE REFORMERS?

A fresh start is badly needed to bring this frustrated effort to effective maturity. And the time may at last be ripe. Until recently there were only a few lonely critics within the ranks of the "housers" themselves. But now some local housing authorities are beginning to question the old formulas. The big push for redevelopment and renewal has also performed an important service in forcing all kinds of civic groups and agencies, including real estate interests and local housing authorities, to face up to hitherto insoluble problems and get together to find solutions. In some areas local and metropolitan planning agencies are beginning to assume some responsibility for determining overall housing needs, and for fitting the bits and pieces of federal aid and private and public initiative together. In several cities, the mayors have appointed housing coordinators for this purpose. And alongside central redevelopment, a new issue is just coming over the horizon officially in fast-growing regions such as California: how to encourage better balanced communities with a wider variety of homes in the fringe areas, to meet the needs of the lower-income and minority families who are more and more likely to find their employment in outlying plants and offices.

All this broader-based civic effort and sharper awareness tends to make the weaknesses in nationally overcompartmentalized federal housing policy more apparent. Sooner or later there will be a grass-roots demand for greater flexibility and better coordination, strong enough to overcome the special-interest lobbies, each trying to maintain its own little preserve. And this is the only effective and healthy way to bring about the necessary changes. For it is only when cities and metropolitan areas know what they need and want in terms of federal housing aid that greater flexibility will be justified.

It is not a matter of substituting a new legal-administrative formula for the old one. Under certain conditions the old formula is still the best answer, perhaps the only possible solution. But what is primarily needed, not only for low-income slum dwellers and minority groups but for the great mass of middle-income families in all their infinite variety of taste and need, is more choice in location, dwelling type and neighborhood character. The kind of home best suited to a given American family can never be decided by officials. Their highest responsibility, rather, is to make sure that public policies keep the "effective market" broad enough to provide some real selection at all economic and social levels.

Freedom and flexibility are probably the hardest things to achieve with public policy. But a country that can devise the insured mortgage (in all its different forms), Fannie Mae, the modernization loan, the annual contribution, the local authority bond, redevelopment and renewal grants, and ingenious methods for local governments to contribute their share, should certainly be able to find some way to make these excellent tools work more freely and more effectively.

17

The Evolution of Public Housing Policy

Eugene J. Meehan

Like so many other social programs in the United States, public housing was a product of the New Deal era. The basic assumptions and procedures that guided its development and operation were hammered out in the 1930s, in the National Recovery Act of 1933, the Housing Act of 1934, and the George-Healey Act of 1936, among others. The approach to public housing that emerged in the Housing Act of 1937 and was reproduced in its essentials in the Housing Act of 1949 dominated the public housing program for the next four decades. Two basic modes of operation were used to supply housing services to low-income families. The original prototype, known as the "conventional" public housing program, was characterized by the use of a public agency to develop, own, and operate the housing facilities; by the end of 1974, more than 860,000 units of housing, amounting to 66 percent of the total public housing supply, had been developed by this method. Another 230,000 units, about 18 percent of the total, were produced by a variant known as "turnkey" housing; the units were developed by private interests, then sold to a public agency, usually a local housing authority. The Housing Act of 1965 authorized an alternative approach to supplying public housing for the poor, lease of privately owned facilities. By the end of 1974, leasing accounted for more than 13 percent of the total supply, some 169,000

Reprinted from *The Quality of Federal Policymaking: Programmed Failure in Public Housing* by Eugene J. Meehan by permission of the University of Missouri Press. Copyright 1979 by the Curators of the University of Missouri.

units of 1,316,000. The changes in operating philosophy introduced by the Housing and Urban Development Act of 1974 foreshadowed a major increase in the role played by leased housing in the overall public housing program. Indeed, if the 1974 act were to be implemented systematically and rigorously and without major change it could put an end to the traditional form of public housing in relatively short order. Some of the reasons for the new approach, and its implications, are explored in this chapter.

CONVENTIONAL PUBLIC HOUSING

The public housing program incorporated into the Housing Act of 1937 was very much a child of the times. The first Roosevelt administration faced a staggering array of problems when it took office in 1933: the economy was stagnant, unemployment was extremely high, wage levels were badly depressed, the monetary and fiscal system was in shambles, and public confidence in government and private enterprise alike had been shaken by the stock-market collapse and its aftermath. The housing industry was but one of many sectors of the economy in urgent need of assistance. In the cities, large concentrations of aged and dilapidated buildings, lacking in amenities and badly needing repairs, posed a hazard to the health of the inhabitants and, so it was believed at least, a danger to the social health of the community. Everywhere there was an acute shortage of decent housing for persons of low income, and overcrowding of the kind indicated by the 1940 census of housing had been common for years. In the circumstances, it is hardly surprising that the public housing program was viewed as a multipurpose activity, a way of simultaneously reducing the level of unemployment in the country, assisting the beleaguered housing industry, eliminating slums and their concomitants, and increasing the supply of cheap and decent housing available to the poor.

Development of a program that could serve a number of masters was very powerfully reinforced by various other circumstances of the times. There were wealthy and powerful interests to be placated—in real estate, banking, construction, and the labor unions—and their aims were not always compatible. The prevailing ideology was characterized by built-in opposition to public ownership or even to extensive governmental intervention into the social and economic life of the nation. The tradition of self-help remained strong, and there was a marked tendency to assume that poverty was deserved and avoidable by hard work. Finally, the superiority of a profit-maximizing economic system, euphemized in school and press as a "free enterprise system," was taken for granted by rich and poor alike. The corollary assumption that private enterprise is invariably more efficient and productive than any form of governmental activity was accepted as an article of faith by most elements of society. While such propositions may be tautologically true in Adam Smith's economics, the empirical evidence is sparse and inconclusive. In any case, even if the superior efficiency of private enterprise could be demonstrated with respect to the past, there is no reason in principle why it should continue into the indefinite future regardless of the direction taken by society as a whole. Nevertheless, these beliefs have been much reinforced, quite illegitimately, by uninformed and irresponsible generalizing about "the failure of public housing," though the evidence suggests quite a different set of conclusions.

Unfortunately for the public housing program, multipurpose activities make for ambiguous policies and uncertain target populations; they in turn make it difficult if not impossible to criticize, evaluate, or improve the program. In both the 1937 and 1949 housing acts, the major articulated concerns were unemployment and slum clearance; the provision of housing for persons of low income was a peripheral rather than a central goal.[1] And with respect to housing, primary emphasis was placed on development and construction and not on the provision of housing services. In consequence, progress tended to be measured in terms of dollars spent, units of housing produced, construction wages generated, or number of units of dilapidated housing demolished rather than the amount and quality of housing-in-use supplied to the poor. Yet measuring the success of a public housing program in terms of employment provided, slums cleared, or even units built is as much a travesty as measuring the success of a medical operation in terms of amount of time taken, number of persons involved, or the surgeon's fee. Indeed, if the emphasis in the legislation is taken literally, the Pruitt and Igoe developments in St. Louis, commonly ranked among the more prominent disasters in the history of public housing, ought properly to be counted among its greatest successes, for they were built at great cost, they lasted a very short time, and they were quite expensive to liquidate. In brief, they contributed more to the local economy in the short run than any other housing development in the city's history.

Ownership and Administration

Given the economic circumstances in which public housing evolved, the locus of ownership and operational control over facilities was a matter of prime importance. Public housing provided a major opportunity for breaking the established mode of economic activity and demonstrating an alternative. The profit-maximizing production and distribution system then operating responded only to effective demand (desire *plus* capacity to pay); it had clearly failed to provide for the housing needs of large segments of the population. That is, it had produced housing that was too expensive for many, as well as the many for whom housing was too expensive. How to deal with the situation? An effort to maintain private ownership and yet to control the price of housing to the consumer would have foundered unless production costs were controlled or rents were subsidized. Cost control was anathema to owners and unions alike. Direct cash subsidies, much favored by real estate interests, were considered far too expensive overall, since they would overstimulate demand for an inadequate supply of decent housing and thus provide unwarranted returns to the owners of old housing of poor or marginal quality. Public ownership offered a more efficient means of divorcing the cost of housing to the tenant from the cost of development. Capital could be obtained at preferred rates, taxes avoided, and the return to capital (profit) retained in the public coffers. In the long run, ownership is cheaper than renting or leasing. Nevertheless, in 1974, pressure from interest groups made public subsidy of privately owned housing the central thrust of the public housing program, suggesting that in economic matters sheer persistence is more likely to be rewarded by government than is good argument.

Given the strength of the opposition to public ownership in American society, congressional agreement to public ownership of housing was a tribute to the strength of the critique launched against the performance of the economic system. Until 1965, public housing in the United States meant publicly owned housing. The program was one of the few large-scale experiments in public ownership in an area traditionally regarded as part of the private sector. In the early days of the New Deal, ownership was vested in the federal government and operations were controlled by a centralized bureaucracy. An adverse court ruling in 1935 that prevented the use of eminent domain to obtain land for public housing sites coupled with popular distrust of "big government" forced a change in the rules. The Housing Act of 1937 gave title to local housing authorities (LHAs) which were agencies of local government, created within a framework of state enabling legislation. If public housing has been a dismal failure, as is often charged, there would be little reason to experiment further along the same lines or in parallel areas. In fact, the failure is grossly exaggerated and misconstrued. What failed was a particular form of public housing, foreseeably programmed for failure no matter how earnest, willing, or competent the administration. The attack on "public housing" is perhaps the most arrant example of condemnation without trial in the annals of the society.

In principle, public ownership of housing facilities enables the government to supply housing to persons according to need rather than capacity to pay, making up the difference between rents charged and actual costs from the public treasury. But public ownership alone is not enough. Other conditions must also be satisfied for the program to succeed. Had the federal government created enough decent housing to supply all of society's needs and underwritten the difference between operating costs and the rent that tenants could afford to pay, program administrators could have simply located the needy and housed them as expeditiously as possible. But to the degree that the available housing was of poor quality or was significantly less than the need, or that operating costs were inadequately subsidized and could not be met from tenant rents without imposing serious hardships, the program could not operate properly.

Tragically, the necessary conditions for a successful public housing program were nowhere met consistently or adequately, primarily because of the way in which the program was designed. The quality of building construction was often

poor and sometimes grossly inadequate. Poor construction and inadequate resources for maintenance, reinforced by a social climate in which vandalism was
sometimes positively encouraged, rather than impeded, produced significantly
accelerated deterioration of facilities in the 1960s. The method of financing
adopted by the Congress forced local housing authorities to transfer the burden of
rapidly increasing maintenance and operating costs, reinforced at times by very
serious inflation, to the tenants. By the end of the 1960s, the combination of
policies and circumstances had brought most of the larger housing authorities in
the nation to their financial knees. Nevertheless, the amount of public housing
actually developed—disregarding quality for the moment—was far less than the
actual need. The absence of accurate data relating to need prevents a precise estimate of the degree of inadequacy. Fewer than 160,000 dwelling units were authorized and built under the 1937 Housing Act; the Housing Act of 1949 generated 1,115,000 units to the end of 1974. But in 1949, it was estimated that
810,000 units of housing, the amount authorized by the 1949 act, was only
one-tenth of the total need. The shortcomings of the public housing program
condemned millions of persons to paying an inordinate share of their income for
shelter of the poorest quality for years and years, despite the humaneness of the
goals articulated by Congress in 1949. Governmental unwillingness to accept responsibility for satisfying the urgent and primary need for decent shelter produced scarcity that was socially induced and therefore avoidable, though at cost.
In time, government policy tended to exclude from public housing the very persons the program was designed to serve—the working poor.

Development Policies

The program created by the 1937 Housing Act was built on a local-federal arrangement from which the state was virtually excluded once enabling legislation
was passed. Over time, Congress tended to concentrate on four basic areas of
housing policy, leaving most other matters for administrative decision: First, the
amount of housing authorized for addition to the public housing stock; second,
the cost of developing the facilities; third, the fiscal arrangements that controlled
program operations; fourth, the conditions of tenancy. Federal administrators
exercised a great deal of control over the program through budgetary oversight,
allocating resources for new development, auditing, and monitoring everyday
operations. Local governments could influence the program in their areas
through the formal cooperative agreement required by statute and, less formally,
through appointment of the governing body that directed the program. In practice, local governments had veto power over certain critical aspects of development, notably the size, location, design, and staffing of the facilities. The local
housing authority, under the overall direction of the governing body, had a voice
in site selection, choice of architect, design, and so on; it also controlled such aspects of daily operations as tenant selection, maintenance and repairs, legal ac-

tions against tenants, staffing, and general administration. Until the 1970s, the LHAs were given wide latitude in operations by the federal administration; central control over details of day-to-day operations increased substantially after 1969.

The direct cost of public housing to the local community was spelled out in the required federal-local agreement. The LHA was granted a tax exemption in return for a payment in lieu of taxes amounting to 10 percent of gross rent less utility costs. Whether the payment covered the actual cost to the community, particularly during those periods when rents were high and occupancy was virtually complete, is much debated and probably not determinable. On the other hand, the collective benefit obtained from public housing development certainly outweighed any additional direct cost to the community. Curiously, the positive benefits derived from public housing were usually ignored. The 1937 act required local governments to eliminate one unit of substandard housing for each unit of public housing built, but the impact of the "equivalent elimination" rule was slight and it was abandoned in 1949. Finally, local governments were to provide such normal municipal services as police and fire protection, garbage removal, paving, and street lighting. In practice, the obligations proved difficult to enforce. In St. Louis, the local authority was forced to employ private security guards by the beginning of the 1960s and complaints about the quality of garbage collection, street lighting, and so on were common. The net effect of such performance failures by local governments was a major increase in the managerial burden placed on the LHA and ultimately a large increase in the cost of operating the facilities.

There were two curious lacunae in the development policies generated within the federal government: first, little effort was made to control the quality of the housing produced; second, the cost of the site was not limited by any of the statutes. The 1937 Housing Act placed a ceiling on the overall cost of each dwelling unit and on the cost per room; established limits could be adjusted upward 25 percent in "high construction cost" areas, usually the larger cities where powerful construction unions operated. In 1949, limits on overall cost per unit were eliminated leaving cost per room as the sole criterion available for controlling development cost. Since room cost limits were included in the legislation, they applied to the country as a whole. In 1970, Congress adopted a "prototype" cost base for dwelling units of various sizes and types of construction and HUD was charged with establishing suitable limits and revising them annually. Again, the limits could be exceeded by 10 percent without waiver and by another 10 percent with federal approval. Land costs remained uncontrolled and no qualitative construction controls were specified in the statutes.

The effect of weak control over development costs and construction quality is readily foreseen. Site costs were often unconscionable, particularly in the 1950s, when the rate of development was high and projects were deliberately located in cleared slum areas—and forced to absorb clearing costs. In the long run, the economic inefficiencies generated by land speculation were probably less important than the common practice of paying premium prices for apartments so shoddily built that a choir of angels could not have abided in them regularly without producing serious disrepair. Poor quality cannot be ascribed to federal miserliness. In St. Louis, the Housing Authority paid for its projects at costs equal to or greater than the cost of luxury housing in the suburbs. It did not receive value for money from the housing industry.

The principle underlying the failure is not hard to find. A profit-maximizing economic system also minimizes performance. Unless performance criteria for the end product are specified fully, in which case there is likely to be a major increase in cost, the producer is bound by the rules of the game and perhaps by the "facts" of economic life to maximize profits within the limits of the contract price. The most accessible route to additional profit is a reduction in the quality of the product. The clearest evidence of the pervasiveness of the principle is found in the recent experience of federal agencies engaged in space exploration or defense whose purposes demand very high levels of performance. To obtain quality performance, specifications must be developed in great detail and with precision, otherwise cost overruns of great magnitude can be anticipated from the effort to achieve required performance through trial and error. The result is in either case a massive increase in end-product cost. The same trend appears in the general market for consumer goods. In principle, the producer whose goods perform poorly or whose services are less than what they should be is supposed to lose his customers to a better producer. In practice, information flow among consumers is incomplete and the gap between promise and performance is so common that it seems to have little impact on consumer behavior, perhaps because advertising practices reinforce unconcern. Whatever the reason, the producer who can choose between a significant improvement in product performance at some known cost and artificial demand stimulation for an unimproved product at much greater cost is apparently well advised to choose the latter. The old adage about building a better mousetrap and having the world beat a path to the door no longer holds, if ever it did. Patent medicine is not always driven from the marketplace by disclosing that it is only patent medicine or even by development of a genuine cure for the illness the patent medicine purports to treat.

Conditions of Tenancy

The more important of the congressional policies relating to tenancy in public housing dealt with eligibility for admission and continued occupancy, rent levels, definitions of tenant income, and priorities assigned to different classes of applicants. The consistent central concerns have been the amount of income that a prospective tenant could earn yet enter or remain in public housing and the kinds of income that could be excluded from such calculations. Under strong pressure from real estate interests, the prime goal of federal policy was to exclude from public housing anyone with enough income to obtain housing on the private market. Understandably, those interests sought to keep the income level of public housing tenants at a minimum. Since income limits were partly determined by local rent levels, which in turn were based on information supplied by local real estate interests, they were often quite influential. Over the long run, pressure for low ceilings on tenant income, taken in conjunction with other fiscal policies, contributed materially to the aggregation in public housing of a highly dependent population whose incomes were very low in relation to the rest of the community and changed much more slowly than general wage and price rates. For example, between the early 1950s and the mid-1970s the consumer price index for St. Louis more than doubled, while the median family income for public housing tenants rose from about $2,400 per year to just over $3,700 per year, far less than was needed to keep pace with inflation even if the initial income level had been adequate—clearly not the case.

The procedure used to determine income limits for those admitted to public housing was fairly complex. The LHA went to the local housing market (newspapers, agents and brokers, and so forth) to determine the current price of decent rental accommodations of various sizes. The income needed to "afford" such housing was calculated by a five-to-one ratio (six-to-one for families with three or more minor children). That is, if the going price for a three-bedroom apartment was $100 per month, it was assumed that a family with an income of $500 per month could afford it ($600 per month when there were three or more minor children). The maximum allowable income for admission to public housing was 80 percent of that amount, or $400 per month. Federal policy required a "20 percent gap" between the income sufficient to afford needed housing and the maximum allowable income for admission to the developments. If other factors remained constant, the tenant whose income increased to 25 percent over admission limits was required to leave public housing. He would then be earning enough to "afford" housing on the private market. In principle, the policy was expected to keep everyone with enough income to purchase housing on the private market out of public housing. However, estimates of available housing tended to significantly overestimate the amount of "decent" housing available and significantly underestimate the going price and thereby to exclude from public housing many of its "best" potential tenants. The relative value of the facilities afforded by public housing, even in areas where they were badly deteriorated, is attested by the length of housing authority waiting lists.

Given the formula used to calculate eligibility for admission to public housing, the question what kinds of income should be excluded from the calculation was a major concern for both tenant and LHA. The 1937 act, which simply counted all income from all sources, soon produced hardships that clearly contravened the spirit, if not the letter, of the program. The 1949 act allowed an exemption of $100 per year for each of the first three children in the family and the first $500 of earnings by a minor. The $100 exemption was later extended to all minors in the family and, over time, exemptions were allowed for child care, tuition costs, medical expenses, certain kinds of work expenses, and so on. In some cases, special arrangements were allowed because of peculiar local circumstances; the arrangements that settled the St. Louis rent strike in 1969, for example, enumerated income exemptions considerably broader than those allowed by normal regulations. The Housing and Urban Development Act of 1974 consolidated and reduced exclusions, allowing (1) $300 for each minor, (2) non-recurring income, (3) the first $300 of earnings by the spouse, and (4) 5 percent of gross income (10 percent for elderly families). The "20 percent gap" was then dropped.

Once prospective tenants satisfied the income limits required for admission, various priorities established by Congress or administrative action came into play. Precedence was given to war veterans and persons displaced from their homes by such public actions as slum clearance in both the 1937 and 1949 housing acts. In 1954, a hostile Congress limited admission strictly to persons displaced by public action, but that policy proved untenable and was rescinded the following year. The impact of such priorities probably varied from city to city but seems not to have been very great. Between 1966 and 1973, for example, fewer than 12 percent of all families entering public housing had been displaced by public action, and only 1.2 percent were uprooted by either urban renewal or housing development. In 1956, the elderly were given priority in admission, and an increase in construction costs of $500 per room was allowed for housing designed specifically for use by the elderly. That priority was extended to the disabled shortly afterward.

The negative priorities involved in racial segregation were ignored by the Congress and by the federal and local administrations. When the public housing program began, developments in many cities were racially segregated and blacks were excluded from white projects, or vice versa, as a matter of course. Formal segregation ended in 1954 when the U.S. Supreme Court refused to overturn a California ruling that admission to public housing could not be refused on racial grounds. Within fifteen years, local social and economic conditions in many areas combined to resegregate public housing, this time with respect to the rest of the community, by aggregating large numbers of minority group members in the developments.

The rent paid by public housing tenants was linked to family income and not to the amount of space occupied. A large family with little income might pay less for a five-bedroom apartment than was charged a smaller family with a larger income for an apartment with a single bedroom. Technically, the portion of tenant income paid for rent was not limited, though in practice the administrators tried to maintain rents at minimum levels. As housing authority operating costs soared after 1960, minimum and average rents climbed steadily, far more rapidly than tenant income. By 1969, such cost pressures had created very serious problems for most housing authorities. Some of the very poorest tenants were forced to pay as much as three-fourths of their income for rent, and payments equal to one-half of gross income were common. That condition, among others, led to the 1969 rent strike in St. Louis and to significant disturbances elsewhere. The outcry produced one of the so-called Brooke amendments in 1969, limiting the amount that could be charged a tenant in public housing to 25 percent of adjusted income— less for persons of very low income. Unfortunately, that limitation sometimes led to reductions in state welfare payments; such reductions were forbidden by another Brooke amendment in 1971. The 25 percent limit was apparently taken from the rent supplement provisions of the 1965 Housing Act. Why it was considered proper is uncertain; by European standards, 25 percent of income is a very high rent level. Perhaps the American propensity to relatively expensive single-family housing accounted for the size of the standard. In 1974, the structure was simplified, though the base was retained: rent could vary from 25 percent of income for persons earning 80 percent or more of the median income in the area to 5 percent of income for persons with very large families (six or more minors) or very low incomes (less than 50 percent of the area's median income). The act required LHAs to fill at least 30 percent of their units with families from the very-low-income group. However, the act also required each LHA to collect at least 20 percent of the total income of its tenants as rent. The confusion engendered by the regulations lasted well into 1977. Median income levels are virtually impossible to determine with any accuracy for a metropolitan area, and the meaning of the median in this context is most uncertain. If the median is calculated from the tax rolls, those who do not file, mainly persons of very low income, are omitted, and that tends to raise the median level. If medians are calculated from census data, the results are even more likely to be artificially high. Neither the method to be used for the calculation nor the reason for using such standards in the first place was made clear in the legislation or in the discussion that preceded it.

Fiscal Policies

The public housing program created by the Congress moved toward financial disaster as inexorably and predictably as any Greek tragedy. Inadequate policies with respect to quality and costs virtually ensured physical structures of minimal quality. The limits imposed on tenant income guaranteed a very modest rent yield to the LHA. The self-destruct system was completed by adopting fiscal policies that were foreseeably unworkable and sticking to them for more than thirty years in the face of all evidence. To put the matter as starkly as possible, the federal government undertook to pay all capital costs on public housing as they came due; it guaranteed the mortgage payment, leaving all other expenses the responsibility of the local housing authority. The LHA's sole source of income was rent. No operating subsidy whatever was provided by Congress until 1961. Had the matter stopped there, the program could not have survived very long. Economic collapse was rendered even more certain by imposing four additional fiscal burdens on the LHA, to be met from its rental income alone.

First, utility costs were included in the rent charged the tenant. From the tenant's point of view, utilities were a free good; rent was unaffected by the amount of utilities used. Predictably, utility costs became a major burden on local housing authorities, even before utility prices began to climb in the energy-scarce climate of the 1970s.

Second, 10 percent of gross income from rent less utility costs had to be turned over to local government each year as payment in lieu of taxes. Until 1937, public housing was owned by the federal government and therefore was automatically exempt from state and local taxes. To offset the cost of municipal services to the developments, 10 percent of gross rent was turned over voluntarily to local governments. When ownership of public housing was vested in local authorities, they became subject to local taxes. However, the Congress required local support for the housing program amounting to 20 percent of the federal contribution, a requirement that local governments could meet in full simply by waiving local taxes. In return, the LHA was permitted to pay 10 percent of gross rent minus utility costs in lieu of taxes. In 1954, the waiver of taxes was made a program requirement and the payment in lieu of taxes was mandated rather than allowed.

Third, the cash reserves that could be accumulated by any LHA were limited by administrative action to 50 percent of one year's rent. That very effectively precluded the LHA from building up the funds needed for capital replacement or even for major maintenance such as roof repairs. As the apartments aged, major maintenance was deferred and handled piecemeal. Unfortunately, an iron law of escalation in damages operates in even the most expensive and luxurious apartments: the amount of damage to a building or area increases directly and exponentially with the time delay between damage and repair. Maintenance deferral is an open invitation to vandalism, regardless of the age, sex, ethnic background, income level, occupation, or rent level of the tenants.

Fourth, in any year in which an LHA "showed a profit," in which rental income exceeded gross expenses plus allowable transfers to reserves, the surplus was used to pay capital costs—to reduce annual contract contributions. From 1945 until 1953, the federal government paid less than 50 percent of the capital costs of public housing, and in the peak years of 1948 and 1949 the LHAs paid nearly 85 percent of their own capital costs. Congress added insult to injury in 1954 by requiring the LHAs to repay 55 percent of capital costs from rental income. The requirement had little practical significance given the steady deterioration in the financial position of LHAs, but it does provide a good indication of the blindness to long-range impact common among those responsible for policy decisions relating to public housing.

The fiscal arrangements made by Congress were the most important single factor in the eventual breakdown of the conventional public housing program. Combined with inadequate control over housing quality and relatively poor administrative performance (HUD inefficiency is notorious, even among Washington bureaucrats, and it was very unlikely that LHAs could recruit adequately trained and experienced administrators given their fiscal position and political vulnerability), they doomed the program, foreseeably and inescapably! The point is vital. It was both humane and reasonable to base the tenant's rent on ability to pay rather than space occupied by the family, and it was altogether appropriate to restrict occupancy to persons of low income. It was also reasonable to expect local housing authorities to operate their developments with the income obtained from rent once capital costs were secured. But imposing both requirements without additional subsidy was an act of folly, particularly in the light of the known periodicity of the economic system. The housing program could succeed only if costs, rents, and tenant incomes remained in relatively stable relationship for fairly long time periods. Since economic activity tends toward very rapid shifts in costs and prices and the incomes of the poor do not keep pace with rising costs, the logic of the fiscal arrangements guaranteed a cost-income squeeze for the LHA in any period of rapidly advancing wages and prices.

Even without inflation, the fiscal apparatus was lethal. The LHA's income was a function of the price of housing on the local market and the income of the tenants. The LHA's expenses depended on the size, quality, durability, design, and so on of the developments; the kinds of tenants who occupied the premises; and basic trends in the overall economy. There was no reason to suppose that the income needed to operate the developments would be generated out of the interplay of this set of pressures. In the private sector, the rental income needed for successful operation of multifamily apartments is calculated by a rule of thumb that states that roughly one-sixth of development costs must be generated each year in rent. In the 1940s and 1950s, about 40 percent of the total rent (6.4 percent of development costs) was needed to cover operating expenses; by the 1960s, it was safer to assume that about 50 percent of rental income was required for that purpose. In effect, the private sector estimated that between 6.4 percent and 8.0 percent of development costs must be yielded each year from rents just to cover operating expenses. An equal amount was needed to pay capital costs, taxes, and return to the investor. Utility costs were normally borne by the tenant and do not figure in the calculation. The gross level of revenues required in the private sector is approximately the same as the HUD estimate that $754 in annual income is needed for each $10,000 of investment in a public housing development.

Public housing authorities rarely obtained as much as 6 percent of their investment costs in annual rentals; in St. Louis, the return averaged just over 4 percent for more than two decades. Moreover, an adjustment is needed to cover the utility costs and lieu of taxes paid by the LHAs; it brings income requirements to about 10 percent of development cost per annum. Such sums were far beyond the capacity of housing authority tenants to pay; and even if that much rent had been collected, regulations governing reserves would not have allowed the LHA to set enough aside to meet future replacement costs. Finally, private sector estimates assume good design, sound construction, and proper care by tenant and management alike—conditions not easily met in public housing, particularly after 1960. In the circumstances, the most surprising thing about the collapse at the end of the 1960s is that anyone was surprised. Mere survival was in some cases a major accomplishment.

CHANGING THE BASIC PATTERN:
SUBSIDIES AND PRIVATIZATION

The operating pattern for public housing established in 1937 continued with only minor changes until the 1960s. Both opponents and supporters of public housing tended to what might best be called "mindless incrementalism" in their approach to policymaking. Reasoned decisions increase or decrease resources allocated to specific purposes on the basis of careful study of the effects of operation. Mindless incrementalism is marked by increases or decreases in allocations that are unrelated to performance or even perverse in the light of performance. Such procedures are a good indication of failure somewhere in the policymaking process, usually in either the supply of information or the manner in which the information is used. In the case of public housing, the failure occurred in both areas: too often, the data needed to correct and improve policy were not available; in most cases the conventional wisdom that served as a base for decision was mistaken or misdirected. Since the initial conditions to which these policies applied were not determined and the target population was only vaguely identified, there was no way to decide the amount and kind of change produced by specific actions, to locate the major side effects of policy, or to make a reasoned assessment of impact. The program was radically incorrigible until it collapsed; the way it collapsed virtually guaranteed that any lessons the experience might have taught would not be learned.

In fairness to supporters of public housing, incrementalism was in some degree forced by the opposition; both nationally and locally, hostility to public housing remained widespread, vocal, powerful, and implacable. It was difficult just to obtain a simple increase in the number of units authorized in a given fiscal year. Supporters of the program may well have felt that asking for policy innovations was too risky. There is considerable evidence to support that point of view.[2] The opposition in Congress and in the country was strong enough to delay enactment of a new housing law from 1945 until 1949, even though the proposed bill had Republican support (from Sen. Robert Taft and others). The public housing provisions of the 1949 Housing Act escaped deletion in the House of Representatives by only five votes. In 1949, Congress authorized development of 165,000 units each year for five years, but only 250,000 units were actually funded in the whole decade of the 1950s. As the Eisenhower administration grew increasingly hostile to governmental intervention in the economic sphere, mere survival of the public housing program became increasingly uncertain.

On the other hand, the special circumstances in which public housing operations began in the 1940s made the first generation of developments (authorized in 1937) conspicuously successful in the early years, masking the fact that the program was living on borrowed time. World War II brought about a rapid shift in population to urban war production centers and placed enormous pressure on the existing housing supply. Relatively full employment and higher earnings, coupled with a special dispensation that allowed the use of public housing by war workers, created a bonanza for local housing authorities not entailed by federal policies. War workers kept the apartments full. Tenant incomes far in excess of the levels intended by regulations meant premium rents and ample incomes for LHAs operating new developments requiring little major maintenance or capital replacement. Even after the war ended, occupancy remained high, some of the overincome workers remained, and most of the tenant body were employed, hence rental income remained relatively high until the end of the 1940s. Difficulties began when overincome tenants were forced from the developments, occupancy began to fall, and maintenance costs and capital replacement needs began to rise rapidly.

Again, the multipurpose character of the public housing program tended to impede evaluation of its performance. Additions to the program were usually sold to the Congress during periods of moderate-to-severe economic recession as a way of stimulating the construction industry while serving good purposes. Even as late as 1974, public housing was linked legislatively to community development and then indirectly to such diverse functions as rational use of land, integration of income groups, and preservation of historic properties. While such mixed associations may help gain votes in Congress, they increase the difficulties associated with performance evaluation. In practice, program supporters tend to emphasize the positive aspects of performance and ignore failures; the opposition follows the same strategy but emphasizes different factors. The balance of benefits and costs, which is crucial to reasoned policy improvement, tends to be ignored by both sides.

The Changing Social Environment

While public housing policy remained more or less frozen in its original mold, operating on principles borrowed from the traditional private sector, social change was proceeding rapidly in the housing developments as in the wider community. World War II much accelerated certain trends established earlier, such as the shift of population from the central city to the suburbs. Persons in the higher income brackets headed for the suburbs early in the century; federal housing and tax policies after 1945 encouraged blue- and white-collar workers to follow. New industries and old industries alike moved to the cheaper land on the city's outskirts as they expanded; a burgeoning trucking industry and an expanded highway construction program hastened the process by increasing accessibility. The erosion of the city's tax base was hastened by urban renewal, transportation construction, and subsidies to housing and other construction. Despite the countless billions of dollars poured into the central cities in an effort to pre-

serve what was mistakenly identified as the city as a whole, anticipated investment did not materialize. The inner city became increasingly an isolated clump of
older business facilities surrounded by a widening belt of deteriorated housing
occupied mainly by the very poor, the black, and the permanently unemployed.
Neighborhoods previously characterized by long-term residence and stable social
behavior crumbled and fragmented as the elderly died off and the younger workers moved to the suburbs seeking homes they could afford, desirable schools and
neighborhoods, and physical separation from the expanding inner-city ghetto.
The end of the World War II employment boom hardened the differences between inner city and suburb. The recession of 1956-1957 had a profound impact
on most large cities, and for some the recession of 1961-1962 was merely a continuation. Lack of employment, particularly among the young, the black, and the
disadvantaged, increased out-migration of the working-age population; those left
behind were mainly the permanent poor, the very young and the very old, the
disabled, the relatively helpless and dependent, the recipients of public assistance.

As in other things, the public housing developments mirrored the course of
events in the wider community. Public housing ceased to be a way station for the
working poor enroute to a family-owned dwelling and became a haven for concentrated masses of dependent persons with little possibility of improving their
lot through their own efforts. The indicators of their helplessness were classic:
real wages that lagged persistently and significantly behind local and national
levels; unemployment rates several times the national average; extreme trans-
ience in employment; marginal jobs; frequent and often sustained reliance on
public assistance; and heavy concentrations of the very young and the very old,
usually members of a minority group. In some cases, two or three generations of
a single family were tenants in the same public housing development. Tragically,
factual helplessness was actually increasing at the very time when the dependent
population was being urged most strongly to entertain rising expectations about
the quality of its own life and the life its children could anticipate. In the past, the
liberal rhetoric of national politics had been counterbalanced effectively by the
conservative practice of local authorities. After 1945, the federal government became a direct and meaningful participant in local affairs, often bypassing state
and local jurisdiction. Unfortunately, the rhetoric of national politics was seldom
funded at a level that allowed the entire poor population to benefit. Most commonly, rhetoric was implemented through lotteries in which a few cities were
successful and most were not or through legal changes that could not be enforced
without costs the government was rarely prepared to accept—the busing controversy of the early 1970s is a good illustration of the process.

Of course, rhetoric has an impact on attitudes, opinions, and behavior that may
exceed the effects of funded programming. To the extent that legalistic liberals
supported the pursuit of principle without regard for the consequences, they
played an important role in the general dissolution of internalized social controls

that characterized the 1960s. The subsequent course of events was dramatic evidence of the inability of such institutions as law, police, courts, schools, churches, and families to maintain stability and order when the underlying priorities of society are challenged blindly and persistently. Crimes against person and property increased relentlessly despite enormous expenditures for security and the introduction of highly sophisticated technologies for maintaining social control. Abandoned houses were vandalized systematically rather than allowed to decay unmolested. Public property of all sorts, and not public housing alone, was subjected to alarming abuse in every area of society. Both personal and collective behavior were freed from a significant range of prior restrictions. Claims to rights and prerogatives increased exponentially while obligations long taken for granted were questioned or simply abandoned. The social climate, in brief, became stormy, threatening, subject to extreme perturbations.

Local housing authorities were caught in a broad flow of events they could not hope to master, bereft of resources, married perforce to inadequate and relatively inflexible federal policies, harassed by a clientele that desperately needed their services yet increasingly could not afford them. The cities were helpless, caught in the same whirlwind; the states, for the most part, looked the other way. Declining productivity in the housing industry worsened the LHAs' situation by increasing capital and maintenance costs without improving quality or increasing productivity. The final costs of housing began to rise rapidly just as public housing development began expanding. Various contributory factors can be identified: profit-maximizing entrepreneurs used technological improvements to maximize profits, union power forced the inefficient use of expensive labor. It cost more and more simply to maintain the quality of a basic unit of housing; the effort to reduce costs apparently led to an overall decrease in construction standards.

A parallel transformation of the population of public housing undermined the survival capacity of the LHAs in every part of the country. There was a steady decline in the number of employed workers, a steady increase in the number of families wholly or partially dependent on public assistance. Predictably, the amount of income available to each family tended to decline relative to incomes and prices in the wider community. The number of female heads of household increased with a concurrent expansion of the number of relatively undisciplined young persons living in the developments. In border cities such as St. Louis, racial segregation based on income became the rule. Public housing became the prime repository for the very poor: the black, the elderly, the female head of household and her brood of children, the unemployed, and the unemployable. Rents declined, expenses soared, the meager reserves were soon expended; the financial position of the LHAs weakened rapidly and seriously. Declining revenues forced deferred maintenance, which led to deteriorating physical conditions, which stimulated vandalism, which further depressed the quality of the housing supply. The end result was too often a ghastly landscape of mutilated buildings, broken glass, empty apartments, abandoned automobiles, litter, and garbage; a wasteland hostage to the criminal, vagrant, truant, and street gang; a hazard to the passerby; and a nightmare to the resident.

Subsidies

Money alone would not have solved the problems of the LHAs; but, without significant additions to their incomes, efforts to improve design, tenant selection, management, maintenance, or other aspects of performance were futile. Public housing deteriorated in a shocking manner predominantly because of the money shortage; so long as funds were available, most developments operated reasonably well. The two St. Louis developments completed in 1942, for example, were exemplars of the kind of public housing intended by the legislators so long as even modest resources were available to maintain them. Although the federal government allowed periodic increases in construction costs, modest rent increases, and in rare cases allocated special funds for refurbishing some of the more conspicuous disasters, no regular operating subsidy of any kind was available until 1961 and there was no effective operating subsidy before 1972. Yet, so long as the LHAs were wholly dependent on rent, the fact of low tenant income meant that they could not obtain enough revenue to operate the developments. Under the pressure of rising costs and deteriorating physical plant, the LHAs were literally forced to behave like the slum landlords they had become, increasing rents and reducing services until the tenants finally balked and refused to pay. The only possible source of relief was a subsidy; the only realistic source of subsidies was the federal government. The poor were being squeezed dry.

Ironically, and it is tempting but perhaps unfair to say typically, the first subsidy, when it finally arrived, did little to ease the basic problem. Instead, Congress subsidized the provision of housing for a whole new class of tenants by offering a bonus for housing elderly families. The Housing Act of 1956 allowed a special premium of $500 per room for the construction of housing for the elderly; the Housing Act of 1961 provided the LHAs with an additional $120 per year for each elderly family housed in the developments. In combination, the two subsidies made the elderly poor into the favored darlings of the public housing program; their numbers increased spectacularly in the 1960s and 1970s. Since the only special features required for ''elderly'' housing seemed to have been a few feet of handrail in halls and bathrooms and a warning device to be pulled (if time permitted) should cardiac arrest set in, the increased construction allowance was a significant windfall for the builder. The operating subsidy provided the LHA with a parallel bonus, doubly sweetened by the highly desirable characteristics of elderly as tenants—they usually have no young children, they are not prone to vandalism or violence, they pay their rent regularly, and they cause little wear and tear on the premises. Moreover, the elderly are almost universally regarded as worthy of assistance, for with few exceptions they *are* someone's mother or father and that, in the American scheme of things, guarantees virtue and deserving. And to ice the cake, the elderly required small apartments, they lived readily in high-rise buildings, hence they were ideally suited to the kind of housing the industry was tooled up to build in the 1960s. The orgy of construction for the elderly that followed was paralleled by a declining rate of construction of "family" housing.

Although the shift to housing for the elderly is readily explained, it is somewhat less easy to justify. Granted immediately the elderly poor required assistance, it is uncertain that their need was greater than the needs of other poverty-stricken families. In any case, no one bothered to inquire, nationally or locally. The change in clientele was made by substitution and not by addition, by diverting resources from one target population to another and not by increasing the total enough to handle the additional burden. The emphasis on new construction was particularly unfortunate. The bulk of the apartments available in the private sector were small in size, therefore it would have been much more reasonable to try and lease existing smaller apartments for elderly tenants. The result of the shift, intended or not, was a major reward for one class of prospective tenants (the elderly) and a significant reduction in the effort to service another class of tenants (dependent families). In St. Louis, for example, the percentage of elderly families in public housing rose from around 15 percent in 1955 to about 30 percent in 1970 and to more than 55 percent in 1975, while the total number of units available actually declined.

The next major change in the public housing fiscal structure was made in 1969. The Brooke amendment to the housing act of that year limited the rent that could be charged any tenant to 25 percent of adjusted income. The maintenance and operations subsidy needed to compensate the LHAs for lost revenue was added in 1970. Significant and regular payments were not made until 1972. When the operating subsidy finally arrived, it was inadequate. Moreover, the Housing Act of 1968 had already authorized a number of activities that increased the fiscal burden on the LHAs by requiring provision of such tenant services as educational and occupational counseling, additional private security guards and recreational equipment and encouraging development of tenant participation in management through stimulation of tenant organizations. In effect, the "social" dimension of housing operations was very substantially expanded while the sources of future revenue, and the level of resources to be supplied, remained uncertain. The level of support required to operate and maintain its developments proved difficult to estimate; the federal government hedged the commitment and kept the LHAs limping along until HUD, aided by the Urban Institute, generated a subsidy formula. In 1972, a subsidy amounting to 3 percent of development costs was set as a base for operating and maintenance expenses, though HUD's own earlier figures suggested that 7.5 percent of investment was a more appropriate figure. The amount of subsidy was later increased to 5.5 percent of development costs, still not enough by standard calculations even if the deferred maintenance problem was ignored. The transition to operating subsidies was painful for everyone concerned; local authorities were caught between mounting costs, diminishing income, and increasing pressure from tenants. The federal government found itself riding the tiger of escalating subsidy costs. By the end of 1972, the Nixon administration had decided to halt expansion of public housing; a moratorium was announced early in 1973 and maintained until the following autumn. When the program was allowed to resume, it was limited to leasing. The pressure for more operating subsidies continued, however, and in 1975 a special utilities payment was made available to adjust the shortfall between LHA income and expenses. Despite the subsidies, the LHA continued to receive the equivalent of a starvation diet.

Beginning in 1970, the federal government tried to improve the physical condition of the developments by providing modernization funds that could be used for capital replacement and major repairs. Some of the larger LHAs also received grants to help restore reserve balances badly depleted during the previous decade. Again, the resources available to HUD were nowhere near the level of funds actually needed. Moreover, some funds were earmarked and had to be used for specified purposes that were not necessarily the first priorities of the LHAs. In St. Louis, for example, nearly $2.5 million was used to remove lead-based paint from about half of the apartments in the two older developments though funds for such fundamentals as plumbing, heating, and electrical renovation could not be obtained. Given the immense gap between resources and needs, there was probably no alternative to the use of lotteries, though how the wheel was spun at HUD remained a mystery. In 1974, for example, a few cities shared in the melon known as the Target Projects Program (TPP). St. Louis, one of the lucky winners, received $1.8 million to supplement capital improvements by training staff, developing new procedures, making minor physical improvements, and employing tenants to assist with the work. So important was the last of these functions that TPP was in some quarters identified as the "Tenants Put on the Payroll" program, perhaps with cause. The fact that St. Louis had just begun a tenant management program may have influenced the decision to make the allocation, but that does not suggest that national spending decisions were based on a careful weighing of the potential benefits and costs of the available alternatives. Such special subsidy programs indicate the nature of the fundamental unresolved difficulty underlying the whole public housing effort in the United States: so long as Congress cannot or will not underwrite a serious effort to supply decent housing to all those who need help, one set of random efforts may be just as good as any other.

Privatization

The second major policy change introduced into public housing during the 1960s was increased privatization of various aspects of operations (transfer of some functions to the private sector), usually by authorizing the LHA to contract with private organizations for performance of needed services. The cause of the change was the obviously distressed condition of most large housing authorities; the justification was implicit in the received wisdom of the society, primarily the belief that private organization is prima facie more efficient than public. Until 1974, legislation tended to foster privatization rather than force it; the Housing Act of 1974 and the administrative regulations that accompanied it made privatization the central thrust of federal policy for the immediate future.

Three basic elements in the privatization of public housing appeared first in the Housing Act of 1965. First, the act authorized "turnkey" construction, the development of apartments by private entrepreneurs on their own sites for sale to LHAs. The private developer contracted with the housing authority to provide a completed development. He obtained a site, arranged for architectural and construction services, and delivered the finished product to the LHAs, ready for use. Ostensibly a response to complaints about the quality of design and construction of conventional housing, the turnkey development proved very popular and, after 1965, most new construction was done by the turnkey method. How closely the program lived up to expectations is uncertain. Development time was probably reduced, but in St. Louis there was little evidence of significant improvements in design, location, or construction. Although site costs were reduced, the cost of construction remained high. There is no good reason to suppose that the LHAs could not have achieved the same results with even greater economy had they been given a freer hand in operations.

The second form of privatization authorized by the 1965 act was the sale of public housing to tenants. Ordinarily, such sales were limited to detached, semi-detached, and row-type housing; high-rise apartments were specifically excluded from the homeownership program. Finally, the 1965 act authorized the sale of public housing to not-for-profit organizations who would provide housing for low-income tenants. Neither procedure was widely used. In St. Louis, one small development served as an experiment in homeownership; none of the housing was actually sold to a nonprofit organization.

In 1967, the federal government authorized contracts between LHAs and private firms for management services. A standard fee was paid for each unit placed under management: if the contract called for "soft" management, the LHA retained responsibility for maintenance; alternatively, a "hard" contract could be negotiated in which the management firm also supplied routine maintenance. In all such cases, responsibility for capital replacement and major repairs remained with the LHA. Contracts were normally written for one year with more or less automatic renewal, though they could be terminated for cause or by consent.

Both turnkey development and contract management have been widely used in public housing, in St. Louis as elsewhere. Their popularity with LHA management is readily accounted for. Private firms have much more latitude in dealing with their employees than do governmental agencies; as legislation against discrimination increased, hard-pressed bureaucrats welcomed the opportunity to escape at least partly from the contradictory pressures. Moreover, private firms do have some genuine operational advantages over public organizations: they can locate and employ needed skills more quickly, purchase with greater facility, experiment more, and cut losses more quickly—there is less inertia effect in private operations, other things equal. But the use of contractual services is not without costs. The LHA can lose much of its control over daily operations. The nature of the contract relation creates a significant lag time between detecting pending trouble and forcing the contractor to produce a solution. The primary weapon available to the LHA is contract termination, and that is not very useful against minor contract infractions such as late reports, modest performance delays, and so on. The development manager who is an employee of a contracting firm is far less accessible to the LHA director than his counterpart who is an employee of the LHA. The most serious fault with contractual management, however, lies in its long-range impact on the quality of governmental services. If it is a fact that governments perform poorly and inefficiently in the managerial arena, than purchasing such services on the private market will only guarantee that the inefficiency is prolonged indefinitely and the long-term cost of operations is increased. If governmental operations were for some reason beyond all hope of improvement, there would be no alternative; otherwise, such a policy of despair is not warranted and short-run contracting merely delays the inevitable. It seems wiser to explore the various means by which governmental performance might be improved before adopting a strategy guaranteed to eliminate future improvements.

Other Changes in Public Housing Policy

Various modifications have been made in the original public housing program over the years, usually in an effort to eliminate observable deficiencies or to respond at least to major complaints. Unfortunately, such changes have all too rarely been grounded in careful study of past experience or parallel operations; most commonly, they have been ad hoc improvisations that rely on current fads in social science or administration, ignoring appropriateness or performance. In 1968, for example, Congress forbade the use of high-rise buildings as family dwellings except in emergency; a careful study of St. Louis public housing indicates that the effect of building height on development performance has been minimal. Again, Congress and HUD have urged the scattering of public housing sites, thus avoiding the large aggregates that characterized building in the 1950s. But a blanket order to scatter all forms of housing is irresponsible and improper, for it ignores the evidence already available about the effects of scattering or concentrating different kinds of populations. Elderly tenants, for example, who formerly lived in scattered (and private) dwellings and now live in relatively small (one hundred to two hundred unit) developments would resist scattering to the death since it would mean the end of valued social services and close association with others. Again, efforts to encourage the development of congregate housing for the elderly without specifying the conditions in which it is most likely to succeed or fail is an invitation to disaster unless they are viewed as deliberate experiments—clearly not the intent of the act. A larger-scale example of the same type of error appears in the housing program for the elderly taken as an entity. The federal government encouraged a vast increase in the number of elderly persons housed in public facilities, but the policies to be followed as elderly tenants lost mobility and required increasing amounts of nursing service were left to be worked out ad hoc between LHAs and state welfare agencies, often at great cost to everyone concerned and without federal fiscal support.

An even more striking example of the wayward character of federal policy-making is found in the field of housing management. In the late 1960s, HUD apparently discovered that the quality of management available in public housing left much to be desired. Substantial sums were set aside for management improvement. Although these expenditures may have been justified, there is little evidence to suggest that the experiments and studies sponsored by HUD have contributed much to operating efficiency. Nevertheless, the Housing Act of 1974 contains a rather pretentious instruction to the HUD secretary to secure "sound management practices" in housing operations. The specifics that flesh out the injunction, however, are less than impressive: LHAs should exercise "good judgment" in tenant selection, collect rent promptly, and evict those who fail to meet their financial obligations. An unkind critic might note that the LHAs did these things very well indeed in the quarter-century before HUD's appearance on the public housing scene.

Having stressed the need for good management and sponsored a special institute devoted to the task (and there is probably no more difficult management problem to be found in the field of rental housing), HUD proceeded to make a mockery of its own arguments. First, it committed the government to a radically new conception of tenant-management relations, and then it accepted and supported the principle of tenant management of public housing facilities. The "expanded social services" conception of housing management began with the Housing Act of 1968; the Housing Act of 1969, doubtless stimulated by tenant disturbances in many of the larger housing authorities, reiterated the need for a new approach to tenant-management relations. The initial watchword was *tenant participation* in operations: new lease and grievance procedures were established, tenant organizations were encouraged, managerial control over the conditions of tenancy was significantly reduced by a combination of statutory changes and court decisions. Courts, federal administration, and legislature, aided and abetted by the youthful lawyers in the legal-aid societies, combined to erode LHA control over the tenant body in the name of tenant participation. Tenants were entitled to adequate counseling, recreational facilities, and, most important of all, a voice in the management of development affairs. Moreover, efforts to organize tenants for such purposes were entitled to formal and financial

LHA support. Title II, section 3(4) of the Housing Act of 1974 is quite explicit:

> The term operation also means the financing of tenant programs and services for families residing in low-income housing projects, particularly where there is maximum feasible participation of the tenants in the development and operation of such tenant programs and services. As used in this paragraph, the term "tenant programs and services" includes the development and maintenance of tenant organizations which participate in the management of low-income housing projects; the training of tenants to manage and operate such projects and the utilization of their services in project management and operation.

The act clearly assumes ultimate transfer of management functions to tenant organizations and directs LHAs to take positive and deliberate action to further that outcome.

The HUD commitment to introducing and extending tenant management in public housing is by all odds the most astonishing development in the program's checkered history. Why did it occur? Certainly not by reason of evidence derived from experience. Tenant management was tried on a small scale in Washington, D.C., and Boston in 1971; the first major program began in St. Louis in the spring of 1973. The Housing Act of 1974 was signed in August of that year, long before any conclusive or even indicative evidence had been obtained from the tenant management program. At the end of FY 1976, the value of the tenant management program in St. Louis remained uncertain. Preliminary experience might have justified further trials, particularly of different forms of manager-housing authority relations, but nothing in the St. Louis experiment justified a full-fledged commitment to the principle. Moreover, normal management practice suggests the contrary: given the complexity of the task, the notion that public housing managers could be recruited and trained in a few short weeks from the tenant population bordered on the ludicrous. The decision at best was ideological; more likely, it was merely a resort to current fad as a way out of a nasty situation.

Since the reasons tenant management was promoted in Congress were not included in the official regulations, aside from nominal references to the need for "more participation" by tenants, the point of breakdown in the decisioning apparatus cannot be located and the motives of those involved remain obscure. Cynicism suggests that tenant management is yet another classic example of co-opting the enemy and sharing the prize, thus solving the dilemma posed for the federal administration by potentially unruly tenants. The procedure operated well in colonial empires as a temporary stopgap but failed eventually, as it did on the American Indian reservations. Unfortunately, the legendary cowardice of bureaucrats and legislators tends to make such temporary solutions attractive. On that interpretation, the Housing Act of 1974 appears as a holding action by the federal government, a delaying tactic that will make Indian reservations of the conventional housing facilities. Handing the reservations over to the Indians is the best cheap strategy available for surviving the economic crisis with fewest casualties. Unfortunately, that approach to the problem does nothing either to improve decent housing for low-income populations or to improve the lot of low-income populations to a point where subsidized housing is no longer needed.

LEASED HOUSING

The long-term future of conventional public housing in the United States dimmed unmistakably in the 1970s. Construction, whether conventional or turnkey, came to a halt; an ominous provision for closing out badly damaged developments was added to the housing legislation. By mid-1976, Pruitt and Igoe in St. Louis were being torn down and carted away. Despite such notorious failures, it would be a serious mistake to label all conventional public housing, however developed, a failure. Nevertheless, that attitude is common among legislators, tenants, the general public, academics, and even former supporters of the public housing program. The distinction between the failure of a specific effort (public housing as it was practiced, in the United States) and the failure of a general strategy for supplying low income housing has been ignored consistently. Some genuine failures, inadequate treatment in the media, and widespread ignorance of the particulars of program operations have combined to reinforce the belief that abandoning conventional public housing is the course of wisdom.

Official policy in the 1970s clearly accepted these faulty premises. When the moratorium on public housing expansion was lifted in the fall of 1973, only the leased housing program was permitted to resume operations. Section 8 of the Housing Act of 1974, which gave legal form to the leasing commitment, has become the principal focus of federal efforts in the public housing field. The message to the LHAs has been unmistakable: the future lies with leasing and not with conventional development or its variants.[3] Concurrently, the channels through which housing assistance is channeled to the population have been shifted from a federal-city axis to a federal-state axis; a Republican national administration, faced with city governments dominated by the opposition party, had no choice but to alter the resource routes so that funds passed through the state governments where some measure of Republican strength remained. The trend is likely to continue, whatever the short-run outcome of national elections, because of the inertia built into the national administrative machinery and the extent to which the federal-city connections have been dissolved. The overall effect of the change is likely to be a sharp decline in the role of the LHA, an increase in the authority and influence of the local HUD agency, and transfer of some housing operations from city to state administration. Paradoxically, an administration dedicated to decentralization of authority and the principle of local autonomy may have created a centralized housing administration with far more power than any of its predecessors managed to exercise and may have done so in the name of small government and decentralization of power.

Leasing of privately owned facilities for use as public housing offers a quick and effective device for transferring public housing into the private sector; the technique has been a rallying point for opponents of public ownership since the mid-1930s. The section 23 leased-housing program was added to the Housing Act of 1965 under cover of the hue and cry raised over the rent-supplement provisions of the housing bill. It was supported by the U.S. Chamber of Commerce, the National Association of Real Estate Boards, and various Republicans in Congress known for their hostility to public housing. Leasing began as a very small-scale program for using housing stock already in existence as a means of supplementing the more conventional developments; the initial quota was a modest 10,000 units per year for a four-year period. It was justified, to Congress and to the public, as a way of reducing costs and making greater use of the existing housing stock, which would enable housing authorities to respond more quickly and efficiently to tenant needs. By limiting the number of units that could be leased in any single facility to 10 percent of the total, the sponsors expected to disperse public housing tenants more widely and thus avoid some of the stigma that had become attached to the projects. In practice, that limit could be waived by the LHA on its own authority, hence it did not serve as an effective control over concentration or dispersal. Finally, supporters of leasing argued that owners of substandard housing would be encouraged to rehabilitate their holdings in order to qualify for the program, hence leasing would contribute to improvement of neighborhoods and upgrading of the housing stock.

If the LHA could control the quality, location, and price of housing units leased for use by low-income families, the section 23 lease program would be a valuable adjunct to conventional housing, assuming that the purpose of the LHA is to supply as much of the need for housing as resources permit. However, the private housing market would have to provide the LHA with a supply of adequate housing that is acceptable with respect to quality, location, size, availability, and cost. In general, leasing is likely to be more expensive than building or purchasing, particularly in the long run, because rents will include profits, local taxes, and the cost of financing on the private money market. Moreover, a number of factors can disrupt the effectiveness of the leasing program: the supply of housing may be inadequate with respect to quality, size, location, or cost; even if housing is available, owners may not be willing to lease their property to public agencies for use as low-income housing; finally, the tenants themselves may object to certain aspects of the program such as dispersal and separation from neighbors, distance from home neighborhood, church, schools, and so on.

As it turned out, the private market did not supply the housing needed by the LHAs, taking the nation as a whole. That opened the door to a line of activity far removed from what Congress had authorized and much more difficult to justify as an alternative to conventional public housing development. As the president of the Section 23 Leased Housing Association pointed out in July 1971:

> The leased housing program, as originally constituted, did not work because it was premised upon the assumption that there was ample housing available for lease.

However, if there was any, very few landlords offered it. Therefore another concept, called "turnkey leasing" was developed. This contemplated leasing of new construction rather than existing units.[4]

What began as a program for leasing existing housing, for which there is ample economic justification, turned very quickly into a program for constructing new housing to be offered for lease, for which little if any real justification can be offered. That required some fundamental changes in the program: The income level of the target population was moved upward, equity funding techniques were applied to public housing, and the state entered the picture as a potential developer and funder. The implications of these changes are uncertain but likely to be very far-reaching indeed!

Lease of Existing Housing

Until 1974, virtually all of the leasing carried out in public housing made use of the section 23 program added to the Housing Act of 1937 by the Housing Act of 1965. An alternative mode of leasing, authorized in section 10(c) of the Housing Act of 1937 was used briefly in the 1960s and then abandoned. Section 10(c), which required exemption from local taxation, a special agreement between local government and LHA, and a payment in lieu of taxes, proved unattractive to both local government and LHA. Only $500,000 worth of annual contract commitments were made under its provisions, all before 1969.

Section 23 leasing required prior approval by local government; it could not be undertaken by the LHA of its own volition. But, since leased property was privately owned and paid full taxes, approval was fairly easy to obtain, other things equal. Of course, some locals would have nothing to do with public housing in any form whether or not taxes were paid, but these were exceptions. Leasing did not require an LHA, but in most cases established housing authorities administered the programs. Leasing authorizations were allocated through the local HUD office. The LHA that received an allocation advertised its readiness to lease and sought owners willing to supply apartments and prospective tenants wishing to rent them. Leases were negotiated for twelve to thirty-six months in the early days of the program, but the time was extended to five years in 1966 and to fifteen years in 1970. While the program was targeted at existing housing, some of the "existing housing" being leased after 1970 was quite new or even built for the occasion.

In most cases, the LHA (or other agency) leased the units from the owner and subleased them to the low-income tenant, but the section 23 program also allowed for a direct lease between owner and tenant. The owner was paid a "fair market rental" set by HUD that included the cost of range, refrigerator, utilities, and management services, less any utilities costs paid directly by the tenant. Rent levels had to be consonant with area rents; the housing had to conform to local standards and building code requirements. Qualitative criteria were minimal:

heating, lighting, and cooking facilities had to be provided; the neighborhood had to be free of "characteristics seriously detrimental to family life"; reasonable access to schools, transportation, shopping, churches, and so on was required. Usually the LHA performed simple maintenance leaving all extraordinary repairs and services to the owner.

Ordinarily, the LHA collected rent from each tenant and paid it to the owner together with an additional subsidy obtained through an "Annual Contributions Contract" with HUD. The amount of the subsidy was calculated using a very complex scheme known as the "flexible formula," intended to ensure that no more was paid for leased housing than would be paid if an LHA had constructed the facility.[5] If the leasing program operated at a deficit, the LHA could also receive subsidies normally provided for very large or elderly families ($120 per year per family). There was understandable concern lest the leasing program drive up the price of existing housing in tight markets, and LHAs were cautioned to proceed carefully if the effects of leasing would drop the local vacancy rate below 3 percent.

Tenant eligibility for leased housing depended on income, and the LHA could apply the standards used in conventional public housing if it chose. However, the "20 percent gap" did not have to be maintained, hence income levels in leased housing could be somewhat higher than in the conventional program. Nevertheless, the 25 percent limit on income instituted by the Housing Act of 1969 applied to leased housing as well. Tenant eligibility was decided by the LHA and in most cases the LHA also selected the tenants. HUD policy allowed the owner to choose the tenants subject to LHA approval or from an LHA-prepared list. Since no rent was paid on vacant units if the owner selected tenants, that method was seldom employed until after 1973, when the rules of selection were changed. Evictions were the prerogative of the LHA alone, though the owner could request eviction of an unruly tenant. Until 1973, the owner could contract with either a private firm or an LHA for maintenance and management services; after 1973, contracts with private firms were no longer permitted.

In 1971 and again in 1973, some major changes were made in the program that controlled lease of existing housing;[6] those changes were consolidated in the Housing and Urban Development Act of 1974. They had the effect of placing complete responsibility for management in the hands of the property owner and significantly reducing the role of the LHA in the lease arrangement. The lease was thereafter made directly between owner and tenant, omitting the LHA. The owner's duties and responsibilities were extended to include paying utilities, taxes, and insurance; performing all maintenance functions; processing tenant applications and selecting tenants; collecting rents and accepting what were called "the risks of loss from vacancies," risks that were moderated somewhat by HUD's agreement to continue payments if the tenant violated the lease. Though rent adjustments were made annually, increases were subject to limits established in the Annual Contributions Contract, hence the owner who wished to raise rents had actually to find tenants with higher incomes to occupy his premises. Calculation of subsidies was much simplified: the fair market rent established by HUD was added to the estimated administrative expenses and the estimated family contribution was subtracted from the total.

The changes placed some definite responsibilities on the tenant family, for the first time in the history of the public housing program. In the past, a prospective tenant had only to apply, establish eligibility, and wait for an opening. Now, qualified tenants were given a certificate of eligibility, good for forty-five days (and renewable in the earlier version of the regulations), which committed the LHA to housing assistance payments in the tenant's behalf. Responsibility for finding an apartment, however, lay with the tenant; the LHA could assist only in hardship cases.

The new regulations significantly reduced the role of the LHA in leasing. Although the LHAs determined tenant eligibility and issued certificates, they had little operational responsibility unless they contracted with the owner to perform managerial services. Otherwise, their principal functions were to conduct an initial inspection of the premises and to process the housing assistance payments. Formally, the LHA also had final control over eviction proceedings.

The Housing Act of 1974 made some major additions to the new administrative regulations. "Low" and "very low" incomes were defined for housing purposes as 80 percent and 50 percent of the median income for the area respectively; "large" and "very large" families were similarly defined as containing six and eight minors respectively. These definitions provided a base for determining rent levels. Families that were very large or had very low incomes (or medical expenses equal to 25 percent of income) were required to pay only 15 percent of the income *before* deductions for rent; all other families were charged 25 percent of income *after* deductions; and no family could pay less than 15 percent of income for rent. The deductions allowed were modest: $300 per minor child, medical expenses in excess of 3 percent of gross income, and "unusual" costs. Each family was given a small utilities allowance. Thirty percent of the families in leased housing were to come from the very-low-income group.

The certificate of eligibility was made valid for a sixty-day period, and an additional sixty days were authorized if the tenant had made a serious effort to locate housing. Each family was to be allowed a "shopping incentive credit," defined in a way calculated to baffle even the most ardent bureaucrat:

> (b) The amount of the monthly Shopping Incentive Credit shall be the dollar amount equal to that percentage of the Gross Family Contribution which the Rent Savings is of the Fair Market Rent. The Rent Savings is the amount by which the Fair Market Rent (1) exceeds the approved Contract Rent (plus any applicable allowance), or (2) exceeds the initially proposed Contract Rent (plus any applicable allowance), if that be higher than the approved Contract Rent (plus any applicable allowance).[7]

The net effect, apparently, was a monthly reduction in rent equal to the percentage of the fair market rent saved by the tenant. That is, if the fair market rent was $200 per month and the tenant obtained the unit for $190 per month, the 5 percent saving translated into a $5 per month rent decrease for the tenant.

The 1974 act further increased the owner's control over the leasing program. An owner could now evict tenants with LHA approval, and such approval was apparently contingent only on the legitimacy of the owner's interpretation of the contract. HUD also agreed to pay up to 80 percent of the rent for a period of sixty days if a tenant vacated a leased apartment in violation of the contract, which was a significant reduction of the amount of risk assigned to the owner. Although the full effect of the 1974 Housing Act on the leasing program remains to be seen, some implications of the new regulations are clear. The authority of the LHA is much reduced; the tenant's responsibilities are greater; the owner controls the bulk of the operation. Indeed, the LHA is specifically enjoined from any action that would "directly or indirectly reduce the family's opportunity to choose among the available units in the housing market." Yet it seems reasonable to assume that the prime limit on the individual's freedom of choice is likely to be the inability of the LHA to intercede on his behalf. While not quite so serious as refusing to allow a physician to choose his patient's medicine, much the same principle seems involved. The potential bargaining power of the LHA as collective purchaser and government agent is much reduced. Granted the LHA's potential has not been fully exploited, the potential remains important even if unused. Finally, the search and lease arrangements are a virtual invitation to collusion between owner and tenant at the expense of the public treasury. If the fair market rents are high enough so that the owner is adequately rewarded from the subsidy payment alone, as seems the case in practice, then the owner's interests are best served by retaining the tenant regardless of whether the tenant's rent is actually collected (by the owner, under the terms of the act). Such arrangements would be almost impossible to detect. Finally, carelessness or bias in the LHA inspection of units would have the effect of converting the program into a support system for marginal local slums with little possibility of forcing an improvement in quality or terminating the lease.

Construction for Lease

The Housing Act of 1965 clearly intended that leasing would be limited to the existing supply of housing and that it would serve as an adjunct to the conventional housing program. That intention was transposed or transformed by HUD into active support for construction of new housing for lease and for substantial rehabilitation of existing housing. The reasoning used in HUD to justify the change would do credit to a correspondence-school lawyer. HUD argued that as soon as new housing was built it became part of the "existing" stock, hence it could be included in the program. Moreover, since the LHAs were creatures of state law and not federal law, nothing prevented them from entering into an agreement with a developer to lease as yet unbuilt property for use in the low-income housing program. Congress, instead of resenting or resisting such blatant flouting of its intentions, changed its legislation in 1970 to legalize the administrative modifications. The LHA was allowed to commit its annual contributions in advance; the developer could use them to obtain financing. The original commitment extended for eight successive five-year periods, a total of forty years; that period was reduced to twenty years by the 1974 Housing Act.

The result of the HUD interpretation was a sharp increase in the amount of new construction for lease as public housing, particularly in states where public housing was difficult to site. Between 1969 and 1974, some 61,000 units of housing were added to the lease program; of that number, more than 75 percent (46,123) were new construction, less than 1 percent (300) were substantially rehabilitated, and 24 percent (14,500) were part of the existing housing stock. This caused some anxiety among program supporters, and an effort was made to maintain an even balance between new construction and lease of existing housing.

Until the Housing Act of 1974, the regulations governing administration of new construction were the same as those applied to lease of existing stock. But the owner of the new apartment complex was in a much stronger position vis-à-vis both tenant and LHA than his counterpart who owned existing housing. Most of the advantages were due to needs arising out of the effort to finance new construction or rehabilitation. The rule that limited the LHA to leasing 10 percent of the units in any one complex was clearly inapplicable to projects built specifically for LHA use. Similarly, new construction financing could not be obtained if HUD gave priority to developments in which fewer than 20 percent of the units were leased by an LHA. Serious financial problems appeared if subsidy payments were stopped during vacancies created by tenant violations of lease provisions. HUD maintained its policies through 1973 in the face of bitter protests from owners, but financing requirements did force some concessions. An automatic inflation adjustment in rent was incorporated into the rules, and further changes were allowed if inflation turned sharply upward—thus nullifying the stabilizing effect of leasing on operating costs. The owner retained total managerial control over newly constructed units and could contract with either an LHA or a private firm for managerial services. In effect, lease of new housing allowed the reintroduction of the traditional landlord system with only minor modifications. The owner paid for taxes, utilities, and other services; was responsible for all maintenance; processed applications; selected tenants; and collected rents. After 1974, he also determined tenant eligibility, verified it periodically, set the amount of each family's contribution and subsidy, and terminated tenancy subject only to delay by the LHA.

The LHA's functions in the new construction-for-lease program were minimal. It could serve as a cosponsor of a development but could then exercise no managerial function over the property. It could manage, but only at the owner's request. HUD regulations made joint sponsorship complex and difficult, and the central administration clearly favored direct applications from developers and individual state agencies. Selection of developers, site and plan approvals, and fiscal arrangements were all made entirely through the local HUD office. The language of the regulations allowed but did not require HUD to notify the LHA when a new construction-for-lease program was announced in its area—a basic indicator of impotence in the bureaucratic world. While the LHAs retained some broad supervisory functions with respect to lease of existing housing, the April 1975 regulations governing lease of new property did not contain even one numbered paragraph enumerating the LHA's responsibilities within the new program.

The key to a strong construction-for-lease program is the availability of financing and the opportunity for profits it provides. From the point of view of the developer, access to capital at preferred rates or the right to depreciate the investment quickly and thus generate tax losses is essential. Both of these techniques found a place in the construction-for-lease program; often they were combined in the same development. To obtain preferred borrowing rates, the LHA's power to issue tax-free bonds was exploited and the creation of state agencies with similar powers was encouraged by HUD. One common procedure was for the LHA to create a nonprofit corporation that built apartments, then leased them to the LHA under an agreement that transferred ownership to the LHA at the end of a twenty-year period. The corporation could issue tax-exempt bonds because of its special relation to the LHA. Since local corporations pay local taxes, that method of financing proved popular with local governments whose tax bases were declining. The same tax break was obtained if the LHA loaned a developer the capital needed for construction using funds obtained by issuing tax-free bonds. The completed development was then leased to the LHA in the normal manner. More than thirty states created financing agencies with the power to issue tax-exempt bonds for specific purposes; they could provide capital for developers using the LHA's pledge of payment as security for a loan at a favored rate of interest.

Even more spectacular returns to the developer were produced by the technique known as "equity syndication." The key to its success was the Internal Revenue Service's willingness to allow accelerated depreciation on multifamily properties intended for use by low-income families. In effect, the IRS ruling allowed the developer to depreciate the combined value of his "up front" investment and his mortgage in a very short time, usually five years. Since this was generally more depreciation credit than one person could use unless his annual income was enormous, a portion of the depreciation credit could be sold or assigned to the members of a limited liability company formed specially for that purpose.

As an example, a developer who invested $500,000 of his own money and borrowed $4,500,000 more to build a $5 million project (a common ratio of investment to borrowing in the industry), could depreciate the property at a rate of $1 million per year for the first five years of operation. In effect, the developer "bought" $500,000 worth of depreciation over a five-year term for only $50,000. He needed only find individuals with large personal incomes and sell them the depreciation cumulated in the development. For the person with a large income, the depreciation would be a good buy; the developer, obviously, could charge rather more than his own investment. At the end of five years, when the property value was reduced to nil, the project could be sold and the return treated as capital gains—taxed at a much lower rate than personal income. The "roll-over" provision that allowed developers to defer taxation on profits simply by reinvesting in new construction (as a private homeowner can avoid taxes on profit from sale of a house by purchasing another) was not extended to construction for lease. Nevertheless, it remained a very attractive investment.

NOTES

1. The best general historical survey of the early days of public housing is Robert M. Fisher's *Twenty Years of Public Housing: Economic Aspects of the Federal Program.* Other useful background works include Robert Ellickson, "Government Housing Assistance to the Poor"; Robert Taggart III, *Low Income Housing: A Critique of Federal Aid;* Leonard Freedman, *Public Housing: The Politics of Poverty*; plus the periodic surveys in the *Congressional Quarterly.*
2. See particularly, Freedman, *Public Housing,* and Daniel R. Mandelker, *Housing Subsidies in the United States and England.*
3. The 1976 housing bill included proposals for allocating new resources for conventional construction, but the amounts involved were small.
4. Cited in Charles L. Edson, *A Section 23 Primer,* exhibit 6A, p. 4.
5. See Circular FHA 7430.3 *Low Rent Housing: Flexible Formula and Revision of Leased Housing Programs.*
6. Edson, *Section 23 Primer.*
7. See *Federal Register,* 5 May 1975, Section 8 Leased Housing Assistance Payments Program, Existing Regulations. The regulation was somewhat simplified in March 1976.

18

Publicly Assisted and Subsidized Housing

U.S. Commission on Urban Problems
(Douglas Commission Report)

Opposition to public housing led many of its advocates to seek alternatives. Public assistance remained necessary to bring decent housing within reach of large numbers of Americans. But the attempt to provide this assistance while avoiding the stigma sometimes associated with public housing led to new paths.

The major new concept was to shift ownership and operation of assisted housing to private individuals and groups. Private interests then would be praised for doing that for which the Government had been condemned. Uncle Sam still would be expected to pick up the check, but his presence around the house was not welcome. His relationship was to be muted. Those through whom the public moneys passed were to be the visible benefactors.

It was felt that this approach would be more acceptable if housing subsidies, instead of aiding chiefly those at the bottom of the economic scale, also benefited those who were not classified as poor but whose incomes in general were still too low to qualify for conventional FHA loan programs. Helping the lower middle-income class to obtain better housing would be regarded as commendable by many who would strongly disapprove of similar aid to the poor.

Attempts to bring a new look to assisted housing for both low- and moderate-income groups included the following:

From U.S. Commission on Urban Problems. *Building the American City*. Washington, D.C.: U.S. Government Printing Office, 1969, 143-51.

- Measures to house the elderly.
- Housing for low- and moderate-income groups through interest-rate subsidies and long-term mortgages.
- Rent supplements.
- Rent certificates, or leased housing.
- Subsidies for homeownership.

There are some ironic twists in this new effort. In the earlier days, rent certificates were opposed on the grounds that such an outward manifestation of poverty was demeaning and that indirect means of paying subsidies was more self-respecting.

MEASURES TO HOUSE THE ELDERLY

Two early measures, outside of public housing, to encourage the construction of dwelling units for the elderly (age 62 and older) were started in 1959 and greatly expanded in 1961. One, a mortgage insurance program under FHA, provides liberal terms. The other, administered by the Secretary of HUD, provides direct loans.

Section 231: FHA-Insured Loans

The purpose of this program is to enable special projects to get favorable mortgage and interest terms if 50 percent or more of the units are to serve the elderly. Eligible applicants for 231 loans may be public bodies, nonprofit organizations, or limited-dividend housing corporations. Projects must include eight or more units. The law provides a limit of 10 percent as an allowance for builder's and sponsor's profit and risk.

FHA is authorized to insure up to 90 percent of the value of these projects for the elderly, but the mortgages may not exceed specified amounts. The mortgage ceiling for walkup apartments ranges from $8,000 for efficiency or no-bedroom units to $19,250 for four-bedroom units. The mortgage ceilings are higher for elevator apartments, ranging from $9,500 for efficiencies to $22,750 for units with four or more bedrooms.

Typical loans under the 231 program have been for 40 years at 5½-percent interest (plus another one-half percent for insurance). The number of units constructed under this program are shown in Table 1. The program hit its peak in 1962 and has been declining ever since, largely because more attractive terms became available under 221 (d) (3) programs which are discussed later.

Section 202: HUD Direct Loans

The purpose of the direct loans also is to help nonprofit organizations and public bodies provide housing for the elderly. There is additional provision for

TABLE 1
Provision of Housing Units Under the 231 Loan Program for the Elderly

Year	New units
1960	2,967
1961	5,177
1962	8,261
1963	7,459
1964	4,912
1965	4,405
1966	1,724
1967	850
Total	35,755

TABLE 2
Provision of Housing Units Under the 202 Loan Program for the Elderly

Fiscal Year	Units Completed
1960	—
1961	—
1962	168
1963	623
1964	2,291
1965	2,737
1966	3,471
1967	4,647
1968 (estimated)	7,200
Total	21,137

housing the permanently handicapped. Cooperatives were added as possible sponsors in 1961.

No dollar ceiling is placed on dwelling unit costs or mortgages by the legislation, which calls for construction in an economical manner without use of elaborate or extravagant design or materials.

The loans are made from a revolving fund, originally set up with $50 million but subsequently increased to $500 million by 1965.

The 202 loans may amount to 100 percent of the development cost and run for a period of up to 50 years.

The interest rate originally was to be·either (a) 2¾ percent or (b) the average rate on all government obligations plus one-eighth of 1 percent, whichever was *higher*. This was modified in 1965 to provide that it was to be the *lower* of these two criteria, with 3 percent substituted for 2¾ percent. A clause that these loans may be made only if comparable terms cannot be obtained from private lending institutions is more or less a face-saving device, since the private market has been unable to match such terms.

TABLE 3
Provision of Units for the Elderly Under Public Housing

Year	Units completed (thousands)
1960	0.5
1961	2.3
1962	4.5
1963	7.2
1964	7.9
1965	13.2
1966	16.1
1967	16.1
Total	67.8

The performance record, indicated by Table 2, shows that, as with many other Federal housing programs, the number of units actually produced is somewhat disappointing.

Public Housing for the Elderly

The units built for the elderly under the 231 and 202 loan programs do *not*, it should be emphasized, include the units built especially for the elderly in public housing projects. Despite the attention focused on the new program, public housing from 1960 through 1967 built approximately twice as many housing units for the elderly as were constructed under the 231 loan program and almost five times as many as under the 202 program. Since 1964, the starts for public housing for the elderly have been half the total number of starts.

The record of public housing in providing completed dwelling units for the elderly is shown in Table 3.

Some Conclusions

A comparison of the 202 direct loan program with public housing, insofar as they both aim to serve the elderly leads to several conclusions.

The public housing effort is proceeding much faster because—

- It is a better deal financially. Construction costs are absorbed by the Government under public housing; such costs must be repaid, plus 3 percent interest, under the direct loan program.
- A public housing administration can make a good showing in the "units completed game" by providing housing for the elderly. It generally costs

less to construct and maintain housing for the elderly than family housing, and the administrative and social welfare problems are less complex when accommodating the elderly rather than poor families.
- Still another incentive for public housing administrations to build projects for the elderly is that such projects typically meet less community resistance than do new projects for families.

For these reasons, units built especially for the elderly account for about half of all the public housing built in recent years and totaled 69,700 units at the end of 1967. Preliminary figures for fiscal year 1968 indicate that about 57 percent of the units started were for the elderly.

But this does not explain why the 202 program, instead of fading away, has moved along at a slow but steady pace. The reasons for this appear to be:

- A number of the elderly do not wish to live in a project designated as public housing. (We have attempted to make clear, of course, that the direct loan projects amount to much the same thing under different guise.)
- Nonprofit groups who wish to offer a useful service have awakened to the special needs of the elderly, and this program has provided one channel for their interest.

HOUSING FOR MODERATE-INCOME GROUPS

Section 221 (d) (3)

Adequate rehousing of persons displaced by slum clearance had become a serious problem. In 1959, FHA was authorized to guarantee mortgages on housing for families "displaced from urban renewal areas or as a result of Government action." This program was broadened in 1961 to include "low- and moderate-income families" generally. This pioneering step was intended to produce housing for those who are literally caught in the middle: The people who are too poor to rent or buy standard private housing but not poor enough to be admitted to public housing.

The approach of the 221 (d) (3) program—widely known as d (3)—instead of opening public housing to higher income groups was to bring rental housing within reach of lower income groups by means of a packet of subsidies to the housing developer.

Sponsors or Developers

The developers who obtain these subsidies as mortgagors may be nonprofit associations, limited-dividend corporations, cooperatives, or certain public bodies. The sponsors agree to pass on the benefits of these subsidies to future renters, and in other ways to carry out the purposes of the program. Limited-dividend sponsors are allowed a 6-percent return on investment, while nonprofit sponsors, mainly religious and philanthropic bodies, are allowed none.

Extended Mortgage Terms

Permanent mortgage financing is offered for 40 years as contrasted with the typical 15- or 20-year mortgages applicable to builders of rental housing.

Below-Market Interest Rates

Initially the interest rate, pegged to the average cost of money to the Federal Government, ranged from 3⅛ to 4 percent. This was almost 2 percent under the going private rate.

The interest formula was changed in 1965 to a maximum 3-percent rate. With an additional waiver of the FHA mortgage insurance premium which, on other programs is one-half of 1 percent, and with the accompanying rise in market interest rates, this interest subsidy cuts the cost of mortgage debt service by approximately 40 percent, as compared with conventional FHA financing terms, and permits rent reductions of about 25 percent.

The FHA insures both the construction advance and the permanent loan. The advance is insured at 100 percent of value for nonprofit sponsors and at 90 percent for limited-dividend sponsors (the profit they are allowed accounts for the different treatment). The permanent FHA-insured mortgage is purchased from the financial institution by the Federal National Mortgage Association (FNMA, or Fannie Mae) under its special assistance program. This so-called Fannie Mae takeout explains how the mortgages with below-market interest rates, which would not be attractive to private lenders, are carried by the Government.

Occupants: How High is "Moderate"?

The 221 (d) (3) program, as noted, soon changed emphasis from displacees to families whose incomes were too high for admission to public housing but not high enough to obtain decent housing. The FHA Commissioner of HUD, who since 1954 has had full authority to fix the occupancy qualifications, interpreted this new intent faithfully. Inevitably, 221 (d) (3) began where public housing left off. The locally-determined maximum income limits for public housing became the minimum incomes for entry into 221 (d) (3) housing. That substantially eliminated this program as a means for helping to house the really poor.

This left the question: What upper income limits should be set for the beneficiaries of this generously subsidized program? The principle finally adopted was that the ceiling would be fixed at the median or midpoint of family incomes in each city. Following local studies, upper limits were established in this way.

Table 4 shows these limits for 50 large cities. (These figures apply only to families with three or four members; different ceilings apply to families in other size categories.)

Provision of decent housing for the lower half of the population (by income) was thus taken on as a public responsibility. Public housing was to assist the poorest quarter of urban families while 221 (d) (3) would assist the next quarter. But limited funds meant that the supply of subsidized housing could not stretch nearly far enough to help this half of the population. Who were to be left out in the rationing process which was accomplished by the sifting of applicants for housing on the part of public and private authorities?

Discrimination on the grounds of race or color is not allowed under Federal law. In all sections of the country, encouragingly, housing programs are found which follow this law to the letter. Yet housing programs in some cities still suffer from the residue of racial segregation policies and attitudes that for years were condoned and even encouraged.

Some sifting in 221 (d) (3) follows the practice of many public housing authorities, the imposition of requirements with respect to character. This is a delicate matter. To fill a project overwhelmingly with broken families, alcoholics, criminals, delinquents, and other problem tenants would hardly make it a wholesome environment. Yet the total exclusion of such families is hardly an acceptable alternative. To the extent this exclusion is practiced, the very people whose lives are described to persuade lawmakers and the public to instigate new programs find the door shut in their faces when such programs come into being. The proper balance is difficult to achieve, but society's neediest families surely should not be totally denied the opportunities for rejuvenation in subsidized housing.

Congress itself also laid down certain priorities. The first priority went to the displaced (original law). Then the elderly and handicapped were included (1964). Other "low- and moderate-income persons" were not to occupy more than 10 percent of the units (1966). In short, except for displaced families, there was a built-in bias against the families in the active years of life with growing children who were in the lower income band of the moderate-income group. Administrators and legislators appeared to be hesitant to take on much responsibility for children of even the lower middle class. The elderly and the handicapped were preferred occupants.

Which income groups should occupy publicly assisted housing is too important an issue to sweep under the rug. Congress in 1968 began to raise the question in earnest. Should the thrust of these housing programs be directed toward the second income quarter of the population; that is, the lower economic middle class and those slightly above? Or should the poor and the near-poor who form approximately the lowest quarter of the population be helped most? To the extent the families in the second income quarter are included, should the emphasis be on helping the upper or lower ranges of that group?

TABLE 4

City	1968 maximum income limit in dollars of 221(d)(3) program for family of 3 or 4*	1968 relation to amounts needed for upper threshold of fringes of poverty; $4,718 equals 100 percent† (percent)	Relation to median family income in United States, 1967; $8,017 equals 100 percent (percent)
Atlanta	$6,500	137.8	81.1
Baltimore	7,000	148.4	87.3
Birmingham	6,200	131.4	77.3
Boston	8,200	173.8	102.3
Buffalo	7,700	163.2	96.0
Charleston, W.Va.	7,550	160.0	94.2
Chicago	8,800	186.5	109.8
Cincinnati	7,850	166.4	97.7
Cleveland	8,600	182.3	107.3
Dallas	7,550	160.0	94.2
Denver	7,500	159.0	93.6
Des Moines	8,300	175.9	103.5
Detroit	8,450	179.1	105.4
Gary	8,000	169.6	99.8
Hartford	7,800	165.3	97.3
Honolulu	10,250	217.3	127.9
Houston	6,950	147.3	86.7
Indianapolis	7,650	162.1	95.4
Jersey City	8,200	173.8	102.3
Little Rock	6,300	133.5	78.6
Los Angeles	8,750	185.5	109.1
Louisville	6,950	147.3	86.7
Memphis	6,450	136.7	80.5
Miami	7,150	151.5	89.2
Milwaukee	8,200	173.8	102.3
Minneapolis-St. Paul	8,050	170.6	100.4
Newark	8,500	180.2	106.0
New Haven	8,100	171.7	101.0
New Orleans	7,950	168.5	99.2
New York	9,050	191.8	112.9
Omaha	8,400	178.0	104.8
Peoria	7,650	162.1	95.4
Philadelphia	7,200	152.6	89.8
Phoenix	7,250	153.7	90.4
Pittsburgh	8,050	170.6	100.4
Providence	8,100	171.7	101.0
Richmond	6,550	138.8	81.7
Rockford	8,000	169.6	99.8
St. Louis	8,500	180.2	106.1
San Antonio	6,650	140.9	82.9

TABLE 4 (Continued)

City	1968 maximum income limit in dollars of 221(d)(3) program for family of 3 or 4*	1968 relation to amounts needed for upper threshold of fringes of poverty; $4,718 equals 100 percent† (percent)	Relation to median family income in United States, 1967; $8,017 equals 100 percent (percent)
San Diego	8,650	183.3	107.9
San Francisco	8,650	183.3	107.9
Seattle	8,500	180.2	106.0
Spokane	8,100	171.7	101.0
Tacoma	7,800	165.3	97.3
Toledo	7,850	166.4	97.9
Topeka	7,700	613.2	96.0
Tulsa	6,650	140.9	82.9
Waco	6,400	135.7	79.8
Washington	8,850	187.6	110.4

*"Maximum Income Limits for Admission to Section 221(d)(3) Housing," (April 1968), HUD
†Mollie Orshansky, "The Shape of Poverty in 1966," Social Security Bulletin (March 1968), pp. 3-32.

The weight of reason is that housing subsidies, at most, should not serve those above the median income. Yet among 50 large cities, 22 place the eligibility ceiling for 221 (d) (3) housing for three- and four-member families above the national median for all families of $8,017. In 12 of these 22 cities, the national median is surpassed by more than 5 percent (see Table 4).

Twelve other cities, however, set upper income limits (for this same family size category) that are more than 10 percent below the national median.

The FHA practice of permitting help for families above the median, according to those who defend it, recognizes that big-city income levels tend to be above those for the country as a whole. They point out that the cities with the very low 221 (d) (3) ceilings, with the exception of Philadelphia, are all in or bordering the South, where income levels are lower.

The various income ceilings for eligibility in 221 (d) (3) for families of three or four in size, compiled from Table 4 data for 50 cities, are grouped as follows:

Upper 221 (d) (3) eligibility limits	Number of cities
$6,000 and under	0
$6,000 to $7,000	10
$7,000 to $8,000	16
$8,000 to $9,000	22
$9,000 and over	2

The two cities with the highest eligibility limits are New York City and Honolulu.

Income ceilings mentioned so far apply to average-size families, those with three or four members. Ceilings for single persons in the same cities range from $4,000 to $7,000, except for Honolulu, where the ceiling exceeds that figure. The limit for families with two members generally is $1,000 to $1,300 higher than for single persons. The next categories have limits that apply to pairs of family sizes, families of three and four members, of five and six members, and of seven and eight members.

Another way of examining the income levels set for 221 (d) (3) occupancy, besides the relationship to median family income, is to note how far these limits exceed the incomes of the urban poor and near-poor. In her classic studies of poverty, Mollie Orshansky in 1966 fixed $1,685 as the upper limit of urban poverty for single members with male head under 65, and $2,185 for families with two members. She then estimated that the near-poor, those on the fringes of poverty, received up to one-third more income than the poverty level. This was $2,045 for single persons and $4,232 for four-member families in 1966. Adjusted for the 6-percent cost-of-living rise, the 1968 figures, below which city persons are counted in the near-poor category, are $2,168 for one person, $3,182 for two-member families, and $4,606 for four-member families.

As noted, the lowest 221 (d) (3) eligibility limits for single persons are $4,000 or more. Occupants therefore may have twice as much income as persons on the threshold of the near-poor in those cities. In 32 cities, where eligibility limits for single persons are between $5,000 and $6,000, occupants may have three times the income of the near-poor. Table 4, column 2, shows the relationship of the eligibility figure and the near-poverty level for three- and four-member families. (The figures admittedly are imperfect approximations, and comparative living costs account for many of the variations.) The median of the 50 cities is 169 percent, or approximiately 70 percent above the national near-poverty threshold.

That FHA tried to do a creditable job under the conditions it has laid down for itself is not questioned. The elderly and small families are generally receiving a greater degree of assistance. This seems to be true through a whole range of public programs from welfare to social security, as well as housing. The Commission does not object to the help provided to these groups, but does not condone the disproportionately large share they have received in admittedly insufficient programs.

Advocates of high eligibility ceilings justify their position on three grounds:

1. Because building costs are so high, those persons who, regardless of income level, cannot afford to buy or rent housing should be in line for subsidies in order to be properly housed.

2. It is highly desirable to have a mixture of middle-income families in projects, as opposed to having them exclusively occupied by the poor.
3. Middle-income families should not only be present but should predominate so they can set the tone for the project.

The following questions may be raised about these points:

1. Since there are not enough funds to help all the needy at once, should we help the most needy last, so that the least needy who get help are, in effect, subsidized by the taxes of persons poorer than themselves?
2. Is it not possible to make available funds stretch further and thus achieve a greater degree of economic integration by using subsidies primarily for the poorer occupants while the higher income families pay their own way?
3. Is there not a tendency to exaggerate the correlation between poor families and "problem" families, and thus to rule out almost all of the poor, even though some of them may be fully acceptable on the basis of their citizenship potential in a project?

Among the advocates of lower eligibility ceilings are both fiscal conservatives and humanitarian liberals. The former call for reduced Government spending and are appalled at the idea of subsidizing middle-class housing in this direct form. The latter, seeing that the amount of public money finally appropriated will be limited and insufficient to meet the needs of all, assume that some rationing system, conscious or unconscious, is inevitable; and they fear that the tendency will be to fill the available 221 (d) (3) housing with middle-income families and the elderly to the detriment of the near-poor and families whose needs are either more severe or less proportionately met.

The fiscal conservatives and humanitarian liberals do not dismiss the housing needs of the middle class, but join hands in the belief that the primary effort on their behalf should be in the direction of reducing the various costs that now make housing too expensive. But policymakers at HUD and among the housing officialdom have been more than skeptical that genuine cost reductions can be effected, and are thereby deeply committed to the subsidy method of reducing the rental or purchase price.

Performance Record

These occupancy issues have deep significance for the Nation's housing programs and urban characteristics in the long run. But the most immediate problem is that the 221 (d) (3) program has produced a relatively small volume of housing. The following statistics show the units started since 1961:

Year	Number of units started
1961	2,320
1962	3,182
1963	6,884
1964	13,906
1965	11,098
1966	12,766
1967	23,660
Total	73,816

Preliminary figures for fiscal 1968 indicate 43,000 new starts.

The record indicates some progress over time. This is especially true in fiscal years 1967 and 1968. But the total is not great in comparison with the need, or with the total volume of private construction. Up to 1967, these units did not represent more than 1 percent of the total volume of private construction and amounted to few more total number of units than had been planned as a yearly total when the program was started. With the increase to over 23,000 units in 1967 and 43,000 in 1968, the 221 (d) (3) program still furnished less than 2 and 3 percent, respectively, of the volume of private construction in those years. Nevertheless, by 1968, the program had achieved the annual total originally planned when it was passed. This was due to special efforts at the White House and the top housing officials to speed up the program.

By July 1967 FHA had given commitments to proceed with a total of 73,000 units in 569 projects. The sponsors of these units were as follows:

Sponsors	Units with FHA commitments	Percent of total
Limited-dividend corporations	33,300	46
Nonprofit organizations	23,600	32
Cooperatives:		
Management or membership types	10,800	15
Investor types	3,100	4
Miscellaneous	2,100	3
Total	72,900	100

Here was a program with little risk to the investors, with insured construction loans, with 3-percent below-market interest rates, with long-term guaranteed mortgages, with a Fanny Mae "take out," with a great deal of public support and publicity, and with little if any public opposition or resistance. Why did it move so slowly and produce so little for so long?

The reasons for the sluggishness of the 221 (d) (3) program include the following:

• Nonprofit sponsors lacked the experience, the building and financing know-how, and often the seed money, necessary to initiate and successfully carry out a housing project.

- The amount of profits that the limited dividend corporations could distribute was restricted to a rate of 6 percent, which discouraged (or at least did not encourage) private enterprisers who are accustomed to 12-percent profits or more. (This is not to suggest the program was unattractive to those who participated; builder profits of 7 percent, architect fees of 4 percent, and other charges or fees were allowable costs.)
- Complexities and bottlenecks in processing applications by FHA often frustrated the program. The manual of successive steps which must be taken under 221 (d) (3) comes, with the illustrative forms, to 283 pages. This discouraged all but the most persistent sponsors. Under pressure from the President and his task force, FHA appeared to be making important strides to overcome these hurdles and delays by late 1968.
- Processing time from original applications with FHA approval to the start of construction was estimated by HUD at 376 working days.
- Some of the advocates of higher income ceilings claim that many of the top limits in certain cities prevent middle-class families from applying and from assuring the success of planned projects. However, FHA surpassed the stated income limits by deducting certain expenses from gross income.

It took the 221 (d) (3) program 6 years to bring into being the number of housing units that were set as the initial *annual* goal.

Many of the projects that have been built under the program are excellent. Much of the nonprofit work involved individuals and organizations in a meaningful way in their communities. Many families and individuals who needed help obtained a real housing bargain. The program has picked up steam in the past 2 years. As a major housing program to produce an abundance of housing, it fell far short of its original goals.

Just as the program finally gained momentum, new law provided that it be phased out as the new 1-percent interest rate subsidy program begins. Because of this, Congress gave generous additional authority to FNMA to assist the program in the interim. Subsequent action by the Appropriations Committees shows how wise this was. They reduced the initial amounts for both the 1-percent sales and rental programs from $75 to $25 million.

The momentum finally achieved under 221 (d) (3) can still continue if the program is nurtured by HUD and, especially, if the Budget Bureau does not cut back on the funds FNMA may use for it.

Rent Supplements

In 1965, after a long internal struggle, HUD came to Congress with a program to subsidize the rents of moderate- and middle-income families. These were to be in new or rehabilitated structures privately owned and managed by nonprofit organizations. This program was apparently intended in part as a substitute for public housing, which was then under heavy criticism.

Instead of being aimed at helping the poor, however, as was public housing, the rent supplement program was designed primarily to help the middle- and moderate-income groups with incomes ranging from $4,000 to $8,000 a year, and possibly even up to $10,000. The general intent was to follow the income patterns of those eligible for 221 (d) (3) housing, which has already been discussed.

When this was discovered by the Senate Banking Committee, the members objected strenuously. The majority maintained that the primary aim should be to help the income group which most needed to be helped—the poor. These Senators insisted, therefore, that the income standards of admission prevailing under rent supplements should be the same as under public housing, not as under 221 (d) (3). HUD vigorously opposed this change. The Secretary, for example, declared in a public speech that while those who wanted to use rent supplements for the poor "might have hearts of gold, they had heads of lead."

The National Association of Housing & Redevelopment officials was opposed to the entire idea of rent supplements, even for the poor. It favored, instead, continuing the orthodox method of public housing.

The Senate committee, on the other hand, supported rent supplements as a supplement to the orthodox public housing system, and this standard finally was adopted. Private and supposedly nonprofit groups were to be encouraged to erect new housing or satisfactorily rehabilitate old housing.

Subsidy Formula

Those who were eligible for public housing could have their rents subsidized by the difference between (*a*) the market rent and (*b*) 25 percent of the family income. The costs allowed in computing market rent were to include up to 6 percent interest plus the half-of-1-percent FHA fee.

For example, if the fair market rent for an apartment were to be $1,320 a year ($110 a month), but the family had an income of only $3,000 a year ($250 a month), it would only be expected to pay 25 percent of this income, or $750 a year ($62.50 a month) toward rent. The monthly subsidy would then amount to the difference between $110 and $62.50, or $47.50.

Subsidized housing was to be privately, not publicly, owned by the same institutions relied upon in 221 (d) (3)—nonprofit sponsors, limited-dividend corporations, and cooperatives.

The rent supplement could not exceed 70 percent of the market rent nor be less than 10 percent. As the income of a family changed, the supplement would vary inversely. To illustrate, if the family income in the previous example were to rise to $3,600, the amount which the family could pay would increase to $900 a year

($75 a month), reducing the supplement to $35 a month. But if the family's income fell to $2,400, it would only be expected to pay annual rent of $600 ($50 a month), requiring the subsidy to rise to $60 a month.

The change in the actual rent payment by a family in this program would only be one-quarter of any rise in income, leaving a strong financial incentive for the family to try to increase its income.

Other programs, in order to encourage low-rent housing, subsidized one or more of the following elements of costs: construction, site, operation and maintenance, tax burden, interest, and so forth. Rent supplements, however, were intended to help tenants directly. One advantage was flexibility, because the supplements could be varied from person to person according to income and available housing.

The supplements also permitted the use of private rather than public financing. This made the program more acceptable to the main body of congressional and public opinion, although, because of the higher interest rates involved, it created large added costs over the long run. It was a price which the program paid for greater private participation. An added inducement to localities lay in the fact that, since the properties were to be privately owned, they would pay full local property taxes. Here, as under 221 (d) (3), there was some opportunity to attract as promoters, organizers, and managers the private profit seekers as well as philanthropists. This could not be done very effectively in the case of nonprofit groups or management and membership cooperatives. But there were possible loopholes under the limited-dividend corporations and investor-sponsored cooperatives. In attempting to check this, the FHA was forced to adopt procedural safeguards. These, together with the natural tendency of bureaucracy toward overelaboration, caused forms and procedures to be multiplied until the sponsors seemed at times to be completely smothered in red tape. Urban America's description of the successive steps which sponsors of rent-supplemented units had to take, and the forms they had to fill out, came to 323 pages.

Racial and Economic Integration

One of the basic, though unavowed, purposes of the rent-supplement program was to promote in a constructive fashion a greater degree of economic and racial integration. It was not intended that a building or project would house only rent-supplement families. On the contrary, it was hoped that a large percentage of the tenants in a building would pay the full economic rent. Those receiving the supplements were to be mixed in among them without being publicly distinguished from them. In this way, it was hoped that the occupants would avoid the stigma sometimes associated with public housing.

It was also hoped that these buildings, with their mixed occupancy, could be diffused through a city and not confined to the slums or gray areas.

These latter purposes were not explicitly avowed but were soon detected. Those who were generally hostile to racial integration were therefore successful in persuading the House to require that the consent of a locality was necessary before rent supplements could be put into effect there. Unfortunately, this virtually barred the program from the suburbs.

Performance Record

Since there was a close connection between rent supplements and the 221 (d) (3) provisions, the administration of the supplement program also was entrusted to FHA. The clients to be served by the supplements were, however, to be virtually identical with the lower income group eligible for public housing.

Congress permitted 5 percent of the rent supplement *money* (not units) to be used for projects which would share in the below-market interest program of 221 (d) (3) where the annual rate was to be only 3 percent. Another 5 percent of the 3-percent money was also allowed for the elderly. This was to provide an alternative to the provisions for the elderly already made by sections 202 and 231.

Congress authorized $150 million for the years from 1965 to 1968, but the actual sum appropriated for this purpose was later reduced to $42 million. HUD states that by the end of March, 1968, a total of 59.9 thousand units were in the pipeline, and that of these 43.2 thousand, or 72 percent, were definitely destined for rent supplements. Of this latter number, 4.3 thousand were classified as being in the formal stage, 31.5 thousand as preliminary and contracts had been let on 7.4 thousand. This did not specify the precise numbers which were actually under management or in operation.

In the spring of 1968, when this Commission sought information from official sources on the total number of units which had actually been constructed under rent supplements, we were informed that as of the end of 1967, only 921 units had been completed in 12 rent supplement projects. But of these, only 365 units were actually earmarked for rent supplements. Some progress has undoubtedly been made since then. But it is also probably true that a considerable number of the units which are currently claimed as being under management are in reality transfers from previous programs for the elderly such as those under section 202 and 231. When HUD was asked by Congressional committees in 1968 how many units could be produced under rent supplements in the first year after the new law went into effect, the department withdrew its earlier estimate and refrained from providing any final figure. It is obvious, therefore, that grave difficulties have arisen in carrying out the program.

Part of the trouble has undoubtedly been caused by the fact that many of the sponsors had not understood the duration and complexity of the process. Many became exhausted and quit. Others were frightened by the prospect that they could not find a sufficient number of tenants to make their project pay and that they would become responsible for the organizing costs.

As the general level of interest rates rose, the gap widened between the cost of

TABLE 5

Processing Time for Application Under Sec. 221 (d)(3)—Mortgage Insurance for Multifamily Rental or Cooperative Housing for Low- and Moderate-Income and Displaced Families

Step	Agency or Office	Action Taken	Days
	PREAPPLICATION STAGE		
1	Local: Local public agencies, nonprofit or limited dividend corporation, or cooperatives	Preapplication analysis request (form 2012) received by FHA local insuring office from nonprofit sponsor	…
	Local/Federal		
2a	FHA local insuring office	Site feasibility study	14
2b	......do	Land use intensity analysis	10
2c	Regional: Assistant regional administrator, FHA	Zone site engineering report	9
2d	National: Office of Assistant Commissioner for Multifamily Housing	Headquarters nonprofit sponsor approval	22
	INITIAL APPLICATION STAGE		
3	Local (same as 1 above)	Sponsor response to invitation to submit preliminary application	70
4a	Local/Federal (same as 2a above)	Site plans examined	12
4b	......do	Prearchitectural analysis	14
4c	......do	Prevaluation analysis	15
4d	......do	Mortgager corporation analysis	8
4e	......do	Chief underwriter review	5
4f	Regional: Assistant regional administrator, FHA	Zone multifamily review	15
	FINAL APPLICATION STAGE		
5	Local (same as 1 above)	Sponsor submits final application package of detailed specifications, drawings, cost, and financing data	77
6a	Local/Federal (same as 2a above)	Final architectural analysis	37
6b	......do	Final cost estimate review	20
6c	......do	Final valuation analysis	8
6d	......do	Final financial and credit analysis	8
6e	National (same as 2d above)	Allocation/reservation of funds	33
7	Local/Federal (same as 2a above)	Commitment issued to mortgagee	…

Note: Preapplication stage, lapsed time: 45 days. Initial application stage, lapsed time: 110 days. Final application stage, lapsed time: 404 days.
Source: Study by Model Cities Systems Improvement Team, HUD, June 23, 1967.

housing and the 25 percent of their income that low-income families were allowed to pay under the program. Since the amount of the subsidy is limited, higher interest rates progressively diminished the number of low-income families who could qualify.

Some sponsors found it difficult to build within the physical limits allowed for rent supplement units and yet make them attractive to the remaining tenants. Some were repelled by what they regarded as cold, bureaucratic, and at times actually hostile treatment at the hands of FHA.

We are confident that this was not the intention of top FHA officials. They seem to have tried to be helpful. But as testimony before our Commission revealed, the rank and file officials in district and local offices were, in many cases, highly unsympathetic. They were accustomed to dealing with the conservative real estate and financial community. They did not feel at home in having business dealings with churches and philanthropists whom they tended to regard as soft and impractical. Nor did they welcome having the poor as their constituents. This was a social class whom they had never served and who seemed alien to their interests and associations. After these attitudes were increasingly revealed by our hearings, the head of FHA reacted vigorously. He called his field representatives together and instructed them to pay special attention to such applications. He warned the field officials that if they persisted in their past course, Congress would undoubtedly transfer the program and reduce the number of FHA employees. This produced a decided change of attitude in many offices, although the old indifference and antagonism linger among many of the personnel.

HUD officials still believe that the rent supplement program will catch on. They point to the 7.4 thousand units of rent supplements for which contracts have actually been let, and insist that the vast majority of the 31.5 thousand in the preliminary stage will ultimately result in actual units. It remains to be seen whether these hopes will materialize. New and favorable factors are, of course, the increased authority provided for the program by the 1968 Act, together with the greater subsidization of interest also continued in that measure.

Of the total number of units which were in the rent supplement pipeline, 27.4 thousand, or 63.5 percent, were sponsored by nonprofit organizations, 15.1 thousand by limited-dividend corporations, and only 640 by cooperatives.

19

Interest Rate Subsidies:
National Housing Policy Review

U.S. Department of
Housing and Urban Development

The Section 235 Program

The Section 235 homeownership assistance program, established in the 1968 legislation, is the largest subsidy program through which the Department of Housing and Urban Development specifically attempts to provide homeownership. The HUD Section 235 Handbook, issued in January 1973, states the objectives of the program succinctly:

> The program is intended not only to produce more homes, but to enable lower income families to become owners of homes and thereby experience the pride of possession that accompanies homeownership. In this way, the program can be a vital influence in promoting personal responsibility and social stability.

The Section 235 program is basically production-oriented both in terms of the stated goals of the program and in its structural and administrative makeup. The program was designed to help achieve the target of 6 million new or substantially rehabilitated units for low and moderate income families by 1978. The subsidy is attached to the house and not to the occupant family. If the occupant family should move, it would lose the subsidy.

The subsidy formula is calculated as the lesser of either (1) the difference be-

From U.S. Department of Housing and Urban Development. *Housing in the Seventies: A Report of the National Housing Policy Review*. Washington, D.C.: U.S. Government Printing Office, 1974, pp. 104-23.

tween (a) 20 percent of monthly adjusted income and (b) the total monthly payment under the mortgage for principal, interest, mortgage insurance premium, taxes, and hazard insurance; or (2) the difference between (a) the monthly payment for principal, interest, and the mortgage insurance premium, and (b) the payment to principal and interest at a 1 percent interest rate.

Viewed one way, the subsidy places a special burden on some Section 235 families. Those receiving the maximum subsidy under the second formula—usually the lower income Section 235 families—must bear increases in taxes and insurance without increased assistance. The higher income families, who usually are subsidized under the first formula, have their subsidy raised to cover the entire increase in taxes or insurance until the second formula subsidy limit is reached.

A builder/sponsor under Section 235 usually has a strong demand for its product if it builds according to HUD regulations. A family must be lucky enough to be the one-out-of-50 income-eligible Section 235 families (on average) selected for homeownership by the builder/sponsor and the mortgagee.

For many of the Section 235 families whose shares of mortgage payments are based on 20 percent of adjusted gross incomes, there is no incentive to be concerned about whether a higher price represents more "house" since they do not pay the additional price themselves. Thus, the builder faced with strong demand may be able to "capture" some of the Government subsidy by encouraging the family to purchase an expensive house, with the higher cost covered by a higher Government subsidy.

This counterproductive incentive structure highlights the crucial role that HUD appraisers and inspectors must play in order to hold down excess profits and to protect the interests of the Government. Abuses and fraud, however, are an inherent and demonstrable danger of such an incentive structure.

For the Section 235 homeowner family, the subsidy is typically large (equal to about one-eighth of the family's average income). There is little financial risk to the homeowner here because his or her initial equity frequently is less than the deposit on an apartment, while the Government assumes almost all the risk of a Section 235 home by providing insurance for the mortgagee. In the past, HUD has not sought deficiency judgments to recover costs against Section 235 homeowners whose homes have been foreclosed.

The income and mortgage limits predetermine most of the characteristics of the participants and the units produced. The mortgage limits range from $18,000 to $24,000, depending on family size and location, and the income limits are set at 135 percent of local housing authority income limits. However, there is a significant exception to this general rule. Twenty percent of the contract authority may assist households with incomes up to 90 percent of the Section 221(d)(3) below-market-interest-rate income limits. The income limits from this program allow higher income families to enter the Section 235 program.

In contrast to such legislatively determined upper limits, the lower mortgage

TABLE 1
Characteristics of the Section 235 Program, 1972

Units assisted through December 31, 1972 (home insurance written)	398,000
Total mortgage amounts through December 31, 1972 (home insurance written)	$7.0 billion
Maximum annual subsidies permitted by law through fiscal year 1973 (contract authority released in appropriations)	$665 million
Median mortgage amount per unit	$18,500
Median buyer income	$6,500
Racial and ethnic compositions of buyers:	
Nonminority white	66%
Black	22%
Spanish American	11%
Other	2%

Source: Department of Housing and Urban Development.

and income limits are set administratively by HUD's Minimum Property Standards for the unit and by mortgage credit standards for the applicant. Given local building costs, the setting of Minimum Property Standards has the effect of establishing minimum cost and, therefore, the minimum mortgage amount: the higher the standards, the more expensive the home. The mortgage amount and the stringency of the mortgage credit standards determine the effective lower income limits. A general rule is that the mortgagor's share of the total mortgage payment, under ordinary circumstances, should not exceed 35 percent of net effective family income. Some major characteristics of the Section 235 program are presented in Table 1.

Major Findings

1. The Section 235 homeownership program has not made significant progress toward achieving equity. Only 12.6 percent of the families served have incomes of less than $5,000 annually. Yet families with annual incomes of less than $5,000 live more often in substandard and low quality housing than families earning more than $5,000 annually. In the income class with greatest participation ($6,000-$6,999), only 2.7 percent of eligible families are served. A household is 5 times more likely to be served if it resides in the South than in the Northeast or Middle Atlantic regions.

2. Subsidies received by recipients actually increase as gross family income increases.

3. The program provides substantial benefits to its recipients. Housing quality of recipients improved by 35 percent and nonhousing expenditures increased by 8 percent.

4. Total Government costs are about 10 percent greater than the cost of the subsidy. Foregone taxes and administrative costs account for most of the difference.

5. A dollar spent by Government on the Section 235 program results in only 82 cents worth of benefits to the recipient.

6. Counterproductive program incentives may reduce the efficiency and equity of the program. These structural "incentives," aimed at builders and developers rather than the intended beneficiaries, may lead to more expensive homes and higher default and foreclosure rates.

7. This study did not demonstrate that Section 235 housing costs more than comparable privately produced units.

8. The insurance fund for Section 235 appeared to be actuarially sound through 1972, but recent trends in foreclosures and assignments throw this conclusion into doubt.

9. The main problems appear to be structural problems inherent in the production subsidy in-kind approach. Some administrative changes could reduce the counterproductive incentives.

Equity

Table 2 shows the distribution of Section 235 participants by gross-income class, and other information on the equity aspects of the program. The table makes apparent the serious horizontal inequity in the program. Very few of the income-eligible families in each income class receive Section 235 benefits. In addition, the average subsidy actually increases in the upper income range. This happens because higher income families tend to be larger, so they have lower adjusted incomes than smaller families with the same gross income, and because higher income families tend to purchase more expensive homes both because of their larger families and their greater financial expectations: The decrease in the Government subsidy that might be expected because of their higher income is more than offset by the more expensive homes that higher income families purchase.

The vertical inequity in the program is best illustrated by column 5 in Table 2, where the total subsidy paid to an income class is spread among all eligible families in their respective class. Families in the $6,000 to $6,999 annual income class benefit most from the program; in other words, the least needy—and the class presumably already living in better housing within the target group of $3,000 to $7,000 income[1]—receive the largest subsidy.

TABLE 2
Distribution of Section 235 Housing, by Income Class,
as of December 31, 1972

(1)	(2)	(3)	(4)	(5)
Gross Income	Percent Distri- bution of Households Served by 235	235 Households as Percent of all Households	Direct Annual Subsidy Per Household Served	Direct Annual Subsidy per Household in the Income Class*
$ 0- 999	Less than 0.05	Less than 0.05	—	—
1,000-1,999	Less than 0.05	Less than 0.05	—	—
2,000-2,999	0.3	Less than 0.05	$720	$0.19
3,000-3,999	2.1	0.2	768	1.52
4,000-4,999	10.2	1.0	780	7.70
5,000-5,999	23.7	2.3	768	18.03
6,000-6,999	26.4	2.7	768	20.83
7,000-7,999	19.3	1.9	792	14.80
8,000-9,999	15.9	0.8	828	6.71
10,000 or more	2.1	Less than 0.05	864	0.21

*Total subsidy paid to an income class spread among all households in that income class.
Source: Department of Housing and Urban Development. National Housing Policy Review estimates based on data from Department of Housing and Urban Development and Department of Commerce, Bureau of the Census, *Current Population Reports,* Series P-60, Nos. 84 and 87, and *1970 Census of Population.*

Table 3 presents a measure of the geographic equity and inequity in the program. The table reveals that about 49 percent of the Section 235 units are concentrated in Regions IV and VI, which have only about 25 percent of the Nation's population and 30 percent of the Nation's population in the $3,000 to $7,000 annual income range. Moreover, Regions I, II, and III have about 9 percent of the units but nearly 31 percent of the total population, and 29 percent of the "eligible" population. The concentration of units in the South—Regions IV and VI—can be explained in part by the statutory mortgage limits and the relatively lower cost of construction in these areas. These factors make new construction more feasible in the South.

Taken together, the tables show that the homeownership assistance program has not made significant progress toward achieving equity.

Impact

One legislative goal of the Section 235 program is to produce more "standard" housing units. A measure of the success of the program presumably could be demonstrated by adding up the number of standard housing units constructed.

In measuring the impact of the Section 235 program, totaling the number of

TABLE 3
Section 235 Regional Distribution, as of December 31, 1972

(1)	(2)	(3)	(4)	(5)
HUD Region	Percent of 235 Units Produced	Percent of U.S. Households	Percent of U.S. Households Having Between $3,000 and $7,000 Annual Income	Units to Target Group (Col. 2 ÷ Col. 4)
I	1.9%	5.7%	5.1%	0.4
II	3.8	13.7	12.4	0.3
III	3.0	11.3	11.3	0.3
IV	29.2	15.2	18.7	1.6
V	17.6	21.1	18.0	1.0
VI	19.4	9.7	11.4	1.7
VII	4.8	5.6	6.2	0.8
VIII	4.3	2.6	3.0	1.5
IX	10.4	11.7	10.8	1.0
X	5.3	3.3	3.1	1.7
Total U.S.	100.0%	100.0%	100.0%	1.0

Source: Department of Housing and Urban Development. National Housing Policy Review estimates based on data from Department of Housing and Urban Development and Department of Commerce, Bureau of the Census, *1970 Census of Population.*

new units would be an overstatement, however, because it is likely that to some extent developers participating in the subsidy program would have produced other housing if the program did not exist. One recent study determined that for every 100 subsidized units undertaken, 86 unsubsidized starts previously planned were canceled, primarily because subsidized starts reduce the amount of mortgage market funds available for unsubsidized starts.[2]

Conceivably, the objective of providing standard housing for the target group specified in the Section 235 program could have been attained without increasing the number of new units if there had been an improvement in the quality of the existing low quality stock. Although any changes in the housing quality of non-program beneficiaries cannot be measured precisely, the improvement in the quality of housing occupied by recipients can be calculated.

The "extra housing" that a Section 235 family receives is measured by the difference between what the unit would cost in the private market and what the owner actually pays toward the mortgage. It is possible that the sum of the Government subsidy and the owner's contribution could be greater than the private market's evaluation of the unit. This would be true if the construction costs of Section 235 housing were more expensive than they would have been in the private market. But a June 1973 study of nine housing markets containing almost

2,000 Section 235 housing units located in three HUD regions indicated that the construction costs for Section 235 units were very similar to those of conventional units.[3]

If Section 235 houses and comparable private houses indeed sell for the same price, that means that the owner receives the full value of the subsidy, in the form of "extra" housing. This amount equals about $948 per year for a sample of 329 Section 235 homeowners in 10 Standard Metropolitan Statistical Areas.

But of more importance in assessing the impact of the program is the percentage of improvement in housing quality induced by the program. This figure is estimated by comparing the housing budgets of families participating with those having the same income but not participating in the program; housing improvement is estimated to be about 35 percent for participants in the Section 235 program.

Not all of the subsidy is taken in the form of better housing. To the extent that a family has flexibility in its spending habits—despite the fact that it must purchase a given amount of housing to participate in the program—it will allocate the funds previously spent on housing for nonhousing commodities. The subsidy is not a simple add-on to their previous housing budget: a figure of 8 percent has been estimated as the increase in nonhousing expenditures for Section 235 families compared to the control group.

Because a Section 235 homeowner family is constrained to purchase a certain type and quality of housing with its subsidy dollars, these funds have less value to the family than do unrestricted dollars. The measure of the value of the subsidy to the recipient is termed the benefit to the recipient. For the Section 235 program, the $948 annual subsidy is valued by the average family at $857 ($71 per month).

Costs

There are five types of costs that the Federal Government must bear in order to provide the services of the Section 235 program. The costs were estimated over the life of the program, using assumptions of income and cost growth rates, based on past experience, of 5.7 and 6 percent, respectively. Where there were startup costs, the costs were amortized over the projected 11-year life of the program, using a 6 percent discount rate.

By far the most important cost to the Federal Government is the direct subsidy cost paid by HUD to the mortgagee. In 1972, the estimated average direct subsidy was $948.

A second important cost to the Federal Government is the taxes that are foregone (not paid) because of the program. Homeowners may deduct mortgage interest payments and property taxes from their taxable income. This cost, however, was not counted, because all homeowners are entitled to this deduction. But Section 235 homeowners—unlike other homeowners—also are entitled to deduct the interest and property taxes that the Government pays by means of the subsidy. The cost to the Government of this entitlement was calculated to be $61 for the average family occupying Section 235 housing in 1972.

The administrative cost of the program was divided into endorsement, maintenance, and settlement costs, and spread over the "expected" life of the units subsidized. For 1972 these costs amounted to $34 per unit. This is an overestimate, however, because the mortgage insurance premium—part of which is paid by the Government to itself—is used to offset administrative expenses connected with the program as well as the specific mortgage losses borne by HUD because of default terminations. This offset was estimated at $15 per unit for 1972 and was subtracted from the total administrative costs.

Based on an admittedly questionable assumption, the special risk insurance fund for Section 235 was found to be actuarially sound in 1972, and no additional adjustments were made to account for foreclosure losses. Specifically, the predicted final default termination rate and average loss per mortgage plus administrative costs were assumed to be equal to the income generated by the 0.5 percent mortgage insurance premium.

Finally, the Government National Mortgage Association (GNMA) from time to time provides an additional subsidy to support Section 235 mortgages when the FHA interest ceiling is below the market interest rate. GNMA issues commitments under the Tandem Plan to buy mortgages at 97 percent of par, and, in turn, sometimes sells them for a lower price. Actual Section 235 Tandem Plan losses for fiscal years 1972 and 1973, and projected losses for fiscal year 1974, were amortized at 6 percent over the "expected" life of the program and allocated evenly over each year. The estimated cost for 1972 was about $24 per mortgage. The estimated total 1972 cost of the program to the Federal Government was $1,051 per unit, or approximately $391 million for the total program.

Efficiency

The efficiency measures relate benefits and costs to estimate an overall evaluation of the program in relation to the private market. An important part of the efficiency aspect of the program is whether counterproductive incentives, departmental red tape, quality standards, and delays increase the cost of subsidized housing in relation to comparable housing in the private market. Theoretically, this might be expected to be the case if the private market were competitive. Several factors mitigate this conclusion, however. First, a Section 235 house is not actually designated as such until an eligible buyer is certified. Thus, the builder is not always assured of subsidy benefits and is more likely to build competitively. Second, HUD's appraisals and cost analyses tend to keep the selling price of Section 235 units in the range of the approximate "market value."

The empirical evidence gathered for almost 2,000 units in nine cities did not show that the average Section 235 house costs more than similar privately constructed housing. This does not necessarily imply that Section 235 construction is as efficient as conventional construction. Alternate explanations are that Section 235 units are located on less desirable and, consequently, lower cost land, or that Section 235 builders accept a lower profit margin because of the lower risk involved in selling subsidized housing.

One significant qualification in this cost study is that there appears to be almost no non-FHA housing in urban areas constructed within the Section 235 mortgage limits apart from mobile homes. Although the cost study attempted to adjust for differences in amenities, it is doubtful that all housing quality as well as neighborhood differences were taken into account in the adjustments. Nevertheless, the net effect on construction costs of the findings is to produce a Construction Efficiency Index of 1.0; consequently, the market value of the subsidy is equal to the dollar value of the subsidy.

Production Efficiency is a measure that depends on the relation between the costs of subsidized housing construction and the costs of identical unsubsidized housing construction, and on the indirect costs of the program. For this program, indirect costs such as taxes foregone, administrative costs, and the Governmental National Mortgage Association Tandem Plan, produce an efficiency of less than 1.0.

$$\text{Production Efficiency} = \$948/\$1,051 = .87$$

A family is constrained in its use of a subsidy when it is provided in-kind—that is, in actual housing rather than in dollars paid directly to the recipient. It is generally agreed that because of the inherent restriction of choice, an in-kind transfer usually is not worth as much to an individual as is an outright cash grant. Transfer Efficiency is a measure that takes this factor into account. The estimate is based on a sample of 329 families in the Section 235 program in 10 cities, and on an estimate that measures the "utility" of the subsidy to the average family. Transfer Efficiency is defined as the ratio of the cash value of the subsidy in-kind related to the market value of the subsidy. In the Section 235 program the market value of the subsidy is assumed to be equal to the dollar amount of the subsidy, because the aforementioned study did not indicate a difference between the construction cost of Section 235 housing and identical, conventionally financed housing.

$$\text{Transfer Efficiency} = \$857/\$948 = .90$$

The overall measure of the efficiency of the program is a combination of Production Efficiency and Transfer Efficiency, called "Program Efficiency." Program Efficiency is the ratio between the cash value of the subsidy to the recipient and the total Federal costs.

$$\text{Program Efficiency} = \$857/\$1,051 = .82$$

This measure represents the net benefits to the private individual relative to the total cost incurred by the Government in providing that benefit. The continuation of the program may be questioned if benefits of $194 per year (the difference between the cash value to the recipient and the total Federal cost) are not provided to the rest of society by the provision of a Section 235 home. Because social benefits are almost impossible to measure, however, this estimate can be used by policymakers as a benchmark to determine the amount of social benefits required in order for the program to be Socially Efficient. Overall, the Section 235 program would have had to produce about $71 million in social benefits in 1972 to be deemed Socially Efficient.

Program Viability

The latest simulations conducted for the program, based on 4 years of experience—and the last 26 years of the Section 203(b) basic mortgage insurance program—indicated that the insurance fund for Section 235 was actuarially sound but at the break-even point. A final default termination rate of 18.6 percent has been calculated and an average life expectancy of 16.1 years generated.

Other data indicate that the average loss to HUD from a default termination is now $4,350 per unit, a figure at the maximum of the 25 percent loss rate sustainable by the mortgage insurance premium given a final default termination rate of 18.6 percent. Therefore, as long as foreclosures and acquisition losses do not increase beyond present estimates, the Section 235 program can be regarded as actuarially sound. The most recent data on foreclosures and acquisition costs, however, have indicated that the fund may become actuarially unsound.

THE SECTION 236 PROGRAM

The Section 236 rental and cooperative housing program authorized by the 1968 act involves the Government in three activities: stimulating housing production; subsidizing housing for rental by low and moderate income families; and insuring multifamily mortgages. The first and third of these activities are designed to promote the second, which is the ultimate goal of the program.

All Section 236 projects are privately owned and financed. FHA mortgage insurance encourages the participation of private lenders by greatly reducing their risks. When the FHA interest ceiling is below the market interest rate, an additional subsidy (GNMA Tandem Plan) is often necessary to obtain private financing. Any nonprofit organization, tenant cooperative group, corporation, partnership, or individual may become the sponsor (owner) of a project. An individual, or profitmaking corporation or partnership, must limit its cash return to 6 percent of invested equity. For this reason, profitmaking entities are called limited dividend sponsors. In addition to their allowed rate of return, investors in limited dividend projects also benefit from special tax advantages and other op-

TABLE 4
Characteristics of the Section 236 Program, 1972
(Including Projects with Units Under Rent Supplement)

Units assisted through December 31, 1972* (Finally endorsed)	142,000
Total mortgage amounts through December 31, 1972* (Finally endorsed)	$2.2 billion
Maximum annual subsidies permitted by law through fiscal year 1973 (Contract authority released in appropriations)	$700 million
Units in process and units finished processing at the end of fiscal year 1973* (Reservations and obligations of contract authority)	451,000
Units completed, by sponsor type:	
Limited dividend	62%
Nonprofit	31%
Cooperative	7%
Median mortgage amount per unit	$16,700
Median income of new tenants	$5,300
Racial and ethnic composition of new tenants:	
Nonminority white	76%
Black	20%
Spanish American	3%
Other	1%

*Excludes units financed through State and local programs and not insured by FHA.
Source: Department of Housing and Urban Development.

portunities for profit during the development of a project. In exchange for its direct regulation of rents and a general determination of tenant eligibility, the Federal Government agrees to subsidize a Section 236 project by paying the difference in monthly installments between (a) amortization of the mortgage at the FHA ceiling interest rate plus FHA insurance premium and (b) amortization at 1 percent.

To be eligible for a Section 236 subsidy, a family's income must be no more than 135 percent of the income limit for low rent public housing in that particular area at the time of initial occupancy. Income is adjusted for family size and limited exceptions to this income rule are permitted. Two rents are associated with each program unit. The "market rent" is equal to the sum of operating expenses, amortization of that portion of the mortgage associated with the unit at the FHA ceiling interest rate, and the mortgage insurance payment. The "basic rent" is equal to operation expenses plus amortization at 1 percent interest. The tenant family must pay the "basic rent," or 25 percent of its adjusted monthly income, whichever is greater. In no case is it required to pay more than the "market rent." The sponsor must turn over to HUD all rent receipts in excess of "basic rent."

A limited percentage of Section 236 families can receive an additional rent supplement subsidy. This "piggybacking" of subsidy benefits substantially increases the depth of the subsidy, with minimum tenant rent falling to 30 percent of the basic rent.

Table 4 provides some general information on the program: its magnitude, project types, and tenant characteristics.

Major Findings

1. The Section 236 program provides sizable Federal housing subsidies, mainly to moderate income households.
2. The Section 236 program serves less than 1 percent of all households earning less than $8,000 per year.
3. Tenants occupy units that are about 50 percent better than the housing they would have occupied in the absence of the program. Expenditures on nonhousing goods have changed little.
4. The "market rent" of a Section 236 unit is higher, on average, than the rent charged for an identical unit in the private market.
5. On average, Section 236 units cost about 20 percent more to construct than comparable privately financed units.
6. Federal costs exceed the market value of the housing provided to the tenant by approximately 40 percent in the regular program and approximately 20 percent in the Section 236 rent supplement "piggyback" program.
7. The main reason Federal costs exceed market value is that Section 236 units are not rent-competitive with identical private units and so the direct subsidy is spent inefficiently. The additional costs of foregone tax revenue, administrative overhead, and foreclosure losses also contribute to the excess of costs over housing value.
8. A Section 236 subsidy is worth only 65 to 70 percent as much to a tenant as its market value because the subsidized unit provided is better housing than he would choose if given a cash grant equal to the subsidy.
9. Tenant welfare is increased by only about 50 cents for every dollar spent because Federal costs are higher than the value of the housing provided and because the tenant places a lower value on the transfer in-kind benefit than on an unrestricted cash grant.
10. Approximately 20 percent of all Section 236 units are expected to fail in the first 10 years of operation. The program does not appear to be actuarially sound.

TABLE 5
Distribution of Section 236 (Including 236 Rent Supplement) Housing,
by Income Class, as of December 31, 1972

(1)	(2)	(3)	(4)	(5)	(6)
	Households Served by 236		236		Direct
			Households		Annual
		Percent	as Percent		Subsidy Per
		Distri-	of all	Residential	Household
Gross Income	Number	bution	Households	Need*	Served
$ 0- 999	220	0.2	0.01	—	$956
1,000-1,999	3,200	2.3	0.08	1,800,000	974
2,000-2,999	11,590	8.2	0.27	5,300,000	1,081
3,000-3,999	16,980	12.0	0.43	9,300,000	1,021
4,000-4,999	28,370	20.1	0.74	13,100,000	980
5,000-5,999	33,710	23.9	0.90	16,700,000	1,011
6,000-6,999	26,290	18.6	0.73	20,300,000	1,093
7,000-7,999	13,590	9.6	0.35	23,700,000	1,233
8,000-9,999	6,410	4.5	0.09	27,400,000	1,455
10,000 or more	640	0.5	Less than 0.005	34,600,000	1,189

*Number of households living in unsubsidized housing earning less than lower limit for that income class, as given in column 1.

Source: Department of Housing and Urban Development, National Housing Policy Review estimates based on data from Department of Housing and Urban Development, Department of Agriculture and Department of Commerce, Bureau of the Census, *Current Population Reports*, Series P-60, Nos. 84 and 87, and *1970 Census of Population*.

Equity

Table 5 shows the distribution of Section 236 tenants on the basis of unadjusted family income. The percentages are based on recent tenant admissions, but earlier admissions show a similar pattern. Unadjusted income was used to allow for comparisons with Census data.

Almost three-quarters of all Section 236 tenant families have annual incomes in the $4,000 to $8,000 range. This distribiution is the result of the program's predominant reliance on newly constructed units and the limited size of the subsidy.[4] Another factor has also diminished the extent to which the program has been able to serve those earning below $4,000: Sponsors have an incentive to serve families that have steady income and are able to afford the rent easily. They may also avoid "problem" tenants. This policy reduces management problems, insures a steady flow of rent receipts, and allows flexibility in raising rents when operating costs increase.[5] Limited dividend sponsors may be more responsive to these incentives. A random sample of projects revealed that the average income of tenants in limited dividend projects is higher by 28 percent than the average income of tenants in nonprofit projects.

The probability of receiving a Section 236 subsidy increases with income through the $5,000 to $6,000 annual income range and declines beyond that (Table 5, column 4). The differences between these percentages are small, however, and may be simply the result of normal variation.

Column 5 of Table 5 delineates the number of Census households in each income group who, although eligible to participate in the programs, are not residents of federally subsidized housing and who earn less than the lower limit of that income group. Although 57 percent of all Section 236 program units are occupied by families with gross annual incomes in excess of $5,000, there are 16.7 million households with lower incomes who do not receive any housing subsidy whatsoever. There are also 13.1 million households earning less than $4,000 who are not living in subsidized housing. In considering these figures, two facts must be noted. Not all households would accept subsidized housing if it were offered to them. Secondly, many of the Section 236 households with incomes above $4,000 or $5,000 may be more needy than some of the unserved households with lower incomes, because of larger household size, limited future income prospects, fewer assets, or because of other reasons. Unfortunately, the data cannot be adjusted to account for these factors. For the same reason, however, some of the unserved households may even be more needy than their income suggests.

The overwhelming majority of all Section 236 tenants earn less than the national median household income ($9,689 in March 1973). The direct benefits accrue chiefly to the $4,000 plus group. Other subsidized housing programs—rent supplement and low rent public housing—serve lower income groups. Deeper subsidies and simpler units explain the differences in population served.

Column 6 of Table 5 indicates that the average Section 236 program subsidy increases slightly and irregularly with income. This result is surprising, because the rent formula indicates that tenant rent increases with income. Most Section 236 program families received the maximum benefits for which they are eligible, i.e. the full difference between market rent and basic rent. The size of this maximum benefit depends upon land and construction costs per unit. Total development costs also determine the income groups that can afford to live in the projects: all tenants, except those with rent supplements, must legally pay at least the basic rent. As a result, projects with high total development costs have higher maximum benefits and serve higher income people; projects with lower total development costs can serve lower income persons but also have lower maximum benefits. Given this interpretation, local differences in development costs could produce the effects noted in Column 6.

Column 4 shows the percentage of households served in each income group. The Section 236 program provides housing for less than 1 percent of families in each income group, even those in the $5,000 to $7,999 range. The ability to

TABLE 6
Monthly Rent Comparison*

Location	Census Mean Gross Rent, 1970	Renter Costs Family of Four BLS Lower Budget, 1972	Average 236 Market Rent, 1972-1973	
			New	Rehab.
Boston	$135	$124	$272	$225
Washington, D.C.	134	117	239	219
Pittsburgh	110	90	251	238
St. Louis	97	94	249	NA
San Francisco	144	130	249	NA
National average	$118	$103†	$208‡	

NA - Not available.
*Including utilities.
†Metropolitan areas only.
‡Based on new admissions, October 1, 1971 to September 30, 1972.
Source: Department of Housing and Urban Development, National Housing Policy Review estimates based on data from Department of Housing and Urban Development, Department of Commerce, Bureau of the Census, *1970 Census of Housing* and Department of Labor, Bureau of Labor Statistics.

serve a large percentage of the needy depends on the average cost per family and on the total level of program funding. Benefits per household under Section 236 are substantial; the average annual subsidy being $907 for a regular unit and $1,757 for a rent supplement piggyback unit. The units are generally more expensive than the average unsubsidized unit. Table 6 compares average Section 236 market rents in five cities with the mean private rent in 1970 and with the Bureau of Labor Statistics estimates of renter costs in its lower budget for a family of four. The national data show a similar pattern. If simpler units could be provided at a smaller subsidy cost per family, then more families could be served from the same budget. Even taking into account that the market rent frequently overstates the quality of the unit (see below), Section 236 units are of higher quality than the average private unit.

Impact

The strategy of the Section 236 program is to relieve housing problems of lower income families by offering them units that provide more housing services than they could purchase with the same rent in the private rental market.[6]

How much "extra housing" does the average tenant family receive? This quantity is measured by the difference between what the Section 236 unit would rent for in the open market and the rent paid by the tenant.

The average subsidy is $907 per year. The average subsidy when the piggyback mechanism of rent supplement is applied is $1,757. These figures, in effect, for the reasons noted above, measure the average difference between market rents (the cost of constructing and operating a unit) and tenant rents. It may cost more, however, to provide a subsidized unit than a conventional unit. Therefore, the stated market rent of a unit may be more than the actual rent that could be demanded for that unit on the open market. In that case, the average subsidy exaggerates the "extra housing" received by the tenant. In fact, the analysis for the Section 236 program establishes that the average tenant in a Section 236 unit without rent supplements receives $703 in extra housing services per year. In the Section 236 piggyback program, the average quantity of extra housing consumed is $1,537.

Another important issue is whether the tenant family is living in better housing under the program than it would have in the absence of the program. On the basis of a sample of tenants and information on how low income persons spend their incomes, it is possible to determine how the program affects the tenant's level of housing. This computation was performed only for the Section 236 program, without rent supplement. In this computation, the average tenant family improves its housing services 51 percent under the program. Expenditures on other goods, however, are virtually unaffected. These results indicate that the program is having the desired impact on the families served—at least in terms of housing. These families are receiving a substantial quantity of "extra housing" and this addition represents a major shift in the quality of housing they occupy, without loss of other goods.

Although society as a whole may benefit from this sharp improvement in housing relative to other goods, the individual Section 236 family may prefer instead a subsidy that consists of somewhat less housing and more other goods. For example, if the tenant family were given a cash grant equal to the housing subsidy, it might elect to spend only 30 percent on housing and the other 70 percent on other goods. The inflexible nature of the transfer-in-kind mandated under the program results in the subsidy being worth less than its cash value to the tenant. The average cash grant equivalent for Section 236 families is approximately $499, which is roughly 70 percent of the market value of the extra housing provided. The cash grant that the tenant would require in exchange for his Section 236 rent supplement subsidy is substantially larger in dollar terms, but is not larger when measured against the extra housing provided. The estimated cash grant is $984—64 percent of the market value of the extra housing provided to Section 236 rent supplement families.

Costs

Besides direct subsidy payments, there are four other costs that must be considered in determining the actual total cost to the Federal Government of a Sec-

TABLE 7
Annual Costs Per Section 236 Unit, 1972

Cost Item	236	236 Rent Supplement
Direct subsidy (Including insurance premium)	$ 907	$1,757
Foreclosure costs (Net of insurance income)	29	29
Administrative Costs	16	16
Subtotal	952	1,802
Tax revenue foregone (Limited dividends only)	99	99
Total	$1,051	$1,901

Source: Department of Housing and Urban Development, National Housing Policy Review.

tion 236 unit (Table 7). In the case of limited dividend sponsors, the tax shelter inducements reduce Federal tax revenues and thus impose a budgetary cost. The GNMA Tandem Plan subsidy and HUD administrative costs also must be taken into account. Finally, the insurance losses caused by the financial failure of projects must be measured. Many of these costs occur irregularly. To facilitate cost-benefit analysis, a fair share of these costs should be allocated to the year being studied. The technique used is to determine the extent of the irregular costs over the life of a project, to discount those costs to the initial year, and, finally, to amortize the sum of those costs over the life of the project.

For units completed through 1972, GNMA Tandem Plan losses were relatively small and may be ignored. This situation may change in the future because of recent deviations between the FHA ceiling and the going market rate of interest for mortgages. Administrative expenditures are also small. It costs $139 in HUD personnel time and overhead to initiate a program unit under Section 236. It costs another $6 a year to monitor the unit. Amortized at a 6 percent discount rate over 35 years (the estimated subsidy life of a typical unit), administrative costs are only $16 a year.

Tax revenue losses for Section 236 projects are a result of several tax shelter inducements. First, certain construction period expenses can be taken as immediate deductions rather than capitalized in the project mortgage for future depreciation. Second, during the operation of the project, the cost basis of the project may be depreciated on an accelerated basis.[7] This usually results in an artificial loss that can shelter other income of the taxpayer-investor. The high loan-to-value ratio and low cash equity required for a Section 236 project provide the investor-taxpayer with a greater ratio of depreciation dollar losses to equity invested than for a conventional project. Third, upon transfer of a Section 236 project, the rate of taxation of gain can be more favorable than for other real property. Moreover, the tax on such gain can be deferred if the project owners transfer it in accordance with the "rollover provision" of the Internal Revenue Code.

Estimates of the tax revenue foregone to induce the participation of limited dividend sponsors have been made.[8] These estimates vary with the assumptions about the availability and rate of return of other tax shelters and the typical point at which a sponsor will sell a project to maximize its returns. A reasonable estimate is that foregone tax revenue—or, from the standpoint of the sponsors, tax savings—for a typical Section 236 limited dividend unit may total $1,446.[9] Amortized at 6 percent over 35 years, the average annual tax loss per limited dividend unit was $99 (Table 7).

Estimates of the losses due to insurance claims on the FHA Special Risk Fund also were made. If these losses are allocated over all units and amortized, the annual cost per unit is $86. Adding this loss to other program costs would involve some double-counting, however. The direct subsidy payment includes an insurance payment that the Government, in essence, makes to itself. Adjusting for this premium income, the annual net foreclosure cost per unit is $29.

Efficiency

Is subsidized housing competitive in price? In 1971, HUD's audit office reviewed Section 236 projects in 21 cities. Each project was matched with two similar conventional projects, and the "market rents" for the Section 236 units were compared to rents of conventional units with the same number of bedrooms. The rents were adjusted for differences in amenities. The survey's data indicate that the market rents of the Section 236 units were 10 percent higher than conventional rents. No adjustments were made for differences in neighborhood quality, but it was the opinion of those conducting the survey that such adjustments would have increased the disparity in rents.

The HUD audit survey is consistent with the results of a special study of construction costs in three regions undertaken in June 1973. This study shows that it cost $3 per square foot, or 20 percent more, to build a subsidized unit than to construct a similar conventional unit.

With information on both costs and benefits, it is possible to determine the efficiency of the program. One important question is how much cost is incurred by the Government to provide the "extra housing" to the tenants. That relationship, which has been defined as Production Efficiency, will differ between Section 236 units with rent supplement payments and regular Section 236 units, and between units in limited dividend projects and units in nonprofit projects. Results of all four possibilities are reported in Table 8.

As Table 8 shows, Production Efficiency varies from 0.67 to 0.85. The lower

TABLE 8
Production Efficiency of the Section 236 Program, 1972

236 without Rent Supplement	
Nonprofits and cooperatives	0.74
Limited dividends	0.67
236 Rent Supplement	
Nonprofits and cooperatives	0.85
Limited dividends	0.81

Source: Department of Housing and Urban Development, National Housing Policy Review.

efficiency for limited dividend sponsors may not be accurate because limited dividend projects seem to have better foreclosure experience. It was not possible to make separate foreclosure cost estimates for limited dividend sponsors.

Production inefficiency can arise from two sources: (1) the indirect costs that accompany the subsidy payments, such as administrative costs and foregone tax revenue, and (2) inefficiency in transforming the subsidy payment into extra housing for the recipient. The second source accounts for approximately 60 percent of the total Section 236 inefficiency.

Earlier it was noted that the "market rent" of Section 236 units is approximately 10 percent more than the rent of similar conventional units. This inefficiency is magnified by a production strategy that requires a family to move into a newly constructed unit rather than to upgrade its present unit. For example, consider a family living in a $120 apartment; society wishes this family to be housed in a unit worth $200. If its present unit could be satisfactorily improved by repairs and modernization with $80, an inefficiency of 10 percent in making such improvements would make the direct cost to the Government $88. The Section 236 program, however, does not improve housing in this way. Instead, the family moves into a subsidized project where a unit that would cost $200 if built for the conventional market costs the Government $220. If the family continues to pay a rent of $120, then the direct cost to the Government to improve the family's housing by $80 is $100. The inefficiency is 25 percent, rather than 10 percent.

The Production Efficiency estimates for the Section 236 rent supplement program are lower because of the deeper subsidy. In the above example, the unit costs the Government $20 more than it is worth. If the subsidy were deeper (for example, if the family's rent were only $90), then this absolute loss would be spread over a large transfer. It would cost the Government $130 to provide $110 worth of housing, an inefficiency of only 18 percent.

The Transfer Efficiency estimates show that the average Section 236 tenant family implicitly values its transfer-in-kind at only 71 percent of its market value and the average Section 236 rent supplement tenant family implicitly values its transfer-in-kind at only 64 percent of its market value.

TABLE 9
Section 236 Efficiency, 1972

Type of Sponsor	Production	Transfer	Program
236 without Rent Supplement			
Nonprofits and			
cooperatives	.74	.71	.52
Limited			
dividends	.67	.71	.47
236 Rent Supplement			
Nonprofits and			
cooperatives	.85	.64	.55
Limited			
dividends	.81	.64	.52

Source: Department of Housing and Urban Development, National Housing Policy Review.

Finally, Program Efficiency indicates how much overall benefit tenants receive in relation to the costs incurred by the Government (Table 9). This ratio ranges from 0.47 to 0.55. In other words, for every $100 in expenditures or tax revenues foregone, the Federal Government improves tenant welfare only $47 to $55.

Program Viability

It is difficult to predict with accuracy what experience the Section 236 program will have with respect to mortgage foreclosures and assignments. Data exist on the program's 5 years of operation, and other data can be obtained for a similar program (Section 221(d)(3) below-market-interest-rate rental housing) through the first 10 years of operation. After that point, forecasts must be based on the experience of an unsubsidized FHA multifamily program (Section 207). The evidence available suggests that approximately 20 percent of all units will fail within the first 10 years. Over 40 years—the life of mortgages issued under the program—the failure rate may be 30 percent or more. This longer-run prediction is obviously less reliable because it is based on the experience of a nonsubsidized FHA program (Section 207).

As of December 31, 1972, HUD owned six Section 236 projects and held assigned mortgages on 60 more—about 2 percent of all insured projects. No foreclosed Section 236 projects had as yet been sold, so estimates of loss in turnover must be based on the experience of another subsidized program. For the Section 221(d)(3) below-market-interest-rate program, the average loss on the acquisition and sale of a unit was approximately 45 percent of the acquisition costs. These projects were held for periods of up to 3 years, and, on the average, rental receipts failed to cover operating costs and maintenance expenditures.

TABLE 10
Characteristics of the Rent Supplement Program, 1972

Units assisted through December 31, 1972* (finally endorsed)	77,000
Total mortgage amounts through December 31, 1972* (finally endorsed)	$1.0 Billion
Maximum annual subsidies permitted by law through fiscal year 1973 (contract authority released in appropriations)	$280 Million
Units in process and units finished processing at the end of fiscal year 1973† (reservations and obligations of contract authority)	119,000
Median income of new tenants	$2,400
Racial and ethnic composition of new tenants:	
Nonminority white	44%
Black	44%
Spanish American	6%
Other	6%

*Excludes units in Section 236 projects. Excludes units financed through State and local programs and not insured by FHA. Includes all units in other rent supplemented projects even where some units may not receive a rent supplement.

†Excludes units in Section 236 Projects. Excludes units financed through State and local programs and not insured by FHA.

Source: Department of Housing and Urban Development.

THE RENT SUPPLEMENT PROGRAM

Although not a production program itself, the rent supplement program always is used in conjunction with Government housing production programs. These include the Section 221(d)(3) market-rate program; Section 236; Section 221(d)(3) below-market-rate; and Section 231 insurance for multifamily projects serving the elderly or handicapped. Section 236 piggybacks were discussed earlier, and because the Section 221(d)(3) below-market-rate and Section 231 combinations are rare, this section will deal exclusively with the combination of rent supplement and the Section 221(d)(3) market-rate program.

The Section 221(d)(3) market-rate program does not subsidize, by itself, the production of multifamily housing. It does provide, however, important inducements to build such housing—a high loan-to-value ratio, a 40-year mortgage, mortgage insurance, special tax advantages, and, in some cases in the past, Tandem Plan assistance.

The rent supplement provides the subsidy in the form of a contract through which the Government agrees to make monthly rent payments on behalf of the tenant. In exchange, the landlord agrees to obtain HUD's approval of rent changes. To be eligible for a rent supplement subsidy, a family must earn, at initial occupancy, less than the local limit for admission to low rent public housing. In addition, the family must satisfy one or more hardship criteria such as (1) having an elderly or handicapped household head as spouse; (2) having a veteran or member of the armed forces; or (3) having been displaced from an urban renewal location.

Each unit has an "economic rent," which is the sum necessary to cover the operating and capital costs associated with that unit. The tenant family is required to pay 25 percent of its income or 30 percent of the "economic rent," whichever is greater. Income is adjusted for family size and tenant rent cannot exceed the "economic rent."

Table 10 provides some basic background information on the program.

Major Findings

1. The rent supplement program serves mainly low income households.
2. Sizable subsidies are provided to rent supplement tenants while many low income households receive no assistance. The rent supplement program serves less than 1 percent of all households earning less than $4,000 per year.
3. There is evidence that the "economic rent" for a Section 221(d)(3) market-rate rent supplement unit is higher than rents for similar units in the private market.
4. Federal costs exceed the market value of the housing provided by approximately 30 percent in the Section 221(d)(3) market-rate rent supplement program.
5. The main reason Federal costs exceed market value is that Section 221(d)(3) market-rate rent supplement units are not rent-competitive with identical private units and therefore the direct subsidy is spent inefficiently. Foregone tax revenue, administrative costs, and foreclosure costs also contribute to the excess of costs over housing value.
6. Forecasts indicate that about 30 percent of all Section 221(d)(3) market-rate rent supplement units will fail in the first 10 years. The program does not appear to be actuarially sound.

Equity

Table 11 shows that most tenants benefiting from the rent supplement program have very low incomes, 82 percent of them below $4,000 in annual income. The probability of being served by the program (Column 4) declines as income increases, but the differences probably are too small to be significant. The rent supplement program is able to serve low income groups for two reasons. First,

TABLE 11

Distribution of Rent Supplement (Excluding 236 Rent Supplement) Housing, by Income Class, as of December 31, 1972

(1)	(2)	(3)	(4)	(5)	(6)
	Households Served By Rent Supplement		Rent Supplement Households as Percent of all Households	Residual Need*	Direct Annual Subsidy Per Household Served
Gross Income	Number	Percent Distri- bution			
$ 0- 999	2,150	2.8	0.13	—	$1,342
1,000-1,999	24,200	31.9	0.63	1,800,000	1,427
2,000-2,999	19,740	26.0	0.46	5,300,000	1,503
3,000-3,999	15,870	20.9	0.40	9,300,000	1,511
4,000-4,999	8,850	11.7	0.23	13,100,000	1,582
5,000-5,999	3,540	4.7	0.09	16,700,000	1,773
6,000-6,999	1,170	1.5	0.03	20,300,000	1,845
7,000-7,999	330	0.4	Less than 0.005	23,700,000	1,744
8,000-9,999	120	0.2	Less than 0.005	27,400,000	1,738
10,000 or more	30	Less than 0.05	Less than 0.005	34,600,000	1,392

Note: Detail may not add to totals because of rounding.

*Number of households living in unsubsidized housing earning less than lower limit for that income class, as given in column 1.

Source: Department of Housing and Urban Development, National Housing Policy Review estimates based on data from Department of Housing and Urban Development, Department of Agriculture, and Department of Commerce. Bureau of the Census, *Current Population Reports*, Series P-60, Nos. 84 and 87, and *1970 Census of Population.*

the subsidy formula allows the Government to subsidize a larger share of the rent, thus requiring a smaller contribution on the part of the tenant. Secondly, units built under the Section 221(d)(3) market-rate program are simpler in amenities than the typical Section 236 unit. In 1971, the average Section 221(d)(3) market-rate mortgage was $13,818, compared to $16,304 under Section 236.

Column 6 of Table 11 shows that the average subsidy increases slightly and irregularly with income.

Horizontal equity is again a problem in the sense that the rent supplement program provides extensive benefits to relatively few families while most receive no assistance. Table 11, Column 5 shows that there are 13.1 million families unserved with annual incomes of less than $4,000. There are two ways to solve this equity problem—either the rent supplement program can be funded at a substantially higher level, or an alternate technique can be found that will provide assistance to more families but at less cost per family. Table 12 indicates, for a sample of four cities, the extent to which the "economic rent" for the typical Section

TABLE 12
Monthly Rent Comparisons*

Location	Census Mean Gross Rent, 1970	Renter Costs Family of Four BLS Lower Budget, 1972	Average 221(d)(3) MR Economic Rent 1972–1973†
Boston	$135	$124	$205
Washington, D.C.	134	117	186
Pittsburgh	110	90	163
St. Louis	97	94	191

*Including utilities.
†New construction only.
Source: Department of Housing and Urban Development, National Housing Policy Review estimates based on data from Department of Housing and Urban Development, Department of Commerce, Bureau of the Census, 1970 *Census of Housing,* and Department of Labor, Bureau of Labor Statistics.

TABLE 13
Annual Costs Per Section 221 (d)(3) Market-Rate Rent Supplement Unit, 1972

Cost Item	Amount
Direct subsidy (including insurance premium)	$1,133
Foreclosure costs (Net of insurance income)	70
Administrative costs	15
Subtotal	$1,218
Tax revenue foregone (Limited dividends only)	92
Total	$1,310

Source: Department of Housing and Urban Development, National Housing Policy Review.

221(d)(3) market-rate unit exceeds the rent for the average private unit or the unit satisfying the housing needs specified in the Bureau of Labor Statistics lower budget for a family of four. Even taking into account that the economic rent frequently overstates the quality of the unit (see below), these units are of higher quality than the average private unit.

Impact

The average rent supplement subsidy in combination with the Section 221(d)(3) market-rate program is $1,133 per year. This deeper subsidy, combined with a less costly unit, results in the Government's paying a larger share of the total unit rent than is the case under Section 236—55 percent compared to 40 percent.

One notable consequence of the deeper subsidy is that the tenant receives more housing services. The average annual transfer-in-kind is $948. In other words, the family receives about $80 more housing per month than it purchases with its own rent. It cannot be determined, however, how much the rent supplement subsidy alters the normal consumption pattern of a recipient family. Data comparable to those used in the Section 236 analysis do not exist. Similarly, there is no information on how much value the family attaches to its subsidy; as a result, it cannot be determined how much impact the program has on the family's welfare.

Costs

In addition to the direct subsidy, there are four other costs that must be considered in calculating the total costs to the Federal Government in providing this transfer-in-kind. These are: (1) Tandem Plan subsidies; (2) administrative costs; (3) insurance claims; and (4) foregone tax revenue (Table 13).

Here, as in the Section 236 program, all cost and benefit data refer to projects completed prior to December 31, 1972. For those projects, GNMA Tandem Plan subsidies were minimal and can be ignored. HUD's internal reporting system collects information on administrative costs for the Section 221 program as a whole. Because this includes data on unsubsidized projects, and because of certain other shortcomings, it seems better to rely on the Section 236 administrative cost data as an indication of costs under the Section 221(d)(3) market-rate program.

Computer simulation of the rent supplement program suggests that the subsidy will be in effect for the full 40 years of the contract. Therefore, the initial administrative costs have been amortized over 40 years. These costs plus the annual monitoring costs total only $15 per year.

Because of a higher failure rate, insurance claims are projected to be larger under the rent supplement Section 221(d)(3) market-rate program than under Section 236. The extra 5 years of subsidy life temper this increase somewhat. The annual per unit allocation of foreclosure costs is $115. After adjustment for premium income, the annual per-unit cost is $70. Here, as in the case of the Section 236 program, the foreclosure calculations imply that the present insurance premium is not large enough to cover anticipated losses over the life of the program.

Limited dividend sponsors of Section 221(d)(3) market-rate enjoy the same tax advantages given to Section 236 sponsors. Because of the lower development cost per unit and the longer period over which to amortize the cost, the average annual cost estimate for foregone tax revenue under the Section 221(d)(3) market-rate program is $92, compared to $99 under Section 236.[10]

Efficiency

The rent supplement program always is combined with a production program, usually either Section 221(d)(3) market-rate or Section 236. Therefore, the effectiveness of the rent supplement program depends on the price competitiveness of the Government-sponsored housing program that it supplements.

As reported in analyzing the Section 236 program, construction costs average 20 percent more for federally subsidized multifamily projects than for conventional units of equal quality. This estimate was obtained from a sample that included both Section 236 and Section 221(d)(3) market-rate units.

The most useful measure of competitiveness is a rent comparison. The "economic rent" of a rent supplement unit is the monthly income necessary to cover the cost of building and operating the unit. If the economic rent is higher than the rent for an identical unit on the private market, then the production program is inefficient and the impact of the rent supplement subsidy is reduced. To make this rent comparison, data on Section 221(d)(3) market-rate units in four cities were collected and compared with private rents for similar units in these cities. These results suggest that Section 221(d)(3) market-rate units are as competitive as Section 236 units. Therefore, the audit finding that Section 236 rents are 10 percent higher than rents on the private market could be applied to the Section 221(d)(3) market-rate rent supplement program as a reasonable approximation.

A series of factors may explain the higher rents observed in both the Section 236 and the Section 221(d)(3) market-rate programs. FHA processing, as a result (at least in part) of the numerous statutory requirements, involves significant paperwork and causes delays at the initial stage, adding to costs. There are undoubtedly instances where the Government has permitted higher land costs or service fees than are typical in conventional building. The Davis-Bacon requirement may increase labor costs in some markets. Concentration of low income families may raise operating costs. Better loan terms, particularly with regard to length of mortgage, partially offset these other factors.

Lack of price competitiveness has a double impact on the rent supplement program. First, the Government subsidy buys less housing. Second, the tenant's own rent contribution is inefficient. Accordingly, part of the subsidy payment must reimburse the tenant family for the loss of efficiency in its own payment. The remaining subsidy is used to buy extra housing for the family.

Having estimated the extra housing provided and the various costs incurred, it is possible to measure Production Efficiency. For nonprofit and cooperative sponsors, the costs incurred were those involving the direct subsidy, administrative costs, and foreclosure costs. These totaled $1,218 which—when divided into the extra housing provided ($948)—yield a Production Efficiency of 0.78. In the case of limited dividend sponsors, foregone tax revenue was also included among the costs. The Production Efficiency ratio then became 0.72. Thus, for every $100 in tax revenue (expended directly or foregone indirectly), the Government could provide between \$72 and \$78 of extra housing under the Section 221(d)(3) market-rate rent supplement program.

It was not possible to estimate Transfer Efficiency for the rent supplement program. If the estimate obtained for Section 236 rent supplement (0.64) were used, the overall Program Efficiency could be estimated. The ratio of benefits (determined on the cash-grant-equivalent basis discussed earlier) to total cost is in the range of 0.46 to 0.50. This means that through the rent supplement Section 221(d)(3) market-rate program, the Government increased tenant welfare by only \$46 to \$50 for every \$100 in costs or foregone taxes.

Program Viability

The longer operating experience of the Section 221(d)(3) market-rate program provides a better data base for estimating foreclosures than was available for the Section 236 program. It is estimated that during the first 10 years of insured life, approximately 30 percent of all Section 221(d)(3) market-rate projects will fail. Projections further into the future must rely on the experience of unsubsidized FHA multifamily housing, and therefore, may be much less reliable. The percentage of financial failures over 40 years—the full term of a Section 221(d)(3) mortgage—is estimated to be approximately 40 percent.

As in the case of the Section 236 program, no foreclosed Section 221(d)(3) market-rate property had as yet been sold. To estimate the Government's loss in the acquisition and sale of foreclosed properties, it was necessary to use the experience of another subsidized program, Section 221(d)(3) below-market-interest-rate. The Government loses approximately 45 percent of the acquisition price on the turnover of these properties. As in the case of the Section 236 program, rent receipts from foreclosed projects are insufficient to cover their operating costs and maintenance expenditures.

The high failure rates reflect the riskiness of the undertaking. Concentrating low income families in one project tends to create problems that add to the costs of operating and maintaining a multifamily structure.

NOTES

1. U.S. Congress, *Report of the House Committee on Banking and Currency on H.R. 17989*, House Report No. 1585, Washington, D.C.: Government Printing Office, 1968.
2. Craig Swan, "Housing Subsidies and Housing Starts," Washington, D.C.: Federal Home Loan Bank Board, Working Paper No. 43, April 1973. This point is discussed later, in the section entitled "Impact on the Housing Stock."
3. Department of Housing and Urban Development Regions III, VI, and IX, Tri-Regional Study conducted for the National Housing Policy Review, June 1973.
4. HUD program data indicates that the great majority of all Section 236 tenants pay only the basic rent. Reliable information as to whether the combination of Section 236 and rent supplement benefits has enabled lower income families to afford Section 236 units is unavailable.
5. When confronted with a potentially serious mortgage default problem, HUD acquiesced in such selectivity and tried to limit participation in the program to families who could afford the basic

rent with less than 35 percent of their monthly income. This regulation was negated by a court ruling.

6. The term "housing problems" refers either to having inadequate housing or to paying an excessive share of the family budget for adequate housing.

7. The Administration's new tax proposal would diminish sharply the advantages of taking accelerated depreciation. Although this change would reduce the revenue loss of limited dividend projects, it would also eliminate a major inducement for participation in the program, because sponsors depreciate their investments rapidly in the first few years, thereby substantially offsetting income from the project or, more importantly, other investments or activities.

8. The tax revenue foregone from all tax shelter advantages, including those available to the conventional builders, was eliminated. It was assumed that in the absence of the program, other tax shelter activity would not have expanded. This overstates to some extent the taxes foregone by reason of the program because in the absence of the program investors would have sought other tax "shelter."

9. Future income was discounted in computing the sum.

10. Foregone tax revenue was estimated in the same manner as in the case of the Section 236 program.

20

Housing Allowances: An Experiment That Worked

Bernard J. Frieden

One of the biggest social experiments ever undertaken, the Department of Housing and Urban Development's experimental housing allowance program began with great fanfare in 1973 and is ending quietly in 1979-1980. It has involved more than 25,000 families in 12 metropolitan areas, at a cost that is expected to add up to $160 million. As is true of most ambitious programs, it owes its origins to the convergence of several different lines of thought on how government should cope with a problem. The problem in this case was how to improve housing conditions for low-income people. Two key ideas prompted the experiment. One was that the best way to help families who needed better housing was to give them money that they could use on their own, instead of building subsidized housing for them. The other was that the best way to learn how a new approach would work in practice was to conduct a large-scale social experiment, following a systematic design and using control groups to check the validity of the results.

Six years later, the data coming off the computers do not provide clear-cut answers to all the questions that were investigated, since the realities of human behavior turned out to be more complicated than the designers of the experiment had assumed. But the experiment produced unexpected results that challenge the traditional conception of low-income housing problems and reveal a sharp conflict between the priorities of federal officials and those of poor families.

Reprinted with permission of the author from THE PUBLIC INTEREST, No. 59 (Spring, 1980), pp. 15-35. © 1980 by National Affairs, Inc.

TROUBLED SUBSIDY PROGRAMS

The underlying cause of the housing allowance experiment was widespread disillusionment with the conventional approach to subsidizing housing for the poor.[1] Ever since the mid-1930's, housing reformers and their political allies had favored a construction strategy. This meant using federal subsidies to build new housing which was then made available to poor people at below-market rents. A series of housing acts from 1937 through the mid-1960's had established first low-rent public housing and then several variations of it, all following essentially the same approach. Yet the flooding tide of housing legislation produced only a trickle of housing. The main problem with this strategy (as has also been said of Christianity) was not that it had been tried and found wanting, but that it had never been tried—at least not on a scale large enough to put it to a real test. Then, in the special political climate of the late 1960's Congress enacted the landmark Housing Act of 1968, interpreted by many as a memorial to Martin Luther King. This act set up two important construction programs backed by the usual federal subsidies. One (known as Section 236) offered rental housing, and the other (Section 235) offered home-ownership opportunities for low- and moderate-income families. Both were designed to attract developers and investors in the hope that private sector involvement would generate a high volume of construction commensurate with the country's needs. The 1968 act, in fact, set a target of 2.6 million subsidized housing units to be built within 10 years.

Beginning in 1969, HUD Secretary George Romney gave top priority to putting the new programs into operation and meeting the ambitious targets of the 1968 act. Between 1969 and 1972, the federal government sponsored more subsidized construction than in the preceding 35 years combined. Yet as the HUD programs, together with their rural counterparts in the Farmers Home Administration, grew to a volume of 400,000 starts per year, both their financial and political costs became troublesome. The new housing required annual federal contributions to help the residents pay the rent or the cost of home ownership. By the early 1970's, yearly outlays began to approach 2 billion dollars. Although this figure was no more than one-fifth of the total cost of federal tax benefits given to middle-income homeowners, it was a natural target for a conservative administration looking for places to cut the federal budget. In addition, poor administration of these programs led to widespread corruption within the Federal Housing Administration that escaped full notoriety only because Watergate created a bigger scandal. President Nixon's annual report on national housing goals for 1972 complained about the rapid growth of future housing subsidy commitments, then estimated at some $12 billion merely to cover housing already approved. These programs were expensive, and getting more so. Worse still, the President's report also noted that the programs were failing to reach the lowest-income families.

Housing experts sponsored by the House of Representatives Subcommittee on

Housing were also finding serious faults with these large-scale programs. A group of researchers at M.I.T. estimated that from one-fifth to one-half the total federal subsidy was not reaching the residents of the new housing, but went for federal and local administrative expenses and for tax benefits to investors. The same study found that subsidy arrangements were regressive, with greater assistance going to families at the upper end of the eligibility range than to low-income families at the bottom. The programs were serving mainly families above the poverty level in lower-middle-income brackets. Further, the families themselves had little freedom of choice in deciding where to live. To get federal housing assistance, they had to move to a designated development whose sponsor had been selected by the local FHA field office. As a result, the allocation of subsidized housing to communities across the country did not correspond as much to the needs of low-income residents as it did to the energy, activity, and political muscle of local sponsors.

An underlying reason for these problems was that the programs were designed to achieve two different purposes that were partially in conflict with each other. One purpose was to encourage new construction; the second to give financial help to families who could not afford good housing on their own. The construction objective overrode the housing assistance purpose at many critical points. The high cost and the generous payments to middlemen were part of the construction strategy. So, too, was the reliance on local sponsors to make key decisions about where to locate projects and whom to admit. Ceilings on the subsidy per family made it hard to bring the cost down low enough for the very poor, and therefore tipped the balance of effort toward families who were better off.

The logic of this critique of production subsidies led toward the conclusion that direct cash payments to low-income families might well be a more effective form of housing assistance. Direct payments to the poor would bypass the project sponsors and other middlemen who were draining off so large a share of the federal housing dollar. Families with cash in hand would be able to make their own decisions about where to live, instead of being limited to designated projects or locations. Rather than having to use their money for costly new housing, they could shop around to find less expensive existing homes. Eligible families would not have to be excluded because they happened to live in communities where developers were not making use of federal housing programs. In addition, direct cash payments could be scaled according to a family's income, rather than following the complicated and regressive formulas that resulted from an attempt to stimulate new construction.

Other analyses presented to the House Subcommittee on Housing pointed in the same general direction. The New York City Rand Institute had made some startling discoveries in its detailed analyses of the New York City housing market during the 1960's. From year to year, a large volume of sound housing was deteriorating in quality and more than 30,000 units per year were being taken off the market through demolition, conversion to non-residential use, or outright abandonment. Between 1965 and 1968, housing losses were greater than new construction by a substantial margin. The main reason for this rising volume of deterioration and abandonment was that a large number of the city's low-income families were unable to pay enough rent to cover the rising costs of operating and maintaining rental property. Landlords who were unable to earn a competitive return were cutting back on maintenance, and, in time, walking away from their buildings.

Ira S. Lowry of the Rand Institute staff concluded from the Rand studies that the most effective way to meet the housing needs of low-income families in New York City was to raise the level of maintenance in existing buildings while they were still in good condition. He estimated that a rent increase of from $400 to $700 per year was needed to support moderate renovation and good maintenance in typical older apartments. Even these small increases, however, were beyond the means of low-income families. Lowry accordingly proposed a housing allowance plan that would make available rent certificates at an average cost of little more than $600 per family.

Proposals for a housing allowance program were timely not only because of disappointments with the prevailing approach to low-income housing, but also because the housing allowance idea had already caught the attention of top policy makers. President Johnson's Committee on Urban Housing (the Kaiser Committee) in its 1968 report had argued the case for housing allowances. The Committee was concerned, however, that a massive housing allowance system could lead to inflation in the general cost of housing and also doubted whether housing allowances would work effectively without parallel measures to counter racial discrimination and provide effective consumer education. It proposed an experimental program to find out. One reason for caution was that the public welfare program, which provided families with cash income intended to cover housing costs as well as other expenses, had many of the characteristics of a housing allowance program. Yet a national survey showed that welfare families had severely inadequate housing, a majority of them living in either substandard or overcrowded conditions. The low level of welfare support did not fully explain this situation. Other families in the same income brackets lived in better housing than those on welfare. It was possible, therefore, that money given to poor families through transfer payments might not open up the same access to housing markets that most people already enjoyed.

Limited trials of the housing allowance idea began in 1970 under the auspices of federally funded Model Cities programs in Kansas City, Missouri and Wilmington, Delaware. The Department of Housing and Urban Development began preliminary studies and designs for a systematic national experiment in 1970 and 1971, and then organized its Experimental Housing Allowance Program.

In January 1973, the Nixon Administration suspended almost all existing federal housing subsidies for the poor and announced its intention to search for more effective programs. The housing allowance experiment, then getting under way in 12 selected cities, took on special importance as part of that search. Meanwhile, Congress enacted a new subsidy program, known as Section 8, to replace those that had been suspended. The new program was a hybrid, based on a flexible financing arrangement that could be used either to promote new construction or, in the manner of a housing allowance, to help people pay for existing houses that met program standards.

DEBATING HOUSING STRATEGIES

While the housing allowance experiments were enrolling families and collecting data, but long before any results were available, policy analysts were carrying on a lively debate over the merits of housing allowances. One school of thought held that housing markets were so restricted and defective that making more money available would still not enable poor people to find decent housing. Others believed that housing markets would respond to a moderate boost in rent levels by increasing the supply of decent, well-maintained housing.

Among the skeptics was Chester Hartman, a long-time critic of federal housing programs, who contended in an article with Dennis Keating that "the shortcomings of the past programs inhere in the nature of the housing market itself." The key assumptions were that little housing is available for the poor, markets are non-competitive, and landlords are dominant. In Hartman's view, the housing allowance approach "pays insufficient attention to the vast shortage of decent, moderate-rent housing in most urban and suburban areas, particularly for groups the market now serves poorly, such as large families." Because of this shortage, he contended, "few doubt that the introduction of housing allowances into a static supply of housing will lead to rent inflation (on a short-term basis at least), not only for recipients, but also for other low- and moderate-income households competing for the same units."

In contrast to this view of a captive market, a series of empirical studies in the 1960's found that landlords were in a precarious position themselves, caught between increasing operating costs and limited rental income. George Sternlieb's study of Newark (*The Tenement Landlord*) and Michael Stegman's study of Baltimore (*Housing Investment in the Inner City*) went a long way toward revising the stereotyped image of the powerful slum landlord who reaped great profits by milking his properties and plundering his tenants. As Stegman described the situation, "Many inner-city landlords are today as victimized as are those to whom they provide inadequate shelter."

Although a casual look at inner-city rent levels might indeed suggest that landlords were succeeding in charging exorbitant and discriminatory rents while giving little service, Stegman found the reality to be different. Inner-city landlords were incurring high operating costs as a result of such factors as non-payment of rent, high vacancy rates, and vandalism to their property. These costs were much higher than in middle-income areas and helped to explain why prevailing rent levels were neither profitable to most landlords nor adequate to provide good maintenance:

> Over 10 percent of cash inflow—an amount equal to about 80 percent of net income—is dissipated on expenditures that do not contribute directly to maintaining or improving resultant flows of housing services. This is why apparently high rents with respect to housing quality can result in little or no profit to the investor. In part, this also explains why housing quality in the inner-city is inferior to that obtainable elsewhere in the city at comparable or only slightly higher rents.

The shortfall between rent collections and maintenance demands suggested that lack of rent money was one of the most important reasons why inner-city housing markets were failing to meet the needs of the poor. Stegman's careful analysis of Baltimore led to conclusions remarkably similar to those of the New York City Rand Institute. Although Stegman himself did not endorse a housing allowance strategy, his findings gave strong support to the view that inner-city housing markets were not locked under the control of powerful slumlords and that public-policy initiatives could indeed create more effective incentives for responsible property management.

In designing the rent allowance experiment, the Department of Housing and Urban Development was concerned with specific questions about how poor families would make use of their housing allowances, how local housing markets would respond to the increased demand generated by direct cash payments, and how different administrative arrangements would influence the results. Accordingly, the program was divided into three parts—a demand experiment, a supply experiment, and an administrative-agency experiment.

In the demand experiment (conducted in Pittsburgh and Phoenix), the research focused on the extent to which eligible families took part in the experiment, changes in housing expenditures for participating families, the choices people made with respect to the quality and location of their housing, and their satisfaction with these choices.

The supply experiment (in Green Bay, Wisconsin and South Bend, Indiana) was designed to test how a large-scale infusion of housing allowance dollars in a single housing market would affect the cost and quality of housing, the behavior of landlords and realtors, and patterns of residential mobility. The supply experiment offered open enrollment to homeowners as well as renters whose incomes were within the established ceilings, and set no limit on the number of families that would be permitted to enroll. (Other parts of the experiment were open to renters only, and the number of participants was limited in advance.)

The administrative-agency experiment selected eight different agencies to carry out housing allowance programs—local housing authorities in Salem, Oregon and Tulsa, Oklahoma; metropolitan government agencies in Jacksonville, Florida and San Bernardino County, California; state community-development agencies in Peoria, Illinois and Springfield, Massachusetts; and the state welfare departments in Durham, North Carolina and Bismarck, North Dakota. In these communities, research focused on the administrative performance of such functions as screening and enrolling applicants, certifying eligibility, providing counseling, and making household inspections.

In all areas, however, the basic requirements were the same. The program was open to families of two or more people and to single individuals who were elderly or handicapped. To receive a housing allowance, a family had to have an income below a ceiling that took into account the local cost of adequate housing and the size of the household. For a family of four, the upper income limit was generally below $7,000. Allowance payments in most cases were set to equal the difference between the estimated cost of adequate housing and one-fourth of the family's income; payments averaged $75 per month. Families in the program were free to spend more or less than the estimated amount for rent, but they had to live in or move to housing that met minimum quality standards set for each part of the experiment. The last requirement was relaxed only for two experimental groups in Pittsburgh and Phoenix that could receive the allowance without meeting any standards of housing quality. Despite the different purposes of the three parts of the experiment, it is possible to consider the twelve demonstration areas as a source of general information on policy issues that cut across the individual experiments.

DID HOUSING ALLOWANCES REACH
THOSE WITH GREATEST NEEDS?

The housing allowance experiment, like other federal housing programs, established income ceilings and payment formulas intended to cover only people who could not afford the cost of decent housing on their own. In other programs, however, project sponsors and local administrators have often screened out those families likely to be most troublesome or most costly to house and have favored people from the high end of the eligible range. As a result, a chronic complaint has been that few of the benefits reached people who were most seriously disadvantaged: the very poor, racial minorities, female-headed households, welfare recipients, large families, and the elderly.

The housing allowance program has had great success in reaching these groups, particularly in comparison with earlier federal housing programs. The average income of families that received housing allowances was about $4,000 (1976 dollars). In contrast, the big subsidy programs of the early 1970's helped mostly lower-middle-income families rather than the poor. The current Section 8 existing-housing program, which has many of the features of a housing allowance, also reaches the poor: In 1977, median income for families in this program was $3,500.

Opponents of housing allowances argued that many families were "hard to house" because of discriminatory practices, and that they would be unable to use housing allowances effectively for this reason. Yet the housing allowance experiment was conspicuously successful in including minority groups, female-headed families, and people on welfare, which meant that a large number of "hard-to-house" people were able to find places of acceptable quality as required by the program.

Minority families—defined here as black or Hispanic—took part in the program fully in proportion to their eligibility. Female-headed families and those getting welfare assistance were the main participants in the housing allowance program. Households headed by women were about half the eligible families, but were half to three-quarters of those receiving payments in the various cities. Welfare families in the experimental cities ranged from 13 to 31 percent of the eligible families, but accounted for one-fifth to one-half of all those who received housing allowances. Large families with limited incomes are also hard to house, but they took part in the housing allowance program in proportion to their eligibility. Only the aged participated in lesser proportion than were eligible, possibly because they are less likely to move than other groups.

Housing allowances not only reached the groups with greatest needs, but they also provided more generous subsidies to those families with the least resources of their own. The big federal housing programs of the early 1970's were criticized for using regressive subsidy structures, with greater benefits for better-off families than for those in the lowest income brackets. Housing allowance payments, in contrast, took into account both income and family size, with larger payments going to lower-income and bigger families. In the eight cities of the administrative experiment, the average monthly payment to families with incomes under $1,000 was $114, while the average payment to families with incomes of $5,000 or more was $53.

DID HOUSING ALLOWANCES REDUCE EXCESSIVE RENT BURDENS?

Housing deprivation can take several different forms, and to reach a fair judgment of the effectiveness of a housing program it is important to look at its impact on each type of deprivation. Governmental concern for the housing of the poor was originally directed at the unhealthy and demoralizing living conditions in the crowded slums of American cities early in the twentieth century. The traditional focus of low-income housing policy since then has been on the substandard physical conditions of slum housing—such as poor ventilation and inadequate plumbing—and on the crowding of families into cramped quarters. More recently, housing conditions have improved for most families, and the supply of low-cost, low-quality apartments has been shrinking steadily. As a result, many people live in housing that meets reasonable physical standards but they spend a third or more of their income for rent—either because low-cost slums are no longer available as an option for the poor or because they have chosen to make financial sacrifices in order to live in better houses.

Low-income families who took part in the housing allowance experiment were originally spending an exorbitant part of their income for housing. Among the 12 cities in the entire program, the median share of total income committed to rental payments varied from 34 percent to 53 percent.

Housing allowance payments did succeed in reducing the share of family income going for rent. In almost all cities, the median rent burden for families who received housing allowances was below 25 percent, with the median in individual cities ranging from 17 to 30 percent. But even with the allowance payments, about half the participating families still spent more than the generally accepted norm of 25 percent of gross income for rent.

The rent burden came down because most families who received housing allowances chose to stay where they were already living and decided not to spend much of the allowance money for improved housing. In order to qualify for housing allowance payments, families had to find housing that conformed to the minimum quality standards established for each part of the experiment. A substantial majority of the families who met these requirements did so without moving from the places where they were living before they enrolled. Of these families that were able to join the program without having to move, most were living in apartments that met the quality standards as soon as they were inspected, but a minority had to make repairs (or get the landlord to make repairs) in order to pass the inspection. The proportion of housing allowance recipients who stayed put, with or without repairs, ranged from 55 percent in the eight cities of the administrative experiment, to 83 percent in the two cities of the supply experiment. Families who stayed where they were paid only minor rent increases.

This pattern of decisions meant that people in the program were using housing allowances mainly to substitute for money of their own that they formerly spent for rent, rather than using it to make a substantial boost in their housing outlays. In Pittsburgh, families in the program used only 9 percent of their payments for rent increases above the normal increase paid by a control group; and in Phoenix, 27 percent of the housing allowance dollars went for housing expenditures above normal increases. The great bulk of the payments went to free family income for other expenses.

DID THE PROGRAM IMPROVE HOUSING QUALITY?

A central purpose of the experiment was to find out whether housing allowances would bring about improvement in the quality of the housing supply. Although a high proportion of participating families lived in housing that met the program's quality standards from the beginning, a majority did not and either had to make repairs or had to move in order to qualify. In the eight cities of the administrative experiment, an average of 57 percent of recipients either moved or upgraded their prior housing; in Pittsburgh and Phoenix, 61 percent either moved or upgraded, and in Green Bay and South Bend, 48 percent either moved or upgraded.

The housing standards that families had to meet varied somewhat in different parts of the experiment, but they were generally in line with local housing codes, model codes recommended by building code administrators, and standards developed by public health organizations.

In order to meet these standards, most families in the program did improve the quality of their housing, either by moving or by repairing their current residences. The substantial minority who upgraded without moving did so mainly by making minor repairs at low costs. Typical repairs involved fixing windows or installing handrails on stairs; some work was also done on structural components, plumbing, and heating systems. In Green Bay and South Bend, landlords and tenants split the work about evenly, using professional contractors for only about 10 percent of repairs. Three out of four below-standard dwellings that were brought up to an acceptable level involved cash costs of less than $25 in Green Bay and less than $30 in South Bend.

In Pittsburgh and Phoenix, tenants and landlords also divided the work of bringing failed units up to standard. Residents typically painted and papered the inside, while landlords did the bulk of the work on plumbing and heating equipment and general repairs. The mean cash cost of the improvement was $92. A control group of families in these cities who did not get housing allowances reported almost the same outlays for repairs, however, and about four-fifths of those in both the experimental and control groups reported that their landlords also made improvements. The main difference was in the kinds of repairs. Families getting housing allowances were more likely to have their houses brought up to "standard" condition as required by the program.

Very few families managed to use their housing allowance payments to switch from rental housing to home ownership. In Green Bay and South Bend, about 300 families who enrolled as renters bought homes while they were in the program; these were less than 3 percent of the renters enrolled. Yet in these cities almost half of the participants in the experiment were already homeowners. Many of these had undoubtedly bought their homes at times in the past when their incomes were higher. But however feasible ownership may be for low-income families, it is clear that housing allowance payments did not raise incomes or assets enough to enable families to improve their housing by becoming homeowners.

A survey of how participating families in Pittsburgh and Phoenix felt about their housing shows that they valued the quality improvements resulting from the program, but it also reveals a deep-seated reluctance to move in order to get quality improvements. Of the families who failed to meet housing standards at the beginning, the most satisfied of all were those who later met them by improving the places where they already lived: 70 percent of these families were "very satisfied" with their housing. But the second most satisfied group were the families who stayed where they were and failed to meet the standards for receiving housing allowances: 45 percent of these were "very satisfied," compared to

30 percent of those who moved and passed and 19 percent of those who moved and failed. The families in the program were strongly attached to their homes. They were pleased if they could make them better at small cost, but giving them up for higher physical standards somewhere else yielded little satisfaction.

For those who could not easily meet the standards where they were, the program required a move that was often unwelcome and unsatisfying. The program's objective of bringing everyone into housing of standard quality was out of touch with the preferences and priorities of many of the families who took part.

NEIGHBORHOODS, HOUSING COSTS, AND PROGRAM EXPENSE

Earlier housing programs usually offered a very restricted choice of neighborhood location, since people who wanted to use the program had to move to designated projects, and as a result of local political pressures the projects were usually concentrated in the worst neighborhoods of the city. The housing allowance strategy, in contrast, promised to open much wider options for neighborhood choice. People in the program could search out moderate-cost housing wherever it was located, and families moving one-by-one were unlikely to arouse the political protests that kept subsidized projects out of many desirable neighborhoods. A general reluctance to move undercut chances for widespread neighborhood mobility, but a sizable minority of families did move: 45 percent in the administrative experiment cities, 39 percent in Pittsburgh and Phoenix, and 16 percent in Green Bay and South Bend.

The housing allowance experiment produced only scattered information on neighborhood conditions, but what there is shows that people who moved tended to go into better neighborhoods than the ones they left. As the Rand Corporation's report summarizes the experience in Green Bay and South Bend, "the worst neighborhoods in each site lost program participants who moved, on balance, to better neighborhoods."

Similarly, in the administrative experiment cities, most people who moved went into census tracts with a higher socioeconomic-index rating (based on resident income, education, and employment) than the places they left. And 39 percent of black households who moved, moved to areas with lower minority concentrations than their original neighborhoods. Black families in the program lived in areas that had an average of 56 percent minority population at enrollment, and moved to areas with an average of 40 percent minority population at the time they got their first payment. In Phoenix and Pittsburgh, black movers also went into neighborhoods with lower black concentrations. The mean reduction was 4 percent in Pittsburgh and 3 percent in Phoenix.

The housing allowance program did not add significantly to opportunities for poor families to live in suburbia. In Pittsburgh, 18 percent of the families originally in the central city moved to the suburbs, and 12 percent of those originally in the suburbs moved to the city. In Phoenix, 33 percent moved from the city to the suburbs, while 6 percent went from the suburbs to the city. In both areas, however, control households with similar incomes who had no housing allowances showed almost exactly the same pattern of movement.

Housing allowances, then, may have widened the locational options open to poor people, but very few took the opportunity to move to different neighborhoods and most families in the program chose not to move at all. For those who did move, the program did not improve access to the suburbs, but it did help them move to better and less segregated neighborhoods in the cities.

The most troublesome fear raised by the idea of a housing allowance program was that pumping new money into malfunctioning central-city housing markets would drive up housing costs both for people in the program and for low-income renters in general. The supply experiment in Green Bay and South Bend was organized above all to investigate the possible inflationary effects of a housing allowance. All those who were eligible in terms of income were invited to apply, the availability of housing assistance was well publicized, and payments were assured for a full ten years. The intent was to saturate both housing markets with housing allowances and then to analyze changes in rent levels.

The results were clear and unequivocal: there was virtually no effect on housing costs. Rents in Green Bay and South Bend increased less rapidly than either regional or national rent averages. Gross rents in Green Bay increased by an average of 7 percent a year from 1974 through 1977, and in South Bend by 5 percent. Higher fuel and utility costs accounted for most of the change in both places.

With hindsight, it is easy to see why housing allowances had no inflationary impact. The tendency of families to stay in their previous homes, plus their reluctance to spend more for rent, meant that allowance payments injected few new dollars into local housing markets. In addition, even with open enrollment in Green Bay and South Bend, relatively few families took part in the program. About 20 percent of the households in the two areas were eligible in terms of income, but only about half the eligible families were enrolled at any given time, and about 80 percent of those enrolled actually met the requirements to receive payments. As a result, even in the supply experiment, housing allowances went to only 8 percent of the households in the area.

In the ten cities for which information is available, allowance payments per family averaged from $888 to $1,632 per year. Administrative costs averaged from $152 to $429 in addition, excluding the cost of research and analytical work commissioned for the experiment. The average cost per household was about $1,150 in 1976 dollars—$900 in cash payments and $250 for administration.

The average cost of $1,150 compares very favorably with the cost of the two earlier programs for comparable income groups, in which public housing cost an average of $1,650 per family, and rent supplements $1,310, both in 1972 dollars. HUD's current Section 8 program is also more expensive than housing allowances. By 1976 estimates, the Section 8 existing-units program—which is most comparable to housing allowances—cost $1,500 per family, and Section 8 new-or-rehabilitated-units cost more than $4,000. HUD budget projections for 1980 placed the cost of Section 8 existing-units at $2,700 per family and new-or-rehabilitated-units at more than $4,500 per family.

WHERE DID HOUSING ALLOWANCES FALL SHORT OF EXPECTATIONS?

To the surprise of many housing experts, less than half the families eligible for housing allowances actually participated in the program.

There are many plausible reasons why poor families who were eligible for housing aid failed to enroll for it, or once enrolled failed to qualify for payments. Case studies indicate that some people who were attached to their homes doubted whether they could pass inspection or whether the landlord would agree to rent to people in the program. Others avoided the program out of pride: They viewed housing allowances as something like welfare, or they feared the agency staff would treat them in demeaning ways. Searching for a new place to live was almost always troublesome; it usually meant having to arrange for baby sitters, getting listings, finding transportation, and dealing with landlords. Often the search had to be completed quickly while places were still available in the local program, and many people had little free time. Even people in the selected groups that were not required to meet any housing standards still had to agree to be interviewed from time to time and to file reports on their finances and their housing. Some people were unwilling to go through the administrative procedures and some were overwhelmed with other problems. One woman who applied but never completed her enrollment told an interviewer later: "I was working hard, I was pregnant and having a nervous breakdown. My two kids had decided to live with their father. I just couldn't get involved in anything else."

Families who were able to meet the housing standards where they were already living had the best prospects for getting payments once they enrolled. In a few cities, many families never did succeed in meeting the housing standards, perhaps confirming the view of critics who had argued in advance that supply shortages would prevent housing allowances from working satisfactorily. In Pittsburgh, 78 percent of the families failed to meet housing standards when they first enrolled, and of these 73 percent still failed to meet them two years later. In Phoenix, 80 percent failed to meet the housing standards at enrollment, and 54 percent of these still did not meet them two years later. The pattern in these cities was not typical, however, and may reflect special enrollment procedures in which people entered the program by invitation instead of on their own initiative. Also in Pittsburgh and Phoenix, moving to another house did not necessarily help people meet the standards. In Pittsburgh, of those not meeting standards at enrollment, 15 percent moved and passed but another 28 percent moved and failed again. In Phoenix, 32 percent moved and passed, and 25 percent moved and failed. Again, however, the experience in these cities was not typical of the entire program.

An important factor influencing participation in the housing allowance program was the severity of the housing standards families had to meet: the tougher the standards, the fewer families took part. In Pittsburgh and Phoenix, one group of participants was not required to meet any housing standards at all: Once enrolled on the basis of income eligibility, they automatically received payments. With no standards, 78 percent of the eligible families in Pittsburgh and 90 percent in Phoenix got the payments. In Green Bay and South Bend, where housing standards were moderately demanding, about 40 percent of the eligible renters received payments. In Pittsburgh and Phoenix, in the group forced to meet the most stringent housing standards, only 30 percent and 45 percent of those offered enrollment actually received payments. The most likely explanation for this trade-off between standards and participation is that most low-income families are reluctant either to pay higher rent or to move in order to upgrade their housing conditions.

One group—minority families—had an especially hard time qualifying for payments. In the administrative experiment, minority families were less likely than other enrollees to meet the standards for payments. On the average, only 53 percent of the black households enrolled (but 79 percent of Hispanic households) eventually got housing allowances, compared to 77 percent of non-minority families. In the severely segregated city of Jacksonville, Florida, only 21 percent of black enrollees got allowances during the first enrollment period, compared to 54 percent of others.

This minority experience partly confirms the views of skeptics who argued that shortages of standard housing and discrimination would offset the value of cash payments to the hard-to-house. But there was also minority experience to the contrary. In Pittsburgh, eligible blacks enrolled to a greater extent than other eligible families, and once enrolled did as well as others in meeting program standards. In Phoenix, minority families (mostly Hispanic) enrolled in proportion to their eligibility, and once enrolled did better than others in qualifying for payments. Since the minority pattern was mixed, it is possible to conclude either that the glass was half empty or that it was half full.

It is also true that almost all social programs for the poor operate far below their authorized levels, because many people who are legally eligible for benefits do not apply. Further, most new programs have increasing enrollment in the first few years before they reach a steady rate of participation. In Green Bay and South Bend, 26 percent of all eligible households took part in the first year, 37 percent in the second year, and 40 percent in the third year. These figures are not out of line with participation rates in other programs for the poor. In New York City, for example, only 52 percent of families eligible for all categories of welfare actually took part in welfare programs in the early 1970's. And participation in the national food stamp program ranges from 12 percent in North Dakota to 58 percent in California, with a national average of 38 percent. Once again, it is an open question whether the glass is half empty or half full.

Before the housing allowance experiment, conventional wisdom held that increases in the income of poor families would lead to nearly proportional increases in their housing expenditures—that a 10 percent increase in income would generate a 10 percent increase in rent payments. A recent Rand Corporation study, based on surveys of a sample of all households in Green Bay and South Bend, estimates the income elasticity of housing demand at only .19 for renters and .45 for homeowners. In these communities, a 10 percent increase in income for renters would lead to only a 1.9 percent increase in rent payments. Elasticities estimated for other cities in the housing allowance program were also low.

An implication is that if families who receive housing allowances are free to decide how much of their payment to spend for housing, they will not increase their rent outlays very much above the prior level. But if rent payments do not increase, giving cash to the poor is not likely to prompt landlords to spend much money for property improvements or better maintenance, as Lowry had anticipated when he proposed housing allowances as a solution to New York City's problems of deterioration and abandonment. Letting consumers make their own decisions regarding how much to spend for rent works against the goal of improving the quality of housing.

The housing allowance program was truly exceptional in allowing families to set their own priorities between spending on housing or spending on other items. Most housing programs sponsor construction to a predetermined standard and require the families involved to use most of their subsidy to pay for a level of housing quality chosen by an administrator. In the case of housing allowances, federal officials expected the typical family to move to better accommodations and to spend most of its subsidy for higher rent. The reality was that most families stayed put, made minor repairs if they were required to meet program standards, got marginally adequate housing if they did not have it to begin with, and used most of the payment to free their own funds for non-housing expenses. As a result, the program had only limited impact on the quality of the housing supply and on mobility; but these were unavoidable consequences of respecting the wishes of families in the program.

LEARNING FROM A SOCIAL EXPERIMENT

The housing allowance experiment did not fully resolve the debates about the nature of inner-city housing markets. The results certainly did not bear out the skeptics' fears of widespread inflation and unavailability of housing. Contrary to their predictions, the hard-to-house were able to find adequate housing through the allowance program or had already found reasonable places earlier. Female-headed and welfare families especially were able to make good use of housing allowances. But there were also results to confirm the skeptics doubts. In some cities enrolled families had severe problems finding adequate housing, depending to a great extent on the standards they had to meet. And minority groups in many cities did not fare as well as others, bearing out the argument that discrimination would blunt some of the desired effects of cash payments for housing.

Housing allowance proponents can take satisfaction in the program's ability to reach and help families with serious housing problems. Yet this success in reaching families with marginal incomes and heavy financial burdens also insured that participating families would be reluctant to increase their rent outlays. Hard-pressed to come up with rent money to begin with, and living in the inflationary economy of the mid-1970s, they used their payments in ways that did not live up to the advocates' hopes of stimulating reinvestment in older housing.

It turned out that letting the poor make their own decisions led to results that ran counter to the goals of federal housing administrators. The Department of Housing and Urban Development has traditionally given top priority to improving the quality of housing, both for the country at large and for the people who take part in its programs. Marc Bendick, Jr., and James P. Zais of the Urban Institute began their own assessment of the housing allowance experiment by noting the goals former Secretary Patricia Harris set for HUD in a recent budget submission: the revitalization of urban areas, the maintenance and expansion of the supply of housing, and the provision of freedom of opportunity in housing. (Freedom of opportunity might conceivably include the freedom to live in housing of marginal quality in order to save on rent, but for HUD they note that this goal implies facilitating the "movement of low-income families outside areas of lower-income, minority concentration.") They argue persuasively that housing allowances do not serve the stated goals of HUD policy: "[T]hey have failed to generate substantial expansion of the housing stock, dramatic revitalization of cities, or major increases in freedom of choice in housing."

Similar results of another housing program are putting HUD's traditional commitments to the test. The Section 8 existing-housing program has many of the characteristics of a housing allowance, and also allows families to use federal subsidies in existing apartments that meet prescribed standards. About half the participants in Section 8 existing-housing do not move from where they lived before, and they use their financial assistance mainly to reduce their rent burden. This program has had great success in reaching the poor, female-headed families, minorities, and the elderly; but it has done little to improve the quality of the housing supply. Not surprisingly, HUD has begun to slow down the existing housing program and to shift most of its housing assistance activity to a different Section 8 program for new construction or substantial rehabilitation.

The housing allowance experience reinforces other analyses that have shown high cost replacing slum conditions as the major housing problem facing the urban poor. If the problem has changed, the search for solutions should not be held captive to HUD's traditional organizational mission. HUD should have a mission that encompasses the range of housing problems, and a capacity to use the right tool for each purpose. There is still need for construction programs, since they are likely to be more effective than housing allowances for such purposes as helping minority families in tight housing markets or opening up the suburbs to the poor. But housing allowances are the right tool for many problems, such as the emerging concern for the victims of "gentrification." The widely heralded rediscovery of city neighborhoods, which is prompting affluent families to refurbish charming brownstones and town houses, is also pushing many poor renters out of their homes. Housing allowances would probably be highly effective in helping these families find other places to live nearby while coping with rising rents.

The most valuable contribution of social experiments may be that they raise new and troublesome questions about the purposes of public policy. A series of education experiments, for example, tried to find ways of helping disadvantaged youngsters learn more in school. Instead of revealing the most promising teaching techniques, these experiments led analysts to question more carefully how to measure learning and how to define what kind of learning we want to achieve. Similarly, the housing allowance experiment began by trying to find answers to questions about the design of a national program of cash assistance for housing. But its operation brought to the surface a serious conflict between the priorities of the poor and those of housing-program administrators.

The poor do not give housing *quality* the high priority that program administrators do. In the long history of housing reform in the United States, this is the first time the beneficiaries of a program have been able to make their views known on how the money should be spent. The views of the reformers have always dominated; in fact, we know almost nothing about whether earlier generations of slum-dwellers would rather have had the cash than either model tenements or public housing projects. But the poor of this generation, at least, have spoken clearly through the housing allowance experiment. Their main problem, as they see it, is cost, not quality. Interestingly, a household survey commissioned by HUD just before the housing allowance experiment began also suggested that housing quality was not a serious problem for the urban poor. In three cities surveyed in 1972, fully 84 percent of the households with incomes below $5,000 rated their housing units as "excellent" or "satisfactory." The housing allowance experience confirms and amplifies this finding. The poor still have serious housing problems, but they are not the ones most public programs address.

The real test of whether the housing allowance experiment was a success will be whether policy makers re-examine the purposes of government action in the light of its unexpected results. An important question for the next wave of housing programs is: Who should decide how much housing a family ought to consume and where it ought to live, the family or an administrator who sets the standards? (And the higher the standards are set, the fewer people will take part.) There may conceivably be public benefits involved that would justify overriding the preferences of the poor themselves and requiring them to pay for better housing than they would otherwise choose to do. If that is so, federal officials have a responsibility to present the case for setting aside the wishes of the poor.

At a minimum, the housing allowance experiment calls into question those housing goals that are based mainly on the weight of tradition or on the organizational mission of an established federal agency. It offers instead a rare opportunity to recognize the changing needs of the clients.

NOTE

1. Many individuals associated with the organizations responsible for the housing allowance experiment generously gave of their time and made available reports and other information. I would like to thank especially Jerry J. Fitts and Howard Hammerman of the Department of Housing and Urban Development, Ira S. Lowry of the Rand Corporation, and Clark Abt and Helen Bakeman of Abt Associates.

Full documentation, including citations and tables, of the findings discussed in this article are presented in my Joint Center Working Paper No. 62, "What Have We Learned from the Housing Allowance Experiment?" (M.I.T.–Harvard Joint Center for Urban Studies, Cambridge, Massachusetts, 1980). That version will be published also in *Habitat International*, Volume 5. No. 1-2 (1980).

21

Housing Allowances: A Bad Idea
Whose Time Has Come

Chester Hartman

If the Reagan administration has its way, we will shortly have a new program to deal with the shelter needs of the nation's poor: housing allowances. The April 1982 *Report of the President's Commission on Housing* offered as its first recommendation: "The primary Federal program for helping low-income families to achieve decent housing should be a Housing Payments program." And last December the Office of Management and Budget proposed a complete transformation of the federal housing subsidy system, substituting housing vouchers (a term used interchangeably with "housing allowances") for the existing programs, which have previously been directed mainly at housing construction and rehabilitation. The 1983 budget takes this recommendation a big step toward reality by halting virtually all government subsidized rental housing construction and authorizing funds to put 106,000 families on a voucher system.

Vouchers appeal to philosophical conservatives on several grounds. Conservatives don't like subsidizing the poor at all, but if pressed they prefer vouchers, on the theory that they are more "marketlike" than direct subsidies or government programs. Under a voucher system, needy people receive cash or cash-like assistance—food stamps, education vouchers, or housing vouchers—to help meet a particular need, and they can purchase the product on the open market. This presumably allows the poor to function just like other sovereign consumers

From *Working Papers Magazine*, Vol. IX, No. 6 (November-December, 1982), 55-58. This article is a review of two books about housing allowances and the *Report* of the President's Commission on Housing (1982).

in a responsive marketplace ruled by the laws of supply and demand. Thus, if housing is a problem, vouchers will increase effective demand, which will send the market a signal to increase supply. If, as the conventional wisdom now has it, the housing problems of the poor are primarily inadequate incomes rather than an inadequate housing supply, vouchers can permit the housing-deprived to consume what the market already has to offer. In theory, vouchers also address the problem of "horizontal equity"—the fact that many direct subsidy programs reach only a fraction of needy people (why should some poor families get heavily subsidized housing while the majority of them get no housing subsidies at all?).

But housing vouchers present two practical problems. First, housing markets are not at all like the free markets of textbook economics. Unlike a food stamp recipient, who can go into a supermarket with $50 worth of stamps and buy virtually the same products as the holder of a crisp $50 bill, the low-income housing consumer does not face a housing supermarket. Decent, moderately priced housing is in very short supply. Discrimination is rampant against minorities, and other "nontypical" households. And, as we shall see, there is no evidence that increasing effective tenant demand via Reagan-style vouchers would call forth new housing supply where it is needed.

Second, "horizontal inequity" is indeed a problem—but not one addressed by the Reagan program. About 3 million families currently live in government subsidized apartments—and an estimated 15 million more pay excessive rents to live in inadequate housing. However, the Reagan administration has no intention of universalizing housing allowances. Far from it—fewer families would be served by the voucher proposals than are aided by past subsidy programs. Most of the 106,000 vouchers would go to families who already live in subsidized apartments; one form of subsidy would replace another. Only about 10,000-30,000 new families would receive the vouchers in the first year, which is far below the recent rate of subsidized housing construction.

The Reagan proposal continues a long term trend toward "privatizing" housing subsidies, much of which has been self-defeating.

Under the Nixon and Ford administrations, the 1974 Housing and Community Development Act introduced a voucher-like mechanism known as "Section 8," under which government paid a developer or landlord the difference between a "market rent" and what a poor family could afford—generally 25 percent of income. After 1974, only token sums trickled into public housing projects built, owned, and operated by local housing authorities.

A housing allowance would complete this shift. It would end government's direct involvement in increasing the supply of housing for low income people. And not only is the administration proposing to shift the form of the subsidy, but also to cut back outlays sharply. Under the voucher plan, the proposed voucher per family has been set arbitrarily at about half of existing per-unit subsidy levels. And the allowance is to be fixed in current dollars for the life of the commitment, rather than rising to reflect inflation.

At the meager levels proposed by the Reagan administration, housing vouchers will reach only a tiny fraction of households now paying burdensome rents for inadequate housing. The rhetoric about free markets working more efficiently mainly serves to camouflage steep cuts in outlays for housing. The more subtle and potentially interesting question is whether even a substantial voucher program would translate into better housing for low income people.

In theory, a voucher program makes sense to the extent the nation's housing problem is really an income problem. If enough money were targeted to housing allowances for low income people, presumably they could afford better housing. But because of the very peculiar nature of housing markets, it does not necessarily follow that housing allowances are an efficient or effective form of housing subsidy. One problem is the risk that rents will merely rise to soak up the additional purchasing power; quality or supply will not necessarily increase. Another problem is that many recipients will decide to stay put, let the vouchers cover part of their rental outlay, and spend the savings elsewhere. Again, there will be no improvement in housing supply—only a disguised income transfer to tenants and perhaps ultimately to landlords.

As it happens, these and other questions were the subject of one of the largest policy experiments ever conducted—HUD's Experimental Housing Allowance Program (EHAP). This $160 million experiment was launched in 1970 by the Nixon administration, which, as older readers will recall, shared some basic philosophies with the current one. The EHAP experiment provided vouchers to more than 30,000 families for three to ten years in twelve cities across the country, with sophisticated permutations and controls. Its findings, as reported in two recent books, provide very little comfort to supporters of the voucher approach:

- When government insisted on standards of housing quality, people declined to participate in the program. Only when recipients were permitted to live in substandard housing (and in effect spend their housing allowances elsewhere) were participation rates high. Very poor people, minorities, large families, and families living in substandard housing had the lowest participation rates.
- Only one-fourth of the allowance actually was spent to obtain better housing. Since recipients were spending an average of 40 percent of their income on rent prior to receiving the allowance, it was hardly surprising that they should use the allowance to reduce this burden rather than to find more expensive housing.
- Not surprisingly, the minimal increase in housing demand created by the allowances had little effect on housing markets. It neither inflated rents nor stimulated new housing construction.

The explanation lies in the nature of housing markets. There often is no direct way for tenants to translate a housing allowance into better housing. It makes little sense for the tenant to invest the allowance in improving the apartment, since the building belongs to the landlord, who may raise the rent or find another tenant. And it may not be possible to move to better quarters or worth the disruption, since the allowance is of limited duration. None of the EHAP variations offered the participants a bonus for moving expenses, nor does the Reagan plan.

Moreover, it makes sense for poor families to avoid spending housing allowances on housing, because when you're poor, you're not just housing poor. Most households living on the margin prefer to ease their heavy rent burden so they can have a little more food, transportation, clothing, and other of life's necessities. In the EHAP experiment, using housing allowance funds for non-shelter items reduced the recipients' average rent-to-income ratio from 40 percent to 25 percent.

Poor people also resist moving up to more expensive housing because housing is not an easily adjustable expenditure. One cannot decide to reduce housing expenses suddenly by consuming one less room or not residing in an apartment for a day or two, in the way one can rapidly and significantly reduce food expenses by eating less or eating cheaper food.

Even more crucially, in most locales there is simply no supply of decent, moderately priced rental housing to choose from. A study released last February, by researchers Frank DeGiovanni and Mary Brooks of Pratt Institute's Center for Community and Environmental Development (*Impact of a Housing Voucher Program on New York City's Population*), found that 36 percent of New York City families given Section 8 certificates were unable to use them because they couldn't find decent vacant units. Minorities and families with children were least able to use their certificates. Another study of Section 8, by the General Accounting Office, demonstrates that vouchers by themselves will not upgrade the quality of housing. Their 1979 inspection of a sample of existing Section 8 units in Massachusetts, Illinois, Georgia, Arizona, and California revealed that "42 percent contained one or more conditions which violated Federal housing quality standards and/or endangered the life, health, safety, or welfare of the occupants or the public."

Nor are the suppliers of housing able and willing to respond to increases in demand like the manufacturers of Wheaties. Unless induced by massive direct or indirect subsidy, private builders of moderate rent apartments respond slowly or not at all. Housing is expensive, it takes a long time to produce, the resource constraints (construction financing, land, etc.) are difficult to overcome.

In short, people avoid spending their housing allowance money on housing not because they don't value housing, but, in large part at least, because they can't get good value for their dollar in the current housing market. They can neither induce significant improvement in their current quarters, or find alternative quarters in that market.

A major housing allowance program that did not substantially increase the supply of housing could well put inflationary pressures on rent. The EHAP experiment did not shed light on this question, however, since recipients spent so little of their allowance on housing, and the program was available to a limited number of households. But clearly a broader housing allowance program, in the absence of government controls on the market, could wind up lining landlords' pockets. According to an essay in the Brookings book, by Harvard economist John Kain, modeling techniques used by the Urban Institute and the National Bureau of Economic Research to simulate the impact on larger cities like Detroit, Cleveland, and Newark "indicated that a full-scale earmarked allowance program might cause significant rent increases for both recipients and non-recipients."

Another serious concern is that a shift to vouchers will accelerate the abandonment of public housing projects, where over three million Americans now live. While some of these are evident failures, most provide decent, low-rent apartments whose appeal is reflected in long waiting lists. The administration's 1983 budget not only eliminated subsidies for new public housing, but substantially cuts operating subsidies for existing projects—many of which are in need of large-scale maintenance investment. Additionally, some 5,000 of the 106,000 vouchers for Fiscal Year 1983 are earmarked for residents of public housing units that are to be demolished.

Many localities would like nothing better than to get rid of some of their older public housing projects that, originally located on unappealing, out-of-the-way sites, are now hot properties, thanks to gentrification, new transit lines, and other factors. Alexandria, Virginia, is a prime example, where as a result of the new Metro system and "in" places like Old Town, developers and the city are teaming up to replace low-rent projects with pricey residences and commercial uses. Boston's Columbia Point—built on a desolate landfill site in 1954 but now neighbor to the John F. Kennedy Library and a new University of Massachusetts campus—is another. The ability to offer housing vouchers instead of project apartments will greatly grease that process. Permanent low-rent units will be removed, and replaced by short-term rent certificates.

Another byproduct of the shift from public housing to housing allowances will be the loss of many important tenants' rights, won after considerable struggle. Public housing tenants are now among the most protected class of tenants in the country, shielded from arbitrary evictions and from retaliatory evictions, guaranteed a notice and hearing when benefits are denied, protected by a warranty of habitability that the quarters are decent, safe, and sanitary that can be used as grounds for withholding rent. These rights are not likely to be built into a housing allowance program that is rooted in free market dogma.

Housing allowances might make sense, strategically, if they were the opening wedge toward an entitlement program—that is, if it were similar to food stamps and Medicaid, which, whatever their inadequacies and current curtailments, are available to anyone and everyone who meets the eligibility criteria. No direct housing assistance program the government has ever mounted is an entitlement program—simply because housing is too expensive a good to guarantee for everyone in the society. Cushing Dolbeare of the National Low Income Housing Coalition and others have suggested we might take a very narrow segment of the population—say, large female-headed households with incomes under 50 percent of the median, or the elderly of similar income levels—and agree to guarantee those people an entitlement to housing allowances.

That would perhaps be politically acceptable, would involve roughly predictable and reasonable budgetary outlay, and would establish the principle of an entitlement to decent housing at an affordable cost. That opening wedge then could be expanded incrementally to different categories and higher income levels. But President Reagan's Commission on Housing has specifically rejected the notion of housing allowances as an entitlement, and it is inconceivable that Ronald Reagan or his Office of Management and Budget would ever agree to such a notion.

Ironically, we do now have one entitlement program in the housing area, as Cushing Dolbeare is fond of pointing out: the tax system provision allowing all qualifying homeowners to deduct mortgage interest and property tax payments from their taxable income. Over 25 million tax returns had one or another of these indirect housing subsidies in 1981, at a cost to the Treasury, in foregone tax revenues, of more than $39 billion in FY 1982 (by comparison, HUD's entire budget for that year was $16 billion). And the regressivity of this entitlement tax expenditure is mind boggling. Thirty percent of all mortgage interest deduction benefits (nearly two-thirds of all homeowner tax benefits) goes to the 5 percent of the population with annual incomes over $50,000; 92 percent goes to taxpayers with annual incomes over $20,000.

In the current debate over federal housing expenditures, this enormously regressive tax expenditure for housing remains unscathed through all the administration's budget cuts and tax reforms, while those who really need housing aid have their much smaller piece of the budget pie cut to the crust. An October 1981 Congressional Budget Office Study, *The Tax Treatment of Homeownership: Issues and Options*, shows how simple reforms like putting a dollar cap on these benefits, eliminating them altogether for second homes, and converting them from a tax deduction to a tax credit could provide substantial additional government tax revenue and eliminate major systemic inequities, while having minimal effect on housing market behavior.

In sum, this administration wants to pull the federal government out of its traditional housing assistance role as rapidly and completely as possible, and the housing allowance proposal is the opening gambit in that move. In a revealing and highly disturbing interview, published in the November 6, 1981, *Washington Post*, right after the release of the Presidential Housing Commission's *Interim Report*, HUD Secretary Samuel Pierce let out what may be the administration's game plan: "We hope that by 1984 or '85, that we will have interest rates down enough that it will stimulate housing so that we don't have to use the voucher system. We hope that maybe we'll even get out of that." The easy way to terminate the nearly fifty-year-old federal role in housing lower income households is to get rid of programs that have long-term commitments, like public housing and Section 8, by substituting very flexible short-term commitments, and gradually phasing them out.

It should be clear that housing allowances do not do the same thing that traditional government housing programs for the poor have done: produce housing for them. As the EHAP experiment has shown, short-term housing vouchers aren't going to motivate anyone to produce new or substantially rehabilitated housing units, which, for all their defects, the older programs, with their fifteen- to forty-year subsidy commitments and direct public construction did. A small scale housing allowance program, which is the most we will get from this administration, will do little for the poor. A large-scale entitlement program of housing allowances might do some good, but unless coupled with a construction program it would entail extraordinary housing inflation and highly inefficient use of government resources.

Housing is an expensive good, and there's little way to get around that fact. To meet the National Housing Goal of "a decent home and suitable living environment for every American family"—which Congress twice promulgated, in 1949 and 1968—will cost lots of money. There are better and worse, cheaper and more costly ways of doing it. And the only way to substantially reduce housing costs and provide decent housing for the poor is to take large elements of housing production, ownership and management out of the profit sector and treat housing as a social good. But that's another article and another administration.

Bibliography

Aaron, Henry J. *Shelter and Subsidies: Who Benefits from Federal Housing Policies?* Washington, D.C.: The Brookings Institution, 1972.

————, and von Furstenberg, George M. "The Inefficiency of Transfers in Kind: The Case of Housing Assistance," *Western Economic Journal*, 9 (June 1971), 184-91.

Abbott, Edith. *The Tenements of Chicago, 1908-1935*. Chicago: The University of Chicago Press, 1936.

Abrams, Charles. *The City is the Frontier*. New York: Harper & Row, 1965.

————. *The Future of Housing*. New York: Harper & Brothers, 1946.

Anderson, Martin. *The Federal Bulldozer*. Cambridge: MIT Press, 1964.

Augur, Tracy B. "Planning Principles Applied in Wartime: An Account of the Planning of a Town for Willow Run Workers," *Architectural Record*, 93 (January 1943), 72-77.

Baratz, Morton S. "Public Housing: A Critique and a Proposal," *Social Research*, 20 (October 1953), 332-44.

Bauer, Catherine. "Cities in Flux," *American Scholar*, 13 (Winter 1943-1944), 70-84.

————, "Planned Large-Scale Housing: A Balance Sheet of Progress," *Architectural Record*, 89 (May 1941), 89-105.

Bellush, Jewel, and Hausknecht, Murray, eds. *Urban Renewal: People, Politics and Planning*. Garden City: Doubleday, 1967.

Bendick, Marc, Jr., and Zais, James P. *Incomes and Housing: Lessons from Experiments with Housing Allowances*. Washington, D.C.: The Urban Institute, 1978.

Birch, Eugenie Ladner. "Woman-Made America: The Case of Early Public Housing Policy," *Journal of the American Institute of Planners*, 44 (April 1978): 130-44.

————, and Gardner, Deborah S. "The Seven-Percent Solution: A Review of Philanthropic Housing, 1870-1910," *Journal of Urban History*, 7 (August 1981), 403-38.

Bowley, Devereux, Jr. *The Poorhouse: Subsidized Housing in Chicago, 1895-1976*. Carbondale: Southern Illinois University Press, 1978.

Bradbury, Katherine L., and Downs, Anthony, eds. *Do Housing Allowances Work?* Washington, D.C.: The Brookings Institution, 1981.

Break, George F., et al., eds. *Federal Credit Agencies: A Series of Research Studies Prepared for the Commission on Money and Credit*. Englewood Cliffs, New Jersey: Prentice Hall, 1963.

Brown, Robert K. *Public Housing in Action: The Record of Pittsburgh*. Pittsburgh: University of Pittsburgh Press, 1959.

Brueggeman, William B. "The Impact of Federally Subsidized Housing Programs: The Columbus, Ohio Case," in Stephen D. Messner and Maury Selden, eds., *Proceedings, American Real Estate and Urban Economics Association, 1970*, 5 (1971), 51-65.

————; Racsler, Ronald L.; and Smith, Halbert C. "Multiple Housing Programs and Urban Housing Policy," *Journal of the American Institute of Planners*, 38 (May 1972), 160-67.

Carlson, David B., and Heinberg, John D. *How Housing Allowances Work: Integrated Findings from the Experimental Housing Allowance Program*. Washington: The Urban Institute, 1978.

Carr, Lowell Juilliard, and Stermer, James Edson. *Willow Run: A Study of Industrialization and Cultural Inadequacy*. New York: Harper & Brothers, 1952.

Clark, Evans. "The Subsidy in Low Rental Housing," *The Annals of the American Academy of Political and Social Science*, 190 (March 1937), 151-61.

Colean, Miles L. *American Housing*. New York: Twentieth Century Fund, 1944.

————. *Housing for Defense*. New York: Twentieth Century Fund, 1940.

————. *The Impact of Government on Real Estate Finance in the United States*. New York: National Bureau of Economic Research, 1950.

Darling, Philip. "A Short-Cut Method for Evaluating Housing Quality," *Land Economics*, 25 (May 1949), 184-92.

Davies, Richard O. *Housing Reform During the Truman Administration*. Columbia, Missouri: University of Missouri Press, 1966.

Dean, John P. "The Myths of Housing Reform," *American Sociological Review*, (April 1949), 281-88.

DeForest, Robert W., and Veiller, Lawrence, eds. *The Tenement House Problem*. 2 volumes. New York: The Macmillan Company, 1903.

deLeeuw, Frank, with Jarutis, Eleanor L. *Operating Costs in Public Housing: A Financial Crisis*. Washington, D.C.: The Urban Institute, 1970.

"Does Housing Offer a Career to Architects: A Symposium," *Architectural Record*, 83 (April 1938), 81-86.

Downs, Anthony. "Housing the Urban Poor: The Economics of Various Strategies," *American Economic Review*, 59 (September 1969), 646-51.

————. "The Successes and Failures of Federal Housing Policy," *The Public Interest*, Volume 34 (Winter 1974), 124-45.

Dunham, H. Warren, and Grundstein, Nathan D. "The Impact of a Confusion of Social Objectives on Public Housing: A Preliminary Analysis," *Marriage and Family Living*, 23 (May 1955), 103-12.

Eccles, Marriner, S. "Inflationary Aspects of Housing Finance," *Federal Reserve Bulletin*, Volume 33, No. 12 (December 1947), 1463-65.

Eckstein, Otto. "The Economics of the 1960's—A Backward Look," *The Public Interest*, 19 (Spring 1970), 86-97.

Everett, Robinson O. and Johnston, John D., Jr., eds. *Housing*. Dobbs Ferry, New York: Oceana Publications, 1968. Originally published as Vol. 32 (Spring 1967) and (Summer 1967) issues of *Law and Contemporary Problems*.

Fish, Gertrude Sipperly, ed. *The Story of Housing*. Sponsored by Federal National Mortgage Association. New York: Macmillan Publishing Company, 1979.

Fisher, Ernest M. *Housing Markets and Congressional Goals*. New York: Praeger, 1975.

Fisher, Robert Moore. *Twenty Years of Public Housing*. New York: Harper & Brothers, 1959.

Foard, Ashley A., and Fefferman, Hilbert. "Federal Urban Renewal Legislation," *Law and Contemporary Problems*, 25 (Autumn 1960), 635-84.

Ford, James. *Slums and Housing, with Special Reference to New York City*. 2 volumes. Cambridge: Harvard University Press, 1936.

Frieden, Bernard J. *The Future of Old Neighborhoods*. Cambridge: MIT Press, 1964.

———. "Housing and National Urban Goals: Old Policies and New Realities," in James Q. Wilson, ed., *The Metropolitan Enigma*. Garden City: Doubleday & Company, 1970.

———. "Improving Federal Housing Subsidies: Summary Report," in U.S. Congress, House, Committee on Banking and Currency, *Papers Submitted to Subcommittee on Housing Panels on Housing Production, Housing Demand, and Developing a Suitable Living Environment*, Part 1, 473-88. 92nd Congress, 1st Session, 1971. Washington, D.C.: U.S. Government Printing Office, 1971.

"Frontiers of Housing Research: A Symposium at Madison, Wisconsin, September 2 and 3, 1948," *Land Economics*, 25 (February 1949).

Funigiello, Philip J. *The Challenge to Urban Liberalism: Federal-City Relations During World War II*. Knoxville: The University of Tennessee Press, 1978.

Furstenberg, George M. von. "Distribution of Federally Assisted Rental Housing," *Journal of the American Institute of Planners*, 37 (September 1971), 326-30.

Gelfand, Mark I. *A Nation of Cities: The Federal Government and Urban America, 1933-1965*. New York: Oxford University Press, 1975.

Glazer, Nathan. "Housing Problems and Housing Policies." *The Public Interest*, 7 (Spring 1967), 21-51.

Gray, George Herbert. *Housing and Citizenship . . . A Study of Low-Cost Housing*. New York: Reinhold Publishing Corporation, 1946.

———. "Public Housing, A Function of Democracy," *Architectural Record*, 93 (September 1943), 52-55.

Grebler, Leo. "Stabilizing Residential Construction—A Review of the Post-War Test," *American Economic Review*, 39 (September 1949), 898-910.

———; Blank, David M.; and Winnick, Leo. *Capital Formation in Residential Real Estate: Trends and Prospects*. Princeton, New Jersey: Princeton University Press, 1956.

Greenwald, William I. *Buy or Rent?* New York: Twayne Publishers, Inc., 1958.

Greer, Guy. *Your City Tomorrow*. New York: The Macmillan Company, 1947.

Grigsby, William G. *Housing Markets and Public Policy*. Philadelphia: University of Pennsylvania Press, 1963.

———, and Rosenburg, Louis. *Urban Housing Policy*. New Brunswick, New Jersey: Center for Urban Policy Research, Rutgers University, 1975.

Grobert, Robert R. "Urban Renewal Realistically Reappraised," *Law and Contemporary Problems*, 26 (Winter 1961), 212-29.

Guttentag, Jack M. "The Federal National Mortgage Association," in George F. Break, et al., eds., *Federal Credit Agencies*. A series of research studies prepared for the Commission on Money and Credit. Englewood Cliffs, New Jersey: Prentice Hall, 1963.

Haar, Charles M. *Federal Credit and Private Housing: The Mass Financing Dilemma*. New York: McGraw-Hill, 1960.

Hartman, Chester W. *Housing and Social Policy*. Englewood Cliffs: Prentice Hall, 1975.

———. "The Housing of Relocated Families," *Journal of the American Institute of Planners*, 30 (November 1968), 266-86.

——— and Levi, Margaret. "Public Housing Managers: An Appraisal," *Journal of the American Institute of Planners*, 39 (March 1973), 125-37.

Heinberg, John D., and Sunley, Emil M., Jr. "Tax Incentives for Rehabilitation Rental Housing," *Proceedings of the American Real Estate and Urban Economics Association*, 6 (1971), 197-218.

Hill, John G. "Fifty Years of Social Action on the Housing Front," *Social Service Review*, 22 (June 1948), 160-76.

Hines, Thomas S. "Housing, Baseball, and Creeping Socialism: The Battle of Chavez Ravine, Los Angeles, 1949-1959," *Journal of Urban History*, 8 (February 1982), 123-43.

Hudnut, Joseph. "Housing and the Democratic Process," *Architectural Record*, 93 (June 1943), 42-46.

Hunter, Robert. *Tenement Conditions in Chicago: Report by the Investigating Committee of the City Homes Association*. Chicago: City Homes Association, 1901.

Isler, Morton L. "The Goals of Housing Subsidy Programs," in U.S. Congress, House, Committee on Banking and Currency, *Papers Submitted to Subcommittee on Housing Panels on Housing Production, Housing Demand, and Developing a Suitable Living Environment*, Part 1. 92nd Congress, 1st Session. Washington, D.C.: U.S. Government Printing Office, 1971.

Keith, Nathaniel S. *Politics and the Housing Crisis Since 1930*. New York: Universe Books, 1973.

Klaman, Saul B. *The Postwar Residential Mortgage Market*. A study of the National Bureau of Economic Research. Princeton: Princeton University Press, 1961.

Kriesberg, Louis. "Neighborhood Setting and the Isolation of Public Housing Tenants," *Journal of the American Institute of Planners*, 34 (January 1968), 43-49.

Kristoff, Frank. "Federal Housing Policies: Subsidized Production, Filtration and Objectives," 2 parts. *Land Economics*, 48 (November 1972), 309-20; 49 (May 1973), 163-74.

———. "Housing Policy Goals and the Turnover of Housing," *Journal of the American Institute of Planners*, 31 (August 1965), 232-45.

Kummerfeld, Donald D. "The Housing Subsidy System," in U.S. Congress, House, Committee on Banking and Currency, Subcommittee on Housing, *Papers Submitted to Subcommittee on Housing Panels on Housing Production, Housing Demand and Developing a Suitable Living Environment*, Part 2. 92nd Congress, 1st Session, June 1971. Washington, D.C.: U.S. Government Printing Office, 1971.

Levitan, Sar A., and Cleary, Karen A. *Old Wars Remain Unfinished: The Veteran Benefits System*. Baltimore: The Johns Hopkins University Press, 1973.

Lewis, Charles F. "An Investment Approach to Housing," *The Annals of the American Academy of Political and Social Science*, 190 (March 1937), 17-23.

Lowry, Ira S. "Filtering and Housing Standards: A Conceptual Analysis," *Land Economics*, 36 (November 1960), 362-70.

Lubove, Roy. "Homes and 'A Few Well Placed Fruit Trees': An Object Lesson in Fed-

eral Housing," *Social Research*, 27 (Winter, 1960), 469-86.
———. "New Cities for Old: The Urban Reconstruction Program of the 1930's," *Social Studies*, 53 (November 1962), 203-13.
———. *The Progressives and The Slums: Tenement House Reform in New York City, 1890-1917*. Pittsburgh: University of Pittsburgh Press, 1962.
McDonnell, Timothy L. *The Wagner Housing Act*. Chicago: Loyola University Press, 1957.
Maisel, Sherman J. *Financing Real Estate*. New York: McGraw-Hill, 1965.
Mandelker, Daniel R. *Housing Subsidies in the United States and England*. Indianapolis: The Bobbs-Merrill Company, Inc., 1973.
Marcuse, Peter. "Housing in Early City Planning," *Journal of Urban History*, 6 (February 1980), 153-76.
Meehan, Eugene J. "Is There a Future for Public Housing?" *Journal of Housing*, 45 (May/June 1983), 73-76.
———. *Public Housing Policy: Convention Versus Reality*. New Brunswick, New Jersey: Center for Urban Policy Research, Rutgers University, 1975.
Meeks, Carol B. *Housing*. Englewood Cliffs: Prentice Hall, 1980.
———. "Review of the Housing Allowance Program," *The Journal of Consumer Affairs*, 10 (Winter 1976), 208-23.
Muth, Richard F. *Public Housing: An Economic Evaluation*. Washington, D.C.: American Enterprise Institute, 1973.
Nenno, Mary K. "The Reagan Housing, CD Record: A Negative Rating," *Journal of Housing*, 45 (September/October 1983), 135-41.
———. "The 10-Year Housing Goals Show a Short Fall in Number of Units and A Need for Links to Fiscal Policy," *Journal of Housing*, 40 (July 1978), 342-46.
Nourse, Hugh O. "The Effect of a Negative Income Tax on the Number of Substandard Housing Units," *Land Economics*, 46 (November 1970), 435-45.
Olsen, Edgar O., and Rasmussen, David W. "Section 8 Existing: A Program Evaluation," in U.S. Department of Housing and Urban Development, *Occasional Papers in Housing and Community Affairs*, 6 (December 1979), 1-32.
Olsen, Edgar O., and Reeder, William J., "Does HUD Pay Too Much for Section 8 Existing Housing? *Land Economics*, 57 (May 1981), 243-51.
O'Toole, William J. "A Prototype of Public Housing Policy: The USHC," *Journal of the American Institute of Planners*, 34 (May 1968), 140-52.
"Our Confused Housing Program," *Architectural Forum*, 106 (April 1957), 126-29ff.
Peterson, George E. *Tax Exempt Financing of Housing Investment*. Washington: The Urban Institute, 1979.
Post, Langdon W. *The Challenge of Housing*. New York: Farrar & Rinehart, 1938.
"The President's Conference on Home Building and Home Ownership. Report." John M. Gries and James Ford, eds. *Home Finance and Taxation*. Washington, D.C.: National Capitol Press, 1932.
———. *Home Ownership, Income and Types of Dwellings*. Washington, D.C.: National Capitol Press, 1932.
———. *Housing Objectives and Programs*. Washington, D.C.: National Capitol Press, 1932.
———. *Slums, Large-scale Housing and Decentralization*. Washington, D.C.: National Capitol Press, 1932.
Ratcliff, Richard U. "Housing Standards and Housing Research," *Land Economics*, 28 (November 1952), 328-32.
Rathbun, Daniel B. "The Veterans' Home-Loan Program: Success or Failure?" *The Appraisal Journal*, (July 1954), 400-8.

Robbins, Ira S. "Housing Goals and Achievements in the United States," *American Journal of Economics and Sociology*, 15 (April 1956), 285-92.

Rosenman, Dorothy. *A Million Homes A Year*. New York: Harcourt, Brace, 1945.

———. "Defense Housing: Are We Building Future Slums or Planned Communities?" *Architectural Record*, 90 (November 1941), 56-58.

———. "The Racket in Veterans' Housing," *The American Magazine*, 142 (September 1946), 26-27ff.

Rowlands, David T. "Urban Housing Activities of the Federal Government," *The Annals of the American Academy of Political and Social Science*, 190 (March 1937): 83-93.

———, and Woodbury, Coleman, eds. *Current Developments in Housing*. Volume 190 of *The Annals of the American Academy of Political and Social Science*, March 1937.

Sands, Gary. "Housing Turnover: Assessing Its Relevance to Public Policy," *Journal of the American Institute of Planners*, 42 (October 1976), 419-26.

Schechter, Henry B. "Federal Housing Programs," in U.S. Congress, Joint Economic Committee, *The Economics of Federal Subsidy Programs: A Compendium of Papers Submitted.* . . . Part 5, "Housing Subsidies." 92nd Congress, 2nd Session, October 1972. Washington, D.C.: U.S. Government Printing Office, 1972.

———, and Schlefer, Marion K. "Housing Needs and National Goals," in U.S. Congress, House, Committee on Banking and Currency, *Papers Submitted to Subcommittee on Housing Panels on Housing Production, Housing Demand, and Developing a Suitable Living Environment*, Part 1. 92nd Congress, 1st Session, Washington, D.C.: U.S. Government Printing Office, 1971.

Schussheim, Morton J. *The Modest Commitment to Cities*. Lexington, Massachusetts: Lexington Books, 1974.

Solomon, Arthur P. *Housing the Urban Poor: A Critical Evaluation of Federal Housing Policy*. Cambridge: MIT Press, 1973.

———, and Fenton, Chester G. "The Nation's First Experience with Housing Allowances: The Kansas City Demonstration," *Land Economics*, 50 (August 1974), 213-23.

Starr, Roger. "Which of the Poor Shall Live in Public Housing?" *The Public Interest*, 23 (Spring 1971), 116-24.

Stegman, Michael A. "Kaiser, Douglas, and Kerner on Low-Income Housing Policy," *Journal of the American Institute of Planners* 35 (November 1969), 422-27.

———. "Slumlords and Public Policy," *Journal of the American Institute of Planners*, 33 (November 1967), 419-24.

Sternlieb, George. "The City as Sandbox," *The Public Interest*, 25 (Fall 1971), 14-21.

———. *The Tenement Landlord*. New Brunswick, New Jersey: Urban Studies Center, Rutgers, State University, 1966.

———, and Hughes, James W. *The Future of Rental Housing*. New Brunswick, New Jersey: Center for Urban Policy Research, Rutgers University, 1981.

Straus, Michael W., and Wegg, Talbot. *Housing Comes of Age*. New York: Oxford University Press, 1938.

Straus, Nathan. *The Seven Myths of Housing*. New York: Alfred A. Knopf, 1944.

Struyk, Raymond J. *A New System for Public Housing: Salvaging a National Resource*. Washington, D.C.: The Urban Institute, 1980.

———. *Reforming Public Housing: An Early Analysis of the Administration's 1983 Proposal*. Washington, D.C.: The Urban Institute, 1983.

———, and Bendick, Marc Jr., eds. *Housing Vouchers for the Poor: Lessons from a Na-*

tional Experiment. Washington, D.C.: The Urban Institute, 1981.

Struyk, Raymond J.; Marshall, Sue; and Ozanne, Larry J. *Housing Policies for the Urban Poor: A Case for Local Diversity in Federal Programs*. Washington, D.C.: Urban Institute, 1978.

Struyk, Raymond J.; Mayer, Neil; and Tuccillo, John A. *Federal Housing Policy at President Reagan's Midterm*. Washington, D.C.: The Urban Institute, 1983.

Surrey, Stanley S. "Federal Income Tax Reform: The Varied Approaches Necessary to Replace Tax Expenditures with Direct Governmental Assistance," *Harvard Law Review*, 84 (December 1970), 352-408.

Swan, Craig. "Housing Subsidies and Housing Starts," *American Real Estate and Urban Economics Association Journal*, 1 (Fall 1973), 119-40.

Taggert, Robert. *Low-Income Housing: A Critique of Federal Aid*. Baltimore: The Johns Hopkins Press, 1970.

Thurow, Lester C. "Goals of a Housing Program," in U.S. Congress, House, Committee on Banking and Currency, Subcommittee on Housing, *Papers Submitted to Subcommittee on Housing Panels on Housing Production, Housing Demand and Developing a Suitable Living Environment*, Part 2. 92nd Congress, 1st Session, June 1971. Washington, D.C.: U.S. Government Printing Office, 1971.

Tough, Rosalind. "The Life Cycle of the Home Owners' Loan Corporation," *Land Economics*, 27 (November 1951), 324-31.

U.S. Congress. House. Committee on Banking and Currency. *Housing Act of 1949: Hearings . . .* 81st Congress, 1st. Session. Washington D.C.: U.S. Government Printing Office, 1949.

———. House. Committee on Banking, Currency and Housing. Subcommittee on Housing and Community Development. *Evolution of Role of the Federal Government in Housing and Community Development: A Chronology of Legislative and Selected Executive Actions, 1892-1974*. 94th Congress, 1st Session. Washington, D.C.: U.S. Government Printing Office, 1975.

———. House. Committee on Banking and Currency. Subcommittee on Housing. *National Housing Goals: Hearings . . .* 91st Congress, 1st Session, May-June 1969. Washington, D.C.: U.S. Government Printing Office, 1969.

———. House. Committee on Banking and Currency. Subcommittee on Housing. *Papers Submitted to Subcommittee on Housing Panels on Housing Production, Housing Demand and Developing a Suitable Living Environment*. 92nd Congress, 1st Session, June 1971. Washington, D.C.: U.S. Government Printing Office, 1971.

———. House. Committee on Banking and Currency. Subcommittee on Housing. *Suspension of Subsidized Housing Programs: Hearings . . .* 93rd Congress, 1st Session, March 20, 1973. Washington, D.C.: U.S. Government Printing Office, 1973.

———. House. Committee on Banking, Finance and Urban Affairs. Subcommittee on Housing and Community Development. *Housing: A Reader*. Prepared by the Congressional Research Service, Library of Congress, for the . . . 98th Congress, 1st Session, July 1983. Washington, D.C.: U.S. Government Printing Office, 1983.

———. Joint Committee on Housing Pursuant to H. Con. Res. 104. *Housing in America: Its Present Status and Future Implications*. A report prepared for the . . . 80th Congress, 2nd Session. Washington, D.C.: U.S. Government Printing Office, 1948.

———. Joint Economic Committee. *The Economics of Federal Subsidy Programs: A Compendium of Papers Submitted . . .* Part 5, "Housing Subsidies." 92nd Congress, 2nd Session, October 9, 1972. Washington, D.C.: U.S. Government Printing Office, 1972.

———. Joint Economic Committee. *Housing and the Economy: Hearings* . . . 96th Congress, 2nd Session, April 16 and September 17, 1980. Washington D.C.: U.S. Government Printing Office, 1980.

———. Joint Economic Committee. *Housing Subsidies and Housing Policies: Hearings* . . . 92nd Congress, 2nd Session, December 1972. Washington, D.C.: U.S. Government Printing Office, 1972.

———. Senate. Committee on Banking and Currency. *Home Owners' Loan Act: Hearings* . . . 73rd Congress, 1st Session, April 1933. Washington, D.C.: U.S. Government Printing Office, 1933.

———. Senate. Committee on Banking and Currency. *Housing Act of 1954, FHA Insurance Provisions: Hearings* . . . 83rd Congress, 2nd Session, April 1954. Washington, D.C.: U.S. Government Printing Office, 1954.

———. Senate. Committee on Banking and Currency. *Mortgage Interest Rate Problem: Hearings* . . . 83rd Congress, 1st Session, January 1953. Washington, D.C.: U.S. Government Printing Office, 1953.

———. Senate. Committee on Banking, Housing and Urban Affairs. Subcommittee on Housing and Urban Affairs. *Hearings* . . . *to Consider Extension and Revision of HUD Housing and Community Development Programs*. 98th Congress, 1st Session, March 1983. Washington, D.C.: U.S. Government Printing Office, 1983.

———. Senate. Committee on Education and Labor. *Creating a United States Housing Authority*, Senate Report No. 933, to accompany S. 1685, 75th Congress, 1st Session, July 1937. Washington, D.C.: U.S. Government Printing Office, 1937.

———. Senate. Special Committee on Post-War Economic Policy and Planning. Subcommittee on Housing and Urban Redevelopment. *Post-War Economic Policy and Planning: Hearings* . . . Part 4, "Housing and Urban Development." 79th Congress, 1st Session, 1944-45. Washington, D.C.: U.S. Government Printing Office, 1945.

U.S. Congressional Budget Office. A Budgetary Framework for Federal Housing and Related Community Development Policy. Staff Working Paper. February 1977.

———. *Federal Housing Assistance: Alternative Approaches*. May 1982.

———. *Federal Housing Policy: Current Programs and Recurring Issues*. June 1978.

———. *Homeownership: The Changing Relationship of Costs and Incomes, and Possible Federal Roles*. January 1977.

———. *Housing Assistance for Low- and Moderate-Income Families*. Budget Issue Paper. February 1977.

———. *Housing Finance: Federal Programs and Issues*. September 1976.

———. *The Long-Term Costs of Lower-Income Housing Assistance Programs*. 1979.

———. *Real Estate Tax Shelter Subsidies and Direct Subsidy Alternatives*. 1977.

U.S. Department of Housing and Urban Development. *Housing in the Seventies: A Report of the National Housing Policy Review*. Washington, D.C.: Government Printing Office, 1974.

———. *Housing in the Seventies: Working Papers*. 2 vols. Washington, D.C.: Government Printing Office, 1976.

U.S. National Resources Planning Board. *Housing, the Continuing Problem*. Washington, D.C.: Government Printing Office, 1940.

U.S. President's Advisory Committee on Government Housing Policies and Programs. *Government Housing Policies and Programs: A Report*. Washington, D.C.: Government Printing Office, 1953.

U.S. President's Committee on Urban Housing. *A Decent Home*. Washington, D.C.: Government Printing Office, 1967.

————. *The Report of the President's Committee on Urban Housing: Technical Studies*. 2 vols. Washington, D.C.: Government Printing Office, 1967.

Vinton, Warren Jay. "Public Housing," *Planning 1958: Selected Papers from the National Planning Conference, Washington, D.C., May 1958*. Chicago: American Society of Planning Officials, 1958.

————. "A Survey of Approaches to the Housing Problem," *The Annals of the American Academy of Political and Social Science*, 190 (March 1937), 7-16.

Walker, Mabel. *Urban Blight and Slums*. New York: Russell & Russell, 1938.

Walzer, Norman, and Singer, Dan. "Housing Expenditures in Urban Low-Income Areas," *Land Economics*, 50 (August 1974), 224-31.

Weaver, Robert C. "Housing Allowances," *Land Economics*, 51 (August 1975), 247-57.

Weicher, John C. *Housing: Federal Policies and Programs*. Washington, D.C.: American Enterprise Institute for Public Policy Research, 1980.

————. "The Rationales for Government Intervention in Housing: An Overview," in U.S. Department of Housing and Urban Development, *Housing in the Seventies: Working Papers*, Volume 2. Washington, D.C.: Government Printing Office, 1976.

Welfeld, Irving. *America's Housing Problem: An Approach to its Solution*. Washington, D.C.: American Enterprise Institute for Public Policy Research, 1973.

Wendt, Paul F. *Housing Policy–the Search for Solutions*. Berkeley: University of California Press, 1963.

————. *The Role of the Federal Government in Housing*. Washington, D.C.: American Enterprise Association, 1956.

Wheaton, William L.C.; Milgram, Grace; and Meyerson, Margy Ellin, eds. *Urban Housing*. New York: The Free Press, 1966.

White, Harrison C. "Multipliers, Vacancy Chains, and Filtering in Housing," *Journal of the American Institute of Planners*, 37 (March 1971), 88-94.

Wolman, Harold. *Politics of Federal Housing*. New York: Dodd, Mead & Company, 1971.

Wood, Edith Elmer. *The Housing of the Unskilled Wage Earner: America's Next Problem*. New York: The Macmillan Company, 1919.

————. *Slums and Blighted Areas in the United States*. Federal Emergency Administration of Public Works, Housing Division, Bulletin 1. Washington, D.C.: Government Printing Office, 1935.

Woodbury, Coleman, ed. *The Future of Cities and Urban Redevelopment*. Chicago: University of Chicago Press, 1953.

————. "Housing in the Redevelopment of American Cities," *Land Economics*, 25 (November 1949), 397-404.

————. "Objectives and Accomplishments of the Veterans' Emergency Housing Program," *American Economic Review*, 37 (May 1947), 508-28.

Wright, Henry. *Rehousing Urban America*. New York: Columbia University Press, 1935.

Index